THE TRADITIONAL COOKING OF
RUSSIA & POLAND

THE TRADITIONAL COOKING OF
RUSSIA & POLAND

Explore the rich and varied cuisine of Eastern Europe in more than
150 classic step-by-step recipes illustrated with over 740 photographs

Elena Makhonko and Ewa Michalik

HERMES
HOUSE

This edition is published by Hermes House, an imprint of Anness Publishing Ltd, Blaby Road, Wigston, Leicestershire LE18 4SE
Email: info@anness.com

Web: www.hermeshouse.com; www.annesspublishing.com

If you like the images in this book and would like to investigate using them for publishing, promotions or advertising, please visit our website www.practicalpictures.com for more information.

Publisher: Joanna Lorenz
Editorial Director: Helen Sudell
Executive Editor: Joanne Rippin
Designer: Adelle·Morris
Food styling: Jenny White, Claire Ptak and Joy Skipper
Food photography: Jon Whitaker
Prop styling: Penny Markham
Production controller: Wendy Lawson

© Anness Publishing Ltd 2011

A CIP catalogue record for this book is available from the British Library.

ETHICAL TRADING POLICY
Because of our ongoing ecological investment programme, you, as our customer, can have the pleasure and reassurance of knowing that a tree is being cultivated on your behalf to naturally replace the materials used to make the book you are holding. For further information about this scheme, please visit www.annesspublishing.com/trees

Previously published in two separate volumes, *Russian Food & Cooking* and *Poland: Food & Cooking*

NOTES
Bracketed terms are intended for American readers.
For all recipes, quantities are given in both metric and imperial measures and, where appropriate, in standard cups and spoons. Follow one set of measures, but not a mixture, because they are not interchangeable. Standard spoon and cup measures are level. 1 tsp = 5ml, 1 tbsp = 15ml, 1 cup = 250ml/8fl oz.
Australian standard tablespoons are 20ml. Australian readers should use 3 tsp in place of 1 tbsp for measuring small quantities. American pints are 16fl oz/2 cups. American readers should use 20fl oz/2.5 cups in place of 1 pint when measuring liquids.
Electric oven temperatures in this book are calculated for conventional ovens. When using a fan oven, the temperature will probably need to be reduced by about 10–20°C/20–40°F. Since ovens vary, you should check with your manufacturer's instruction book for guidance. The nutritional analysis given for each recipe is calculated per portion (i.e. serving or item), unless otherwise stated. If the recipe gives a range, such as Serves 4–6, then the nutritional analysis will be for the smaller portion size, i.e. 6 servings. The analysis does not include optional ingredients, such as salt added to taste, etc.
Medium (US large) eggs are used unless otherwise stated.

Main front cover image shows Roast Partridges with Sage, Thyme and Garlic – for recipe, see page 128.

PUBLISHER'S NOTE

Contents

Introduction

Mention Russian food, and most people will conjure up an image of a tureen of ruby-red borscht served with sour cream, imperial salmon pie, tiny little dumplings, or chilled champagne and caviar. Polish cuisine uses many of the same elements, and both of these countries share not only similar dishes but also a great pride in their traditional cuisine, handed down from one generation to the next, using ingredients that follow the seasonal rhythms of the year.

Climates

Poland is more or less on the same latitude as southern and western Russia, where most of the Russian population, its industry and its agriculture are to be found. This means that both Poland and southern Russia enjoy warm summers and suffer long, cold, bleak winters, with the briefest of spring or autumn seasons to divide them. The crops that are grown, therefore, are those that can withstand the onslaught of the cold winter weather, such as root vegetables, or that flourish during the short summer growing season and come to fruition well before the snows fall, such as cereal crops.

Preserving food

There are years in both countries when the crops fail, or prolonged snow or ice prevents the farmer from ploughing his land. But both Russians and Poles have developed skilful ways of preserving the food for such eventualities, and these traditional recipes for pickled vegetables, smoked fish, cured meat and sausages are the lifeblood of both cuisines.

Wild food

The other natural resource that links the two countries is the vast larder of wild food to be found in the forests. Russians and Poles love to hunt, whether it's

mushrooms or rabbits, and this tradition is maintained today, by local people and by tourists who come to these ancient woodlands to experience the thrill of the chase. There are plenty of recipes in both cuisines for delicious game pies, stews and soups made with wild boar, venison, hare and game birds, or using the

Above: A typical farming village in the north of Russia, one of the most fertile areas of the country.

freshwater fish from the rivers and lakes. These tend to be flavoured with the tasty field mushrooms, herbs, spices and berries just waiting to be picked.

Another well-loved tradition is for whole families, from the youngest to the oldest, to spend a day in the brief autumn season wandering in the deciduous woodlands, berry-picking or foraging for mushrooms in the undergrowth, with a delightful picnic of cold pies and sweet pastries to sustain the hard workers.

Left: The many varieties of delicious dried and cured meats and sausages are still very popular in Poland, even though it is no longer necessary as a method of preserving meat. Many of them are also exported to Russia.

Foreign influences

Southern and western Russia's strongest trading routes have always been with Europe, and through these they have had access to goods from far-flung countries all around the world. Poland, too, sits in a prime position for trading, alongside the Baltic Sea, with the thrusting economy of Germany to the west, the developing Baltic states to the east, and the stability of Denmark, Sweden and Finland to the north. This means that links with other countries are well established, and trading of food and culinary ideas from and through Poland has been conducted for hundreds of years.

However, northern and eastern Russia suffer extreme Arctic temperatures. These parts of the country are much more remote from world commerce, and have to rely on their own foodstuffs and traditional cuisines, owing to the difficulty of transporting goods. Despite this, there are still delicious recipes from Siberia to enjoy, such as the much-loved dumplings, pelmeni, known in Poland as pierogi.

Below: Classic recipes, such as borscht, rely on the best seasonal ingredients.

Above: The forested areas of Poland are huge, and people still fish, hunt game and gather fruit and mushrooms there.

About this book

Most Russian and Polish food is based on good-quality, fresh ingredients, enhanced by preserved vegetables such as sauerkraut or dried mushrooms, or cured meat such as sausage and ham. Here you will find recipes that reflect this tradition.

All the recipes are carefully explained with simple step-by-step instructions and colour pictures. The final appearance of the dish is an important element for every cook – Russians and Poles have a good eye for presentation – and the vivid colours of beetroot (beets), black rye bread, white sour cream, green herbs and rich dark meat stand out on the plate.

Russian and Polish cooking is all about enjoying the taste, texture and aroma of these hearty traditional foods. The reward for the cook comes from making an impressive dish that sustains good health while pleasing the senses.

Below: Both Russia and Poland have many recipes for little pies and dumplings.

Religious traditions

Russians have their own religious faith, based on the Eastern Orthodox Christian tradition. Even though this was suppressed during the 20th century under Communism, the rituals of the church year were preserved by many families. The main festivals, with their major family feasts, were celebrated quietly in people's homes, with the traditional dishes associated with each one, such as Pashka (above), made for the Easter holiday, or roasted carp, eaten on Good Friday. In Poland, too, the Communist years meant that Catholic rituals had to be celebrated quietly at home, but the Christmas and Easter festival meals were carefully prepared in the same way as they had been for centuries, with delicious treats such as Christmas almond soup or angels' wings biscuits.

Below: Salmon pie, or koulibiac, was devised for the Russian imperial court.

Russian Land and History

The huge land mass that is Russia spreads out across a great proportion of the Northern Hemisphere. It touches Europe at one end and Japan at the other. Its history is similarly complex, holding together extremes of class, income, religion and ethnic diversity, as well as the cultural characteristics of East and West. The resulting culinary inheritance of this nation is one of its unifying factors, with Russians sharing a love of their recipes and the joy of hospitality.

Left: The distinctive towers of The Kremlin, Moscow. Now the seat of Russia's democratic government, it was once the stronghold of the Communist regime, and before that the palace of the tsars.

foods in the cold winter months became a matter of life and death, and from this necessity arose many delicious recipes for pickled or preserved foods that are still made and enjoyed in Russian households today.

The rise of the tsars

The first time the whole of Russia was pulled together into one country was in the 16th century, when Ivan the Terrible began his reign. His brutal regime enforced obedience over a vast land mass containing many different tribes and religions, with their own customs. Later, the more settled reigns of Peter the Great and Catherine the Great allowed for more interaction with other countries, and at this point a European influence arrived in Russian cuisine. It is difficult to believe that wheat was unknown in Russia before the 16th century; it is now one of Russia's major exports and makes up half the country's grain crop. At the same time,

Russia's beginnings

The first settlements in Russia grew up on the western side of the country, where the warmer weather and abundant wild food make it easier to have permanent arrangements for living, working and feeding the family. Moscow grew out of one of these early settlements, developing as the centre of power and government in the 16th century. The wonderfully fertile 'black earth' of the surrounding countryside enabled the first farmers to grow plenty of rye, oats, barley and buckwheat to make dark, tasty bread, pancakes, dumplings and grain spirits such as vodka, the staples of the Russian diet. The freshwater fish in many rivers and lakes, plus the wild game from the forests, formed the protein element of people's diet. Learning to preserve these

Below: Many city dwellers also own a smallholding in the country that supplies the family with fresh fruit and vegetables.

Below: Buckwheat in blossom, one of the earliest cereal crops grown in Russia and still a staple ingredient today.

Below: The once familiar symbol of the Communist Party was the national flag of the Soviet Union.

Above: The vast forested taiga region in the north is an area still abundant with wild food, including fish and game.

Above: The fertile land on the banks of the Volga River in western Russia provides rich pasture for sheep and cattle.

green vegetables and salads first appeared on the tables of the nobility, as well as chocolate, sweet pastries and other luxurious delicacies that have since become great favourites.

Turmoil and revolution

The upheavals of the 20th century, the Russian Revolution, Communism and the subsequent collapse of the Soviet Union by the end of the century, caused many hardships all the way from west to east. The Russian people generally had enough to eat, although the diet of most people was rather monotonous, being based on bread, potatoes, cabbage and vodka. It was supplemented, as it had been through the centuries, by wild produce such as mushrooms, honey, berries and game to be found in the forests, according to the annual rhythm of the seasons.

The 21st century

Life since the end of the Cold War and the fall of Communism has been extremely hard for many Russians. While a few people made huge fortunes in the rush to embrace capitalism, others were left without savings, pensions or any income. The beginning of the 21st century has seen an upturn in Russia's fortunes and a more equable regime has begun to emerge. Luckily, many Russians have access to a small plot of land that

they can cultivate for food. A quite astonishing 80 per cent of the country's vegetables are grown on these individual smallholdings, and are then used fresh, preserved in people's own kitchens, or sold to their neighbours.

The traditions of the Russian way of life have been maintained through all these upheavals. Religious festivals are still extremely important markers throughout the year, and are celebrated with

Below: Grayling are hung to dry during the brief Siberian summer, to be stored for the long, harsh winter months.

reverence for the old ways, using recipes handed down through the generations. With the recent expansion of links with the outside world, Russian food culture has exploded into life, and today the people of this huge country once more take great pride in their national cuisine.

A giant among countries

The sheer size of Russia is astonishing. Even after the break-up of the Soviet Union and its satellite states, Russia still stretches over 8,000 kilometres (4,971 miles), covering 11 time zones from the Baltic States and the Black Sea in the west to the Sea of Japan in the east. There are 40 National Parks and more than 100 nature reserves in this wild, sometimes bleak landscape. The most important

element, which dominates life in Russia, is the climate, which is influenced by the mountain ranges that encircle the country.

The mountains of Russia

The Urals run roughly north to south, dividing the western, European part of Russia from the eastern, Siberian plains. By far the majority of Russia's population lives in the shelter of the more temperate western side of the mountains. Here it is possible to grow a very good variety of crops to feed millions of people, and therefore this is where most people have chosen to settle.

Much higher than the Urals, the Caucasus mountains form the south-western border between Russia, Georgia and Azerbaijan. This region has a warmer climate and provides the people of Russia with wheat, vegetables, herbs, honey and dairy produce. Vineyards, orchards and olive groves have been established here in the sheltered foothills for centuries.

Below: Russia's size and geographical complexity is unique, and this, combined with the climate, and the influences of its many neighbours, has given the country a rich and varied cuisine.

Russia's two capitals

Moscow (seen above at night) and St Petersburg are the two main power centres of the Russian Federation. Moscow is by far the older settlement, with records going back to the 12th century, whereas St Petersburg was constructed on the barren, waterlogged landscape of the far northern Baltic coast. It was founded in the early 18th century, on the orders of Peter the Great, one of Russia's most innovative and dynamic tsars. Both cities have at one time or another been the nation's capital. Moscow, with its vast size and longer history, finally won out in 1918 and is the bustling, thriving centre of government and commerce today. St Petersburg's position on the Baltic Sea means that it has become a major hub for importing and exporting goods, but its main attraction is as the artistic centre of Russia. Its citizens are proud of their wonderful art, music and theatres, and the well-developed and cosmopolitan cuisine in its many restaurants.

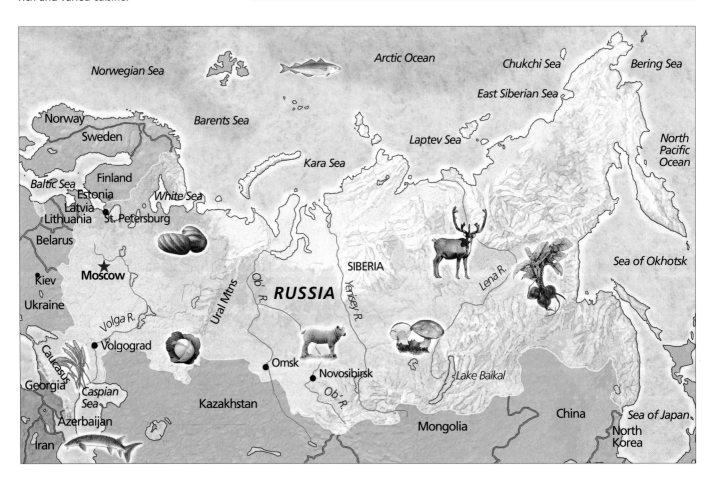

Above: This riverside village is typical of the Russian settlements found in the fertile valleys of the Ural mountains.

To the south of Russia, running roughly along its border with China and Mongolia, lies a vast mountainous region, which has had an even stronger influence on the way Russia has developed over the centuries. These unmapped and often un-named mountain ranges prevent the warmer tropical air currents from the Pacific Ocean and the Chinese mainland from reaching Russia from the south, while there is no corresponding mountain range to protect the country from the Arctic winds blowing from the north. This is the main reason why so much of northern Russia is unproductive tundra, a land of permafrost where the low temperatures, as well as the many swamps and lagoons dotting the landscape, make it impossible to grow any kind of crops or to keep animals for food.

Agriculture in Russia
Below the northern tundra belt, stretching across most of Russia, is a more temperate zone known as the taiga. Here, forests of pine trees lie undisturbed for thousands of kilometres (miles). The taiga protects the more productive agricultural land to the south from the harsh climate of northern Russia. Hunters love the taiga for its sources of game and freshwater fish, which thrive in its cold temperatures, and there are many wonderful Russian recipes for warming stews and soups using game and fish as the main ingredients. The taiga also contains an

abundance of wild berries, many of which find their way into both savoury and sweet dishes. Local people have always known the best way of using the sparse produce of the taiga, from adding juniper berries and wild mushrooms to flavour hunter's stew, to savouring wild strawberries, sweetened with local honey, in a tangy dessert.

Further south still, the landscape softens into a more productive zone known as the 'steppe'. Western Russia, in particular, has a fantastic natural resource in the 'black earth' zone to be found around Moscow, fed by the long Volga River. This black earth, or *chernozem*, allows the farmers to grow nourishing food crops such as grains of all kinds, vegetables, sunflower seeds and pasture for cattle, sheep and pigs. The collapse of the Communist system of collective farms left much of this fertile land uncultivated

for a few years, but now both local and European entrepreneurs are beginning to see its potential and are working on bringing the land back to life.

Northern Russia, including the whole of Siberia, is very sparsely populated, even in the 21st century, when transport links have traversed the wildest places on Earth. Here time seems to stand still, and life is very harsh. Meat is a rarity and is enjoyed only on special occasions. People in Siberia eat the same type of food that people in this region have always consumed: a relatively restricted, but healthy, diet of dark rye bread, root vegetables, game, fish and dairy products.

The fishing industry
Fishing is a very important food industry in Russia. The country adjoins three major oceans: the Arctic, the Atlantic and the Pacific. Russia also has borders with the smaller Caspian Sea and the Black Sea, and contains hundreds of lakes and rivers teeming with freshwater fish.

Russian fishing fleets go out to sea every day of the year, and come back loaded with cod, herring, crab and haddock from the cold northern waters. Russian caviar, renowned all over the world, comes from sturgeon that grow to a great size in the warm Caspian Sea. All of these different kinds of fish and shellfish are used in traditional recipes, particularly on those days when meat is banned by the church for religious reasons, such as the period of Lent.

Below: In contrast to Russia's fertile areas is the harsh and extensive Baikal steppe of the Chinese-Russian borderlands.

Russian Cuisine

The cooking of Russia has its roots in how to make the most of a sometimes limited number of local ingredients and how to sustain the body against the bitter cold of a Russian winter. There is still time and energy, however, to express the Russian love of food and hospitality.

The cuisine of the past

Many years ago, this huge country had a largely rural population. The peasants would work on land owned by the nobility, and traditional methods of food production lasted for centuries. All kinds of grain, particularly wheat, corn and buckwheat, were grown on the wide, flat fields, and this encouraged the development of recipes for different kinds of bread, pastry and cakes. Bread is an absolute staple of the Russian diet – no meal would be complete without it.

21st-century changes

The hoarding instinct became more pronounced, if anything, during the food shortages of the 20th century, when Communism changed the way the land was farmed, not always for the better as far as feeding the people was concerned. When Communism fell in the late 20th century, a small but influential new upper class appeared, the 'new Russians', along

Below: The samovar may have been replaced by the electric kettle, but it is still held in great affection by Russians.

with a growing lower class, whose access to wealth was strictly limited. The new Russians are affluent, sometimes super-wealthy, and this spending power has introduced a new spectrum of luxury items in the food stores as well as Western-style restaurants and cafés.

Eating out

When Russians cook at home they do not think or care about which region the dish originates from. That is not the case when eating out, as restaurants are strictly of a type: a Georgian restaurant would never dream of serving a course from Ukraine, for example.

As well as these specialist regional restaurants, in recent times Russian fast-food places have become popular. Here a buffet of hot and cold traditional Russian courses is offered for a low price. The most perfect Russian fast food is actually a traditional dish, pelmeni, which can be made with around 20 different fillings. Another Russian classic to be found on the streets of most towns is the beer stand, the beer being served warm when the weather is cold, and always accompanied by a salty snack such as salted fish or boiled crayfish.

Above: There are many different versions of the famous Russian borscht.

Shopping and cooking

Russians love to eat and drink, especially in the company of family and friends. Hence they are also very generous and hospitable hosts, and eating at home with family and friends is an important part of life. Many Russians today shop at supermarkets, where they can buy typical Russian fare as well as imported delicacies. But special food-market stalls entirely devoted to either pickled vegetables or many kinds of dried fruit still thrive, while fresh bread is usually bought every morning from the baker.

The typical Russian way of cooking is to make large batches of food at one time. Casseroles and soups are made in large 7-litre (12-pint) pans and nobody thinks twice about eating the same food for four consecutive days.

Food of the day

Breakfast is usually a cup of tea with sugar and a slice of lemon, and maybe a piece of bread or cake to go with it. The classic Russian lunch is often taken in a *stolovaja*. These are simple cafeterias where students and employees eat an inexpensive lunch of genuine Russian food. Usually there are three dishes to choose from, inevitably including a soup. As always in Russia, bread and tea is served with the meal.

Dinner is the main meal of the day. In past times, when many people were working hard on the land, it would be a substantial affair to keep up the energy levels. The nobility stretched this meal into several courses, while peasants might be on basic rations of bread and soup, maybe with a little meat or fish.

These days, if it is a special occasion there will be some appetizers (zakuski), a thick, rich soup, then a main course of meat, fish or poultry. Desserts are usually light and based on fruit after the rich and substantial savoury courses.

Pelmeni

These tiny pasta rolls, filled with meat and eaten all over Russia, are something between dim sum and ravioli and originally came from China.

Pelmeni are at their best when home-made, but these days they can be bought frozen. Making these snacks is a fantastic way of spending quality time with friends and family, as pelmeni are usually made in big batches, often around 100 at a time. There is always a bottle of vodka and a plate of simple zakuski around to help yourself from while the baking goes on. One person takes care of the dough, another mixes the meat, and a third fills the little rolls with the filling. Once ready, pelmeni are placed in perfect straight rows on cutting boards, carefully counted and placed in the freezer. They taste best 'frost-bitten', according to the Russians.

When it is time to eat, the pelmeni are boiled from frozen in water and stock, and served with refreshing sour smetana, a couple of drops of vinegar, salt and ground black pepper – simple, yet elegant. Around 20 pelmeni per person is a normal portion, and vodka is the only possible drink to go with them.

Blinis

For Russians, blinis have symbolized life and fertility since pagan times. Perfectly round, golden and warm, the blini also symbolizes the sun. During Maslenitsa, a happy festival where the return of the spring is celebrated, blinis are the main food for a whole week. They are also

Above: Russian vodka must be served ice cold and in large quantities.

eaten to excess before the start of Lent. In the old days they were served to women in childbirth to help them gather their strength and sustain them through labour. 'Life begins and ends with blini', according to the Russians.

Champagne, vodka and tea

Russian champagne is often served throughout a good dinner; it is sweet and served at room temperature, but the new generation has learned to appreciate French champagne served chilled.

Vodka is made from wheat grain and often has a touch of sweetness from sugar, berries or fruits. Roots and herbs are also used to season vodka. Chilli pepper vodka is bottled with a whole red chilli. Vodka is usually enjoyed straight, and Russians always have a piece of dark

Below: Frost-bitten pelmeni ready to be dropped in boiling stock.

bread or a salted cucumber to go with it. To have a toast with vodka is a way of showing respect for the host. The tradition is to empty the glass in a single gulp. There is a Russian saying, 'To leave vodka in the glass is to leave tear drops for the host'.

Tea, served from the samovar, once had almost ritual status. Today kettles and tea bags are commonplace, but the samovar, also now likely to be electric, is still used at parties. Russians take their tea with sugar and lemon rather than milk.

Zakuski

The tradition of zakuski first appeared in Russian manor houses when a table of food and drink was always ready in the hallway, to greet guests any time of day or night. On the table a carafe containing vodka was given the place of honour, and during the winter the samovar was constantly sizzling with hot tea, together with dishes of salted cucumbers, smetana (sour cream), pickles, black bread and a simple fish or meat dish. Gradually the number of dishes on the table increased, and eventually people were sometimes too full to eat dinner once it was time to sit down for the main meal of the day.

Nowadays zakuski often consists of black sourdough bread, boiled potatoes mixed with dill, salted herring and smoked fish. There should also be some sort of caviar on the table. Often the famous salat olivje is included, and there will be some kind of 'poor man's caviar' made of vegetables.

Pickles are always a part of the zakuski table. Sauerkraut should be there, of course, but also marinated tomatoes and pickled mushrooms.

Russian Festivals and Celebrations

Hospitality is very important in most Russian households, and food and drink must be offered to visitors as they arrive to celebrate any holiday. As in most countries, special recipes are connected to the various festivals and religious ceremonies, and even at christenings no one would expect to leave without a glass or two of vodka and a plate or two of food.

New Year
According to the Russian calendar, New Year is before Christmas. During the years when Christmas was banned, some of the activities that belonged to Christmas were transferred to the New Year celebration, so now the decorated fir tree and Father Frost (Ded Moroz), are part of the New Year celebrations. On New Year's Eve, 31 December, Russians like to celebrate with a party of vodka and zakuski. At midnight there is champagne and festive fireworks.

The highlight of New Year for children is the arrival of Father Frost. According to Russian tradition he is offered a glass of vodka at every place he visits and cannot refuse without being rude. Father Frost carries a staff and wears a long blue coat. His helper, the Snow Maiden, represents frozen rivers and lakes and is dressed in a sparkling blue gown.

Christmas
Orthodox Christians follow the Julian calendar, so Christmas Day falls on 7 January, and is a quiet family celebration in comparison to the more extravagant New Year celebrations.

Above: Father Frost, the Russian equivalent of Father Christmas, and his assistant, the beautiful Snow Maiden, arrive in central Moscow for the traditional New Year parade on 31 December.

During the Soviet era it was actually forbidden to celebrate Christmas for several years. However, many people continued to celebrate in secret. Today, Christmas once again is regarded as a religious festival and a national holiday. Many people follow the tradition of fasting before Christmas, when they will avoid dishes that contain fat and meat. Many traditional Russian dishes have been specifically created to be eaten during the fasting period, including the 'caviars' made from vegetables, especially beetroot (beets) and mushrooms. A meal of 13 of these dishes is eaten on Christmas Eve, one of which is kutja, a porridge made with honey and raisins that is also served at funerals. The meal begins with zakuski, after which there will be a borscht, or another rich soup. Pasties with mushrooms, fish or cabbage are served with the soup.

On Christmas Day the fast is finally over and a huge meal is served featuring the foods that were forbidden during the past few weeks. The main course is often roasted goose, suckling pig or turkey. Finally the dessert table is laid with gingerbread, fruit compotes and kiselj, a soup made of cranberry juice thickened with cornflour (cornstarch).

Below: A girl lights a candle in St Petersburg's Cathedral. In the Orthodox church Christmas Day falls on 7 January.

Below: An impressive display of New Year fireworks begins over St Basil's Cathedral in Moscow's Red Square.

Right: A lavishly spread Easter zakuski table, decorated with Fabergé eggs.

Maslenitsa

Originally an ancient pagan festival to welcome spring, today Maslenitsa is a big public party for both children and adults, with theatrical performances, dances and lots of games.

During the week of Maslenitsa, also known as 'Butter Week', the children ride sledges, build snow forts and have snowball fights, while the adults take sleigh rides and drink cognac served from samovars. Outside the cities, large bonfires are built and people burn *tjutjelo*, dolls made with straw symbolizing winter.

Blinis are the absolute favourite food during Maslenitsa. In Russia it is said that when you eat a blini you get a share of the warmth and the strength from the sun, and during the week of Maslenitsa everyone eats them to excess.

Lent

During Lent the rule for Orthodox Christians is to abstain from meat and eggs. Instead they are allowed to eat food such as fresh and pickled vegetable and mushrooms fried in vegetable oil. Over the centuries, much creativity has gone into inventing filling dishes avoiding the proscribed meat and fish: stews, pelmeni, soups, vegetable caviar, pastries with vegetables, mushrooms and fruits.

Easter

Called Pascha in Russian, Easter is the most important festival in the Christian calendar. In Russia it occurs at the same time of year as an old pagan feast marking the end of winter. One Easter

tradition is to select perfect, white eggs to cook and paint. The eggs can also be dyed red by boiling them with onion skins. These brightly painted eggs are used to brighten up the table and are also given as presents to friends and family. Tsar Nikolai II gave bejewelled eggs made by Fabergé in St Petersburg to his wife and his mother. Today these extravagant eggs represent a piece of Russian imperial history and the tradition of giving bejewelled eggs has been revived.

The grand pashka, the Easter dessert, dominates the festive table. It is made in a wooden pyramid mould decorated with religious symbols and the letters 'XB',

meaning 'Christ is Risen'. Another favourite Easter cake is kulich, a tall, round confection glazed with sugar and filled with raisins and nuts.

A modern Easter party in the 21st century starts with vodka and zakuski (often including chicken liver mousse, marinated mushrooms, and fish salad) and ends with pashka and kulich. In between come many different meat, poultry or fish dishes which have been off the menu for the last seven weeks, such as rabbit in smetana, roast chicken stuffed with sauerkraut and dried fruits, or oven-baked fish. Family and friends are invited to share the Easter feast.

Below: Russian monks enjoy traditional Easter foods; cake, red caviar and wine.

Below: Street parades in traditional costume often mark national holidays.

Polish Land and History

Surrounded on most of its borders by powerful neighbouring countries, Poland was for centuries subjected to repression and occupation by other nations. This is not surprising, for it was a prize worth capturing: the fertile countryside abounds with all manner of good things to eat – from vast fields of grain and lakes and rivers teeming with freshwater fish, to large forests inhabited by animals and birds suitable for the table.

The first Polish kingdom

Prior to 966, the year of the earliest recorded historical event and first written reference to a Polish state, the region that is now known as Poland was inhabited by various tribes, including the Polanie, Wislanie, Pomorzanie and Mazovians. With the baptism of Mieszko I, duke of the Slavic tribe of Polans, in 966, the tribes, known collectively as the West Slavs, were united, and within 25 years had become one of the most powerful states in eastern Europe.

For the next 800 years Poland was a flourishing sovereign state, which made trade and cultural links with other countries through a combination of adventurous exploration and royal marriages. In addition, from 1569 to 1791 Poland joined with Lithuania to form a commonwealth that was beneficial to both countries and made them a strong force in eastern Europe.

With hunting parties providing venison, hare, pheasant and duck from the woods; mushrooms and herbs growing abundantly in the deep forests; and fish filling the lakes, ready to be fried, simmered, or made into soup, medieval Poland already had a strong and diverse culinary culture.

With the formation of strong links with the rest of Europe, however, cooking techniques and ingredients from western and southern Europe, especially Italy and France, started to have a huge influence on Polish food. In addition, spices from the East started to be incorporated, being used, in particular, to disguise the flavour of any meat or game that was perhaps past its best.

With the arrival in 1518 of an Italian princess, Queen Bona Sforza, to marry King Sigismund I, Polish cooking began to evolve into the rich cuisine of today. Homesick for Italy, the new queen encouraged French and Italian cooks to travel to Poland, bringing with them more delicate recipes for soups and stews, as well as new ingredients, including cabbage, leeks, lettuce and celeriac, which were adopted with enthusiasm.

Division of the spoils

From the end of the 18th century until the end of the 20th century, the history of Poland has been one of occupation and turmoil. For many years the land was controlled by different powers, including Russia, Prussia and Austria. This was followed by a brief period of independence in 1918–39, which ended abruptly when Nazi Germany invaded in 1939. After the war the country fell under Communist rule and the domination of the USSR until 1989.

Over 20 per cent of the population of Poland died during World War II, most of them Jews and members of other ethnic minorities who were transported to concentration camps. Survivors had their natural food stocks to fall back on when imports became scarce, but even these were often taken from them in the later 20th century to feed other mouths, or wasted under the centralized Communist system. Despite an attempt to establish collective farms under this system after 1945, however, the traditional Polish system of small-scale agriculture somehow survived, along with many closely guarded age-old local recipes and ingredients.

The 21st century

Poland has changed radically since the uprising against the Communist leaders in the 1980s, which was led by Lech Walesa and the Solidarity trade union, based in the Gdansk shipyards. It now has its own democratic government, although several Communist party members have been returned to power now that the people are free to choose their own representatives. It has also joined NATO and the EU, and a free flow of goods and people passes once again into and out of the country.

Left: Deer have been hunted in the forests of Poland since medieval times, and venison is still very popular.

As with many changing countries in Eastern Europe, a large number of Polish workers go abroad to further their careers in more prosperous parts of the world. And wherever Polish workers go, they take cultural traditions with them. As a result, although Polish restaurants and food stores have long been a feature of the larger cities in Europe, especially since World War II, these outlets are now spreading further afield as they find new opportunities for work abroad.

The geography of the country

Poland's shape – a square with the south-western corner chewed away – is dominated by the natural boundaries of

Below: Carp, a favourite on the Polish table at Christmas, are found in the many lakes.

Above: The stunning Baltic coastline is home to many different types of fish.

the Baltic Sea to the north and the Sudeten, Tatra and Carpathian mountain ranges to the south. On its western and eastern borders, however, there are no such physical delineations. On the western border the only sign that you are passing from Germany to Poland is the Oder river, which winds its way from south to north towards the sea. On the eastern side,

nothing separates Poland from its neighbours, Kaliningrad, Lithuania, Belarus and Ukraine.

This lack of natural boundaries has proved inviting to Poland's neighbours, who have, in the past, been tempted to take advantage of Poland's abundant natural resources for their own use.

Below: Because it is bordered by seven other countries, Poland has enjoyed the influence of many different cultures.

However, Poland's position as a kind of pivot nestling between Western and Eastern Europe, as well as between the warm south and the chilly north, also has its advantages. One of these is the country's exposure to different cultures and their corresponding trade links. As a result, Poles have been able to adapt their cuisine to mix local ingredients with imported crops, such as potatoes and salad vegetables, which now flourish in the fertile soil.

Southern mountains
To the south, Poland's natural border is formed by the spectacular mountain ranges that divide the country from the Czech Republic and Slovakia. With most of Poland's hills rarely rising to more than 300m/1,000ft above sea level, the

Above: The beautiful Tatra mountain range forms a natural border with Slovakia.

contrast between the plains and the southern fringe is extreme. The highest mountain, Mount Rysy, in the Tatra range on the border with Slovakia, is 2,499m/8,200ft above sea level, while the lowest point, located west of the village of Raczki Elblaskie, plunges to 1.8m/5.9ft below sea level.

The foothills to these mountains support a range of animals, including sheep, pigs and cattle. Hay fields rising gently up the slopes are a common sight and are cultivated in order to feed the animals. Despite the abundance of sheep, lamb is not a favourite meat in Poland – and flocks of sheep are more often kept for their wool, to be made into clothing

City life
The capital city, Warsaw, like many of the other major cities of Poland, is situated in the central region of the country. Now that the restrictions of earlier years have been lifted, there is a flourishing restaurant trade in these cities, and people love to go out on special occasions to eat their favourite foods – dumplings (pierogi) filled with savoury or sweet mixtures, filling soups, hunter's stew (bigos) and the delectable cakes and pastries made by the many bakers to be found in Polish cities.

ready for the cold winters, and their milk, to be made into a much-loved sharp-tasting sheep's cheese.

Despite the winter cold, the southern mountain region is well-populated, with family farms predominating. Some entrepreneurial inhabitants now take advantage of their position in the fresh mountain air to encourage tourists to stay for walking holidays, fortified by hearty stews and maybe the fierce local plum brandy (Sliwowica Lacka). Other local industries include food-processing plants, which now package and despatch the abundant meat, dairy and food crops of the region.

Left: The sweeping grasslands of Poland provide hay to feed the cattle, sheep and pigs throughout the winter.

A good farming climate

Temperatures and growing conditions in Poland vary only slightly from one side of the country to the other, with warmer, wetter weather in the south-west and colder, drier areas in the north-east. The whole country can be very cold in the winter as the biting north-westerly winds sweep across mainland Europe and Scandinavia, picking up rain and snow clouds from the Baltic.

Summer temperatures are rather more variable, depending on the prevailing air currents, although the reliable gentle summer rains bring stable growing conditions for the crops of central Poland and ensure that there is always enough summer pasture for the cattle and food for the pigs.

To make the most of such fertile conditions the people of Poland developed many ways of working with the climate to maximize crop yields from the land. They also knew how to make sure there was enough food to see them through the lean times of year, and this led to many excellent, tasty recipes based on meat, game, root vegetables, grains and freshwater fish, combined with preserved foods such as sauerkraut, curd cheese, sour cream and, of course, the famously potent local vodka.

Northern lakes

The region in northern Poland that borders the Baltic Sea is a flat wetland dominated by waterways and home to many of the country's 10,000 lakes. These lakes are teeming with a great variety of freshwater fish, a fantastic source of protein that has been part of Polish cuisine since the earliest days. Pike, carp and trout in particular grow to a good size, and are served to the whole family on feast days such as Christmas, where carp is set in jelly or simmered in a wine stock. In the past a successfully caught carp was kept alive until the last moment before it was cooked to ensure its freshness – often even swimming in the family's bathtub!

The Baltic coastline is smooth, with the strong currents of the Baltic driving shoals of fish past Poland and on to the Baltic states and Scandinavia. Poland's relatively short sea border ends with a swirl at Gdansk, where the Vistula river meets the sea and a long spit of silt from the river has formed a natural lagoon.

Above: The fertile grasslands in central Poland are ideally suited for farming.

Poland's fishing fleets based on the coast still catch sardines, haddock, lobster and other seafood, but over-fishing and pollution in the Baltic means that many have to travel much longer distances to find enough fish.

In this spongy northern terrain, some of which is below sea level, there is little room between the lakes and forests for large-scale agriculture. Farms tend to be very small family affairs, with just a few pigs and cattle and the growing of root crops, particularly potatoes – a staple of many Polish dishes, including pancakes and dumplings.

Central plains

Like the northern lake region, the central part of Poland is also very flat, but less liberally sprinkled with lakes. This gives the farmers more room to grow cereals and to keep cattle, although family farms tend to be rather small and many still produce only enough food for their owners and for local markets, rather than trading on a national scale.

Shaped by the glaciers of the Ice Age, this flat landscape is rich in natural resources, particularly coal, and this led to considerable industrialization during the 19th and 20th centuries. In later years, these heavy industries have moved elsewhere, leaving a legacy of pollution, run-down housing and a lack of jobs for the local people.

Church festivals

The Catholic church – a hugely important part of life in Poland throughout its recorded history – retains its influence today. Nearly all Poles regard themselves as Catholics, with 75 per cent of them being regular churchgoers. A symbol of hope, the church helped to preserve traditional feast days and foods, and provided something to look forward to in the long dark years of food shortages and repression.

Polish Cuisine

In a country where the people have had to battle for independence, it is a matter of national pride that the traditions of Polish cuisine have been so well preserved. Faced with bitterly cold winters, the Poles know how to make expert use of their natural resources to produce hearty and sustaining meals. Polish food is not for slimmers!

Family life – the daily routine

From the shipyard communities of Gdansk in the north to the villages in the Tatra mountains in the south, Polish people take their daily meals seriously. Many dishes require long, slow cooking, and as most meals are eaten at home (restaurants are mainly for special occasions), time must be taken to plan, shop and cook for the family.

Breakfast

Although breakfast can be quite a quick meal – the working day often starts at 8am – it is still quite substantial. Poles like to base their morning meal on dark rye bread, cooked meats, hard-boiled eggs, cheese or jam. In the old days, people ate soup for breakfast, often thickened with grains (kasza) or based on sweetened milk with rice – a sustaining bowl of goodness to start the day. These days the liquid is more likely to be a cup of tea or coffee.

Lunch

Traditionally the main meal of the day in Poland, lunch is often eaten at home, although people who travel long distances to work might take lunch with them. If at all possible, everyone in the family will

Right: Steaming, hearty soups are often served in bread as a nourishing winter meal.

return home sometime between 1pm and 3pm to eat a two- or three-course meal that is designed to set them up with enough energy for the rest of the day.

The first course of this meal is nearly always soup. Poles love hearty vegetable and meat soups, and also make a range of chilled ones for summer. The famous soup borscht (barszcz), based on the beautiful ruby-red colour of beetroot (beets), is a universal dish, which pleases the eye as well as the stomach. Other favourite appetizers might be fish in aspic or a selection of cold cooked meats and vegetable side dishes. Next comes a sustaining main dish, such as hunter's stew (bigos) or pork cutlets served with sauerkraut and other vegetables. This course is generally based on meat, apart from on fasting days ordained by Catholic ritual, where fish takes its place.

Finally, the Poles love their desserts and will often find room for a cake such as poppy seed cake (makowiec), a substantial pastry such as plum dumplings (knedle ze sliwkami), or a dish of ice cream in hot weather.

Supper

At the end of the long working day, families will gather together again to eat supper, normally between 6pm and 8pm This is usually a lighter meal than lunch, with similar dishes – soup, fish, sweet desserts – being served, but this time omitting the heavier main course. Both lunch and supper may be accompanied by wine, vodka or fruit juice.

Snacks

Apart from the three main meals of the day, Poles enjoy eating snacks. Many Polish people have a sweet tooth, and there are a multitude of bakeries in every town and village. These bakeries sell a range of breads, of course, but their speciality is more often the delectable cakes and pastries that are so popular with their clientele.

Many of these delicacies are based on yeast dough, for example doughnuts (paczki z roza) or jam puffs, plum cake and seasonal favourites such as babka, an Easter cake made with citrus fruit, raisins and spices. Other sweet snacks are pastry-based, such as mazurek, a delicious tart

Far left: There is an abundance of fresh produce available at Polish markets.

Left: Bakeries selling bread and a range of cakes are visited on a daily basis.

Polish vodka

Picasso once said that 'the three most astonishing things in the past half-century have been the blues, cubism and Polish vodka'. This endorsement is well founded, as the amazingly strong spirit, made from potatoes and selected grains, flavoured with herbs, berries and spices, is now popular around the world and has a reputation for quality. In Poland, vodka is often drunk with meals as well as at other times.

made of pastry enriched with egg yolks and topped with all kinds of sweet things – soft cheese, honey, fruits, jam or nuts.

Preserving food

In any country that has extremely cold winters and where very little fresh food is available for weeks on end, techniques for preserving food needed to be developed to make sure everyone had enough to eat through the bleak months. This tradition is still practised in Poland today, and there are a range of pickled foods that feature on the winter menu.

Sauerkraut is perhaps the most famous of these. It originated as a way of preserving cabbage for use when fresh vegetables could not be dug from the snow-covered fields, but has now become a staple ingredient that is used in all types of weather. In past times, country households would keep a barrel of the pickle in the kitchen, while townspeople could buy a ladleful at a time from a similar barrel in the grocer's shop. Today,

Right: The oven is the key feature of this beautiful traditional Polish kitchen.

sauerkraut is widely available in jars and cans. Other vegetables, such as cucumbers, gherkins, beetroot (beets) and kohlrabi, can also be pickled, while others, such as the many varieties of mushrooms found in the forests, can be dried and added to marinades and stews.

In past years, before fresh fish could be easily and quickly transported around the country, only people who lived near the coast could eat seafood all year round, until a recipe for soused herring made with spices and vinegar was developed. Like sauerkraut, this is a staple dish that is found in most European countries with a Baltic Sea or North Sea coastline, ranging from Belgium to Norway.

Regional and ethnic dishes

The shape and terrain of Poland means that it has always been well served by trade links within and outside of the country. Linked by the mountain ranges to the south to its Czech and Slovak neighbours, and with no geographical barriers further north, Poland trades freely with Germany and France on one side and Russia on the other. With such open borders, any localized recipes soon spread over the whole country.

Despite this, some regions are known for certain foods. The northern lakes produce freshwater fish in abundance, and these became a major part of many

Above: Hot doughnuts filled with rosehip jam are a favourite snack in Poland.

Christmas feasts. Further south, fields of grain provide the basic ingredients for all sorts of bread, particularly the dense, robust rye bread found throughout Poland and its neighbouring countries. In the high southern mountains, sure-footed sheep provide milk to be made into a fresh, sharp cheese (oszczypek).

The influence of the many Jewish people who lived in Poland before World War II can be seen in several dishes, especially the traditional Jewish fish dish, pike or carp in aspic, which has been incorporated into Polish Catholic tradition and has become a regular part of Christmas feasts.

Polish Festivals and Celebrations

Many of the festivals celebrated in Poland are linked to the rituals of the Catholic calendar, with its emphasis on Christmas and Easter. These two major Christian celebrations are marked with a quite magnificent seriousness in Poland, and the religious basis is never forgotten. Other, more secular celebrations are also noted during the year, including hunting feasts in rural areas and name-day parties everywhere, as well as weddings and other family get togethers.

Christmas

Celebrations start early in Poland, with St Nicholas arriving on his sleigh on 6 December to hand out presents of honey and almond cookies and apples to the children, along with religious pictures of the Nativity. Traditionally, good children were rewarded for reciting their prayers to St Nicholas; naughty ones who had not bothered to learn them by heart could expect a severe rebuke, and no presents!

After a few weeks' wait the biggest celebration of the year on Christmas Eve (Wigilia) takes place. Wigilia means 'waiting', and it is the anticipation of Christ's birth that is all-important.

Wigilia is a huge affair of long meals and family rituals involving dressing the tree and opening gifts. The presence of as many family members as possible is a vital element, and guests and strangers are welcomed in as part of the family, sometimes with an ulterior motive – to make up the numbers – odd numbers at the table are thought to bring bad luck.

In past times, people in rural areas would bring a sheaf of corn into the house or spread hay under the white tablecloth to remind them of the manger in the stable where Jesus was laid. Most of all it is a day for telling the story of the Christmas angel, Aniolek, who brings the presents (and sometimes the sparkling tree, too) into the house while no one is looking; for dressing up in your best clothes; for waiting for the appearance of the first star in the sky, which signals the beginning of the feast; and, most of all, for eating the traditional food of this special day.

The Wigilia feast

This Christmas Eve meal is a major event in the Polish calendar. No meat is eaten, according to religious tradition, and people even try to avoid using animal fats

Above: Honey and almond cookies are given to children during Advent.

in the cooking. In past years, the feast was a huge affair of 12 courses (to represent the 12 apostles), but nowadays three or four courses are considered plenty. First, the family and guests will break and share a plate of oplatek, the thin wafers associated with the

Below: Carp in aspic is just one of the many dishes served for the Wigilia feast.

Below: A decorated Christmas tree in Bytom market square in Silesia, Poland.

communion service in church. Then follows a warming beetroot (beet) or sweet almond soup and some dishes of vegetables from the surrounding fields, such as sauerkraut, stuffed kohlrabi, mushrooms and potatoes.

The main dish is usually a magnificent whole carp or pike, and the meal ends with a dried fruit compote, and then the special Christmas pudding, kutia, made from wheat grains, honey, poppy seeds, cherry jam, dried fruit and nuts. Those who are still hungry might nibble the traditional honey cookies or a yeasty poppy seed roll, and the grown-ups can open their presents with a glass or two of fiery vodka to hand.

After the feast
Midnight Mass follows the Christmas Eve celebration, and the family service is a chance to focus on the real reason for the feast. It also marks the end of Wigilia as the birth of Christ is celebrated by the

A Wigilia feast
This joyful family feast will include some of the following:
• Christmas borscht
• Christmas Eve almond soup
• Herring in sour cream
• Carp in aspic, or wine sauce, or fried in breadcrumbs
• Pike with hard-boiled eggs and parsley
• Dumplings (pierogi)
• Sauerkraut with mushrooms
• Noodles with poppy seeds
• Dried fruit compote
• Poppy seed rolls
• Christmas pudding (kutia)
• Wine with the savoury dishes and vodka with the pudding

Above: At Easter time Polish women and girls traditionally spend Good Friday hand-decorating eggs. These are then used as table decorations or gifts.

congregation. After all this splendour, Christmas Day lunch is often a smaller and quieter affair. Some families eat a roast turkey, but more often the meal consists of leftovers from the previous day served cold with plenty of salad and vegetables. It is a time to enjoy visiting friends or family, where you will be offered a piece of honey cake or cookies.

New Year's Eve
This is a time to shake off the excesses of Christmas and start afresh with a party, either at home or out at a restaurant if you are lucky enough to be able to book a place. There may well be a full dinner during the evening, followed by champagne and a buffet after midnight.

Twelfth Night
Christmas finally winds down on 6 January, with a quiet celebration marking the arrival of the wise men at Christ's nativity. On this day, known as Twelfth Night, many families still mark the initials of the three kings above their front door with chalk, and burn incense in order to protect the home and family against hardship during the coming year.

Good Friday
On Good Friday, the main focus is religious. Many families visit several churches, to pray, but also to inspect and compare the decorated tombs found in each church, with an effigy of the Christ figure surrounded by flowers. A simple meal will follow that evening – maybe soused herring and potatoes – and the women spend the day decorating eggs.

Easter
It's hard to know how to top the festivities of Wigilia, but Polish people certainly try to go one better at Easter (Wielkanoc), when this most important Christian festival is celebrated with lavish feasting and partying alongside the traditional religious ritual.

There is a longer build-up to Easter than at Christmas, starting with the quiet and serious weeks of Lent. During this period everyone tries to give up some favourite food, and meat is eaten far less often than at other times of the year.

Easter also coincides with the annual spring cleaning season, a ritual that symbolizes death and re-birth. In Holy Week, just before Easter, the cooking and cleaning in every household rises to such a pitch that many men take themselves quietly out of the way to the local tavern or restaurant for a restorative meal or just some shots of excellent vodka.

Easter weekend

Saturday is a day of anticipation. In past times, the local priest would visit as many houses as possible to bless the family and the Easter feast laid out on the table, ready for the following day's celebrations. Finally, at midday on Easter Sunday, after another church service in the morning, the family gather for a long feast lasting through to the evening.

In the centre of the Easter Sunday table there is often a white lamb made of sugar or butter, usually standing on a little hill of greenery made of cress grown specially for the occasion, and surrounded by sweetly scented hyacinths. Once the

Above: The Easter table is laid on Easter Saturday and is often blessed by a priest.

Left: Lambs made from sugar or butter are sold during Easter.

family has gathered, a plate of quartered hard-boiled eggs is passed around and the feast can begin. This consists of cold meats including sausage, roast pork, turkey and ham; cold vegetables and salads; mazurki, the sweet, decorated pastries; and the Easter cake known as babka, baked in a special tall tin with fluted edges.

Harvest festival

A traditional rural feast day, the harvest festival is celebrated in most parts of the world. In Poland, the most popular and hardworking girl in a village (or maybe just the prettiest?) is chosen to represent the farm workers, and will carry a harvest wreath on her head from church to present to the local landowner. He will then reward the company with an array of dishes containing all the good things gathered during the harvest – grains, fruit, nuts and plenty of vodka.

Weddings and christenings

The traditional family celebrations of weddings and christenings are, of course, another good excuse for a great

Left: The annual harvest is a time of celebration and feasting.

meal with family members and friends, as they are everywhere in the world. In Poland, wedding traditions dictate that the bride and groom must pass a bottle of vodka to their neighbours before they can be allowed to walk through the spectators into the church.

After the ceremony there is a lavish wedding banquet for all the family and friends. Before it starts, however, another little ritual is always carried out, whereby the respective parents of the bride and groom offer them bread (ensuring that they always have plenty to eat); salt (to remind them of the hardships they may have to overcome); and a bottle of champagne (to celebrate the good things in life). The couple then drink the champagne and throw the glasses over their shoulders – if they smash, that will bring good luck.

Christenings follow a similar pattern to weddings: following a ceremony in church, christening parties often move on to the local tavern, where the godparents are expected to pay for the guests to toast the baby's health with vodka. These celebrations often used to extend over several days, but in busy modern times they are more likely to take up only one day. The traditional gifts of linen robes and caps for the baby have also changed over the years into gifts of cash.

Hunting feasts

In the old days, when rich landowners owned large tracts of Polish countryside, they would organize communal hunting parties to spend the day on the trail of wild boar, game birds and other delicacies of the forest. The whole male population of the village would be co-opted to help in shooting or beating, bringing their hunting dogs with them.

After all this effort and fresh air, the hunters would return ready for some good hot food and drink. This appetite, in conjunction with the mixture of meats from the day's hunt, gave rise to the famous Polish hunter's stew *bigos*. This rich and satisfying mixture of different kinds of meat, sauerkraut, mushrooms and stock is well spiced with juniper berries and peppercorns. Today, both hunting and the stew are still popular, accompanied by a glass of chilled vodka.

Name days

Polish people celebrate their name days rather than their birthdays. Most people are called by biblical names, and the corresponding saint's day is usually the most important secular day of the year for each individual. The day is marked by a feast or party, involving a good spread of food, plus plenty of alcohol, chocolates and presents. The guests may also sing the traditional song 'Sto lat', wishing them 100 years of happy life.

Secular festivals

Although religious occasions are marked with the best feasts, Poles do celebrate other events throughout the year. Some follow the rhythm of the seasons, such as hunting feasts and the Midsummer festival on 24 June, others are political. These include Consitution Day on 3 May and Independence day on 11 November.

Left: A traditional Polish wedding in the mountains in the south of the country.

CLASSIC INGREDIENTS

For centuries the difficult terrain and climate caused most of Russia to be quite isolated, and the rural population survived exclusively on locally grown produce. Gradually, as communications were established with its neighbours, new ingredients such as wheat and green vegetables were introduced to the Russian diet. Poland, on the other hand, has had access to a greater variety of ingredients since medieval times, as well as a kinder climate with fewer extremes. The climate in Poland, with its humid summers and wet, cold winters, gives ideal growing conditions for many seasonal crops and supports the yearly cycle of rearing farm animals for food, resulting in a natural abundance of locally grown produce such as grain and many varieties of fruit and vegetables. In Russia, the western side of the country has a similar climate, but further east and north, agriculture is more restricted. The ingredients in Siberian recipes, for instance, tend to be more earthy – potatoes, cabbage, honey, fish and game.

Fish and Shellfish

Recipes using fish and seafood are very popular in both Russia and Poland, and there is a big variety of species caught and sold. Russian fishermen have access to three major oceans, a host of smaller seas and hundreds of large lakes and rivers. Polish fishermen, however, set out from only a relatively short section of the Baltic Sea coast, and are therefore more dependant on the abundance of freshwater rivers and lagoons in this low-lying land.

Freshwater fish

The rivers and lakes that thread their way through the countryside of both Russia and Poland contain a fantastic source of protein that has long been incorporated in family meals.

Pike, carp and perch live in the still, deep waters of huge lakes and slow-running waterways such as canals, while trout and salmon leap and flash their silvery scales in the shallow, fast-flowing rivers. Carp and pike are both cooked for celebration meals, roasted whole with a tasty herb or horseradish dressing, marinated in red wine, dressed with chopped hardboiled eggs or even jellied in aspic. These impressive large fish make a great centrepiece for a Christmas or Easter feast, particularly when meat is off the menu for religious reasons. The Poles say that a shiny scale from the Christmas Eve carp, hidden in your wallet, will guarantee wealth for the coming year. Perch is also very popular – it is a common river fish and easily caught, even by inexperienced anglers. It is served in all sorts of ways – marinated, fried or

Above: Dried fish, displayed at a fish market in Ukraine.

poached with a mushroom and dill sauce. Trout and salmon tend to be treated very gently and simply baked in the oven to let their fresh flavour shine through. Garlic and herbs make a splendid dressing for the delicate flesh. Salmon is also used in a tasty pie with puff pastry.

Sea fish

Many varieties of sea fish are cooked and eaten by the Poles and the Russians – and coastal fishing dates back to the very earliest days of settlements around the coastline. People who live on the northern shores of Russia, in particular, rely on fish as a major source of protein, since meat is scarce in these chilly latitudes.

The subtle flavour of a piece of fresh fish straight from the ocean is often combined with dill, the most commonly used herb of these regions, whose feathery fronds are sprinkled liberally over the finished dish. Fillets of haddock, cod, sole or halibut are usually simply fried in breadcrumbs, grilled (broiled) or poached and served with a tangy sauce seasoned with lemon or sour cream. Smaller fish such as sardines are grilled and served whole, fresh from the sea, with just some melted butter and parsley as a dressing. Fish soup made of halibut, turbot or any other firm white fish is another favourite dish, and the Russian twist is to cook it with chopped salted cucumbers and capers to sharpen the flavour.

Below: White fish steaks, such as cod, are usually served fried in breadcrumbs.

Below: River trout are eaten simply baked whole with butter and parsley.

Below: Both Poles and Russians enjoy pike, a fearsome-looking freshwater fish.

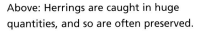

Above: Herrings are caught in huge quantities, and so are often preserved.

Shellfish

Although both Russians and Poles eat many different types of shellfish, such as lobster, oysters and crab, their main focus is on the larger fish to be found in the sea. One favourite dish, though, is crab salad. This creamy mixture dressed with parsley might grace the zakuski table as an appetizer, and will usually be made of ready-prepared or canned crab mixed with chopped cabbage and mayonnaise.

Caviar

The roe from cod or pike used to be the single most important dish on the Russian table. Over time, sturgeon caviar became the most popular variety, and in the 1800s a well-to-do family might present a bowl containing 20 kilos (45lb) of caviar on their zakuski table, with a large silver spoon so that their guests could help themselves to this salty treat. In the West, caviar has come to represent utter luxury, and is usually served in small portions or as a dressing on top of a plainer fish, for example in a special-occasion recipe for sole with vodka sauce and caviar. Today wild sturgeon are nearly extinct, and real, original Russian caviar is more expensive than ever. However, a lesser quality black sturgeon roe can still be found at a lower price and is almost equally delicious.

Preserved fish

Fish can be canned, salted, pickled, smoked or dried in Russia and Poland. The Russian tradition of zakuski, a table groaning with delightful mouthfuls of hot

Above: Caviar is still Russia's most popular and extravagant indulgence.

Above right: Blinis with salmon and caviar.

and cold snacks arranged to please the eye as well as the tastebuds, relies heavily on mouthwatering preserved fish.

Salted herring is served quite plainly with golden mustard sauce or with smetana (sour cream). Sometimes it is covered in a dressing of chopped hardboiled eggs and vegetables, which is known as sjuba, meaning 'fur' – herring in a fur coat. Blinis are often topped with little pieces of smoked salmon, and chopped smoked or salted fish makes a frequent tasty addition to a salad of mixed vegetables.

Below: Fish is often smoked or salted to preserve it, but also because it tastes good. Russians especially adore smoked salmon.

Fish stock

Makes about 1 litre/2 pints/ 6 cups stock
1kg/2lb white fish bones, heads and trimmings
1 litre/2 pints/6 cups cold water
6 white peppercorns
a bouquet garni
3–4 mushrooms
1 leek, roughly chopped
1 onion, roughly chopped
1 celery stick, roughly chopped

1 Wash the fish heads and remove the gills. Chop heads and bones if necessary. Place in a large pan.

2 Add the other ingredients, bring to the boil, lower the heat and simmer for 20 minutes (no longer or the flavour will be unpleasant). Strain. Season to taste.

Meat and Poultry

The people of Poland and Russia love meat. It often forms the main course for lunch or supper, and always for large celebratory meals, when the religious calendar allows. On these important occasions the meat is often prepared whole, and roasted suckling pig, chicken or goose are characteristic dishes for Easter Sunday or New Year feasts. The lesser cuts need tenderizing, and this is achieved by simmering on a low heat for a long time in a covered pot.

Pork

A plump pig, carefully fattened through the summer and autumn and eaten during the cold winter months, is still found in many a backyard and smallholding. During the years of massive collective farms in Russia in the 20th century, pork meat and pork sausage was less easy to find, but in Poland, this tradition survived in the countryside throughout the Communist era. Pork is cooked in all kinds of delicious ways – fried in breadcrumbs, roasted as a large joint with prunes or apple stuffing, stewed with vegetables, minced (ground) as a filling for rolled cabbage leaves, or even combined with several other meats in a tasty hunter's stew.

Pork sausage and ham are the most common forms of cured pork. They, too, feature in hunter's stew, lending their smoky flavour to the dish. Ukrainian cooks make a particularly piquant form of sausage blended with peperivka, or spirits flavoured with cayenne pepper, which gives the meat a definite kick. Polish sausage (kielbasa) is such an important part of the diet that it was one of the

Above: A cow herder moves cattle to new pastures in a Russian Federation village.

essential ingredients to make its way abroad with emigrating families. It is added to stews and soups or simply eaten sliced, as a snack, with a glass of vodka.

Beef

There are many Russian and Polish recipes for delicious beef dishes, from beef stroganoff to steak tartare. It is said that the Tartars, who first brought beef cattle

to Poland, used to tenderize their beef steaks by placing them under the saddle – inspiring the recipe for raw steak tartare. Lesser cuts of beef are minced together and often mixed with pork to make succulent burgers, served with buckwheat or mashed potato, or to form the filling

Below: Pork chops make a frequent appearance on the Polish table.

Below: Smoked sausage can be served in slices with vodka or added to stews.

Below: Lamb or mutton is not such a favourite in Poland as it is in Russia.

Above: Smoked meat, especially chicken, is often eaten with salad in Russia.

for the little dumplings (pelmeni) so beloved of the Russians. Beef can also be simmered gently in a thick tomato, red wine and paprika sauce to make goulash, topped with a spoonful of sour cream for each portion.

Veal

Poles and Russians love veal, especially veal cutlets, which they eat in the same way as pork chops, simply fried in breadcrumbs. Veal liver, kidneys and brains, which make a luxurious savoury treat served on toast, are also popular.

Lamb

Although this is not quite such a popular meat as pork and beef, lamb features in many Polish and Russian recipes. It can be cooked as a whole roasted joint with

Below: Roast goose is served for special celebrations in both countries.

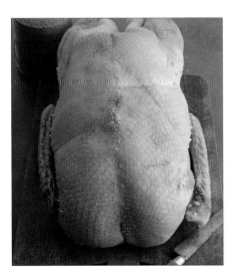

plenty of garlic and herbs, or as part of a meat soup, or a braised casserole, where its sweet taste blends well with aubergines (eggplants) and tomatoes.

Poultry

Many people still keep their own hens for fresh eggs and tasty meat. There are hundreds of recipes for using all parts of the chicken, from a whole roasted bird, stuffed with herbs and fruits, to a casserole or even a simple vegetable soup based on the stock from the carcase. However, the stronger flavours of goose and turkey are highly prized for special occasions, and potted goose, sealed and preserved in its own fat, is a winter favourite in Russia.

Game birds

Polish cuisine is full of recipes for partridge, pheasant, quail, pigeon and wild duck. The skill of plucking, dissecting, hanging, marinating and then cooking these wild birds is still one that is found in many kitchens. Juniper berries and other spices and herbs are often used to marinate the birds before cooking.

Game meat

Both Poland and Russia are full of wild places where hare, rabbit, deer and wild boar can be hunted. These strong-tasting meats are generally cooked in the oven to tenderize them and make the most of the fragrant gravy. Venison steaks are the exception; they are best pan-fried with strong wild mushrooms, and served with a red wine sauce.

Below: Partridges have less fat and a stronger taste than farm-reared birds.

Chicken stock

Makes about 1.5 litres/2½ pints/6½ cups
a whole chicken or 900g/2lb
  chicken wings and drumsticks
2 leeks, roughly chopped
1 large carrot, roughly chopped
1 celery stick, roughly chopped
2 bay leaves
2 sprigs fresh thyme
1.75 litres/3 pints/7½ cups water

1 Put all the ingredients into a large pan. Bring slowly to the boil, then use a spoon to skim.

2 Reduce the heat and simmer the stock very gently for 2–3 hours, skimming occasionally if necessary. Rapid boiling will make the stock cloudy.

Below: Venison is still hunted in both Russia and Poland.

Dairy Produce and Eggs

The farmers of Poland and western Russia have always kept extensive sections of their land as pasture for cows, sheep and goats. The lush green fields of grass in the plains and on the lower mountain slopes, particularly in the Caucasus near Russia's south-western border, are watered by the plentiful rain and snow of these parts. Sheep and goats, as well as cows, are milked to make yogurt, cream, sour cream (smetana), butter and soft cheeses.

Fresh cream

The Russians and Poles are very fond of sweet food, in the form of gooey cakes and rich desserts. Fresh cream makes the perfect accompaniment, whether it is whisked to soft peaks and then spread between the layers of sponge cake, or heated with vanilla sugar to make a custard topping for Easter pastry.

Sour cream (smetana)

This tangy, smooth cream is a real feature of Russian and Polish cooking. Preserving food is a vital element of the cuisine, and sour cream tends to last a lot longer than the fresh variety. It is almost ubiquitous in Russian and Polish recipes, both sweet and savoury.

Sour cream is stirred into nearly every soup pan just as it is ready to serve, or added in spoonfuls on top of each individual portion. It is also a main ingredient in the sauce when cooking rabbit casserole or beef stroganoff. And there are yet more savoury uses for this delicious dairy product: as a dip for

Above: Cows grazing on hillside pastures in the Tatra Mountains of Poland.

cheese dumplings, for instance, or a light dressing for salad, or forming the sauce for a panful of courgettes (zucchini).

Sour cream can also be used in a multitude of sweet dishes. It blends with soft cheese in a baked cheesecake, or with potato flour to make the succulent wrapping for a whole stuffed plum dumpling, or with butter, sugar and flour

Above: Whipped fresh cream accompanies desserts and cakes in Russia and Poland.

for the deep-fried little treats eaten at Christmas, known as angels' wings.

Sour cream is quite high in fat, but if calories are an issue, crème fraîche can be used instead. However, this does not give quite such a rich texture to the dish.

Below: Yogurt is sometimes used as an alternative to sour cream.

Right: Sour cream is used in Russian cuisine in a huge variety of ways.

Above: Curd cheese is used to make dumplings and a range of desserts.

Above: Cottage cheese is a lighter alternative to curd cheese.

Above: Butter is used in cooking rather than spread on bread.

Yogurt

This is sometimes used as a lighter alternative to the sour cream (smetana) so beloved of both Russians and Poles. It can be stirred into soup in exactly the same way as sour cream, but does not blend quite so well and has a more astringent taste. It is often used in recipes from the Caucasus, for example in yogurt and barley soup, or as a topping for lamb dishes. It also has a longer shelf life so is more common in isolated areas.

Butter

Fresh country butter is most often used in baking. It lightens and enriches potato cakes and biscuits, and forms a major part of the creamy custard poured into a baked shell for the special Easter pastry.

Below: Eggs symbolize new life and spring in Polish and Russian traditions.

Cheese

While the favourite cheese for cooking in Poland and Russia is the soft variety, traditional types of harder cheese do exist. They are made of cow's, goat's or sheep's milk and tend to be quite smooth, yellow and creamy in texture. Mature varieties, such as Polish Tylzycki or Bursztyn, sometimes contain caraway seeds for a particularly zesty flavour. They are generally eaten with dark rye bread for breakfast or for a lunchtime snack.

The main form of cheese in Russia and Poland, however, is the soft kind, from the uneven texture of cottage cheese to smoother, richer curd cheeses. Like sour cream (smetana), it adds a velvety consistency to many dishes, and there are hundreds of recipes, both sweet and savoury, involving this useful ingredient with its bland flavour.

Soft cheese can be the main ingredient in baked cheesecake, a Russian favourite with a cup of tea in the afternoon, or form the filling for crêpes, blended with egg yolks and sugar. One of the traditional recipes eaten at Easter is a dome-shaped pudding called pashka, which is formed from a mixture of strained cottage cheese, eggs, butter and sugar, dotted with dried fruit.

In its savoury form, soft cheese appears in several Polish and Russian dumpling recipes, either as a filling mixed with onion and mashed potatoes, or as part of the dough.

Right: Hard-boiled eggs are used extensively in Russian cooking.

Eggs

'Round as an egg' was an old Russian saying to describe a beautiful young girl. This was a great compliment, as eggs were very precious. They are also an important part of the Russian Orthodox Church's Easter celebrations.

A perfect, cheap Russian dinner might consist of a couple of fried eggs, a piece of bread and two or three fried sausages or some tasty fried onions. Eggs are indispensable in baking as part of the pelmeni dough, and also in sweet cakes and gateaux, omelettes and pancakes.

Polish cooks also find a place for eggs in the form of baked goods such as cakes and desserts, but in Poland they are very often hard-boiled, sliced in two and served cold as part of a salad. Chopped hard-boiled eggs also make a great thickener for a creamy white sauce or mayonnaise, and add nutritional value.

Vegetables and Grains

The fertility of the black, humus-rich soil in the most populated parts of Russia and Poland, and the culture of maintaining a kitchen garden, have led to an emphasis on vegetables of all kinds in Russian and Polish cuisine. Before trading links were forged with the rest of the world in the 16th century, both countries tended to rely on the sturdy root vegetables, wild mushrooms and nourishing grains that were the only crops that grew reliably in the difficult climate. More delicate salad vegetables, grown in hothouses, appeared in the 17th and 18th centuries.

Beetroot (beets)

This ruby-red vegetable is much loved by both Poles and Russians for its sweet taste and nutritional qualities, not to mention its reputation as an aphrodisiac! It was first mentioned as being cultivated in Poland and the Ukraine as far back as the 11th century. Beetroot makes a lovely rich and satisfying hot soup with sour cream (borscht), and it also blends beautifully with sour cream and hard-boiled eggs to make a fragrant cold soup. Chopped beetroot is a favourite ingredient in salads, and seems to offset the texture of oily fish particularly well. Russians mix it with chopped hard-boiled eggs, apples and strips of salted herring and pile it into a dome shape for the famous dish, Russian salad. They also use finely diced beetroot as a tasty topping for blinis, when it is known as beetroot caviar.

Potatoes

It is quite surprising that the potato, now found in so many Polish and Russian recipes, was unknown in both countries until the 17th century. Peter the Great introduced it to Russia and it has become ubiquitous in Russian cooking, whether as

Above: Seasonal vegetables and fruits piled high on a market stall in Krakow, Poland.

a separate vegetable accompaniment, in a stew, or cooked and cooled as part of a salad. Cold boiled potatoes with a sour cream dressing and plenty of feathery dill are a favourite part of the zakuski table.

Polish cooks tend to use potatoes in all sorts of ways too – as a thickener in soups, as a main course with mushrooms, mashed and made into pancakes and dumplings – all of which are substantial and filling dishes suitable for the cold weather. Potato pies, pirojki, consist of a yeast pastry encircling a filling of mashed potatoes and fried onion. Soup is sometimes poured into a hole at the top of these little baked or fried treats.

Left: Beetroot is one of the main ingredients of the world-famous borscht.

Right: Red and green cabbage keep well through the long winter months.

Other root vegetables

Many of these feature in Russian and Polish recipes, usually as a basic ingredient of soups and stews, where they blend into the liquid and add flavour and health-giving qualities. Carrots, kohlrabi, swede (rutabaga), celeriac, black radish and turnips are ideal crops for growing in a smallholding and also are stored away to last through the winter.

Onions are found in most savoury dishes. They can be chopped small and blended with meat to make a juicy burger or a stuffing for roast meat, or sliced into stock for soups and stews.

Cabbage

The aroma of cabbage soup simmering on the stove must have filled many a Russian or Polish house over the last few centuries. Cabbage is a nutritious vegetable that grows through the winter and keeps well once cut. The traditional cabbage soup is a peasant dish that can contain a variety of ingredients depending on what is available: carrots, potatoes, celeriac and herbs. Like most Russian and Polish soups, it is served topped with a spoonful of sour cream.

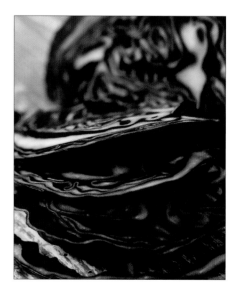

Above: Potatoes were introduced to Polish and Russian kitchens in the 17th century.

The large outer leaves of green cabbage are rolled around minced (ground) meat or fish mixtures and baked in the oven, and the more delicate inner leaves are popular served raw, shredded and dressed with creamy mayonnaise in a salad. Red cabbage has its own distinctive flavour, and also looks stunning as an accompaniment to roast meat when braised with apples, herbs, honey and spices, and even a dash of red wine.

Sauerkraut

The best way to preserve cabbage if there is a glut is to pickle it in brine, after which it can be kept for up to seven months. Sauerkraut is made by slicing the cabbage

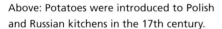

Below: White cabbage is grown in huge quantities and preserved in brine.

Above: Swedes are an important part of the winter diet in both countries.

finely, seasoning it with salt and then letting it mature in an oak barrel or a glass jar. Nowadays sauerkraut is more often bought ready prepared from the market, in a jar or a can.

This pungent mixture is used in all sorts of ways in Polish and Russian kitchens, helping to preserve health and enliven the taste of blander ingredients. It can be served as a side dish with sausages or poultry, stirred into a bubbling hunter's stew, blended with the stuffing for dumplings or mixed with other cold ingredients to make a tasty salad. Its strong flavour is an acquired taste for anyone not brought up to eat this typical Eastern European delicacy.

Below: Green cabbage is prized for its ability to grow through the winter.

Cooking with sauerkraut

Although often eaten cold, gentle simmering in a stew is a simple and delicious way to use sauer-kraut. These casseroles become even tastier when left to stew overnight. As with all kinds of slow home cooking, the results vary according to the taste of the cook and the ingredients that are available. Sauerkraut can also be fried with onions and then cooked in wine or water. Some Russians cook sauerkraut in champagne.

Salted cucumbers

This is a Russian speciality. Salted cucumbers are made by preserving them with salt, spices, herbs and sometimes

Below: Russians are very fond of salted cucumbers dipped in honey and smetana.

Above: Cultivated mushrooms may not involve the thrill of the hunt but are almost as popular a cooking ingredient.

garlic or horseradish. They are set in layers in oak casks, interleaved with oak and cherry tree leaves. These strongly flavoured ingredients have many uses in Russian cuisine. They can be eaten quite plain, dipped in honey or sour cream, as part of a zakuski spread, or added to soups such as soljanka or rassoljnik. They are also sometimes even added to hot or cold sauces to spice up the mixture and add some texture.

Mushrooms
A staple of the kitchen, mushrooms grow wild and abundant in the forests of Poland and Russia. Many families still make expeditions to the countryside in autumn to pick mushrooms, using the knowledge of which varieties are good and safe to eat that has been handed down through the generations. Mushrooms are earthy, rich vegetables, which form an integral part of many savoury recipes. The flavour goes so well with robust dishes, for instance in a wild boar casserole or a sturdy, filling soup with pasta.

The best-loved mushrooms in Russia are porcini and ceps. They are delicious accompaniments to most food, and of all wild mushrooms they are the easiest to dry, making them available all year round. Their flavour seems to become even more

intense after drying, and once hydrated, they can be added in small quantities to enliven soups, sauces and pie fillings.

Salad vegetables
The Italian Queen Bona Sforza brought her retinue to Poland in the 16th century when she married King Sigismund I. Among her servants were several chefs, who delighted the court with their light, airy dishes and their talent for making refreshing salads from tender vegetables such as lettuce, spinach and leeks, previously unknown in the chilly, damp

Below: Wild mushrooms, such as chanterelles, are hand picked and added to stews or served as a side dish.

Above: Apple and leek salad is said to be one of the dishes that was introduced to Poland by their queen, Bona Sforza, who came from Italy.

Polish climate. These ingredients are still known in Poland as wloszczyzna, or 'Italian vegetables'.

Russians tend to use the sturdier vegetables such as carrots and cabbage in their salads, rather than delicate lettuce. Both Polish and Russian recipes for appetizers and side dishes are often based on cold salads and mixtures of fruit and vegetables, such as apple and leek salad, which makes the perfect accompaniment to cold meat and fish.

Wheat
Like potatoes, wheat made a late appearance in this corner of Eastern Europe, but has since become an absolute favourite. Half of the wheat crop of the world is now grown in Russian fields and used for home and export markets.

Poles love to use refined wheat flour in their white bread, which is eaten for breakfast and is also made into breadcrumbs, used in many dishes as a topping or a coating for pan-fried meat or fish. Plain (all-purpose) white wheat flour is often used in pastry and cakes, and makes superb Polish dumplings.

Russians also make kvass, a sweet low-alcohol drink, from wheat. It can be drunk as a refreshing pick-me-up or added to a cold soup for a little extra kick.

Above: Although the grain was introduced relatively recently, wheat crops now take up a very large proportion of Russian and Polish farmland.

Buckwheat

The grains originally grown in Russia and Poland were the earthier, stronger ones such as buckwheat. In its milled form it has a slightly grey colour that is not so appealing to the eye as white wheat flour or dark rye flour. However, it has a distinctive taste that Russians love in pancakes, and Poles know best in the form of kasha, a porridge-like side dish.

Below: The distinctive, almost triangular, shape of grains of buckwheat.

Rye

The word 'bread' in Russia and Poland often means a dark, dense rye loaf. The Russian obsession with rye bread is so all-consuming that in the past, people tended to eat as much as 1 kilogram (2lb) of it every day. It was also discovered that rye bread made with a sourdough mixture remained fresh for a long time.

Black rye bread is still the most popular kind of bread in Russia and Poland, even today, and no meal, at any time of day, is complete without it. Rye bread is an excellent accompaniment to smoked and pickled fish.

Like wheat, rye can be fermented and turned into a mixture that forms the base of a special soup. White borscht is made with fermented rye flour stirred into a vegetable stock. Its sharp, tangy taste is quite distinctive.

Barley

This grain has traditionally been grown in the wide, flat pastures of rural Poland and Russia, and in fact, Russia is the world's largest producer of barley.

As pearl barley it often adds welcome carbohydrates to soups. Pearl barley is barley that has been polished, or processed, to remove the nutritious hull and bran. It doesn't need pre-cooking, just simmering gently in the stock.

Below right: Barley is the perfect ingredient to add to soups and stews. Some of the best vodka in Poland is made from barley.

Below: Rye flour is used for making bread and white borscht in Poland.

How to cook buckwheat

Despite its name, buckwheat is not related to wheat and is often sought as a gluten-free alternative to wheat. High in manganese, iron, magnesium, phosphorus, copper and zinc, buckwheat is eaten as a side dish or added to soups and stews.

1 To cook buckwheat as a side dish, first measure how much you need, then wash it in several changes of cold water.

2 Put the buckwheat in a pan and add twice as much water, bring to the boil, cover, and simmer for 10–15 minutes until all the water has been absorbed. Season and serve immediately.

Fruit and Nuts

One of the great blessings of the Russian and Polish climate is its suitability for growing fruit and nuts. The temperate zones of Poland and south-western Russia contain orchards full of apples, grapes, plums and almonds; the woods and forests further north overflow with juicy berries and nuts in the autumn. Even in the colder areas of both countries, some low-growing berry bushes have become used to the frost and snow and in fact cannot tolerate any hot sun in the summer.

Left: A fruit farm in Russia, growing orchard fruits such as apples and pears.

Orchard fruits
Polish orchards are full of apple, pear and plum trees covered in blossom in the spring. So long as a cold April wind or a sudden frost does not destroy the crop, these will produce a huge number of delicious fruits in the autumn. Poles and Russians are particularly fond of blending sweet fruits with savoury meats, for instance in a fruity stuffing for roast goose, pork or duck, or as a tart plum

sauce for beef kebabs. Polish fruit soup is a particular speciality, made of mixed plums, pears and cherries with water, sugar and sour cream. It is served cold as a summer treat, with potato dumplings.

Some of the most traditional recipes are for fruit desserts and cakes, such as an apple pie studded with raisins and enclosed in puff pastry, or simple baked apples. Plum dumplings contain a hidden treasure – a whole plum is encased in

potato and sour cream pastry, with a spoonful of cinnamon and sugar tucked inside the fruit. At harvest time in Poland, cooks make a cake with a sweetened yeast dough topped with halved plums, which is often served as a dessert with cream or ice cream.

Berries
Russians and Poles are very diligent at finding and cooking what nature provides, and berry picking is one of their great pleasures in the autumn. Some of the more delicate fruits, such as strawberries and raspberries, are only found in the warmer areas of the country. Tiny wild strawberries, which do grow in the cooler forests, are quite tart, and need plenty of sugar to make them palatable.

Perhaps the best known fruits of the berry crop are dark red cranberries, with their astringent flavour. Russians love to make their own cranberry juice mixed with sugar and served with ice on the zakuski table, alongside the vodka. Cranberries also add a sharp note to a

Below: Strawberries are often grown in Polish gardens and made into jam.

Below: Apple pie is a favourite dessert in both Poland and Russia.

Below: Plums are often dried to become prunes, and enjoyed through winter.

Summer berry jam

675g/1½lb/6 cups raspberries
675g/1½lb/6 cups strawberries
300ml/½ pint/1¼ cups water
1.3kg/3lb/6½ cups granulated
  (white) sugar, warmed
juice of 2 lemons

Use whichever summer berries are
in season: strawberries and raspberries as here, or red currants,
blackberries, or blueberries.

1 Put the berries and water in a
large pan on a low heat, cover and
cook gently for about 15 minutes.

2 Add the sugar and lemon juice
to the pan and cook over a low
heat, stirring frequently, until the
sugar has dissolved. Bring to the
boil and cook for 5–10 minutes, or
until the jam reaches setting point
(105°C/220°F).

3 Remove the pan from the heat
and skim using a slotted spoon.
Leave to cool for 5 minutes, then
stir gently and pour into warmed
sterilized jars. Seal and label.

strongly flavoured sauerkraut salad. For a
change of colour, purple blueberries are a
favourite filling for sweet pies, topped
with a sour cream and icing sugar glaze.

Dried fruits
Raisins and prunes, thriftily made from the
autumn crop of grapes and plums, are
used in both sweet and savoury recipes,
particularly those that mark the religious

Above: The intense red of cranberries
makes them a Christmas favourite.

high points of the year. Polish Easter
pastries and Christmas poppy seed cake,
as well as the Russian Easter dessert,
pashka, contain raisins – not too many,
but just enough to add a background
sweetness and a deliciously different
texture. Prunes are a favourite with
savoury recipes such as roasted pork or
sauerkraut stew, where the strong
flavours blend so well. All kinds of dried
fruits are used in a compote for dessert,
mixed together with cinnamon and
reconstituted in citrus-flavoured juice.

Nuts
The subtle flavour of nuts is part of many
Russian and Polish dishes. Like dried fruit,
nuts are used in celebration dishes such as
Christmas Eve almond soup, a sweet and
sour mixture containing ground almonds,
currants for sweetness and egg yolks as a

Below: Almonds are often ground and
used in baking recipes.

Above: Prunes, raisins and dried apricots
are often poached for dessert.

thickening agent. Whole or chopped nuts
are also sprinkled on top of Easter pastries
alongside the dried fruits. A delicious
mixture of chopped almonds and
cinnamon works well as a stuffing for
baked apples, and a single halved almond
makes a crunchy topping for honey and
cinnamon cookies. Nut rolls, or kolachi,
are well known in Russia to accompany a
cup of tea or coffee. They are made with
a sweet yeast dough wrapped round
ground nuts, sugar, milk and butter.

Nuts can also be found in savoury
recipes, particularly those from Georgia
and the south-west of Russia. Chicken
with walnut sauce uses the nuts as the
main thickening ingredient in a sauce
made fragrant with onion, garlic,
coriander (cilantro) and spicy cayenne
pepper. This kind of nut sauce can
accompany chicken fillets or pork chops.

Below: Walnuts are grown in Georgia and
feature in local dishes.

Condiments and Flavourings

Russian and Polish food relies on good-quality basic ingredients – fresh fish, meat, mushrooms, root vegetables and berries – and dishes are not highly spiced or seasoned. A selection of herbs and other flavourings are used judiciously to enhance rather than hide the main ingredients and to enliven the meal: a delicate sprinkling of parsley or some fronds of dill, for example, alongside more piquant flavours such as garlic, capers, horseradish and juniper berries.

Dill

This is the favourite herb in Poland and Russia. It grows well in the cool climate of both countries. Its slightly aniseed flavour adds a tart accent to blander foods such as plain white fish or boiled potatoes, where it really shines and is used in great abundance. But dill also has an important role to play as a garnish, with its feathery leaves decorating anything from cold Russian salad to hot cabbage soup.

Parsley

Although dill has the reputation of being the Eastern European herb par excellence, parsley is the flavouring automatically added to every hotpot, soup, vegetable, meat and fish dish. It almost goes without saying that a few sprigs or chopped sprinklings of this gently peppery herb will be needed every day in the kitchen. The flat leaf kind is most often used, with its slightly stronger flavour, and this is also ideal as a garnish for cold dishes such as veal brawn or crab salad.

Other green herbs

Many other herbs have their place in Russian and Polish cuisine. Coriander (cilantro) has a particular affinity with the spicier dishes of the south-west of Russia,

Flavoured vodkas

Both Russian and Polish vodkas are famous for their taste and strength, and in each country they are thought of almost as a national drink, with rituals and traditions of their own. Many flavoured vodkas are produced, including red pepper, ginger, fruit flavours, vanilla, chocolate (without sugar), and cinnamon. In Russia and Ukraine, vodka flavoured with honey and pepper is also popular.

such as Georgian bean salad or Georgian chicken with walnut sauce. Marjoram, thyme, sage and bay leaves blend well with the meaty braised dishes such as hunter's stew or anything containing wild mushrooms. Chives have a rich onion flavour and as such they are best suited to the well-defined flavour of a whole roasted carp.

Garlic

Western Russian cooks from the areas around the Caucasus mountains use lots of garlic. While it is not such a feature of recipes that come from the eastern side of Russia, nor of Polish recipes, where the flavourings tend to be a little more subtle, garlic makes a real impact in dishes such as Georgian pressed fried chicken with garlic sauce. The distinctively aromatic flavour is also an integral part of lamb dishes such as Uzbekistani pilaff or a roasted lamb joint brushed with garlic butter and studded with rosemary.

Horseradish

The horseradish root has a very tangy, almost bitter flavour. It is freshly grated and mixed with stock or sour cream for a robust sauce that goes well with game or one of the more meaty fish dishes, such

Below: Dill is a favourite herb with most types of fish dish.

Below: Coriander is a popular cooking ingredient in the south-west area of Russia.

Below: Garlic is one of the ingredients that Uzbekistan has introduced to Russia.

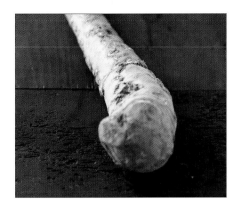

Above: The knobbly horseradish root, when grated, gives a powerful flavour.

as roasted carp. It can also be used to flavour pickled vegetables, such as beetroot (beets). A very little grated horseradish goes a long way.

Juniper berries
Traditionally the main flavouring in marinades for game such as hare, pheasant or wild boar, these small dried berries have a pungent, spicy taste that lends a distinctive note to meat and sauces. They are used widely in both Poland and Russia. The berries need to be gently crushed before adding to a stew or marinade to release their full flavour.

Poppy seeds
These aromatic little black seeds are added to many baked goods such as breads, sweet cakes and puddings. In Russia they are often sprinkled over the top of cakes and breads, and their fragrant taste is mixed with wheat kernels, nuts and honey in a Polish dish known as kutia, part of the traditional Christmas Eve feast.

Below: Black poppy seeds are used to flavour cakes and breads.

Above: The distinctive taste of juniper berries flavours many savoury stews.

Other spices
Cinnamon and cloves are often used in both savoury and sweet dishes, including flavouring marinades or compotes of dried fruit. Vanilla is added to many desserts and cakes, especially traditional festive baked goods such as Polish Easter cake. Savoury spices include allspice, with its peppery flavour, which is ideal for enlivening a marinade for game and blends very well with juniper berries. Capers add a tangy, vinegary note to fish dishes, including fish soup.

Honey
In the past, honey was used as a preservative as well as a sweetener. In Poland, honey is particularly associated with Christmas, in the form of honey and almond cookies and angels' wings biscuits. It is also added to vodka with cloves and cinnamon for a Polish Christmas drink and for the Russian sbitenj (see box).

Below right: Versatile and delicious, honey is used in baking and to make drinks.

Below: Inside the dried husks of the vanilla pod lie the fragrant, pungent seeds.

Spiced honey drink

This spiced drink, sbitenj, is one of Russia's oldest drinks.

Serves 4–6
150g/5oz/generous ½ cup honey
100g/3¾oz/generous ½ cup sugar
500ml/17fl 2 cups water

For the spice mixture
10ml/2 tsp St John's wort
2 cloves
5–6 black peppercorns
1.5ml/¼ tsp ground ginger
5ml/1 tsp ground cinnamon
10ml/2 tsp dried mint
1 litre/1¾ pints/4 cups water

1 Put all the ingredients for the spice mixture in a pan. Bring to the boil, simmer for 5 minutes, then remove from the heat.

2 Mix the honey and sugar and water in a separate pan. Bring to the boil, stirring. Lower the heat and simmer for 10 minutes. Strain the spiced water into the pan and heat gently, without boiling. Serve warm.

SOUPS

Both Russians and Poles have a passion for soups, whether hot or cold. Piping hot, filling soups are served during the harsh winter months, when there is a special need for sustaining food that warms from the inside out. Borscht, the famous beetroot (beet) soup with its splendid ruby-red colour, is perhaps the best known and has several variations, including White Borscht from Poland, but Cabbage Soup is also very popular, especially in Russia. Even Catherine the Great enjoyed cabbage soup, and developed a ritual for serving it to her guests. Poland enjoys hearty main course soups too, such as Chicken Noodle Soup, which is an entire meal in a bowl. There are also recipes for cold soups, and two Russian favourites are okroshka, made with the nation's favourite beer, and svekoljnik, made from beetroot. Both of these are popular as a refreshing appetizer during the summer.

Fish Soup with Salted Cucumber and Capers

This fish soup is considered to be the queen of Russian soups. Its lovely, rich flavour is accentuated by the addition of salted cucumbers, capers and olives. If you can find sturgeon, use that instead.

Serves 4

2 onions
2–3 carrots
1 parsnip
200g/7oz Salted Cucumbers (page 79)
30–45ml/2–3 tbsp rapeseed
  (canola) oil
15ml/1 tbsp tomato purée (paste)
1 bay leaf
4–5 black peppercorns
1 litre/1¾ pints/4 cups home-made or
  good-quality fish stock
400–500g/14oz–1¼lb salmon, halibut
  and turbot fillets, skinned
8 green olives
8 black olives
30ml/2 tbsp capers plus 5ml/1 tsp juice
  from the jar
4 thin lemon slices
60ml/4 tbsp smetana or crème fraîche
45ml/3 tbsp chopped fresh dill,
  to garnish

1 Finely chop the onions. Dice the carrots, parsnip and finely dice the cucumbers.

2 Heat the oil in a large pan, add the onions and fry over a medium heat for 2–3 minutes, until softened.

3 Add the carrots and parsnip to the onions, and fry over a medium heat, stirring all the time, for a further 5 minutes until softened.

4 Add the cucumbers, tomato purée, bay leaf and peppercorns to the pan and fry for a further 2–3 minutes. Add half of the stock, cover and bring to the boil. Reduce the heat and simmer for 10 minutes.

5 Meanwhile, cut the fish into 2cm/¾in cubes. Add the remaining stock, green and black olives, the capers and the caper juice to the pan.

6 Return to the boil and add the fish. Reduce the heat and simmer for 5 minutes, until the fish is just tender, being careful not to overcook the fish.

7 To serve, spoon the soup into warmed bowls, add a slice of lemon, a spoonful of smetana or crème fraîche and dill.

VARIATION Soups with salted cucumbers as an ingredient are often called soljanka. Soljankas can also contain cooked meat. Just substitute the fish with a mixture of boiled beef, ham and cooked sausages.

Energy 389kcal/1613kJ; Protein 24.5g; Carbohydrate 9.1g, of which sugars 7.2g; Fat 28.5g, of which saturates 7.7g; Cholesterol 73mg; Calcium 74mg; Fibre 3.1g; Sodium 361mg.

Chicken Noodle Soup

The Russians are masters at making excellent stock and this recipe is a good example. It is said that the stock should be translucent and as clear as a teardrop. This clarity is achieved by keeping the heat low when cooking the chicken – you need to aim for a very gentle simmer.

Serves 4

1 small chicken
1.5 litres/2½ pints/6¼ cups water
1 onion, cut into wedges
1 carrot, peeled and sliced
1 parsnip, peeled and sliced
1 leek, white parts only, cut
   into chunks
5ml/1 tsp salt
45ml/3 tbsp finely chopped parsley,
   to garnish
60ml/4 tbsp smetana or crème fraîche,
   to serve

For the noodles
150g/5oz/1¼ cups plain white (all-
   purpose) flour
1 egg
30–45ml/2–3 tbsp cold water
1.5ml/¼ tsp salt

1 Put the chicken in a large pan, add the water and bring to a slow boil. Reduce the heat and simmer. Skim the surface.

2 Add the onion, carrot, parsnip, leek and salt to the pan, cover and simmer very gently for 45 minutes, or until the chicken is tender. Using a slotted spoon, remove the vegetables from the pan and discard.

3 Transfer the chicken to a plate and leave to cool. Pass the stock through a sieve (strainer) and pour back into the pan. When the chicken is cool, cut into bitesize pieces.

4 To make the noodles, put the flour, egg, water and salt in a food processor and blend to a smooth dough.

5 Put the dough on a floured surface and knead for 2–3 minutes. Wrap in clear film (plastic wrap) and leave to rest in the refrigerator for 30 minutes.

6 Divide the dough into four even pieces. Using a rolling pin or pasta machine, roll out one piece at a time until very thin, and then cut into 5–6cm/2–2½in strips. Leave the strips to dry for 5 minutes.

7 Place a few strips on top of each other and shred them diagonally into very thin strips. Toss in flour and allow them to dry.

8 To serve the soup, put the chicken pieces into four individual serving bowls. Bring the stock to the boil, add half the noodles and cook for 5 minutes. Pour into the soup bowls, garnish with chopped parsley and accompany with smetana or crème fraîche.

COOK'S TIP Only half the noodles are required for this recipe. Keep the remaining noodles in an airtight container for up to a week in the refrigerator, or freeze. Substitute ready-made noodles if you are short of time.

Energy 427kcal/1805kJ; Protein 54.5g; Carbohydrate 40.2g, of which sugars 7.8g; Fat 6.4g, of which saturates 1.7g; Cholesterol 152mg; Calcium 76mg; Fibre 5.3g; Sodium 237mg.

Georgian Meat Soup

With its lovely aroma of garlic, and its smooth, creamy texture, this is the king of soups in the Russian province of Georgia. It is one of the most popular dishes served in Russian restaurants and is served on both festive occasions and weekdays.

Serves 4

1.2kg/2½lb chunky pieces breast or shoulder lamb, on the bone
1.5 litres/2½ pints/6¼ cups water
3 large onions
½ mild chilli
5 garlic cloves
2 tomatoes
45–60ml/4–5 tbsp olive oil
15ml/1 tbsp tomato purée (paste)
45–60ml/4–5 tbsp chopped fresh parsley
45–60ml/4–5 tbsp long grain rice
salt
60ml/4 tbsp Plum Sauce (page 143), to serve

VARIATION Instead of serving the soup with Plum Sauce, try adding 3–4 chopped fresh plums to the soup at the same time as the rice is added.

4 Add the tomatoes and tomato purée to the pan and fry, stirring all the time, for a further 1 minute. Add the onion and tomato mixture to the pan containing the meat and stock. Then add the parsley, chilli and garlic.

5 Add the rice to the pan. Season with salt to taste and cook for 20–25 minutes.

6 To serve, divide the meat between four soup bowls, pour the soup on top, and accompany with the Plum Sauce.

1 Put the meat in a large pan, add the water and bring to the boil. Reduce the heat and simmer for 5 minutes. Skim the surface, cover with a lid and simmer for 50–60 minutes, until the meat is tender.

2 Meanwhile, roughly chop the onions. Remove the seeds from the chilli. Finely chop the garlic. Slice the tomatoes into rough wedges.

3 Heat the oil in a large frying pan. Add the onions and fry for about 5 minutes, until golden brown.

Energy 433kcal/1801kJ; Protein 27.6g; Carbohydrate 24g, of which sugars 12g; Fat 25.5g, of which saturates 8.1g; Cholesterol 95mg; Calcium 72mg; Fibre 2.6g; Sodium 369mg.

Veal Kidney and Cucumber Soup

Many Russians prefer this soup to be as thick as porridge (kasha), but a thinner consistency may be more to your taste. It is important that you don't bring the soup back to a boil after the Lezjen sauce has been added, otherwise it may curdle.

Serves 4

1.5 litres/2½ pints/6¼ beef stock
50g/2oz/generous ¼ cup pearl barley
4–5 potatoes
1 onion
1 small leek
2 carrots
50g/2oz celeriac
3–4 Salted Cucumbers plus
  30ml–45ml/2–3 tbsp juice
600g/1lb 6oz calf's kidney
45ml/3 tbsp rapeseed (canola) oil
2 bay leaves
5 black peppercorns
2 allspice berries
25g/1oz chopped fresh dill

For the Lezjen sauce
15g/½oz/1 tbsp butter
1 egg yolk
75ml/5 tbsp double (heavy) cream

1 Heat half of the stock in a large pan. Add the barley and cook for 35–50 minutes until soft.

2 Meanwhile, cut the potatoes into small wedges and add to the barley for the last 10 minutes of cooking.

3 Meanwhile, chop the onion, slice the leek, finely slice the carrots and celeriac, and dice the Salted Cucumbers.

4 Cut the calf's kidney into small chunks, trimming away and discarding any fat.

5 Heat the oil in a large frying pan. Add the onion, leek, carrots and celeriac and fry over a medium heat, stirring occasionally, for about 10 minutes, until the onions and leeks are softened.

6 Add the Salted Cucumbers, bay leaves, peppercorns and allspice to the pan, and fry for a further 1–2 minutes, stirring.

7 Add the vegetable and cucumber mixture to the pan together with the cooked barley and potatoes. Add the kidney and the remaining stock. Bring to the boil, then reduce the heat and simmer for 20 minutes.

8 Just before serving the soup, make the Lezjen sauce. Melt the butter in a pan. Remove the pan from the heat and mix in the egg yolk and cream.

9 Alternatively, make the sauce in advance and keep warm in a bowl, uncovered, standing over a pan of hot water at a maximum of 55°C/130°F, until ready to serve.

10 Add the dill or parsley to the soup and season with the Salted Cucumber juice, according to taste.

11 Bring the soup back to the boil, stirring all the time. Remove from the heat and serve immediately, topped with a spoonful of Lezjen sauce.

COOK'S TIP Do not boil the soup after the sauce has been added as it might curdle.

VARIATION As a quick alternative to making the Lezjen sauce, you can also top the soup with a spoonful of smetana or crème fraîche.

Energy 515kcal/2152kJ; Protein 29.7g; Carbohydrate 38.5g, of which sugars 8.6g; Fat 27.9g, of which saturates 11.4g; Cholesterol 684mg; Calcium 107mg; Fibre 4.7g; Sodium 340mg.

Tripe Soup

Firm and white ox tripe can be used to make an economical and nourishing meal. In Poland, it is usually prepared with spices and served as a soup. Although it takes some time to prepare, it is a great delicacy and is well worth the effort.

3 Cut the cooked tripe into slices. Pour the cooking liquid into a measuring jug (cup) and add enough water make up the volume to 1.75 litres/3 pints/7½ cups. Return the tripe and liquid to the pan.

4 Add the carrots, celeriac and leeks to the pan and cook for 15 minutes, or until tender. Add the chopped onions.

Serves 4–6

1.3kg/3lb scalded and cleaned ox tripe
pinch of salt
2 carrots, cut into matchsticks
½ medium celeriac, cut into matchsticks
2 large leeks, cut into matchsticks
2 small onions, chopped
75g/3oz/6 tbsp butter
40g/1½oz/⅓ cup flour
2.5ml/½ tsp ground ginger
1.5ml/¼ tsp freshly grated nutmeg
1.5ml/¼ tsp ground black pepper
8 allspice berries
5ml/1 tsp sweet paprika
10ml–15ml/2–3 tsp dried marjoram
rye bread and shots of vodka, to serve

1 Rinse the tripe several times in cold water, draining well each time. Put in a pan and add enough water to cover the tripe. Bring to the boil and cook for 20 minutes, then drain.

2 Cover the tripe with fresh boiling water, add a pinch of salt, and cook again over a low heat for about 3 hours, or until the tripe is tender.

COOK'S TIP There are two types of tripe: the smooth type, known as 'blanket' tripe, which comes from the first stomach, and 'honeycomb' tripe, which comes from the second. Both types should be thick, firm and white in appearance; avoid any that is grey or slimy.

5 Make a roux by melting the butter in a small pan over a low heat, then add the flour and mix to a smooth paste. Stir a small amount of the broth into the roux, then add to the pan containing the tripe and the vegetables.

6 Add the ginger, nutmeg, pepper, allspice, paprika and dried marjoram, and cook over a low heat for 20 minutes.

7 Serve the soup immediately with rye bread and some ice-cold vodka.

VARIATION Some cooks like to add a glass of dry white wine to the broth at step 5.

Energy 234kcal/977kJ; Protein 18.3g; Carbohydrate 13.5g, of which sugars 5.8g; Fat 12.3g, of which saturates 7.1g; Cholesterol 165mg; Calcium 168mg; Fibre 3g; Sodium 202mg

Barley Soup

This tasty soup, which has many variations all over Eastern Europe, is ideal for keeping out the chill on bitterly cold winter days. Combining economical cuts of meat and staple winter vegetables, this version is a favourite in Poland and is eaten all over the country.

Serves 4–6

800g/1¾lb pork ribs
2.25 litres/4 pints/10 cups water
2 bay leaves
2.5ml/½ tsp dried marjoram
2.5ml/½ tsp salt
6 peppercorns
2 carrots, chopped
2 celery sticks, chopped
2 parsnips, chopped
2 leeks or 1 large onion, chopped
4 small dried boletus mushrooms, soaked and sliced into thin strips
75ml/5 tbsp pearl barley
25g/1oz/2 tbsp butter
2 potatoes, peeled and diced (optional)
chopped fresh parsley, to garnish

VARIATION You can use beef ribs in place of the pork, if you like.

1 Put the pork ribs in a large pan and pour in the water. Add the bay leaves, marjoram, salt and peppercorns, then cover the pan and cook on a low heat for about 1 hour.

2 Lift the ribs out of the liquid, remove the meat and discard the bones. Cube the meat, then return it to the pan and add the carrots, celery, parsnips, leeks or onion and mushrooms. Cover and simmer for 30 minutes, until the vegetables are tender.

3 Add the pearl barley, butter and potatoes (if using) to the pan and cook over a gentle heat for a further 15–20 minutes, or until the barley is tender. Serve the soup immediately, garnished with chopped parsley.

Energy 282kcal/1184kJ; Protein 31.3g; Carbohydrate 18.3g, of which sugars 5.5g; Fat 9.7g, of which saturates 4.2g; Cholesterol 93mg; Calcium 51mg; Fibre 3.5g; Sodium 137mg.

Fresh Cabbage Soup

Soups play an important part in both Russian and Polish cuisine and this simple cabbage-based vegetarian soup is one of the most popular everyday soups in Russia. Every housewife has her own recipe and the variations and adaptations are endless.

Serves 4

40g/1½oz/3 tbsp butter
1 onion, sliced
1 head white cabbage, total weight
   750g/1lb 10oz, shredded
1 carrot, shredded or grated
1 piece celeriac, total weight 50g/2oz,
   shredded and grated
2 bay leaves
5 black peppercorns
1.5 litres/2½ pints/6¼ cups
   vegetable stock
5 new potatoes, diced
15ml/1 tbsp sunflower oil
1 (bell) pepper, cored and sliced
2 tomatoes, chopped
salt and ground black pepper
45ml/3 tbsp chopped fresh dill,
   to garnish
smetana or crème fraîche and rye
   bread, to serve

4 Heat the oil in a frying pan over medium heat. Add the pepper and tomatoes and fry for 2–3 minutes, until softened. Transfer to the soup and simmer for 5 minutes. Season to taste.

5 Spoon the soup into bowls and sprinkle with the chopped dill. Top with smetana or crème fraîche and serve with rye bread.

1 Melt the butter in a large pan over a medium heat. Add the sliced onion and cook, stirring, for 3 minutes, until softened but not browned. Add the shredded cabbage, carrot and celeriac and cook for 3 minutes.

2 Add the bay leaves, peppercorns and 200ml/7fl oz/scant 1 cup of stock to the cabbage. Bring to the boil, then reduce the heat, cover and simmer for 15 minutes, stirring occasionally.

3 Add the remaining stock and the potatoes and simmer for a further 10 minutes until the potatoes are soft.

Energy 273kcal/1141kJ; Protein 6g; Carbohydrate 36.7g, of which sugars 17.4g; Fat 12.2g, of which saturates 5.8g; Cholesterol 21mg; Calcium 122mg; Fibre 7.2g; Sodium 106mg.

Mushroom Soup

In the damp, dark woods of Russia, there are plenty of wild mushrooms. The best time to pick them is early autumn, and these are then often marinated, pickled or dried to make sure that there is an ample supply throughout the year. This soup is made with dried porcini mushrooms.

Serves 4

30g/1¼oz dried sliced porcini
  mushrooms
1.5 litres/2¼ pints/6¼ cups water
75–90ml/5–6 tbsp pearl barley
1 onion, finely chopped
1 large carrot, diced
1 parsnip, diced
4 potatoes, diced
45ml/3 tbsp rapeseed (canola) oil
2 bay leaves
5 peppercorns
salt and ground black pepper
60ml/4 tbsp smetana or crème fraîche,
  and 45–60ml/3–4 tbsp dill, to serve

1 Put the mushrooms in a pan, add the water and soak for 3 hours or overnight. Bring the liquid to the boil, reduce the heat and simmer for about 10 minutes. Then remove the mushrooms from the pan, reserving the cooking liquid. If using whole mushrooms, slice them.

4 Add the fried vegetables to the mushrooms, stock and pearl barley. Add the potatoes, bay leaves and peppercorns, bring to the boil and cook for 15 minutes. Season with salt and pepper to taste.

5 To serve, pour the soup into individual soup bowls, and top each with a spoonful of smetana or crème fraîche. Sprinkle with chopped dill to garnish.

VARIATION Instead of pearl barley, use small pasta, such as orzo or conchiglie, and add to the soup towards the end of the cooking time.

2 Add the barley to the stock, season and cook for 30 minutes or until soft.

3 Heat the oil in a frying pan, add the onion, carrot, parsnip and fry, stirring, over a medium heat, until golden brown.

Energy 196kcal/828kJ; Protein 4.1g; Carbohydrate 37g, of which sugars 1.8g; Fat 4.5g, of which saturates 0.6g; Cholesterol 0mg; Calcium 20mg; Fibre 1.4g; Sodium 11mg

Mushroom Soup with Pasta

This fragrant Polish soup is served with sour cream, chopped fresh herbs and delicate flakes of home-made pasta, making it both sustaining and delicious.

Serves 4

50g/2oz/1 cup dried ceps
1.5 litres/2½ pints/6¼ cups water
1 carrot, roughly chopped
1 parsnip, roughly chopped
½ celeriac, roughly chopped
1 large onion, roughly chopped
15g/½oz/1 tbsp butter
6–8 black peppercorns
juice of 1 lemon
salt, to taste
sour cream and chopped fresh
    parsley or dill, to garnish

For the pasta

115g/4oz/1 cup plain (all-purpose)
    flour, plus extra for sprinkling
1 egg, beaten
2.5ml/½ tsp salt
15–30ml/1–2 tbsp water

1 Rinse the dried mushrooms, then place in a large pan with the water, heat until warm and leave to soak for 30 minutes.

2 Bring to the boil. Cover and simmer for 25–30 minutes, or until the mushrooms are soft. Strain the stock into a clean pan, reserving the mushrooms.

3 To make the pasta, sift the flour into a bowl, make a well in the centre and add the egg, salt and 15ml/1 tbsp water. Mix to a dough, adding more water if needed.

4 Transfer the dough to a lightly floured surface and knead for about 5 minutes, or until the dough is firm.

5 Roll out the dough as thinly as possible, then sprinkle the surface with flour and leave to dry out.

6 Add the carrot, parsnip, celeriac, onion, butter, peppercorns and salt to taste to the pan containing the mushroom stock. Simmer gently over a low heat for a further 20 minutes.

7 Strain the stock into a clean pan, discarding the other vegetables. Slice the reserved mushrooms into thin strips. Cut the pasta dough into 1cm/½in squares.

8 Bring a large pan of lightly salted water to the boil, add the pasta squares and cook for about 4 minutes. Drain, rinse in cold water, then drain again.

9 Bring the pan of stock back to the boil, then add the lemon juice, the sliced mushrooms and cooked pasta, and heat through. To serve, ladle the soup into warm bowls, then swirl a little sour cream in the centre of each and garnish with chopped parsley or dill.

Energy 265kcal/1111kJ; Protein 7.4g; Carbohydrate 31.3g, of which sugars 0.9g; Fat 13.2g, of which saturates 7.4g; Cholesterol 75mg; Calcium 72mg; Fibre 2.4g; Sodium 343mg.

Polish Easter Beetroot Soup

Two versions of borscht have formed an intrinsic part of Polish cuisine for centuries, with the oldest-known recipe dating back to the 16th century. One is made specially for the Christmas Eve feast, while this one is for eating at Easter, and is made with fermented juice.

Serves 4–6

1kg/2¼ lb beef bones
1 leek, roughly chopped
1 large onion, roughly chopped
2 slices of celeriac or parsnip
2 carrots, roughly chopped
5ml/1 tsp salt
5–6 dried wild mushrooms, rinsed and soaked in warm water for 30 minutes
juice of ½ lemon (optional)
pinch of sugar (optional)
175ml/16fl oz/¾ cup dry red wine (optional)
1 garlic clove, crushed (optional)
chopped fresh dill, to garnish
Dumplings Stuffed with Mushrooms (page 184), to serve

For the fermented beetroot juice
1.8kg/4lb raw red beetroot (beets)
1.5 litres/2½ pints/6¼ cups boiled water, allowed to cool until just lukewarm
1 slice wholegrain (whole-wheat) bread
4–5 garlic cloves, peeled
10 black peppercorns
4–5 allspice berries
2–3 bay leaves

1 To make the fermented beetroot juice, carefully wash the beetroot, then peel and slice them thinly.

2 Place the beetroot slices in a large glass jar or a bowl and cover completely with the lukewarm water.

3 Place the bread on top, then add the garlic, peppercorns, allspice and bay leaves. Cover the jar or bowl with a piece of muslin (cheesecloth) and put in a warm place. Leave to ferment for 3 days.

4 Skim off the foam that will have risen to the surface and strain the ruby-red juice into a bowl, then transfer to clean bottles or jars. Cork and keep in a cool place until required. (It will keep for several months, if stored in a cool place.)

5 Put the bones in a large pan, pour over 600ml/1 pint/2½ cups of water and add the chopped vegetables and salt. Bring to the boil and simmer for 15 minutes, or until the vegetables are cooked.

6 Put the dried mushrooms and 475ml/16fl oz/2 cups water in a separate pan, bring to the boil and simmer for 5 minutes, until the mushrooms are cooked.

COOK'S TIP Red borscht is sometimes served in a cup as a drink at a wedding, or as a hangover cure after a party.

7 Strain the meat stock and the mushroom cooking liquid into a measuring jug (cup) to measure the final quantity. Pour into a large, clean pan, and add 600ml/1 pint/2½ cups of fermented beetroot juice for every 300ml/½ pint/1¼ cups stock. Heat gently until the borscht just boils, then remove from the heat.

8 Taste the borscht and add lemon juice or sugar, as you prefer. To enhance the acidity, add a glass of red wine, or for extra flavour and aroma, add crushed garlic about 15 minutes before serving.

9 Serve in warmed bowls with Dumplings Stuffed with Mushrooms, garnished with chopped fresh dill.

Energy 84kcal/348kJ; Protein 0.5g; Carbohydrate 0.5g, of which sugars 0.1g; Fat 9g, of which saturates 3.4g; Cholesterol 8mg; Calcium 2mg; Fibre 0g; Sodium 672mg.

Russian Beetroot Soup

This famous soup is the centre and highlight of the Russian meal. There are many versions of the recipe. The secret behind a good borscht is the home-made stock and the high quality of the root vegetables.

Serves 4–6

5–6 beetroot (beets), total weight
  500g/1¼lb
3 carrots, total weight 250g/9oz
1 cabbage wedge, total weight
  300g/11oz, shredded
3 potatoes, diced
2 onions, sliced
45ml/3 tbsp tomato purée (paste)
15ml/1 tbsp sugar
5ml/1 tsp salt
60–90ml/4–6 tbsp smetana or
  crème fraîche
chopped fresh dill, to garnish
4–6 lemon wedges, to serve

For the stock

1kg/2¼lb beef on the bone
2 litres/3½ pints/8 cups water
1 carrot
1 parsnip
1 piece celeriac
1 onion
2 bay leaves
4–5 black peppercorns
2–3 fresh parsley stalks
5ml/1 tsp salt

COOK'S TIP It is a good idea to make double the quantity of this recipe and freeze what you don't need. The soup is easy to heat up for a quick meal.

1 To make the stock, put the beef and bones in a large pan, add the water and bring to the boil. Lower the heat and simmer for 10 minutes, skimming the surface of any residue.

2 Add the carrot, parsnip, celeriac, onion, bay leaves, peppercorns, parsley and salt to the pan. Cover and simmer gently for 1 hour. Remove the vegetables and herbs from the pan and discard. Remove the meat from the pan and dice.

3 To make the soup, add the beetroot and carrots to the stock, bring to the boil then simmer for about 40 minutes, until the vegetables are tender. Remove the beetroot and carrots from the pan.

4 Add the shredded cabbage, potatoes and onions to the stock, bring it back to the boil then simmer for 15–20 minutes.

5 Grate the cooled beetroot and carrots. When the cabbage and potatoes are tender, add the beetroot, carrots and meat to the stock with the tomato purée, sugar and salt. Simmer for 10 minutes.

6 To serve, pour the soup into warmed bowls. Top each serving with 15ml/1 tbsp smetana or crème fraîche and dill. Accompany with a lemon wedge.

Energy 127kcal/535kJ; Protein 4g; Carbohydrate 20.2g, of which sugars 17.7g; Fat 4g, of which saturates 2.3g; Cholesterol 9mg; Calcium 60mg; Fibre 5g; Sodium 143mg.

White Borscht Soup

This light, sour soup from Poland is made from a fermented rye flour, water and bread mixture, which needs to be prepared several days before you want to make the soup.

2 Transfer to a large, sterile glass jar, cover with muslin (cheesecloth), then close the lid and leave to ferment in a warm place for at least 3 days.

3 To make the stock, put the celeriac, carrots, leek, onion, parsley, garlic, bay leaves and water in a large pan.

4 Bring to the boil, then simmer for 20 minutes, or until the vegetables are tender. Strain, discarding the vegetables.

5 Add the dried, soaked mushrooms and 600ml/1 pint/2½ cups of the white borscht to the hot stock. Bring to the boil, then season to taste.

6 Add the potatoes and hard-boiled eggs. Serve immediately, garnished with fresh marjoram or dill.

Serves 4

50g/2oz/2 cups rye flour
1 rye bread crust
1 celeriac, roughly chopped
3 carrots, roughly chopped
1 leek, roughly chopped
1 onion
2 parsley sprigs
4 garlic cloves, crushed
4 bay leaves
1.2 litres/2 pints/5 cups water
5–6 dried mushrooms, soaked in
  warm water for 30 minutes
4 small boiled potatoes, cubed
2 hard-boiled eggs, cut into quarters
salt and ground black pepper, to taste
marjoram or dill, to garnish

1 To make the white borscht, put the rye flour in a large, heatproof bowl and stir in enough boiling water until the flour forms a thin paste. Leave it to cool, then add 1.2 litres/2 pints/5 cups lukewarm water and the bread crust.

Energy 133kcal/561kJ; Protein 6g; Carbohydrate 19.1g, of which sugars 1.5g; Fat 4.2g, of which saturates 0.9g; Cholesterol 95mg; Calcium 26mg; Fibre 1.1g; Sodium 1109mg.

Ukrainian Borscht

This borscht is flavoured with salo, salted pig's lard. If you can't find genuine Ukrainian salo, use Italian lardo, often sold in delicatessens, or other cured pork fat, instead.

Serves 4

2 potatoes
1 red (bell) pepper
juice of ½ lemon
300g/11oz cooked boiled beef
60–75ml/4–5 tbsp rapeseed
  (canola) oil
4–5 medium beetroot (beets), grated
1 carrot grated
1 small piece celeriac, grated
1 small onion
1 small wedge cabbage, finely sliced
30ml/2 tbsp tomato purée (paste)
1.5 litres/2½ pints/6¼ cups beef stock
3–4 garlic cloves
50g/2oz salo or lardo
15ml/1 tbsp sugar
salt

1 Peel and cut the potatoes into wedges and finely slice the pepper, discarding the core and seeds. Cut the boiled beef into small chunks.

2 Heat the oil in a large frying pan. Add the grated beetroot, carrot and celeriac, the onion and cabbage, then stir-fry for 10 minutes, until softened.

3 Add the potatoes, tomato purée and half of the stock to the beetroot mixture. Bring to the boil, then reduce the heat and simmer for 15 minutes.

4 Add the remaining stock and the slices of red pepper to the pan and simmer for a further 5–10 minutes, until all the vegetables are tender.

5 Meanwhile, chop the garlic. Put in a mortar with the salo or lardo and grind together with a pestle.

6 Add the meat to the soup, bring to the boil, then turn off the heat. Stir in the lemon juice, sugar and garlic mixture, and season to taste.

Energy 483kcal/2015kJ; Protein 22.4g; Carbohydrate 36.5g, of which sugars 20.8g; Fat 28.4g, of which saturates 9g; Cholesterol 55mg; Calcium 75mg; Fibre 5.7g; Sodium 169mg.

Christmas Eve Almond Soup

A traditional part of the Christmas Eve feast in Poland, this nourishing, slightly sweet almond soup is made with rice and currants and is often served with an egg yolk. It makes a hearty appetizer for a winter meal, or can be eaten on its own as a snack.

Serves 4

500ml/17fl oz/generous 2 cups milk
225g/8oz/2 cups ground almonds
115g/4oz/1 cup cooked rice
    (50g/2oz/¼ cup raw weight)
a drop of almond extract
50g/2oz/¼cup currants
    or raisins
15ml/1 tbsp sugar (optional)
4 egg yolks (optional)

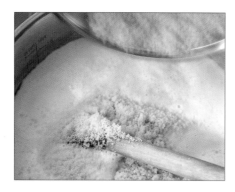

VARIATION You may find that the dried fruit gives the soup enough sweetness for your taste, in which case omit the sugar.

COOK'S TIP Only use the freshest free range eggs for this recipe, as they are served raw.

1 Bring the milk to the boil in a large, heavy pan. Add the ground almonds and cook gently, stirring often, over a low heat for 15–20 minutes, or until slightly thick.

2 Mix together the rice, almond extract, currants or raisins and sugar, if using.

3 Place a heaped tablespoon of the rice and currant mixture in the base of each of four bowls.

4 Ladle the soup into the bowls. If you like, place a raw egg yolk into each one before serving immediately.

Energy 480kcal/1999kJ; Protein 17.3g; Carbohydrate 28.2g, of which sugars 16.7g; Fat 33.6g, of which saturates 3.8g; Cholesterol 7mg; Calcium 299mg; Fibre 4.4g; Sodium 64mg.

Sorrel Soup with Eggs

Sorrel grows wild in grassy areas in Poland, but it is also cultivated commercially for use in a range of dishes, including soups, sauces and salads. It has a pleasant, slightly sour taste, which is complemented by the richness of the sour cream and hard-boiled eggs in this dish.

Serves 4

15ml/1 tbsp butter
400g/14oz fresh sorrel leaves,
  chopped
15ml/1 tbsp plain (all-purpose) flour
1 litre/1¾ pints/4 cups beef or
  vegetable stock
45–60ml/3–4 tbsp sour cream
4 hard-boiled eggs, chopped
salt and ground black pepper,
  to taste

1 Melt the butter in a large pan, then add the chopped sorrel leaves and a pinch of salt. Stir well so that all the leaves are coated in the melted butter.

2 Cook the sorrel over a low heat for 5–7 minutes, until the leaves have just wilted.

3 Put the flour in a small bowl and gradually add 60ml/4 tbsp stock, mixing constantly to make a paste.

4 Add the flour mixture to the pan and stir to combine with the sorrel. Stir in the remaining stock, bring to the boil and simmer for 10 minutes.

5 Season the soup to taste with salt and ground black pepper, then gradually add the sour cream, whisking well between each addition.

6 Transfer the soup to warmed soup bowls and top with a spoonful of chopped hard-boiled egg.

VARIATION If you are unable to find sorrel leaves, you could use rocket (arugula) or large basil leaves, although this will alter the flavour.

Energy 162kcal/673kJ; Protein 9.8g; Carbohydrate 5g, of which sugars 2g; Fat 11.7g, of which saturates 5g; Cholesterol 205mg; Calcium 215mg; Fibre 2.2g; Sodium 238mg.

Cold Beetroot Soup

All year round, soup is the heart of every Russian meal. In the summer the soups are often served chilled, as in this recipe, to be enjoyed in the summer heat. You will need to leave plenty of time between making this soup and serving it so it has time to chill properly.

2 Put the eggs in a pan, cover with cold water and bring to the boil. Reduce the heat and simmer for 10 minutes. Drain and put under cold running water. Remove the shells and chop the eggs.

3 When the beetroot are cold, pour the beetroot stock into a jug (pitcher) or bowl and put in the refrigerator. Remove the skin from the beetroot, and coarsely grate it into a large serving bowl.

4 Dice the cold potatoes and add them to the grated beetroot together with the cucumbers, eggs, spring onions and the mustard. Mix together.

5 To serve, pour the beetroot stock over the beetroot in the serving bowl, add the smetana or crème fraîche and mix gently together. Season with the lemon juice, sugar and salt to taste. Sprinkle the chopped dill on top to garnish.

Serves 4

800g/1¾lb small raw beetroot (beets)
1.2 litres/2 pints/5 cups water
3 eggs
4 medium potatoes, cooked
2–3 cucumbers, total weight
  300g/11oz, cut into thin strips
1 bunch spring onions (scallions),
  finely chopped
15ml/1 tbsp mustard
60ml/4 tbsp smetana or crème fraîche
15–30ml/1–2 tbsp fresh lemon juice
5–15ml/2–3 tsp sugar
salt
60–75ml/4–5 tbsp fresh dill, chopped

1 Put the beetroot and water in a pan, add 5ml/1 tsp salt and boil for about 50 minutes. Leave to cool in the stock.

COOK'S TIP
This soup can be prepared in advance up to step 5 until ready to serve.

Energy 215kcal/908kJ; Protein 11.8g; Carbohydrate 28.9g, of which sugars 19.9g; Fat 6.8g, of which saturates 2.3g; Cholesterol 147mg; Calcium 122mg; Fibre 6.3g; Sodium 311mg.

Cold Kvass Soup

Kvass is a fermented low-alcohol drink enjoyed in Russia. It is also used as a base for this soup, known as okroshka. The soup is very easy to make and is perfect for a light lunch on a lazy summer day. When chilled, tasty okroshka will cool you even in the hottest weather.

Serves 4

2 eggs
15ml/1 tbsp mustard
100ml/3½fl oz/scant ½ cup smetana or crème fraîche plus 60ml/4 tbsp, to serve
1 litre/1¾ pints/4 cups kvass or buttermilk (see Cook's tip)
250g/9oz cooked meat, such as unsmoked ham or roast pork, or cooked sausages, diced
1 cucumber, total weight 250g/9oz, very finely sliced
1 bunch spring onions (scallions), finely sliced
15ml/1 tbsp sugar
45ml/3 tbsp finely chopped fresh dill
salt

COOK'S TIP If you cannot find kvass, which is a sweet, wheat-based Russian drink, buttermilk will give a different but equally good flavour.

1 Put the eggs in a pan, cover with cold water and bring to the boil. Reduce the heat and simmer for 10 minutes. Drain and put under cold running water. Shell the eggs and separate the yolks from the whites. Reserve the whites.

2 Put the egg yolks in a soup tureen or bowl and mash until smooth. Add the mustard and the 100ml/3½fl oz/scant ½ cup smetana or crème fraîche and mix together. Slowly add the kvass or buttermilk, and blend.

3 Finely chop the reserved egg whites. Add the diced meat, sliced cucumber, spring onions and chopped egg to the egg yolk and kvass mixture and mix together. Finally add the sugar and dill and season with salt to taste.

4 To serve, pour the soup into soup bowls and top with the remaining smetana or crème fraîche.

Energy 353kcal/1473kJ; Protein 27.6g; Carbohydrate 17.6g, of which sugars 17.3g; Fat 19.8g, of which saturates 10.3g; Cholesterol 169mg; Calcium 363mg; Fibre 0.8g; Sodium 305mg.

Fruit Soup with Sour Cream

The wealth of forests and gardens provides an abundance of summer fruits in Poland, and this has greatly influenced the cuisine. Made with a mixture of fresh, seasonal fruit, this delicious soup is ideal for a summer meal. Serve it cold with Grated Potato Dumplings or sweet rolls.

Serves 4

4 cups mixed fresh fruit, such as
  pears, plums and cherries
1 litre/1¾ pints/4 cups water
5 cloves
1 cinnamon stick
45ml/3 tbsp plain (all-purpose) flour
250ml/8fl oz/1 cup sour cream
90g/3½oz/½ cup sugar, or to taste
175ml cherry vodka (optional)
Grated Potato Dumplings (page 173),
  or sweet bread rolls to serve

VARIATION You can also serve this refreshing soup with some noodles or crispy croûtons.

1 Wash and peel the fruit, remove the cores and stones (pits) and cut larger fruits into even-sized pieces. Put in a pan, add the water, cloves and cinnamon, and simmer for about 10 minutes.

2 When the fruit is tender, strain the liquid into a large bowl and reserve. Push the fruit in the sieve (strainer) so that all the juice is squeezed out. Then return the pulp together with the liquid to the pan and bring to the boil.

3 In a small jug (pitcher), mix the flour with the sour cream. Pour the mixture into the pan, gradually, and stir to mix. Bring back to the boil, stirring constantly.

4 Remove from the heat and add sugar to taste. Add the cherry vodka, if using. Serve immediately with Potato Dumplings or sweet rolls.

COOK'S TIP If the soup tastes a little too sweet, squeeze some lemon juice into the mixture before serving.

Energy 299kcal/1258kJ; Protein 3.4g; Carbohydrate 45.8g, of which sugars 37.2g; Fat 12.7g, of which saturates 7.8g; Cholesterol 38mg; Calcium 91mg; Fibre 2.4g; Sodium 30mg

Mini Bread Rolls with Garlic Sauce

These soft little rolls are called pampushki in Russian. They are small, sweet and fluffy and are delicious served warm, dipped into an aromatic garlic sauce. They are often served with soups or to accompany main-course dishes, and are traditionally eaten with Ukrainian borscht.

Makes 60 rolls

25g/1oz/2 tbsp butter
250ml/8fl oz/1 cup milk
420–480g/14½–1lb 1oz/heaped 1⅔–2
   cups plain white (all-purpose) flour
5g/⅛oz easy-blend (rapid-rise)
   dried yeast
2.5ml/½ tsp salt
5ml/1 tsp sugar
1 egg

For the garlic sauce
3 garlic cloves
pinch of salt
30ml/2 tbsp rapeseed oil
75ml/5 tbsp lukewarm water

1 Melt the butter in a small pan. Pour in the milk and warm until it reaches blood temperature. Remove from heat.

2 Put 420g/14½oz/heaped 1⅔ cups of the flour, yeast, salt and sugar in a large bowl. Add the warmed milk mixture and mix well together, then knead for about 5 minutes, until the dough is smooth, adding more flour if necessary. Cover the bowl with a clean dish towel and leave in a warm place for about 40 minutes, until doubled in size.

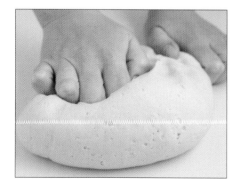

3 Preheat the oven to 230°C/450°F/Gas 8. Line a large baking tray with baking parchment. Transfer the dough to a lightly floured surface and knead lightly. Divide the dough into four pieces then roll out each piece between your fingers, into a long thin roll.

4 Cut each roll into 15 small pieces and form each piece into a small ball. Put the rolls on the prepared baking tray. Brush the tops with beaten egg. Bake in the oven for 10-15 minutes until golden brown. Transfer to a wire rack, cover with a clean dish towel and leave to cool.

5 To make the garlic sauce, crush the garlic into a bowl and mix with the salt, oil and water.

6 Serve the warm rolls with the Garlic Sauce as a dip.

Energy 34kcal/143kJ; Protein 0.9g; Carbohydrate 5.8g, of which sugars 0.4g; Fat 1g, of which saturates 0.4g; Cholesterol 4mg; Calcium 15mg; Fibre 0.2g; Sodium 7mg

APPETIZERS

The tasty appetizers, known in Russia as zakuski, are served at the beginning of most Russian meals. For an everyday meal, zakuski will not be too filling or very numerous, perhaps just two or three different little dishes, but for parties and celebrations, zakuski become much more elaborate and can consist of ten or more different recipes, both hot and cold. Often they contain a salty fish or shellfish, such as herring or crab, or a selection of vegetable 'caviars', and they are carefully chosen to complement the main course. However, these delicate dishes are also ideal for a light lunch or supper in their own right, and are sometimes used for the whole meal. Favourite Polish appetizers are more like the first course to a meal, rather than a buffet of several dishes. They also often include fish, especially herring – frequently marinated in spices and sour cream – and potato pancakes. The Poles also enjoy game pâtés and terrines.

Chopped Herring Salad

Although the ingredients for this Russian dish are simple, it is usually served at festive occasions. The herring fillets must be soaked overnight, so allow time to do this. You can buy ready-made forshmak in Russian delicatessens. It is delicious served with ice cold vodka.

3 When the eggs are cooked, drain and put under cold running water. Remove the shell and separate yolks from whites.

4 Peel, core and chop the apple and put in a food processor. Add the salted or pickled herring fillets, egg yolks and the butter and process briefly. Transfer to a bowl and mix in the fried onion.

5 Finely chop the reserved egg whites and finely slice the spring onions. Put the salad on a serving plate and serve garnished with the egg whites and spring onions.

Serves 6

250g/9oz salted or pickled
  herring fillets
2 eggs
45ml/3 tbsp rapeseed (canola) oil
1 onion, finely chopped
1 Granny Smith apple
40g/1½oz/3 tbsp butter, at
  room temperature
1–2 spring onions (scallions),
  to garnish

1 If using salted herrings, soak the fillets in cold water overnight. The next day, rinse the herring fillets under running water and then drain.

2 Put the eggs in a pan, cover with cold water and bring to the boil. Reduce the heat and simmer for 10 minutes. Meanwhile, heat the oil in a frying pan, add the chopped onion and fry for about 5 minutes, until softened but not browned. Set aside.

Energy 212kcal/875kJ; Protein 7.6g; Carbohydrate 3.2g, of which sugars 2.8g; Fat 18.9g, of which saturates 4.6g; Cholesterol 97mg; Calcium 32mg; Fibre 0.3g; Sodium 223mg.

Polish-style Herrings

Herrings, prepared in many different ways, are a firm favourite in Poland. They are particularly popular during Lent, on Christmas Eve and on Ash Wednesday, when meat is not allowed. This dish of herrings marinated with spices can be made in advance and kept for a week.

Serves 4

4 medium herrings, cleaned, or 8
  boneless fillets
2 large onions, thinly sliced
2 lemons, cut into thin slices
10 black peppercorns
5 allspice berries
4 bay leaves, broken into pieces
juice of 3 lemons
150ml/¼ pint/⅔ cup sour cream
2.5ml/½ tsp sugar
4 large potatoes, peeled and sliced
¼ tsp caraway seeds
90ml/6 tbsp vegetable oil
salt and ground black pepper, to taste
chopped fresh parsley, to garnish
lemon wedges, to serve

1 Soak the herrings in cold water for at least 24 hours and up to 36 hours, changing the water several times.

2 Drain the water and carefully remove the skin by sliding a sharp knife between skin and flesh.

3 If using whole herrings, cut off the head and tail. Divide the fish into fillets and remove all the bones, using tweezers or your fingers.

4 Place a layer of fillets in the base of a large glass jar with a lid, then add a thin layer of onions and lemon slices, some peppercorns, allspice berries and bay leaf. Add another layer of herring and repeat the layers until all the ingredients have been used.

5 In a small bowl or a jug (pitcher), mix together the lemon juice, sour cream and sugar, then pour the mixture into the jar, giving it a little shake as you pour.

6 Screw on the lid and turn upside down a few times to make sure the sour cream mixture covers the fillets evenly. Leave to marinate in a cool place for 24–36 hours.

7 Preheat the oven to 200°C/400°F/ Gas 6. Layer the potatoes in a greased ovenproof dish, sprinkle over the caraway seeds, drizzle with vegetable oil and season to taste. Bake for 35–40 minutes, until the potatoes are tender and golden.

8 Spoon the herrings on to four serving plates and garnish with chopped parsley. Serve with the hot potatoes and lemon wedges for squeezing.

Energy 508kcal/2098kJ; Protein 19.5g; Carbohydrate 5.4g, of which sugars 4.2g; Fat 45.5g, of which saturates 10.9g; Cholesterol 73mg; Calcium 108mg; Fibre 0.7g; Sodium 137mg.

Russian Salad with Herring

This salad looks like a cake, and is internationally called herring à la Russe. The cover under which the herrings dwell is made from several layers of vegetables and mayonnaise, and is always topped with grated hard-boiled eggs. Every Russian cook has their own recipe. This herring dish is served both on the zakuski table and as a main course. Many Russians would also gladly eat what is left for breakfast.

**Serves 8 as an appetizer,
4 as a main course**

250g/9oz salted herring fillets
3 carrots, total weight 250g/9oz
4 eggs
1 small red onion, finely chopped
200g/7oz/scant 1 cup mayonnaise
5–6 cooked beetroot (beets), total
  weight 300g/11oz
2 Granny Smith apples
45ml/3 tbsp chopped fresh dill

VARIATION Replace the cooked beetroot with pickled beetroot if you want to add the tang of vinegar to this dish.

1 Soak the herring fillets in water overnight. The next day, rinse the herring under running water and then drain. Cut into small pieces and put in a bowl.

2 Put the whole carrots in a pan of cold water, bring to the boil, then reduce the heat, cover and simmer for 10–15 minutes, until just tender. Drain and put under cold running water. Set aside.

3 Meanwhile, put the eggs in a pan, cover with cold water and bring to the boil. Reduce the heat and simmer for 10 minutes. When the eggs are cooked, immediately drain and put under cold running water. Set aside.

4 Add the chopped onion to the herrings with 15ml/1 tbsp of the mayonnaise. Spread the mixture over a serving dish measuring about 25cm/10in in diameter.

5 Coarsely grate the carrots, beetroot and apples into small piles or bowls. Add a layer of grated beetroot over the herring mixture and spread 45–60ml/3–4 tbsp mayonnaise on top. Repeat with a layer of grated carrots and mayonnaise and then a layer of grated apple.

6 Spread a thin layer of mayonnaise to cover the salad. Cover with clear film (plastic wrap) and chill in the refrigerator overnight, or for at least 1 hour.

7 Just before serving remove the shell from the eggs and grate coarsely. Sprinkle the grated egg all over the salad so that it covers it completely and creates a final layer, then garnish with chopped dill.

Energy 130kcal/544kJ; Protein 12.1g; Carbohydrate 9.3g, of which sugars 8.7g; Fat 5.3g, of which saturates 0.8g; Cholesterol 95mg; Calcium 96mg; Fibre 2.2g; Sodium 1697mg.

Cold Cod Salad

This salad, with its golden top, was created during Russia's Soviet era when there was a shortage of food. If nothing else, cod, carrots and onions were always to be found in the supermarket 'Gastronom'. The salad is best if chilled overnight, so make it in advance.

Serves 6–8

  600g/1lb 6oz cod fillets, skinned
  5ml/1 tsp salt
  4–5 black peppercorns
  1 bay leaf
  200ml/7fl oz/scant 1 cup rapeseed
    (canola) oil
  3 large onions, diced
  3 large carrots, grated
  45ml/3 tbsp water
  200g/7oz/scant 1 cup mayonnaise

1 Put the cod fillets in a pan and add the salt, peppercorns and bay leaf.

2 Just cover the cod with water, bring to the boil, then reduce the heat and simmer for 5–10 minutes. Drain and leave to cool.

3 Heat half of the oil in a large frying pan. Add the onions and fry, stirring, until golden brown. Remove from the pan and set aside to cool.

4 Grate the carrots. Heat the remaining oil in the frying pan, add the carrots and stir-fry over medium heat for 10 minutes.

5 Add the water to the carrots and continue cooking for 5–10 minutes, stirring, until the water has completely evaporated. Set aside.

6 Use your fingers to divide the cooled fish into small chunks, removing all bones as you do so, and spread in a shallow serving dish.

7 Cover the fish with the onions and then spread the carrots on top. Cover the top with mayonnaise.

8 Chill the salad overnight, or for at least 2–3 hours before serving with bread.

VARIATION As an alternative, you can substitute the cod with perch, pike or other white fish.

Energy 528kcal/2179kJ; Protein 15.3g; Carbohydrate 9.5g, of which sugars 7.5g; Fat 47.9g, of which saturates 6.6g; Cholesterol 63mg; Calcium 38mg; Fibre 2g; Sodium 225mg.

Crab Salad

The famous Russian crab meat, charka, is sold in food shops all over the world. The high quality merits the price. However, inventive Russian housewives found a way to supplement the expensive crab meat by adding finely cut, fresh white cabbage. The result is surprisingly good.

Serves 4–8

1 wedge white cabbage, about 250g/9oz total weight
250g/9oz can crab meat, preferably Russian charka crab meat in its own juice
100g/3³⁄₄oz/scant ½ cup mayonnaise
salt
30ml/2 tbsp finely chopped fresh parsley, to garnish
French bread, to serve

VARIATION This salad can also be served on pieces of very thin, crispy toast, which makes a perfect snack to hand round with drinks.

1 Finely shred the cabbage, discarding the thick stalk. Put in a large bowl and cover with just boiled water from the kettle.

2 Leave the cabbage to soak for 2–3 minutes. Drain off the water and squeeze the cabbage dry with your hands, transferring the handfuls to a dry bowl as you do so. Set aside and leave to cool.

3 When the cabbage is cool, add the crab meat and mayonnaise to the bowl and stir until mixed together. Season and transfer to a serving plate. Garnish with chopped parsley and serve with French bread.

Energy 121kcal/501kJ; Protein 6.4g; Carbohydrate 1.9g, of which sugars 1.8g; Fat 9.8g, of which saturates 1.5g; Cholesterol 32mg; Calcium 66mg; Fibre 1g; Sodium 232mg.

Chicken Liver Pâté

This easy-to-make pâté, with fried onion, melts in your mouth and is one of the most popular dishes on the Russian zakuski table. In restaurants the mousse is often served in shells made out of frozen butter.

Serves 4–6

2 eggs
400g/14oz chicken livers, rinsed
2.5ml/¹/₂ tsp salt
1 onion, chopped
45ml/3 tbsp rapeseed (canola) oil
100g/3³/₄oz/7¹/₂ tbsp butter, softened
salt and ground black pepper
bread slices, to serve

For the garnish
2 onions
45ml/3 tbsp rapeseed oil
4–6 sprigs flat leaf parsley

1 Put the eggs in a pan, cover with cold water and bring to the boil. Reduce the heat to low and simmer for 10 minutes. When the eggs are cooked, drain and put under cold running water. Remove the shell from the eggs, then cut them in half.

2 Put the livers in a pan and cover with boiling water from the kettle. Simmer for 5–8 minutes, until the livers are cooked.

3 Heat the oil in a small frying pan, add the chopped onion and fry over medium heat, stirring constantly, for 5 minutes until softened and golden brown.

4 Using a slotted spoon, put the livers in a food processor. Add the fried onion, egg halves and butter and process to form a smooth paste. Season the mixture with salt and pepper to taste.

5 Spoon the mixture into a serving bowl, cover and chill in the refrigerator for at least 3–4 hours or overnight.

6 When ready to serve, make the garnish. Finely chop the onions. Heat the oil in a small frying pan, add the onions and fry, stirring occasionally, for about 5 minutes until softened and golden brown. Remove the onions from the pan and leave to cool.

7 Remove the pâté from the refrigerator, garnish with the fried onions and parsley sprigs and serve with slices of crusty bread or hot toast.

Energy 263kcal/1088kJ; Protein 14.1g; Carbohydrate 0.9g, of which sugars 0.7g; Fat 22.6g, of which saturates 10.3g; Cholesterol 352mg; Calcium 20mg; Fibre 0.1g; Sodium 175mg.

Russian Salad with Chicken

The creamy Russian salad was devised in the 1880s by Lucien Olivjer, French chef of the Hermitage Restaurant, in Moscow. The dish has since travelled the world under the name Salade Russe. To serve it as they would in Russia, try heaping the salad into a pyramid shape.

Serves 4

3 potatoes
4 carrots
400g/14oz/3½ cups frozen peas
3 eggs
150g/5oz Salted Cucumbers
175g/6oz/¾ cup mayonnaise
200g/7oz cooked or smoked game, wild poultry, turkey or chicken, thinly sliced
2 spring onions (scallions)
salt and ground black pepper
5–6 fresh dill sprigs, to garnish

COOK'S TIP Do not peel the vegetables before cooking as, if you do, they will lose some of their valuable vitamins. Save some slices of carrot, egg and some peas to garnish the salad.

1 Put the potatoes in a pan of salted water, bring to the boil, then cook for about 20 minutes until tender. Drain and leave to cool.

2 Put the carrots in a separate pan of salted water, bring to the boil and cook for 25 minutes.

3 One minute before the end of the cooking time, add the peas to the carrots, return to the boil and continue cooking. Drain and leave to cool.

4 Put the eggs in a pan, cover with cold water, and bring to the boil. Reduce the heat to low and simmer for 10 minutes. When the eggs are cooked, drain and put under cold running water.

5 Cut the cooled potatoes, carrots and the Salted Cucumbers into small dice and place in a large bowl with the cooked peas. Mix together. Shell and chop the hard-boiled eggs and fold these into the potato mixture.

6 Add the mayonnaise to the vegetables, season with salt and pepper to taste and stir gently together. Turn the salad on to a serving dish.

7 Thinly slice the meat of your choice and place on top of the salad. Thinly slice the spring onions and sprinkle over the top. Serve garnished with dill sprigs.

Energy 455kcal/1890kJ; Protein 28.1g; Carbohydrate 12.8g, of which sugars 5g; Fat 32.8g, of which saturates 5.7g; Cholesterol 387mg; Calcium 162mg; Fibre 4.3g; Sodium 963mg.

Salted Cucumbers

Salted cucumbers are the most popular zakuski dish and a cherished ingredient in Russian cooking. This way of serving them, prepared in just a few minutes, arouses all the taste buds, especially when they are served with shot glasses of ice cold Russian vodka.

Makes 1kg/2¼lb

1kg/2¼lb mini cucumbers or medium, fresh gherkins, or regular cucumbers
10 blackberry leaves
10 garlic cloves
3–4 dill sprigs with flowers
1–2 bay leaves
50g/2oz fresh horseradish, finely diced
20 black peppercorns

For the marinade
1 litre/1¾ pints/4 cups water
2.5ml/½ tsp red or white wine vinegar
45ml/3 tbsp salt

To serve 2 as an appetizer
4–6 salted cucumbers
5ml/1 tsp lemon juice
60ml/4 tbsp smetana or crème fraîche
60ml/4 tbsp clear honey
Russian vodka

1 To prepare the marinade for the cucumbers, put all the ingredients in a pan, bring to the boil, then remove from the heat and leave to cool.

2 If you can find mini cucumbers or fresh gerkins, prick all over with a fork; if you are using a large cucumber, cut it into thick fingers.

3 Put the cucumbers into one or several clean, dry glass jars, layering them with blackberry leaves, garlic cloves, dill sprigs, bay leaves, horseradish and peppercorns.

4 Pour in the marinade to cover and seal the jars. Leave to marinate for 5–6 hours. Then store the jars in the refrigerator for at least 2–3 weeks.

5 To serve, place the cucumbers in a serving bowl, cutting into fingers if they were salted whole. Mix the lemon juice with the smetana or crème fraîche. Put the honey in a separate small serving bowl. To eat, dip the cucumbers in honey or smetana or crème fraîche. Serve with ice-cold vodka.

COOK'S TIP These days the use of blackberry leaves as a herb has almost disappeared. In fact, the young leaves have a pronounced blackberry flavour and can be useful for flavouring syrups and jams. They can also be dried to make a country tea.

Energy 503kcal/2086kJ; Protein 8.8g; Carbohydrate 62.7g, of which sugars 61.6g; Fat 25.1g, of which saturates 16.3g; Cholesterol 68mg; Calcium 238mg; Fibre 6.5g; Sodium 80mg.

Hare and Calf's Liver Terrine

Hare and other furred game is popular all over Poland, where it has been hunted and cooked for centuries. For tender meat and a good flavour, use young hare that has been hung. However, you can use slightly older animals for this terrine, as the meat is minced finely.

Serves 4

5 dried mushrooms, rinsed and soaked in warm water for 30 minutes
saddle, thighs, liver, heart and lungs of 1 hare
2 onions, cut into wedges
1 carrot, chopped
1 parsnip, chopped
4 bay leaves
10 allspice berries
300g/11oz calf's liver
165g/5½oz unsmoked streaky (fatty) bacon rashers (strips)
75g/3oz/1½ cups soft white breadcrumbs
4 eggs
105ml/7 tbsp 95 per cent proof Polish spirit or vodka
5ml/1 tsp freshly grated nutmeg
10ml/2 tsp dried marjoram
10g/¼oz juniper berries
4 garlic cloves, crushed
150g/5oz smoked streaky (fatty) bacon rashers (strips)
salt and ground black pepper, to taste
redcurrant jelly and salad, to serve

1 Drain the mushrooms and slice into strips. Put the pieces of hare in a large pan and pour in enough water to just cover. Add the onions, carrot, parsnip, mushrooms, bay leaves and allspice. Bring to the boil, then cover and simmer gently for 1 hour. Add a pinch of salt and allow the meat to cool in the stock.

2 Slice the liver and 50g/2oz unsmoked bacon into small pieces and put in a medium pan. Add a ladleful of the stock and simmer for 15 minutes.

3 Preheat the oven to 180°C/350°F/Gas 4. Put two ladlefuls of the stock in a bowl, add the breadcrumbs and leave to soak.

4 Remove the hare pieces, liver and bacon from the stock and chop finely with a large knife. Transfer to a large bowl, then add the soaked breadcrumbs, eggs, Polish spirit or vodka, nutmeg, marjoram, juniper berries and crushed garlic. Season to taste and mix well to combine thoroughly.

5 Line a 1.2 litre/2 pint/5 cup ovenproof dish with the smoked and remaining unsmoked bacon rashers, making sure they overhang the edges.

6 Spoon the meat mixture into the dish and fold the overhanging bacon over the top. Cover with buttered baking parchment, then cover with a lid or foil.

7 Place the dish in a roasting pan containing boiling water, then put in the oven and bake for 1½ hours, or until a skewer pushed into the centre comes out clean and the juices run clear. Remove the baking parchment and lid or foil about 15 minutes before the end of cooking to allow the terrine to brown.

8 Remove from the oven, and take the dish out of the roasting pan. Cover the terrine with baking parchment and a board and weight down with a 900g/2lb weight (such as two cans).

9 Leave the dish until it is completely cool, then turn the terrine out on to a serving dish. Serve in slices with redcurrant jelly and a green salad.

Energy 370kcal/1544kJ; Protein 25g; Carbohydrate 14.1g, of which sugars 2.5g; Fat 18.1g, of which saturates 6.4g; Cholesterol 291mg; Calcium 52mg; Fibre 1.3g; Sodium 851mg.

Veal Brawn

On the Russian zakuski table, brawn – cooked meat set in jelly – is much enjoyed. Pig's trotters are vital, as they provide the jelly in which the veal sets. Brawn should be served with hot mustard or horseradish.

Serves 8–12

700g/1lb 10oz veal pieces, such as leg, on the bone,
3 pig's trotters (feet), split lengthways
1 onion, cut into wedges
2 carrots
6 white peppercorns
6 black peppercorns
1 bay leaf
about 1 litre/1¾ pints/4 cups water
2 eggs
salt
3–4 fresh parsley sprigs, to garnish
hot mustard or finely grated fresh horseradish, to serve

1 Put the meat, trotters, onion, 1 carrot, sliced, 10ml/2 tsp salt, white and black peppercorns and bay leaf in a large pan and add enough water to cover the meat. Bring to the boil and cook for 2–3 minutes. Skim the surface, cover with a lid and cook over a medium heat for 2 hours, until the meat begins to fall off the bones.

2 Using a slotted spoon, remove the meat from the pan. Separate the bones and gristle and return to the pan, putting the meat on a chopping board.

3 Boil the stock with the bone and gristle for a further 1 hour. (This will extract more flavour from the bones and also produce more jelly for the brawn.)

4 Put the remaining carrot in a pan of salted water, bring to the boil and cook for 15 minutes. Drain and leave to cool.

5 Meanwhile, cut the cooled meat into very fine pieces. When cool enough to handle, thinly slice the cooked carrot.

6 Put the eggs in a pan, cover with cold water and bring to the boil. Reduce the heat to low, cover and simmer for 10 minutes. When the eggs are cooked, immediately drain them and place under cold running water. Remove the shell and slice the egg.

7 Pour the stock through a sieve (strainer) into a measuring jug (cup). Measure the stock, then pour into a bowl. Measure the same quantity of meat and add to the stock. Season with salt to taste.

8 You are now ready to assemble the brawn. Arrange the slices of carrot and egg in an attractive pattern in the bottom of individual soup plates. Gently pour the meat and stock into the plates, trying to preserve the pattern. Place the plates in the refrigerator for at least 4 hours until the brawn is firm and set.

9 Serve from the bowl or turn out on to plates. Garnish with parsley and accompany with mustard or grated horseradish on the side.

VARIATION As an alternative to veal, you could use either beef or chicken. Pig's trotters are the traditional way to make the jelly set, and they give extra flavour. However, if you can't get hold of them, gelatine can be used, in which case you may need to increase the seasoning.

Energy 101kcal/423kJ; Protein 10.6g; Carbohydrate 1.1g, of which sugars 0.9g; Fat 6.1g, of which saturates 2.2g; Cholesterol 51mg; Calcium 9mg; Fibre 0.3g; Sodium 52mg.

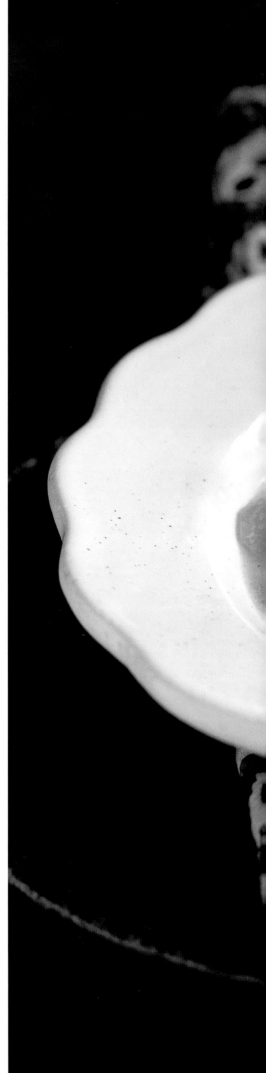

Potato Pancakes

This dish was especially popular in Russia during World War II, when there was little to buy in the shops, and it was served as a treat for children. These pancakes are still enjoyed today, and taste delicious with sugar, apple sauce, or sour cream and a dash of paprika.

3 Put the bacon fat or oil in a large, heavy frying pan and heat over a high heat until it is almost smoking.

4 Carefully put a large spoonful of the potato mixture into the pan and flatten it slightly with a fork. Repeat until you have about four pancakes in the pan.

5 Fry each pancake until it is golden brown on both sides, then remove from the pan with a slotted spoon and drain on kitchen paper.

6 Keep the cooked pancakes warm in a low oven while you cook the rest of the mixture in the same way.

7 Serve the pancakes warm, with a topping of your choice.

Serves 4–6

4–5 large potatoes, peeled and grated
1 large onion, grated
2 eggs
60ml/4 tbsp plain (all-purpose) flour
120ml/4fl oz/½ cup melted bacon fat
  or oil
salt and ground black pepper
  (optional)
sour cream and paprika, or sugar, or
  apple sauce to serve

1 Rinse the grated potatoes and onion, then squeeze in your hands to remove the excess liquid.

2 Put the potatoes and onion in a large bowl with the eggs, flour, and salt and pepper if serving with a savoury topping. Mix to combine thoroughly.

Energy 291kcal/1221kJ; Protein 6g; Carbohydrate 35.4g, of which sugars 2.9g; Fat 15g, of which saturates 2.2g; Cholesterol 63mg; Calcium 36mg; Fibre 2.1g; Sodium 42mg.

Russian Pancakes

These little pancakes are called blinis. Often served with caviar or smoked salmon, or with smetana, soused herring and chopped onion, blinis can be served with a topping already added, or in a pile – with toppings provided separately – so people can make their own.

Makes 20

25g/1oz fresh yeast
5ml/1 tsp caster (superfine) sugar
50ml/2fl oz/¼ cup warm (37°C/98°F) water
2 egg yolks
250ml/8fl oz/1 cup warm (37°C/98°F) milk
2.5ml/½ tsp salt
175g/6oz/1½ cups plain white (all-purpose) flour
3 egg whites
150ml/¼ pint/⅔ cup rapeseed (canola) oil

For the toppings

slices of smoked salmon
pickled herring, chopped
chopped onion
smetana or crème fraîche
caviar
lemon wedges and dill, to garnish

1 Put the yeast, sugar and warm water in a small bowl and blend until smooth. Leave in a warm place for 20 minutes until frothy.

2 Mix together the egg yolks, 200ml/ 6fl oz/¾ cup of the warm milk and the salt in a large bowl. Stir in the yeast mixture and the flour, a little at a time, to form a smooth batter. Leave the batter to rise in a warm place for 4–5 hours, stirring three or four times during that time.

3 Stir the remaining 50ml/2fl oz/¼ cup of the milk into the batter.

4 Whisk the egg whites in a dry bowl until they form soft peaks. Fold into the batter and set aside for 30 minutes.

5 Heat the oil in a frying pan and add 25–30ml/1½–2 tbsp of batter for each blini. Fry over a medium heat until set, then flip and cook the other side. Continue to make 20 blinis.

6 Serve with a selection of toppings. Your guests can choose their own or you can assemble the blinis yourself.

COOK'S TIP Russians would never serve onion with caviar on the same blini. If you have real Russian black caviar, serve it by itself on the blini, with a spoonful of smetana or crème fraîche on the side.

Energy 89kcal/372kJ; Protein 2g; Carbohydrate 7.6g, of which sugars 0.7g; Fat 5.9g, of which saturates 0.9g; Cholesterol 21mg; Calcium 30mg; Fibre 0.3g; Sodium 16mg.

Aubergine Bake

This Russian aubergine dish comes from Samarkand, Taskjent and Bochara – ancient cities in the Central Asian part of the former Soviet Union. It is as filling and satisfying as a meat dish. Serve at room temperature, spread on bread or warm as a main course with potatoes.

Serves 8

1 onion
2 (bell) peppers, preferably
    different colours
3 tomatoes
1 bunch fresh dill
2 aubergines (eggplants)
100ml/3½fl oz/scant ½ cup rapeseed
    (canola) or olive oil
salt and ground black pepper
45ml/3 tbsp chopped fresh parsley
    and 4 lemon wedges, to garnish

1 Preheat the oven to 200°C/400°F/Gas 6. Slice the onion, peppers and tomatoes. Chop the dill. Cut the aubergines into 1cm/½in thick slices and brush with half of the oil.

2 Heat a large frying pan, add the aubergine slices and fry over medium heat, covered with a lid, for 1 minute on both sides, until golden brown. Alternatively, grill (broil) the slices on each side until golden brown. Season with salt and pepper and set aside.

3 Heat the remaining oil in the frying pan, add the onion slices and fry until softened but not browned. Using a slotted spoon, remove from the pan and set aside. Add the peppers to the pan and cook in the same way, then cook the tomatoes, keeping each vegetable separate.

4 Starting with half of the aubergines, layer the vegetables in an ovenproof dish, so that you have two layers of each vegetable. Season each layer with salt, pepper and the chopped dill. Cover the dish with foil.

5 Bake the vegetables in the oven for 10 minutes. Leave to cool, before serving garnished with chopped parsley and lemon wedges.

COOK'S TIP The dish can be cooked on top of the stove instead of in the oven. When all the vegetables have been fried, return them to the pan, in layers. Add 30-45ml/2–3 tbsp water and simmer the vegetables, covered, over a low heat, making sure that they do not burn.

Energy 118kcal/486kJ; Protein 1.4g; Carbohydrate 5.5g, of which sugars 5.1g; Fat 10.2g, of which saturates 1.5g; Cholesterol 0mg; Calcium 25mg; Fibre 2.4g; Sodium 7mg

Beetroot and Vegetable Salad

A ruby-red beetroot salad is a must on the table at any Russian dinner party, forming part of the traditional zakuski. Every hostess has her own variation of the recipe and sometimes the salad is garnished with pieces of pickled herring and surrounded by little mounds of sauerkraut.

Serves 4–6

2 potatoes
2 carrots
4–5 cooked beetroot (beets)
2–3 Salted Cucumbers (page 79)
1 red onion
30–45ml/2–3 tbsp sunflower oil
30–45ml/2–3 tbsp sauerkraut
salt and ground black pepper

VARIATION For a creamier salad, replace the oil with150g/5oz/⅝ cup mayonnaise.

1 Halve the potatoes, put in a pan of cold water, bring to the boil, then simmer for about 15 minutes. Put the whole carrots in a separate pan of cold water, bring to the boil, then reduce the heat, cover and simmer for 10-15 minutes. When the potatoes and carrots are cooked, drain and put under cold running water.

2 Dice the beetroot, potatoes and carrots. Chop the Salted Cucumbers and thinly slice the onion. Put all the vegetables in a large serving dish and mix together.

3 Add the oil and sauerkraut to the vegetables. Season with salt and pepper and stir together.

Energy 130kcal/546kJ; Protein 3g; Carbohydrate 21.5g, of which sugars 10.7g; Fat 4.1g, of which saturates 0.6g; Cholesterol 0mg; Calcium 40mg; Fibre 3.6g; Sodium 100mg.

Marinated Mushrooms

With the possible exception of Italians, Russians are the most enthusiastic mushroom pickers in the world. In the mushroom season the best-looking mushrooms are preserved in a spicy marinade to be served on the zakuski table during winter.

3 Add the remaining salt, the vinegar, sugar, allspice, peppercorns, bay leaves, cinnamon stick and whole garlic clove to the mushrooms. Simmer for 10 minutes.

4 Put the dill and the blackcurrant leaves, if using, in the bottom of clean, sterilized glass jars. When the spiced mushrooms are completely cool, pour into the jars and seal tightly. Store in a cool, dark place or in the refrigerator.

Makes 1 litre/1³/₄ pints/4 cups

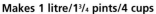

500g/1¼lb mixed wild mushrooms, such as porcini
500ml/17fl oz/generous 2 cups water
25ml/1½ tbsp salt
30ml/2 tbsp red or white wine vinegar
15–30ml/1–2 tbsp sugar
5–6 allspice berries
5–6 black peppercorns
2 bay leaves
1 small piece cinnamon stick
5–6 cloves
1 garlic clove
2–3 stems fresh dill
2 blackcurrant leaves (optional)

1 Wipe the mushrooms with kitchen paper to remove any dirt or traces of soil. If the mushrooms are large, cut them in half, but leave small mushrooms whole.

2 Put the mushrooms in a large pan, add the water and 15ml/1 tbsp salt. Bring to the boil, then reduce the heat and simmer for 30 minutes, stirring occasionally and skimming the surface.

COOK'S TIP Serve these aromatic sweet-sour mushrooms on your zakuski table or as an accompaniment to meat dishes, such as roast beef. The mushrooms will keep for 2–3 months but once opened should be eaten in 3–4 days.

Energy 183kcal/779kJ; Protein 9.2g; Carbohydrate 33.4g, of which sugars 32.4g; Fat 2.5g, of which saturates 0.5g; Cholesterol 0mg; Calcium 48mg; Fibre 5.5g; Sodium 8673mg.

Beetroot Caviar

The delicacies of the sea or Russian inland waters, such as caviar, are often a part of the zakuski table, but chopped vegetable dishes, known as 'poor man's caviars', are also popular alternatives. As with other vegetable caviars, this beetroot caviar is served on rye bread.

Serves 4–8

1 onion, total weight 150g/5oz
4 medium beetroot (beets), cooked
  and peeled
45ml/3 tbsp rapeseed (canola) oil
30ml/2 tbsp tomato purée (paste)
salt and ground black pepper
rye bread, to serve
finely chopped fresh parsley,
  to garnish

VARIATION Add 1–2 crushed garlic cloves to the caviar, either cooked with the onion or, if you prefer it, raw, added with the salt and pepper in step 4. You can also use fresh dill instead of parsley.

1 Chop the onion and coarsely grate the cooked beetroot. Heat the oil in a medium pan, add the onion and fry gently for 5–8 minutes, until softened and golden brown.

2 Add the grated beetroot to the onion and fry, stirring all the time, for a further 5 minutes.

6 To serve, pile the beetroot caviar on to the squares of rye bread and sprinkle with chopped parsley to garnish. Add another little sprinkle of black pepper, if liked.

3 Add the tomato purée to the pan and stir into the onion and beetroot mixture. Cover the pan and simmer gently for about 10 minutes.

4 Season the mixture with salt and pepper to taste. Transfer to a bowl and leave to cool completely.

5 Cut the rye bread into slices, and then cut each slice into squares.

Energy 60kcal/251kJ; Protein 1.1g; Carbohydrate 4.9g, of which sugars 4.2g; Fat 4.2g, of which saturates 0.5g; Cholesterol 0mg; Calcium 14mg; Fibre 1.1g; Sodium 34mg.

Aubergine Caviar

This is one of several Russian recipes for so-called vegetable caviars. The tastiest aubergines (eggplants) are imported to Russia from the Middle East and Georgia and the recipes for vegetable caviars also stem from these regions. Serve with rye bread in the traditional way.

Serves 4–8

2 aubergines (eggplants)
1 red onion
30–45ml/2–3 tbsp rapeseed oil
salt and ground black pepper
rye bread, to serve

COOK'S TIP If preferred, you can mix the ingredients in a blender or food processor to make the caviar into a smooth paste.

1 Preheat the oven to 180°C/350°F/Gas 4. Pierce the aubergines with a fork to prevent them from bursting when baked. Put them in a roasting pan and bake in the oven for 20–30 minutes, until completely soft. Leave to cool.

2 When the aubergines are cool enough to handle, cut them in half lengthways and with a metal spoon scrape out the soft insides. Discard the skins. Chop the flesh into very small dice and put in a large bowl.

3 Finely chop the onion and add to the aubergine. Add the oil and mix well.

4 Season well with salt and pepper to taste and turn into a serving dish. Serve with rye bread.

Energy 35kcal/145kJ; Protein 0.5g; Carbohydrate 1.7g, of which sugars 1.4g; Fat 3g, of which saturates 0.4g; Cholesterol 0mg; Calcium 7mg; Fibre 1.1g; Sodium 1mg

Georgian Bean Salad

A delicious fresh bean salad, with a touch of spice, is an excellent contribution to the zakuski table. This Georgian-style bean salad is also a very good accompaniment to many meat dishes, especially roast lamb, or one of the many burger recipes that the Russians enjoy making.

Serves 4–6

500g/1¼lb/3 cups broad (fava) beans
1–2 large onions
45ml/3 tbsp olive oil
45ml/3 tbsp red wine vinegar
15g/½oz/¼ cup finely chopped fresh
    coriander (cilantro) or parsley
1 small red onion

1 Put the broad beans in a pan, cover with water and bring to the boil. Reduce the heat and simmer for 3 minutes. Drain.

2 Chop the onions. Heat the oil in a frying pan, add the onions and fry, stirring all the time, for about 5 minutes until softened. Add the cooked beans and mix together. Remove the pan from the heat and leave to rest for 5 minutes.

3 Turn the bean mixture into a bowl. Add the vinegar and chopped herbs and stir together. Put the bowl in the refrigerator to chill overnight.

4 To serve, finely slice the red onion. Add to the bean salad shortly before serving and mix together.

VARIATION You can combine several types of beans for this salad, such as flageolet or cannellini beans.

Energy 145kcal/609kJ; Protein 7.6g; Carbohydrate 15.9g, of which sugars 5.4g; Fat 6.2g, of which saturates 0.9g; Cholesterol 0mg; Calcium 71mg; Fibre 6.6g; Sodium 10mg

FISH

Fish has always played an important role in Russian cooking. It has been a staple food ever since people first settled along the many rivers and lakes in its extensive rural landscape. Today fish is still a very popular element of the lunch or dinner table and is prepared in many different and interesting ways. Fish dishes are often accompanied by boiled potatoes sprinkled with dill, and served with a sharp and spicy tartare sauce or with a rich creamy sauce such as Sole with Vodka Sauce and Caviar.
Polish cuisine is more dependent on freshwater fish than seafood, and although it will never supersede meat as the favourite choice for Polish main courses, fish such as carp or pike come into their own for Christmas and Easter celebrations, and during times when meat is forbidden by the Catholic Church. During the rest of the year, most fish is simply fried or grilled and served with butter and herbs, or simmered in a robust sauce such as in the recipe for Haddock and Beer Casserole.

Marinated Perch in Tomato Sauce

In Russia it is quite common to eat cold main course dishes with really hot accompaniments. This fish dish, cooked in advance and garnished with lots of fresh herbs, is often served chilled or at room temperature with some freshly cooked, hot boiled potatoes. Making it a day in advance means that the flavours develop beautifully.

Serves 4–6

---

2 onions
3–4 carrots
600–700g/1lb 6oz–1lb 10oz perch fillets, skinned
45–60ml/3–4 tbsp plain white (all-purpose) flour
100ml/3½fl oz/scant ½ cup rapeseed (canola) oil
30ml/2 tbsp tomato purée (paste)
2 bay leaves
5–6 black peppercorns
200–300ml/7–10fl oz/scant 1–1¼ cups water
salt
chopped fresh parsley to garnish
hot boiled potatoes, and 4–6 lemon wedges, to serve

1 Chop the onions and coarsely grate the carrots. Cut the fish fillets into large chunks, allowing about three pieces per serving. Season the fish pieces with salt and then coat each side in the flour.

2 Heat half of the oil in a large frying pan. Add the fish and fry for about 1 minute on each side until golden brown. Transfer the fish to a large pan.

3 Add the remaining oil to the frying pan, heat until hot, then add the onions. Fry for 1–2 minutes.

4 Add the carrots to the onions and fry for a further 3–5 minutes, stirring all the time, until soft and golden brown.

5 Add the tomato purée, bay leaves and peppercorns to the onion and carrot mixture and fry for 1 minute. Add 200ml/7fl oz/scant 1 cup of the water and cook the sauce, over a medium heat, for 5 minutes.

6 Add the sauce to the fish, cover the pan and simmer, over a low heat, for 5–10 minutes, adding the remaining water if the sauce is too thick. Leave to cool.

7 Turn the fish and sauce into a serving dish and garnish with parsley. Serve with hot boiled potatoes and lemon wedges.

VARIATION Russians use pike for this dish, but if perch or pike are not available you can substitute any firm-fleshed white fish.

Energy 212kcal/881kJ; Protein 19.9g; Carbohydrate 3.9g, of which sugars 0.1g; Fat 13g, of which saturates 1g; Cholesterol 0mg; Calcium 16mg; Fibre 0.2g; Sodium 56mg

Fried Fish with Tartare Sauce

Deep-fried fish – most often perch or pike – served with a tartare sauce is a favourite in Russian restaurants. Here a delicious light beer batter is used to coat the fish, but Russians often use smetana as a coating for fried food, which you might like to try instead.

Serves 4

700g/1lb 10oz perch fillet, skinned and boned
5ml/1 tsp salt
15ml/1 tbsp fresh lemon juice
115g/4oz/1 cup plain white (all-purpose) flour
150ml/¼ pint/⅔ cup light beer
1 egg white
about 1 litre/1¾ pints/4 cups rapeseed (canola) oil
lemon wedges, to serve

For the tartare sauce

3 large pickled gherkins
200g/7fl oz/scant 1 cup mayonnaise
15ml/1 tbsp capers
5ml/1 tsp finely chopped fresh dill
15ml/1 tbsp finely chopped fresh parsley
2.5ml/½ tsp mustard
1.5ml/¼ tsp salt
1.5ml/¼ tsp ground black pepper

COOK'S TIP Try garlic mayonnaise instead of tartare sauce to accompany the fried fish. Simply crush half a clove of garlic into 200g/7fl oz/scant 1 cup mayonnaise.

1 To make the tartare sauce, peel and finely chop the gerkins. Put in a bowl with the mayonnaise, capers, dill, parsley and mustard. Mix together. Add salt and pepper to taste, and transfer the sauce to a serving bowl.

2 Cut the fish fillets into pieces measuring about 3cm/1¼in and put on a plate. Sprinkle the fish pieces with the salt and lemon juice.

3 Put the flour and beer in a bowl and whisk together until it forms a smooth batter. In a separate bowl, whisk the egg white until it stands in soft peaks, then fold into the batter.

4 Heat the oil in a deep fryer to 180°C/350°F or until a cube of bread browns in 1 minute. Dip and turn the fish pieces in the batter and then drop into the hot oil. Fry for 1–2 minutes, until golden. Using a slotted spoon, remove from the pan and drain on kitchen paper.

5 Serve the fish hot with lemon wedges and the tartare sauce.

Energy 719kcal/2986kJ; Protein 36.7g; Carbohydrate 24.3g, of which sugars 2.1g; Fat 53.4g, of which saturates 7.6g; Cholesterol 118mg; Calcium 95mg; Fibre 1.8g; Sodium 352mg.

Fried Carp in Breadcrumbs

This farmhouse dish is often served as the main course of the 12-course Christmas Eve feast in Poland, but it makes a delicious meal at any time of the year. Chunks of carp are coated in breadcrumbs and fried in oil, and served simply with lemon wedges.

Serves 4

1 carp, about 900g/2lb, cleaned and filleted
2.5ml/¹/₂ tsp salt
50g/2oz/¹/₂ cup plain (all-purpose) flour
pinch ground black pepper
1–2 eggs, lightly beaten
115g/4oz/1³/₄ cups dry breadcrumbs
90ml/6 tbsp vegetable oil, for frying
lemon wedges, to serve

1 First scald the carp by putting it into a large heatproof dish or roasting pan and pouring boiling water over it. Turn and repeat on the other side. Drain.

2 Cut the cleaned and scalded carp into even portions and sprinkle lightly with salt. Leave to stand for about 30 minutes. Remove the skin, if you like.

3 Mix together the flour and pepper in a medium bowl. Put the beaten egg in another, and the breadcrumbs on a plate.

4 Dip the fish pieces first into the bowl of flour, then into the beaten egg, and then into the breadcrumbs, coating them evenly at each stage.

5 Heat the oil in a large, heavy pan, until very hot. Carefully add the coated fish pieces and cook for about 5 minutes on each side, until golden brown all over.

6 Remove the fish pieces using a slotted spoon and drain on kitchen paper. Serve hot with lemon wedges.

Energy 479kcal/2008kJ; Protein 32.3g; Carbohydrate 32g, of which sugars 0.9g; Fat 25.6g, of which saturates 4.1g; Cholesterol 148mg; Calcium 133mg; Fibre 1g; Sodium 301mg.

Grilled Sardines with Parsley

Sardines are easy to cook, nutritious, good value for money and extremely tasty, so it is little wonder that they are very popular in Poland. Here, they are simply grilled and served with lemon wedges to squeeze over. This recipe also works well on a barbecue.

Serves 4–6

900g/2lb fresh sardines,
    gutted and scaled
30ml/2 tbsp melted butter
salt and ground black pepper,
    to taste
60ml/4 tbsp chopped fresh parsley,
    to garnish
lemon wedges, to serve

1 Preheat the grill (broiler) to high. Wash the prepared sardines under cold running water and dry with kitchen paper.

COOK'S TIP To butterfly sardines, place the sardines, belly side down, on a board. Run a thumb along the spine to press out. Turn over and pull out the backbone.

2 Brush the fish with melted butter or oil, then season to taste with salt and pepper.

3 Place the sardines on the grill pan and put under the preheated grill. Cook for about 3–4 minutes on each side, until the skin begins to brown.

4 Transfer the sardines to warmed plates, sprinkle with parsley, and serve immediately with lemon wedges.

Energy 327kcal/1362kJ; Protein 35g; Carbohydrate 0.3g, of which sugars 0.3g; Fat 20.5g, of which saturates 8g; Cholesterol 16mg; Calcium 192mg; Fibre 0.5g; Sodium 240mg.

Fish Kebabs

To cook fish outside on skewers over coals or a wood fire and then serve with squeezed lemon and fresh tomato, is an ancient Russian tradition. Although incredibly simple to prepare, this dish is a popular choice in many Caucasian restaurants in Russia.

Serves 4

30ml/2 tbsp fresh lemon juice
60ml/4 tbsp smetana or crème fraîche
1kg/2¼lb firm white fish fillets, such
  as halibut or monkfish
25g/1oz/2 tbsp butter
salt

For the garnish
25g/1oz/2 tbsp butter
4 spring onions (scallions), sliced
1 lemon, cut into wedges
4 tomatoes, cut into wedges
30ml/2 tbsp finely chopped
  fresh parsley

VARIATION In Russia, sturgeon is often used for this dish but any firm, white fish is suitable. You can also use salmon.

1 Heat a barbecue or preheat the oven to 240°C/475°F/Gas 9.

2 Put the lemon juice and smetana or crème fraîche in a large bowl and mix. Cut the fish into small chunks, season with salt, add to the marinade and stir to coat all over. Leave for 10–15 minutes for the fish to absorb the flavours.

3 Melt the butter. Thread the fish chunks tightly on to four metal skewers or wooden skewers that have been soaked in water. Heat the grill (broiler) if using.

4 Cook the skewers on the barbecue, or under the grill for about 10 minutes, turning every few minutes. Baste occasionally with the melted butter and the remaining marinade.

5 To serve, put the skewers on a large serving dish and sprinkle over the sliced spring onions and chopped parsley. Arrange the lemon and tomato wedges around the fish skewers.

Energy 303kcal/1267kJ; Protein 46.1g; Carbohydrate 0.4g, of which sugars 0.4g; Fat 12.9g, of which saturates 7.6g; Cholesterol 145mg; Calcium 32mg; Fibre 0g; Sodium 191mg.

Roasted Carp with Smetana

Roasting a whole fish in the oven, covered with smetana to stop the fish from drying as it cooks, is an old Russian method. A more modern way is to use fish fillets, instead of a whole fish, and bake them in ramekin dishes on top of a base of boiled buckwheat.

Serves 4–6

40g/1½oz/3 tbsp butter, plus extra
  for greasing
1 whole carp, bream or trout, gutted,
  total weight 1–1.5kg/2¼–3¼lb
45ml/3 tbsp plain white
  (all-purpose) flour
300ml/½ pint/1¼ cups smetana or
  crème fraîche
100ml/3½fl oz/scant ½ cup water
salt and ground black pepper
5–6 fresh parsley sprigs, to garnish
salad leaves and hot boiled potatoes,
  to serve

VARIATION In Russia, mayonnaise is sometimes used instead of the smetana.

1 Preheat the oven to 230°C/450°F/ Gas 8. Generously grease an ovenproof dish with butter. Season the whole fish on the inside and outside with salt and pepper, then coat both sides in the flour. Place the fish in the prepared dish.

2 Melt the butter in a small pan. Spread the smetana or crème fraîche over the prepared fish, making sure that it is covered completely.

3 Pour the melted butter over the fish and pour the water around it.

4 Bake in the preheated oven. A 40–50cm/16–20in thick fish will need around 20 minutes and a 60cm/24in thick fish will need 30 minutes.

5 The fish is cooked when the flesh is white and not translucent. Test by inserting a fork in the backbone of the fish where it is thickest.

6 Serve the fish in portions straight from the dish, garnished with parsley and accompanied by salad leaves and boiled potatoes tossed in oil and salt.

Energy 395kcal/1640kJ; Protein 22.3g; Carbohydrate 7.1g, of which sugars 1.2g; Fat 31.1g, of which saturates 18.1g; Cholesterol 149mg; Calcium 96mg; Fibre 0.2g; Sodium 102mg.

Baked Trout with Garlic Butter

The rivers in Poland abound with trout, making them a popular choice in a country with only one seaboard. In this delicious recipe they are simply baked in the oven, drizzled with hot garlic butter and served with sprigs of parsley and wedges of lemon.

Serves 4

2 garlic cloves, crushed
50g/2oz/¼ cup butter, softened,
 plus extra, for greasing
4 medium-sized trout, about
 300g/11oz each, cleaned and gutted
1 lemon
salt and ground black pepper, to taste
fresh parsley sprigs, to garnish
lemon wedges, to serve

1 Mix together the garlic and butter in a bowl. Set aside until required.

2 Preheat the oven to 200°C/400°F/ Gas 6. Grease a large baking dish.

3 Place the fish in the baking dish. Squeeze lemon juice all over and inside the trout, then season with salt and pepper and put in the oven.

4 Bake the trout for 15–20 minutes, or until the flesh flakes easily when you insert the point of a sharp knife. Place on warm serving plates.

5 Melt the garlic butter in a pan, then pour over the fish. Garnish with parsley and serve with lemon wedges.

Energy 205kcal/853kJ; Protein 19.5g; Carbohydrate 0.1g, of which sugars 0.1g; Fat 14.1g, of which saturates 6.5g; Cholesterol 27mg; Calcium 11mg; Fibre 0g; Sodium 132mg.

Foil-baked Salmon

Baking the whole salmon in a foil package ensures that the flesh remains wonderfully moist, and is a favourite cooking method in both Russia and Poland. It can be served hot, with new potatoes and cucumber salad, or cold with a salad, for a summer lunch.

3 Spread the mixture inside the cavity of the fish, and all over the outside. Put the peppercorns and bay leaves inside the cavity, then season the skin with salt and pepper, to taste.

4 Bring the edges of the foil up and seal to make a loose parcel. Put the fish in the preheated oven and cook for about 30–40 minutes, or until the fish is tender and cooked.

5 Remove from the oven, lift out of the foil and divide the fish into six portions. Transfer to warmed plates.

6 Pour over any juices caught in the foil, and serve immediately with lemon wedges, boiled new potatoes and Polish-style Cucumber Salad.

Serves 6

1 salmon, about 1kg/2¼lb, cleaned and trimmed
1 small bunch fresh dill, roughly chopped
4 garlic cloves, finely chopped
115g/4oz/½ cup unsalted butter
50ml/2fl oz/¼ cup dry white wine
juice of ½ lemon
10–12 black peppercorns
4–5 fresh bay leaves
salt and ground black pepper, to taste
lemon wedges, boiled new potatoes and Polish-style Cucumber Salad (page 193), to serve

1 Preheat the oven to 200°C/400°F/ Gas 6. Place the salmon in the centre of a large piece of foil.

2 In a bowl, mix together the dill, garlic and butter, to form a smooth paste. Add the wine and lemon juice, and combine.

Energy 242kcal/1005kJ; Protein 20.3g; Carbohydrate 0.1g, of which sugars 0.1g; Fat 17.9g, of which saturates 6.2g; Cholesterol 68mg; Calcium 23mg; Fibre 0g; Sodium 96mg.

Sole with Vodka Sauce and Caviar

In Russia, caviar was once served only with silver spoons to protect the taste. Today, caviar is served on white buttered toast or blinis, or as a luxurious garnish to a delicious fish. Sole is traditionally used for this recipe, but you can substitute any other flat fish.

Serves 4

500–600g/1lb 4oz–1lb 6oz sole, flounder or plaice fillets
200ml/7fl oz/scant 1 cup fish stock
60ml/4 tbsp caviar
salt
fresh dill, to garnish
lemon wedges and hot boiled potatoes, to serve

For the vodka sauce
25–40g/1–1½oz/2–3 tbsp butter
5–6 shallots, finely diced
5ml/1 tsp plain white (all-purpose) flour
200ml/7fl oz/scant 1 cup double (heavy) cream
200ml/7fl oz/scant 1 cup fish stock
100ml/3½fl oz/scant ½ cup dry white wine
30ml/2 tbsp vodka
salt and ground black pepper

1 Season the fish fillets with salt. Roll up and secure each fillet with a cocktail stick (toothpick).

2 Heat the stock in a small pan. Place the fish rolls in the pan, cover and simmer for 5–8 minutes, until the fish is tender. Remove from the pan and keep warm.

3 Meanwhile, make the sauce. Melt the butter in a pan, add the shallots and fry gently for 3–5 minutes, until softened but not browned. Add the flour and stir until well mixed.

4 Gradually add the cream and stock until smooth. Slowly bring to the boil, stirring, until the sauce bubbles. Reduce the heat and simmer for 3–5 minutes, until the sauce thickens. Remove the shallots with a slotted spoon. Add the wine and vodka and bring to the boil. Season to taste.

5 Pour the sauce over the base of four warmed plates. Place the fish rolls on top and add a spoonful of caviar to each. Garnish with dill and serve with the lemon wedges and potatoes.

Energy 470kcal/1952kJ; Protein 27.9g; Carbohydrate 3.2g, of which sugars 1.9g; Fat 35g, of which saturates 20.4g; Cholesterol 188mg; Calcium 103mg; Fibre 0.3g; Sodium 548mg.

Halibut Steaks with Lemon Butter

Poles often simply grill or fry fresh fish, and this elegant dish is a good example. Spreading the steaks with parsley, lemon and butter before cooking ensures the flesh is moist and enables the flavours to permeate the fish without overpowering its delicate flavour.

2 Soften the butter in a bowl with a fork or wooden spoon, then add the parsley and lemon juice, mix together, then spread over both sides of each fish steak.

3 Line a grill pan with foil, then put the steaks on the foil. Place under the hot grill and cook for 3–4 minutes.

4 Turn the fish over and cook for a further 3–4 minutes on the other side. Check with the point of a sharp knife that the fish is cooked but still tender.

5 Transfer to warmed plates. Serve immediately, with lemon wedges for squeezing over, and garnished with parsley sprigs if using.

Serves 4

4 halibut steaks, weighing about
    185g/6½oz each
150g/5oz/10 tbsp butter
30ml/2 tbsp chopped fresh parsley
30ml/2 tbsp lemon juice
salt and ground black pepper,
    to taste
lemon wedges, to serve
parsley sprigs, to garnish (optional)

VARIATION This butter and lemon sauce can be used for all white fish. Use hake or cod steaks if halibut is not available.

1 Season the fish with a generous amount of salt and pepper on both sides. Preheat the grill (broiler) to medium.

Energy 464kcal/1928kJ; Protein 38.2g; Carbohydrate 0.6g, of which sugars 0.5g; Fat 34.3g, of which saturates 20.1g; Cholesterol 141mg; Calcium 83mg; Fibre 0.6g; Sodium 337mg.

Haddock with Dill Sauce

Dill is Poland's favourite herb, especially when it is served with fish dishes. Here it is used to lift the simple cream sauce that accompanies the moist fillets of poached haddock. Serve the fish on its own, or accompanied by seasonal vegetables.

Serves 4

50g/2oz/¼ cup butter
4 haddock fillets, about
    185g/6½oz each
200ml/7fl oz/scant 1 cup full fat
    (whole) milk
200ml/7fl oz/scant 1 cup fish stock
3–4 bay leaves
75ml/5 tbsp plain (all-purpose) flour
150ml/¼ pint/⅔ cup double
    (heavy) cream
1 egg yolk
30ml–45ml/2–3 tbsp chopped
    fresh dill
salt and ground black pepper,
    to taste
dill fronds and slices of lemon,
    to garnish

1 Melt half of the butter in a large frying pan, then add the haddock fillets, milk, fish stock, bay leaves, and a generous amount of salt and pepper.

2 Bring the liquid to a simmer, then poach the fish gently, uncovered, over a low heat for 10–15 minutes until tender.

3 Meanwhile, melt the remaining butter in a small pan, add the flour and cook, stirring, for 2 minutes.

4 Remove the pan from the heat and add a spoonful of double cream. Beat the cream into the flour and butter, then slowly add the rest of the cream, whisking constantly, so that no lumps form.

5 Stir the egg yolk and chopped dill into the cream and butter mixture, then return to the heat and simmer for 4 minutes, or until the sauce has thickened. Do not boil.

6 Remove the haddock fillets to a serving dish or warmed plates.

7 Taste the sauce and add salt and pepper if needed, then pour it over the fish.

8 Garnish the fish with dill fronds and slices of lemon and serve immediately on warmed plates.

COOK'S TIP A member of the cod family, silver-skinned haddock is sold whole, as steaks or as fillets. It is suitable for grilling (broiling), frying or smoking. This sauce can also be used for any other type of white fish.

Energy 503kcal/2097kJ; Protein 36.6g; Carbohydrate 15.5g, of which sugars 1.2g; Fat 33.2g, of which saturates 19.6g; Cholesterol 191mg; Calcium 92mg; Fibre 1g; Sodium 207mg.

Fish with Mushroom and Dill Sauce

Dill and flat leaf parsley are the herbs most commonly used in Russian cuisine, and both go superbly with most fish dishes. In this recipe the fish is accompanied by a creamy mushroom sauce with a rich taste of dill.

Serves 4

4 perch fillets, total weight
  500–600g/1lb 4oz–1lb 6oz, skinned
5ml/1 tsp salt
plain white (all-purpose) flour, to coat
35–50g/1½–2oz/3–4 tbsp butter
hot boiled new potatoes, to serve

For the dill sauce
2 onions, finely chopped
20 fresh mushrooms, thinly sliced
45ml/3 tbsp rapeseed (canola) oil
15ml/1 tbsp plain white
  (all-purpose) flour
200ml/7fl oz/scant 1 cup fish stock
250ml/8fl oz/1 cup double
  (heavy) cream
100ml/3½fl oz/scant ½ cup smetana or
  crème fraîche
100ml/3½fl oz/scant ½ cup dry
  white wine
1 large bunch fresh dill, chopped
1–2 dashes mushroom or soy sauce
salt and white pepper

3 Stir the cream and smetana or crème fraîche into the sauce. Reduce the heat and simmer for 3 minutes. Add the white wine, soy sauce, salt and pepper and dill.

4 Meanwhile, season the fish fillets with the salt and coat with the flour. Heat the butter in a large non-stick frying pan over a medium heat. Add the fish and fry for 3 minutes on each side or until golden brown and crisp.

1 First make the sauce. Heat the oil in a large frying pan, add the onions and fry, over a medium high heat, for 3–5 minutes until softened but not browned. Add the sliced mushrooms and fry for a further 5–10 minutes.

2 Sprinkle the flour into the onions and mushrooms and stir until mixed. Gradually stir in the stock until smooth. Slowly bring to the boil, stirring all the time, until the sauce boils and thickens.

5 Spoon the sauce over the fish in the pan, reheat gently and serve with hot boiled new potatoes.

Energy 706kcal/2924kJ; Protein 31.2g; Carbohydrate 15.6g, of which sugars 7.5g; Fat 56.3g, of which saturates 30.7g; Cholesterol 191mg; Calcium 98mg; Fibre 1.8g; Sodium 137mg.

Carp with Horseradish Sauce

Carp is a traditional fish on both Russian and Polish menus, and has been farmed in Poland since the 13th century. There are several varieties, the best being the mirror or king carp. The horseradish sauce in this recipe complements the fish perfectly.

Serves 4

750ml/1¼ pints/3 cups cold water
120ml/4fl oz/½ cup vinegar
1 medium carp, about 400g/14oz,
    cut into 4 fillets
115g/4oz/1 cup plain (all-purpose)
    flour
115g/4oz/½ cup butter
250ml/8fl oz/1 cup dry white wine
30ml/2 tbsp fresh horseradish
2 egg yolks, beaten
30ml/2 tbsp chopped fresh chives
salt and ground black pepper,
    to taste

1 Mix the water and vinegar in a large bowl or platter, place the carp fillets in the liquid, turning so each side is coated, and then leave to soak for 1 hour.

2 After an hour, remove the fish from the liquid and pat them dry on kitchen paper.

3 Coat the fillets in seasoned flour. Melt the butter in a frying pan over a high heat, and when foaming add the fish. Fry the fillets for 3–4 minutes on each side, until golden brown.

4 Add the wine to the frying pan and season with salt and pepper. Cover and simmer for 10–15 minutes.

5 When the fish is cooked, transfer it to a serving dish and keep warm.

6 Peel and grate the horseradish. Return the pan to the heat, add the horseradish and egg yolks to the juices and simmer for 5 minutes, or until thickened.

7 Pour the hot sauce over the warm fish and garnish with chopped chives. Serve immediately.

COOK'S TIP Soaking the carp in water and vinegar takes away the muddy taste that river-caught fish sometimes has.

VARIATION If you are unable to buy carp, use river trout instead.

Energy 500kcal/2083kJ; Protein 22.3g; Carbohydrate 23.2g, of which sugars 1.3g; Fat 31.6g, of which saturates 16.7g; Cholesterol 229mg; Calcium 135mg; Fibre 1.5g; Sodium 229mg.

Carp in Wine Sauce

This old Polish carp dish from Krakow forms part of the Christmas Eve meal. Traditionally, the carp was killed and the blood collected in a cup containing lemon juice. This was then added to the sauce. The following version does not require you to do this!

Serves 4–6

400g/14oz carp, cut into thick steaks
750ml/1¼ pints/3 cups water
350ml/12fl oz/1½ cups red wine
30ml/2 tbsp lemon juice
1 small celeriac, sliced
2 onions, sliced
6–8 black peppercorns
2.5ml/½ tsp ground ginger
grated rind of 1 lemon
salt and ground black pepper, to taste

For the sauce

15ml/1 tbsp butter
15ml/1 tbsp plain (all-purpose) flour
45ml/3 tbsp lemon juice
15ml/1 tbsp redcurrant jelly
15ml/1 tbsp clear honey
120ml/4fl oz/½ cup red wine
30ml/2 tbsp currants
30ml/2 tbsp chopped blanched
  almonds

1 Rinse the fish pieces under cold running water, then sprinkle with salt and leave in a cool place for 20 minutes.

2 Meanwhile, make the stock. Put the water, wine, lemon juice, celeriac, onions, peppercorns, ginger, seasoning and lemon rind in a large pan. Bring to the boil and simmer, uncovered, for 15 minutes.

3 Place the fish in a shallow pan and pour over the stock and vegetables. Simmer, uncovered, over a low heat for about 15 minutes, or until the fish flakes easily.

4 Remove the fish to a serving plate using a slotted spoon, and keep warm.

5 Skim out the vegetables and press through a fine sieve (strainer) to form a purée. Add the purée to the stock in the pan. You should have 500ml/17fl oz/2¼ cups stock. Add more water to make up the volume if necessary.

6 To make the sauce, melt the butter in a pan over a medium heat, then add the flour and cook, stirring, for 2 minutes. Stir in the stock. Add the lemon juice, redcurrant jelly, honey and red wine, and cook for 7 minutes.

7 Stir in the currants and almonds, then bring to the boil. Pour the sauce over the carp and serve immediately.

Energy 213kcal/891kJ; Protein 13.2g; Carbohydrate 9.5g, of which sugars 7.5g; Fat 8g, of which saturates 2.1g; Cholesterol 50mg; Calcium 58mg; Fibre 0.6g; Sodium 52mg.

Pike with Hard-boiled Eggs

This dish of poached pike with hard-boiled eggs and parsley is a traditional part of the Polish Christmas Eve meal, although it is eaten at other times of the year, too. Like carp, pike is another very popular freshwater fish in both Poland and Russia.

1 Put the carrots in a large pan and add the parsnips, celery, leek, onion, peppercorns, bay leaves and fish.

2 Pour over enough cold water to just cover. Bring to the boil and simmer, uncovered, for 15–20 minutes, or until the fish flakes easily.

3 Meanwhile, melt the butter in a small pan, then add the chopped hard-boiled eggs and parsley, and heat through.

4 Remove the fish from the pan with a slotted spoon and transfer to a warm serving plate.

5 Liberally sprinkle the fish with the lemon juice, top with the hot egg and parsley mixture and serve immediately.

VARIATION If you are unable to buy carp, use river trout instead.

COOK'S TIP The addition of egg makes this a nourishing and sustaining dish, perfect for the cold Polish winter.

Serves 4

2 carrots, roughly chopped
2 parsnips, roughly chopped
¼ celery stick, roughly chopped
1 leek, roughly chopped
1 large onion, roughly chopped
4–5 black peppercorns
2–3 bay leaves
1.8kg/4lb pike, cleaned, scaled and
  cut into 4 steaks
25g/1oz/2 tbsp butter
3 hard-boiled eggs, chopped
15ml/1 tbsp chopped fresh parsley
juice of 2 lemons

Energy 327kcal/1368kJ; Protein 39.8g; Carbohydrate 0.2g, of which sugars 0.1g; Fat 18.8g, of which saturates 6.2g; Cholesterol 290mg; Calcium 124mg; Fibre 0.2g; Sodium 178mg.

Haddock and Beer Casserole

The earthy flavour of wild mushrooms perfectly complements the delicate taste of the haddock steaks and creamy sauce in this satisfying dish. This Polish recipe, using beer, ensures that the flesh is moist and makes a distinctive and delicious addition to the sauce.

Serves 4

150g/5oz/2 cups wild mushrooms
50g/2oz/¼ cup butter
2 large onions, roughly chopped
2 celery sticks, sliced
2 carrots, sliced
4 haddock steaks, about 185g/6½oz each
300ml/½ pint/1¼ cups light lager
4 bay leaves
25g/1oz/¼ cup plain (all-purpose) flour
200ml/7fl oz/scant 1 cup double (heavy) cream
salt and ground black pepper, to taste
dill sprigs, to garnish

1 Preheat the oven to 190°C/375°F/ Gas 5. Brush the wild mushrooms to remove any grit and only wash the caps briefly if necessary. Dry with kitchen paper and chop them.

2 Melt half the butter in a flameproof casserole, then add the onions, mushrooms, celery and carrots. Fry for about 8 minutes, or until golden brown.

3 Place the haddock steaks on top of the vegetables, then slowly pour over the lager so it doesn't fizz.

4 Add the bay leaves to the casserole and season well with salt and pepper.

5 Put the casserole in the preheated oven and cook for 20–25 minutes, or until the fish flakes easily when tested.

6 Remove the fish and vegetables from the casserole with a slotted spoon and transfer to a serving dish. Cover and keep warm while you make the sauce.

7 Melt the remaining butter in a medium pan, then stir in the flour and cook, stirring constantly, for 2 minutes.

8 Gradually pour in the liquid from the casserole, a little at a time, blending in well each time. Simmer, stirring, for 2–3 minutes until the sauce has thickened.

VARIATION You can replace the beer with the same amount of white wine, if you prefer.

9 Add the double cream to the sauce and reheat briefly, without boiling. Serve the fish and vegetables on warmed plates, accompanied by the sauce and garnished with sprigs of dill.

Energy 564kcal/2346kJ; Protein 37g; Carbohydrate 17.9g, of which sugars 10.5g; Fat 38.8g, of which saturates 23.5g; Cholesterol 158mg; Calcium 106mg; Fibre 3.4g; Sodium 231mg.

Salmon Pie

This Russian speciality is a puff-pastry pie filled with cured salmon, hard-boiled eggs and rice. Pastry of all kinds is very popular in Eastern Europe and it is especially enjoyed in Russia. In the times of the tsar, elaborate pastries were sent as party invitations.

Serves 4

4 eggs
50g/2oz/¼ cup long grain rice, cooked
300g/11oz gravlax or smoked salmon
15g/2oz/¼ cup chopped fresh dill
45ml/3 tbsp smetana or crème fraîche
1 sheet ready-made puff pastry,
   measuring about 40x20cm/16x8in
salt and ground black pepper
1 egg yolk
5ml/1 tsp water
15ml/1 tbsp fresh white breadcrumbs

1 Put the eggs in a pan, cover with cold water and bring to the boil. Reduce the heat to low and simmer for 10 minutes. When the eggs are cooked, drain and put under cold running water. Remove the shell, and chop the eggs into small pieces.

2 Cut the gravlax or smoked salmon into strips and put in a large bowl. Add the eggs, rice, dill and smetana or crème fraîche and mix together. Season with salt and pepper to taste.

3 Preheat the oven to 220°C/425°F/Gas 7. Put the sheet of pastry on a dampened baking tray. Spread the filling lengthways on one half of the pastry sheet.

4 Brush the edges with water and fold the other side over to enclose the filling. Seal together by pressing with a fork along the join. It should be like a tightly packed loaf.

5 Whisk together the egg yolk and water. Brush the pastry with the glaze and make some small holes in the top with a fork. Sprinkle the breadcrumbs over the top.

6 Bake the pie in the oven for 12–15 minutes, until golden brown. Leave the baked pie to rest for 5–10 minutes, then cut into slices and serve.

VARIATION Instead of mixing the filling ingredients, place them in layers. Start with rice, then salmon, then smetana or crème fraîche, then eggs and finally dill.

Energy 624kcal/2606kJ; Protein 32.7g; Carbohydrate 45.6g, of which sugars 1.6g; Fat 36.4g, of which saturates 5.6g; Cholesterol 280mg; Calcium 121mg; Fibre 0.3g; Sodium 1786mg.

POULTRY AND GAME

Poland is a superb hunting country. Its relatively sparsely populated countryside is covered with forests and fields, where hare, deer, wild boar and many game birds flourish, and hunting for the pot is still a popular pastime. Many traditional ingredients of Polish cooking feature in their recipes for game, from juniper berries and herbs to sour cream and mushrooms. Poultry also has a good flavour in Poland, where intensive farming methods are rare, and chicken, geese and ducks are reared on rural smallholdings, eating their natural diet. Russia also enjoys poultry and game recipes, although its hunting traditions are less universal. Venison and rabbit are probably the most common game. Chickens, however, are still often kept in country homes, for eggs as well as for the pot, and there are some typically Russian signature dishes such as Chicken Kiev and Chicken with Walnut Sauce in this chapter.

Chicken Kiev

These classic Ukrainian chicken breasts, filled with garlic butter and then deep-fried, are often accompanied with mushroom sauce. Prepare the chicken parcels well in advance to allow them to chill in the refrigerator before frying. You can also freeze them and cook from frozen.

Serves 4

4 skinless chicken breast fillets
65g/2½oz/5 tbsp cold butter
1.5ml/¼ tsp ground white pepper
4 cloves garlic, peeled and crushed
150g/5oz/3 cups fresh white
　breadcrumbs
2–3 eggs
750ml/1¼ pints/3 cups rapeseed
　(canola) oil
salt
cooked rice and sugarsnap peas,
　to serve

For the mushroom sauce

250g/9oz fresh porcini, chopped
25g/1oz/2 tbsp butter
15ml/1 tbsp plain white (all-purpose)
　flour
300ml/½ pint/1¼ cups whipping cream
salt and ground black pepper

1 Separate the small finger-thick chicken fillets from the larger fillets. Put one fillet at a time between sheets of oiled clear film (plastic wrap) and beat with a rolling pin until the large fillets are 5mm/¼in thick and the smaller fillets 3mm/⅛in thick. When flat, remove from the clear film and put on a board.

2 Cut the butter into four sticks. Put the white pepper, crushed garlic and 1.5ml/¼ tsp salt on a plate and mix together.

3 Roll the butter sticks in the mixture and then place one stick in the centre of each large fillet.

4 Cover the butter with a small fillet and fold the edges of the large fillet up to form a tight parcel. If necessary, secure with a cocktail stick (toothpick). Sprinkle with salt. Chill until ready to cook.

5 To make the sauce, melt the butter in a frying pan, add the mushrooms and cook over a medium heat, stirring frequently. Add the flour and stir until mixed.

6 Gradually stir the cream into the mushroom and flour mixture, a little at a time, until smooth.

7 Slowly bring the sauce to the boil, stirring. Reduce the heat and simmer for 10 minutes. Season to taste.

8 Preheat the oven to 220°C/425°F/Gas 7. Line a baking sheet with foil. Spread the breadcrumbs on a plate.

9 Lightly beat the eggs in a small bowl. Brush the chicken parcels with the beaten eggs, then roll in the breadcrumbs to coat on all sides. Brush again with the beaten eggs, and roll again in the breadcrumbs until thickly and evenly coated.

10 Heat the oil in a deep fryer to 180°C/350°F or until a cube of bread browns in 1 minute. Add the chicken parcels to the hot oil and deep-fry for 3–4 minutes, until golden brown.

11 Remove from the pan and place on the prepared baking sheet. Fold in the foil to cover. Bake in the oven for 5–10 minutes (20 minutes if cooking from frozen). Serve with the mushroom sauce.

Energy 938kcal/3901kJ; Protein 46.2g; Carbohydrate 31.5g, of which sugars 3.3g; Fat 70.7g, of which saturates 33.9g; Cholesterol 327mg; Calcium 122mg; Fibre 1.5g; Sodium 568mg.

Pressed Fried Chicken with Garlic Sauce

This famous dish from Georgia is truly delicious. Whole chickens are flattened, seasoned and fried under a weight so that they are evenly browned. The meat is then crisp on the outside, and juicy inside. Anything you have to hand will do as a weight, from a full jar to a brick.

Serves 4

2 small chickens, each weighing about 750g/1lb 10 oz
5ml/1 tsp salt
2.5ml/½ tsp ground black pepper
10 garlic cloves
50–65g/2–2½ oz/4–5 tbsp butter

For the garlic sauce
200ml/7fl oz/scant 1 cup smetana or crème fraîche
2 garlic cloves
3–4 dashes Tabasco sauce

1 Put the chickens breast-side down on a chopping board and cut open lengthways, through the back. Prise open, turn skin-side up and press down firmly to flatten. Season with the salt and pepper and tuck the chopped garlic under the skin.

2 Melt the butter in two frying pans. Add a chicken to each pan, skin-side down, and fry for about 10 minutes, until lightly browned. Place a weighted plate on top of the chicken. Fry over a low-medium heat for 20 minutes. Turn the chickens, replace the weights and fry the other side for a further 20 minutes, until cooked. If necessary, lower the heat.

3 Meanwhile, make the garlic sauce. Put the smetana or crème fraîche into a bowl. Crush the garlic cloves, add to the bowl with the Tabasco sauce and mix together.

4 Place the fried chickens on a warmed serving dish, allow to rest for 5–10 minutes, then serve with a spoonful of garlic sauce.

Energy 826kcal/3417kJ; Protein 47.9g; Carbohydrate 3.2g, of which sugars 1.3g; Fat 68.9g, of which saturates 31.6g; Cholesterol 325mg; Calcium 52mg; Fibre 0.5g; Sodium 293mg

Chicken Casserole

Warming and nourishing, this casserole consisting of plenty of vegetables as well as chicken, and enriched with egg yolk and cream, is ideal comfort food during cold weather. Served with Buckwheat Kasha it makes a delicious and sustaining main meal.

Serves 4

50g/2oz dried mushrooms, rinsed and
   soaked in warm water for 30
   minutes
800g/1¾lb chicken pieces
550ml/18fl oz/2½ cups water
2 celery stalks, chopped
1 carrot, chopped
30ml/2 tbsp chopped fresh parsley
25g/1oz/2 tbsp butter
25g/1oz/2 tbsp plain (all-purpose)
   flour
120ml/4fl oz/½ cup dry white wine
2 egg yolks
salt and ground black pepper, to taste
Buckwheat Kasha (page 192), to serve

1 Strain the mushrooms, reserving the juices, then chop finely.

2 Put the chicken in a flameproof casserole, add the water and bring to the boil. Simmer for 10 minutes.

3 Add the mushrooms, celery, carrot, parsley and reserved mushroom juices to the casserole. Season, then cover and simmer for 30–45 minutes.

4 Meanwhile, make the roux. Melt the butter in a small pan, add the flour and cook, stirring, for 1 minute.

5 Remove the chicken from the casserole with a slotted spoon and set aside on a warm plate.

6 Add the roux to the casserole and stir. Add the wine and bring to the boil. Remove the casserole from the heat.

7 Put the egg yolks in a small bowl and add a ladleful of the hot juices, stirring constantly. Add to the casserole and stir to combine.

8 Return the chicken to the sauce and heat gently to warm through. Serve with Buckwheat Kasha.

Energy 285kcal/1196kJ; Protein 38.3g; Carbohydrate 6.7g, of which sugars 1.8g; Fat 9.7g, of which saturates 4.5g; Cholesterol 219mg; Calcium 43mg; Fibre 0.8g; Sodium 148mg.

Chicken Burgers with Mushroom Sauce

Burgers made with minced meat, fish or vegetables, are popular everyday food in Russia. Chicken burgers are served in restaurants coated with crisp snippets of toasted bread rather than breadcrumbs, and are delicious eaten with puréed potatoes.

Serves 4

600g/1lb 6oz minced (ground)
  chicken breast
1 egg
75g/3oz/1½ cups fresh white
  breadcrumbs
40g/1½oz/3 tbsp butter
salt and ground black pepper

For the mushroom sauce
25g/1oz dried sliced mushrooms, such
  as porcini, soaked for 2–3 hours
700ml/1 pint 3½fl oz/scant 3 cups
  water
30ml/2 tbsp rapeseed (canola) oil
1 onion, chopped
15ml/1 tbsp plain white (all-purpose)
  flour
45ml/3 tbsp smetana or crème fraîche
salt and ground black pepper

For the puréed potatoes
1kg/2¼lb floury potatoes
200–250ml/7–8fl oz/scant 1–1 cup
  milk, warmed
15g/½oz/1 tbsp butter
salt

COOK'S TIP Turkey breast can be substituted for chicken in this recipe.

1 For the mushroom sauce, put the soaked mushrooms and the water in a pan and simmer for 40 minutes. Using a slotted spoon, remove the mushrooms from the pan, reserving the water.

2 Heat the oil in a large frying pan, add the onion and fry, stirring frequently, for 3 minutes until golden brown. Add the mushrooms and fry, stirring all the time, for a further 5 minutes. Sprinkle the flour over the mushrooms and stir until mixed.

3 Gradually stir all the reserved water into the mushrooms and flour mixture, a little at a time, until smooth. Slowly bring to the boil, stirring all the time, until the sauce boils and thickens.

VARIATION For garlic mash, steep a clove of garlic, peeled and cut in half, in the milk as you slowly warm it on a low heat. Leave the milk to stand for 5–10 minutes, then reheat when you are ready to add it to the mashed potatoes.

4 Reduce the heat and simmer the sauce for 10 minutes. Add the smetana or crème fraîche and simmer for a further 5 minutes. Season with plenty of salt and pepper to taste.

5 Meanwhile, prepare the potato purée. Peel and cut the potatoes into chunks. Put in a pan of salted cold water, bring to the boil, then reduce the heat and simmer for 15–20 minutes, or until soft.

6 Drain the potatoes, return to the pan and mash with a potato masher or a fork. Add the warm milk and butter, beating with a wooden spoon all the time, until the butter is melted and the purée is smooth. Season with salt.

7 Put the minced chicken, egg, salt and pepper into a bowl and mix well. Form the mixture into eight to ten burgers.

8 Spread the breadcrumbs on to a plate. Turn the burgers in the breadcrumbs until coated and then place them on a plate.

9 Heat the butter in a large frying pan until melted. Add the burgers and fry, in batches if necessary, for about 3 minutes on each side.

10 When all the burgers are cooked, return them to the pan, cover with a lid or folded aluminium foil, and cook over low heat for a further 5 minutes. Serve the burgers hot with the mushroom sauce and potato purée.

Energy 588kcal/2479kJ; Protein 46.6g; Carbohydrate 61.6g, of which sugars 7.3g; Fat 19g, of which saturates 7.8g; Cholesterol 178mg; Calcium 131mg; Fibre 3.3g; Sodium 331mg.

Chicken with Walnut Sauce

Sacivi is a Georgian dish that is popular at the end of the summer, when walnuts are ready to be picked. You need to make the dish a day in advance to give the chicken time to chill.

Serves 4–6

4 chicken breast fillets, total weight 500g/1¼lb
500ml/17fl oz/generous 2 cups water
5ml/1 tsp salt
45ml/3 tbsp rapeseed (canola) oil
2 onions, chopped
2 garlic cloves, finely chopped
100g/3¾oz/1 cup walnut halves, plus 5–6 halves, to garnish
5ml/1 tsp ground coriander
pinch of cayenne pepper
45ml/3 tbsp finely chopped fresh coriander (cilantro), to garnish

1 Put the chicken in a medium pan and pour over enough cold water to cover. Bring to the boil, reduce the heat and simmer for 5 minutes. Skim the surface if necessary and add the salt. Cook for a further 15 minutes then remove the chicken from the pan, reserving the stock.

2 Heat the oil in a small frying pan. Add the chopped onions and garlic and fry for 5 minutes, until they are softened, but not browned.

3 Transfer the onions and garlic to a food processor. Add the walnuts, coriander and cayenne pepper and half of the stock from the chicken.

4 Process until a smooth paste is formed. Add the remaining stock, a little at a time, until it reaches the consistency of a thick sauce. Transfer to a large bowl.

5 Cut the cooked chicken into 3cm/1¼in chunks. Add to the sauce and stir until the chicken is coated in the sauce. Cover and chill overnight.

6 To serve, turn the chicken into a serving dish. Garnish with walnut halves and chopped coriander.

VARIATION Sacivi can also be made with a firm white fish such as halibut.

Energy 285kcal/1187kJ; Protein 23.7g; Carbohydrate 7.4g, of which sugars 5.3g; Fat 18.1g, of which saturates 1.8g; Cholesterol 58mg; Calcium 58mg; Fibre 2.2g; Sodium 384mg.

Stuffed Roast Turkey

Turkey is one of the cheaper types of poultry in Poland and is often used to replace more expensive goose. It is best to buy birds that are between seven and nine months old. In this recipe the bird is stuffed with a rich herb stuffing and served with cranberry jelly.

Serves 6

1 turkey, about 4.5–5.5kg/10–12lb, washed and patted dry with kitchen paper
25g/1oz/2 tbsp butter, melted
salt and ground black pepper, to taste
cranberry jelly, to serve

For the stuffing
200g/7oz/3½ cups fresh white breadcrumbs
175ml/6fl oz/¾ cup milk
25g/1oz/2 tbsp butter
1 egg, separated
1 calf's liver, about 600g/1lb 6oz, finely chopped
2 onions, finely chopped
90ml/6 tbsp chopped fresh dill
10ml/2 tsp clear honey
salt and ground black pepper, to taste

1 To make the stuffing, put the breadcrumbs and milk in a large bowl and soak until swollen and soft. Melt the butter in a frying pan and mix 5ml/1 tsp with the egg yolk.

2 Heat the remaining butter in a frying pan and add the liver and onions. Fry gently for 5 minutes, until the onions are golden brown. Remove from the heat and leave to cool.

3 Preheat the oven to 180°C/350°F/Gas 4. Add the cooled liver mixture to the bowl of soaked breadcrumbs.

4 Add the butter and egg yolk mixture to the stuffing together with the dill, honey and seasoning. Mix well.

5 Whisk the egg white to soft peaks, then fold into the stuffing mixture.

6 Stuff the turkey cavity, then weigh to calculate the cooking time. Allow 20 minutes per 500g/1¼lb, plus an additional 20 minutes. Brush the outside with melted butter, season with salt and pepper and transfer to a roasting pan. Place in the oven and roast for the calculated time.

7 Baste the turkey regularly during cooking, and cover with foil for the final 30 minutes. To test if the turkey is done, pierce the thickest part of the thigh with a knife; the juices should run clear.

8 Remove the turkey from the oven, cover with foil and leave to rest for about 15 minutes. Carve, spoon over the juices and serve with stuffing and cranberry jelly.

Energy 740kcal/3126kJ; Protein 112.3g; Carbohydrate 35.9g, of which sugars 7.3g; Fat 13.5g, of which saturates 6.6g; Cholesterol 507mg; Calcium 122mg; Fibre 1.7g; Sodium 517mg.

Roast Goose with Apples

In Russia the goose is viewed as the king of poultry, and it is traditional to serve your guests roast goose with apples on New Year's Eve. The goose will be served with much excitement and flourish, often on a silver platter, and certainly carved with much ceremony at the table.

Serves 4–6

65g/2½oz/5 tbsp butter
1 goose
8–10 Granny Smith apples, peeled, cored and cut into wedges
200ml/7fl oz/scant 1 cup water
salt and ground black pepper
boiled or roasted potatoes with fresh dill, Sauerkraut Stew (page 188) or boiled buckwheat, to serve

1 Preheat the oven to 180°C/350°F/ Gas 4. Grease a roasting pan with 25g/1oz/ 2 tbsp of the butter, then season the goose inside and out with plenty of salt and black pepper.

2 Peel, core and quarter four of the apples and stuff them inside the neck end of the goose. Fold the neck skin over, then truss the goose, making sure that the legs are close to the body.

3 Weigh the goose to work out cooking time, and calculate 15 minutes per 450g/1lb, plus a further 15 minutes.

4 Melt the rest of the butter. Put the goose in the pan and brush with the butter. Pour the water around the goose.

5 Roast for 1½ hours. Core the remaining apples and place in the pan. Return to the oven for the rest of the cooking time.

6 When cooked, rest the goose for 20 minutes, then carve into slices and serve with the apples and accompaniments.

Energy 822kcal/3437kJ; Protein 54.8g; Carbohydrate 44.1g, of which sugars 21.8g; Fat 48.7g, of which saturates 0.9g; Cholesterol 0mg; Calcium 87mg; Fibre 3.1g; Sodium 486mg.

Potted Goose

The season for shooting wild geese starts in autumn. If a Polish housewife is lucky enough to have more birds than she can roast, she will probably pot one of them. Sealing goose meat in fat is a traditional way of preserving, and is an incredibly delicious treat on hot toast.

Serves 6

5kg/11lb goose, boned and fat
  reserved (see Cook's Tip)
5ml/1 tsp salt
5ml/1 tsp fresh thyme leaves
5ml/1 tsp chopped fresh dill
4 bay leaves
5ml/1 tsp ground allspice
toasted rye bread, to serve

1 Cut the goose into large pieces and place in a large bowl.

2 Sprinkle over the salt, thyme, dill, bay leaves and allspice. Toss to coat the meat, then cover, place in the refrigerator and leave to marinate for 48 hours.

3 Place the goose fat in a large pan with a lid and melt gently. Add the goose portions to the pan, cover and simmer very gently for 2–3 hours.

4 Remove the meat from the pan. Pour a layer of fat into the bottom of a 2 litre/3½ pint/8 cup stoneware pot or preserving jar.

5 Place the goose portions on top of the fat, slice or shred first if you prefer. Pour in enough fat to fill the jar to the top.

6 Seal and keep in a cool, dark place for up to 2 months, until required.

7 Remove the goose from the jar and scrape off any excess fat. Serve cold, or heat through slowly if you prefer, before serving with toasted rye bread.

COOK'S TIPS It is very easy to remove the bones from the goose yourself, if you prefer. Once the goose portions have been marinated, drain them and pick out the bones with your fingers.

The potted goose will keep for a couple of months if stored in a dark, cool place.

Energy 903kcal/3735kJ; Protein 41.3g; Carbohydrate 0g, of which sugars 0g; Fat 82g, of which saturates 23.8g; Cholesterol 200mg; Calcium 18mg; Fibre 0g; Sodium 153mg.

Roast Partridges with Sage, Thyme and Garlic

It is important that you select young birds for this simple Polish recipe. Basting the meat regularly during the cooking time prevents the flesh from drying out and adds a lovely buttery flavour, and the herbs and garlic add a subtle yet distinctive note.

Serves 2

2 small partridges, cleaned
  and gutted
4 slices pork fat or streaky
  (fatty) bacon
50g/2oz/¼ cup butter, softened, plus
  5ml/3 tbsp melted butter, for basting
6 fresh sage leaves, roughly chopped
1 bunch fresh thyme
4 garlic cloves, roughly chopped
salt and ground black pepper, to taste
cranberry preserve, to serve (optional)

1 Preheat the oven to 190°C/375°F/ Gas 5. Wash the cavities of the partridges, then dry with kitchen paper. Season the birds well, inside and out, then place in a roasting pan.

2 Lay the slices of pork fat or bacon over the birds, making sure the breasts are completely covered.

3 Shred the leaves of thyme from the stalks and discard the stalks. Mix together the softened butter, herbs and garlic, and use to stuff the cavities of the birds.

4 Place in the oven and roast for about 1½ hours, until cooked through, basting often with the melted butter.

5 Remove from the oven, cover with foil and allow to rest for 15 minutes.

6 Serve with cranberry preserve, if you like.

COOK'S TIP To test if they are cooked, pierce the thickest part of the thigh; the juices should run clear.

Energy 866kcal/3619kJ; Protein 118g; Carbohydrate 0.1g, of which sugars 0.1g; Fat 43.6g, of which saturates 16.1g; Cholesterol 59mg; Calcium 145mg; Fibre 0g; Sodium 1006mg.

Roasted Pheasants

Poland still has a strong tradition of hunting for food, and pheasants are a favourite game bird. Juniper berries, allspice, cloves and bay leaves are the key components of the marinade for this delicious dish. Long marinating ensures the flavours permeate the flesh.

Serves 4

2 medium pheasants, cleaned and
   gutted (ask your butcher to
   do this)
150g/5oz streaky (fatty) bacon, cut
   into thin strips
4–5 dried mushrooms, rinsed
   and soaked in warm water for
   30 minutes
150g/5oz/10 tbsp butter, melted
15ml/1 tbsp plain (all-purpose) flour
300ml/½ pint/1¼ cups sour cream
salt and ground black pepper, to taste
Beetroot Salad (page 195), to serve

For the marinade

175ml/6fl oz/¾ cup dry white wine
200ml/7fl oz/scant 1 cup water
90ml/6 tbsp vinegar
1 large onion, roughly chopped
1 carrot, roughly chopped
½ celeriac, roughly chopped
1 parsnip, roughly chopped
5–8 juniper berries, crushed
4 bay leaves
6 allspice berries
6 whole cloves
5ml/1 tsp sugar
salt and ground black pepper, to taste

1 To make the marinade, put all the ingredients in a large pan and bring to the boil. Once the liquid has boiled, remove from the heat.

2 Place the pheasants in a large dish or stainless steel pan and pour over the hot marinade. Cover and leave to cool, then place in the refrigerator and leave to marinate for 2–3 days, turning the pheasants occasionally.

3 Preheat the oven to 220°C/425°F/ Gas 7. Lift out the pheasants and season all over.

4 Place in a roasting pan with the vegetables from the marinade. Roll up the bacon strips and place inside the cavities of the birds.

5 Drain and chop the mushrooms. Pour the melted butter over the pheasants and sprinkle the mushrooms over the top.

6 Place in the oven and roast for about 1 hour. To test whether they are cooked, pierce the thickest part with a knife; the juices should run clear.

7 Mix the flour with the sour cream, then pour over the pheasants. Cover with foil and cook for a further 10 minutes, or until the sauce is thick.

8 Remove from the oven and leave to rest for 15 minutes. Remove the foil, carve, then serve with the vegetables, sauce and Beetroot Salad.

Energy 1114kcal/4636kJ; Protein 89.9g; Carbohydrate 6.3g, of which sugars 3.4g; Fat 78.3g, of which saturates 40g; Cholesterol 149mg; Calcium 212mg; Fibre 0.1g; Sodium 996mg.

Roast Duck with Fruit Stuffing

Duck is considered a luxury in Poland, and is usually reserved for special occasions. Often, as in this recipe, the duck is roasted, stuffed and served with a range of different fruits.

Serves 4

1 large duck, about 2.75kg/6lb
3 apples, chopped
2 whole oranges, chopped
12 prunes, chopped
12 fresh or dried apricots, chopped
175ml/6fl oz/¾ cup fresh orange juice
30ml/2 tbsp clear honey
Spiced Red Cabbage (page 181),
    to serve

For the marinade
1 lemon
5ml/1 tsp dried marjoram
salt and ground black pepper, to taste

COOK'S TIP Duck is a fatty bird, so it is best roasted with a stuffing that will cut the fat, such as this fresh, fruity one.

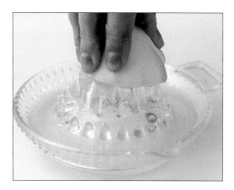

1 Squeeze the lemon and mix the juice in a bowl with the majoram and pepper.

2 Wash the duck and pat dry with kitchen paper, then put it into a large dish. Rub the lemon marinade over the duck. Cover and leave to marinate for 2 hours, or overnight in the refrigerator.

3 Preheat the oven to 180°C/350°F/Gas 4. Mix together the apples, oranges, prunes, apricots, orange juice and honey, then stuff into the cavity.

4 Weigh the duck and calculate the cooking time: allow 20 minutes per 500g/1¼lb, plus an extra 20 minutes.

5 Put the duck in a roasting pan and place in the hot oven. To test whether it is cooked, pierce the thickest part with a knife; the juices should run clear.

6 Cover with foil and allow it to rest for about 15 minutes. Remove the fruit from the cavity and carve the meat.

7 Transfer the meat to a serving platter and arrange the fruit around it. Serve with Spiced Red Cabbage.

Energy 468kcal/1983kJ; Protein 43.5g; Carbohydrate 54.1g, of which sugars 54.1g; Fat 13.7g, of which saturates 2.6g; Cholesterol 220mg; Calcium 99mg; Fibre 7.8g; Sodium 241mg.

Wild Boar with Sweet-and-sour Sauce

Harking back to ancient days when hunters caught wild boar in the forests around Poland, this old Polish recipe involves marinating for several days before roasting and serving it with a flavoursome sauce.

Serves 4–6

1 piece wild boar rump, about
  2kg/4½lb
115g/4oz/⅔ cup lard
30ml/2 tbsp plain (all-purpose) flour
15ml/1 tbsp rosehip preserve
5ml/1 tsp ground cinnamon
5ml/1 tsp sugar
5ml/1 tsp salt
redcurrant jelly, to serve

For the marinade
500ml/17fl oz/2¼ cups water
500ml/17fl oz/2¼ cups dry red wine
90ml/6 tbsp vinegar
2 strips of lemon rind
2 onions, sliced
3 large garlic cloves, chopped
1 carrot, chopped
½ celeriac, chopped
1 parsnip, chopped
15 prunes
10 black peppercorns
10 allspice berries, cracked
4–5 whole cloves
20 juniper berries
4 bay leaves
1 piece fresh root ginger, chopped

1 Place all the marinade ingredients in a stainless steel pan and bring to the boil. Simmer for 5 minutes, then cool.

2 Add the meat to the marinade, cover and chill. Leave to marinate for 3–4 days. This helps to tenderize the meat.

3 Preheat the oven to 180°C/350°F/ Gas 4. Heat the lard in a flameproof casserole. Add the meat and brown all over. Scoop out the vegetables and lemon from the marinade and add to the meat in the casserole.

4 Strain the marinade. Add to the casserole. Cook for 2 hours. Lift out the meat, cover and rest for 15 minutes.

5 Mix together the flour, rosehip preserve, cinnamon, sugar and salt, then add to the casserole. Stir to mix and return to the oven for 10 minutes.

6 Carve the meat into slices, then transfer to plates and spoon over the sauce. Serve with redcurrant jelly.

Energy 655kcal/2734kJ; Protein 73g; Carbohydrate 17.4g, of which sugars 8.8g; Fat 33g, of which saturates 12.5g; Cholesterol 228mg; Calcium 63mg; Fibre 3.3g; Sodium 578mg.

Rabbit in Smetana

Smetana, the Russian version of sour cream, is an ingredient in many of the country's dishes. Cooking rabbit in a sauce of smetana helps to keep the meat tender and also gives it a delicate, mild flavour. In Russia, boiled potatoes are the traditional accompaniment to this dish.

2 Add the shallots and water and half the beef stock to the pan, cover and cook over a low heat for 1–1½ hours, until the meat is tender. If necessary, add a little additional water.

3 Put the rest of the beef stock, the smetana or crème fraîche and the chopped parsley in a jug (pitcher) and mix together.

4 Add the cream and parsley mixture to the meat, bring to the boil, then reduce the heat and simmer for 10–15 minutes.

5 To serve, put the rabbit on a warmed serving dish and spoon over the sauce. Garnish the rabbit with parsley sprigs and accompany it with boiled potatoes, rice or pasta.

COOK'S TIP If you have difficulty in buying rabbit from a supermarket, you can order it from a butcher or often find it at a food market. Chicken can be used instead.

Serves 4–6

40g/1½oz/3 tbsp butter
1 rabbit, total weight about
  1.5kg/3¼lb, boned and cut
  into chunks
12 shallots
45–60ml/3–4 tbsp water
200ml/7fl oz/scant 1 cup beef stock
300ml/1/2 pint/1¼ cups smetana or
  crème fraîche
15g/½oz/¼ cup finely chopped fresh
  parsley, plus 4–5 sprigs, to garnish
salt and ground black pepper
boiled potatoes, rice or pasta,
  to serve

1 Heat the butter in a large frying pan. Add the rabbit pieces and fry over a medium heat, stirring occasionally, for 10 minutes, until browned on all sides. Season with salt and pepper.

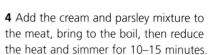

Energy 436kcal/1809kJ; Protein 33.9g; Carbohydrate 6.7g, of which sugars 5g; Fat 30.5g, of which saturates 19.5g; Cholesterol 193mg; Calcium 121mg; Fibre 1.4g; Sodium 129mg.

Venison Ragoût

Bear meat was originally used in this recipe, which dates from the times when bears were hunted for food in Russia, but other game such as elk or venison can be substituted. In some Russian restaurants today bear ragoût made with imported meat is served.

Serves 4

600g/1lb 6oz venison or elk fillet
2 onions
500g/1¼lb turnips
5–6 juniper berries
40g/1¼oz/3 tbsp butter
30ml/2 tbsp rapeseed (canola) oil
1 beef stock (bouillon) cube
60–75ml/4–5 tbsp tomato purée (paste)
15ml/1 tbsp plain white (all-purpose) flour
2–3 bay leaves
4–5 black peppercorns
500ml/17fl oz/generous 2 cups water
300ml/½ pint/1¼ cups double (heavy) cream
salt and ground black pepper
mashed or boiled potatoes to serve

1 Cut the meat into chunky pieces. Chop the onions, dice the turnips and crush the juniper berries. Heat the butter and oil in a flameproof casserole. Add the meat and fry, stirring frequently, for about 10 minutes, until browned on all sides.

2 Add the onions to the pan and fry for 3–5 minutes. Add the turnips and fry, stirring all the time, for a further 5 minutes. Crumble in the stock cube and add the tomato purée.

VARIATION If you do use bear fillet for this recipe, you will need to increase the cooking time by about 1½ hours.

3 Sprinkle the flour over the meat and fry, stirring, for 1 minute. Add the juniper berries, bay leaves, peppercorns and gradually stir in the water. Bring to the boil, then reduce the heat, cover and simmer for about 1½ hours.

4 Stir the cream into the pan and cook for a further 10 minutes. Season to taste and serve hot with boiled or mashed potatoes and Marinated Mushrooms.

Energy 758kcal/3148kJ; Protein 37.6g; Carbohydrate 19.1g, of which sugars 13.7g; Fat 60.7g, of which saturates 32.4g; Cholesterol 199mg; Calcium 139mg; Fibre 4.7g; Sodium 200mg.

Venison with Wine Sauce

Tender venison steaks are the perfect partner to the wild mushrooms that abound in Poland's forests. Here the steaks are cooked simply and served with a rich wine sauce. If venison is out of season or not available you can replace it with beef; sirloin or rump would be the best cuts.

Serves 4

100g/3½oz fresh wild mushrooms, cut in half
4 venison loin steaks, 2cm/¾in thick
25g/1oz/¼ cup plain (all-purpose) flour
25g/1oz/2 tbsp butter
1 large onion, sliced into rings
5ml/1 tsp fresh thyme leaves
5ml/1 tsp juniper berries
5–6 allspice berries
5 bay leaves
4 garlic cloves, crushed
175ml/6fl oz/¾ cup white wine
salt and ground black pepper

1 Brush the mushrooms to remove any grit, and wash the caps briefly if necessary. Dry with kitchen paper. Lightly dust the venison steaks with the flour.

2 Heat the butter in a heavy pan with a lid, then add the onion rings and venison, and fry for 5 minutes, until the onions have softened and the steaks are brown.

3 Add the remaining ingredients to the pan and season to taste. Cover and simmer for 30 minutes.

4 Taste and adjust the seasoning, if necessary. Serve immediately.

Energy 303kcal/1276kJ; Protein 45.1g; Carbohydrate 5.2g, of which sugars 0.4g; Fat 9.6g, of which saturates 4.9g; Cholesterol 113mg; Calcium 24mg; Fibre 0.2g; Sodium 150mg.

Marinated Hare

In this delectable Polish dish, the saddle and thighs of a hare are marinated in buttermilk and vegetables, before being roasted and then baked with a cream sauce. The marinating process helps to tenderize the meat. Wild boar could be used in place of hare in this recipe.

Serves 4

saddle and thighs of 1 hare
120ml/4fl oz/½ cup vinegar
900ml/1½ pints/3¾ cups buttermilk
175g/6oz/¾ cup butter
5 large dried mushrooms, rinsed and
  soaked in warm water for 30
  minutes, thinly sliced
15ml/1 tbsp plain (all-purpose) flour
200ml/7fl oz/scant 1 cup thick
  sour cream
175ml/6fl oz/¾ cup white wine
salt and ground black pepper
cranberry preserve, to serve (optional)

For the marinade:
10–15 juniper berries
2 large onions, cut into slices
½ celeriac, chopped
2 parsnips, chopped
2 carrots, chopped
3 large garlic cloves, crushed
5 bay leaves

1 Place the hare pieces, vinegar and all the marinade ingredients in a large dish and pour in enough buttermilk to cover.

2 Add salt and pepper, cover, and place in the refrigerator. Leave to marinate for 2–3 days. Change the buttermilk after day 1.

3 At the end of the three days, drain off the marinade and buttermilk. Preheat the oven to 180°C/350°F/Gas 4. Transfer the hare pieces to a roasting pan, rub with 15ml/1 tbsp salt, and dot with the butter.

4 Sprinkle the mushrooms over the hare. Cover and roast for 1–1½ hours.

5 Mix the flour with the sour cream and white wine, then add to the roasting pan.

6 Shake the pan so that the hare is covered with the sauce, then cover the pan with foil and replace in the oven. Cook for a further 15–20 minutes, or until the sauce is thick and bubbling.

7 Transfer the pieces of hare to a warm serving dish and spoon over the creamy sauce. Serve immediately, with cranberry preserve, if you like.

COOK'S TIP An important part of Polish cuisine involves marinating game before it is cooked. This process helps to tenderize the meat and also adds flavour to the finished dish.

Energy 581kcal/2423kJ; Protein 62.9g; Carbohydrate 6.9g, of which sugars 3g; Fat 29.5g, of which saturates 8.4g; Cholesterol 40mg; Calcium 118mg; Fibre 0.5g; Sodium 111mg.

MEAT

Russians and Poles are both nations of meat lovers, and enjoy it roasted whole or in casseroles. Russian meat recipes often go right back to the days when the large wood-burning stove, which was kept alight the whole year round, was also used for slowly braising delicious stews. Most of these recipes also contain mixtures of vegetables and grains to add bulk and create an entire meal in a pot. Mushrooms, tomatoes, potatoes and cabbage are frequently included for colour and flavour as well as nutritional qualities. Russians are particularly fond of beef and lamb recipes, while Poles have a special love for pork in all its many forms. Both rural communities developed recipes for using all parts of the animal, including offal, which is a highly prized delicacy often eaten as a snack in Poland, and the hearts, which are enjoyed in Russia. The addition of sour cream to many of the following meat dishes helps to give them a particularly Russian and Polish taste.

Little Beef Dumplings

These tiny Siberian dumplings are traditionally accompanied by red wine vinegar, melted butter and ground black pepper. Russians expect to eat about 40 pelmeni at a time, but this is, of course, not obligatory, and here we suggest 20. Leftover pelmeni are delicious fried in butter. It is customary to make pelmeni in advance and freeze them, to be cooked as needed.

Makes 80–100
Serves 4–6

2 eggs
150ml/¼ pint/⅔ cup water
15ml/1 tbsp rapeseed (canola) oil
2.5ml/½ tsp salt
360g/12½oz/3⅛ cups plain white (all-purpose) flour, plus extra for dusting

For the filling
1 onion, total weight 100g/3¾oz
200g/7oz minced (ground) beef
200g/7oz minced (ground) pork
7.5ml/1½ tsp salt
2–2.5ml/⅓–½ tsp ground black pepper
red wine vinegar, melted butter, salt and ground black pepper, and smetana (optional), to serve

COOK'S TIP The best pelmeni are always handmade but, if you want to save time, you can roll the dough through a pasta machine and cut the pieces into rounds using a 5cm/2in round cutter. Fill them with the meat mixture and seal by pressing the edges firmly together.

1 First make the pastry. Put the eggs, water, oil, salt and half of the flour in a food processor and process until well blended. Add the remaining flour, in batches, to form a smooth pastry.

2 Turn the pastry on to a lightly floured surface and knead for 5 minutes. Put in a plastic bag and leave to rest for 30 minutes, or overnight, in a cold place.

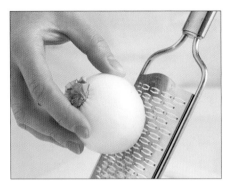

3 To make the filling, finely grate the onion and put it in a bowl. Add the minced beef and pork, salt and pepper and mix together. Set aside.

4 To make the dumplings, cut the pastry into eight pieces. Work with one piece at a time, keeping the remaining pieces in the plastic bag to prevent them from drying out.

5 On a floured surface, roll the piece of pastry into a roll, the thickness of a finger. Cut the roll into 10–12 small pieces.

6 Flatten out each piece to a round, about 3cm/1¼ in in diameter, and then roll out into a thinner round, 5–6cm/2–2½in in diameter.

7 Spread each round with 5m/1 tsp of the meat mixture, leaving a small uncovered edge. Fold and pinch together the rounds to form a half-moon shape.

8 As you make the dumplings, put them on a floured baking sheet. When the sheet is full, put it in the freezer.

9 When the dumplings are completely frozen, transfer them to a plastic bag and keep frozen until required.

10 When you are ready to serve the dumplings, take the amount you need from the freezer and put in a pan of lightly salted boiling water.

11 Simmer until the dumplings float to the surface, then simmer for a further 1 minute. Using a slotted spoon, scoop out of the water and serve immediately, sprinkled with red wine vinegar, melted butter, salt and pepper.

12 A small amount of the cooking water mixed with smetana may be served on the side, if wished.

Energy 381kcal/1605kJ; Protein 20.9g; Carbohydrate 47.9g, of which sugars 1.8g; Fat 13.1g, of which saturates 4.4g; Cholesterol 105mg; Calcium 103mg; Fibre 2.1g; Sodium 74mg.

Roast Beef Roll

This traditional Polish dish is a combination of fine steak and stong-flavoured mushrooms. Stuffed meat dishes such as this have been a part of Polish cooking since the 17th century, and they are usually served on festive occasions or as part of a special Polish dinner.

3 Using a mallet, pound the steak to the thickness of your little finger. Spread the stuffing all over the meat, then roll tightly. Tuck the edges in and tie with scalded white cotton thread.

4 Heat the butter in a large pan. Sprinkle the roll with salt, then add to the pan and seal on all sides. Add the stock, cover and simmer for 30 minutes. Preheat the oven to 180°C/350°F/Gas 4.

5 Transfer the beef roll and the juices to a roasting pan and roast for 30 minutes. Add more stock if required.

6 Remove the thread and cut into thin slices. Ladle over the juices and serve with Buckwheat Kasha and a green salad or poached beetroots.

Serves 4–6

1.3kg/3lb piece boneless rump steak
25g/1oz/2 tbsp butter
120ml/4fl oz/½ cup beef stock
pinch of salt
Buckwheat Kasha (page 192) and a
  green salad or poached beetroots
  (beets), to serve

For the stuffing
50g/2oz/½ cups dried mushrooms,
  soaked in warm water for
  30 minutes
25g/1oz streaky (fatty) smoked bacon
15g/½oz/1 tbsp butter
½ onion, finely chopped
15ml/1 tbsp fresh breadcrumbs
1 egg, beaten
15ml/1 tbsp sour cream
15ml/1 tbsp finely chopped
  fresh parsley
salt and ground black pepper, to taste

1 To make the stuffing, strain the mushrooms and put into a food processor with the bacon. Process to form a paste, then scrape into a bowl.

2 Heat the butter in a pan, then add the onion and fry for 5 minutes. Leave to cool, then add to the bowl with the breadcrumbs, egg, sour cream, parsley and seasoning. Use your hands to knead the mixture to combine.

Energy 360kcal/1510kJ; Protein 50.1g; Carbohydrate 2.9g, of which sugars 0.8g; Fat 16.6g, of which saturates 8g; Cholesterol 177mg; Calcium 23mg; Fibre 0.3g; Sodium 267mg.

Kebabs with Plum Sauce

At weekends, Russian families love to go on a picnic. Other family members, friends and colleagues are all invited to go to a sjasliki – cooking food on skewers. The best sjaslik are made over the glowing cinders left from an open fire.

Serves 4

800g–1kg/1¾–2¼lb beef fillet
1 onion, finely sliced
200ml/7fl oz/scant 1 cup red wine
15g/½oz/1 tbsp butter
salt and ground black pepper
lemon wedges, to garnish

For the plum sauce
300g/11oz fresh green or red plums
400ml/14fl oz/1⅔ cups water
2 garlic cloves
45ml/3 tbsp chopped fresh
  coriander (cilantro)
small pinch of cayenne pepper

1 Cut the meat into chunks. Put in a large bowl with salt and pepper, the onion and wine. Cover with clear film (plastic wrap) and leave in the refrigerator for 3 hours.

2 For the sauce, put the plums in a pan. Add the water, bring to the boil, reduce the heat, then cover and simmer for 20 minutes. Remove the plums from the pan and set aside. Reserve the liquid.

3 When the plums are cool, remove the stones (pits) and put the flesh in a food processor. Add the garlic, coriander and about 75ml/5 tbsp of the plum liquid and blend. Add more liquid to the purée, until it is the consistency of thick cream. Add cayenne pepper and salt to taste.

4 Heat a barbecue, if using, or preheat the grill (broiler). Melt the butter. Thread the marinated meat chunks on to long metal skewers.

5 Brush the meat with the melted butter. Place on the grill and cook the skewers for about 10–15 minutes, turning to cook the meat on all sides.

6 Serve the skewers with the plum sauce and garnish with lemon. Russians would add plain boiled rice and a green salad.

VARIATION You can cook skewers of lamb, such as lamb fillet or boneless loin of lamb, in the same way.

Energy 325kcal/1364kJ; Protein 43.4g; Carbohydrate 8.2g, of which sugars 7.8g; Fat 12.5g, of which saturates 5.6g; Cholesterol 122mg; Calcium 48mg; Fibre 2g; Sodium 95mg.

Burgers with Buckwheat and Fried Onions

Kotletki are Russia's fast food. Russians love them and eat them for both lunch and dinner. Although they can be bought ready-made from the meat counter in the supermarkets, the best kotletki are home-made. Here they are served with buckwheat and fried onions.

Serves 4

1 potato
1 onion
300g/11oz minced (ground) beef
300g/11oz minced (ground) pork
5ml/1 tsp salt
heaped 1.5ml/¼ tsp ground
   black pepper
75g/3oz/1½ cups fresh breadcrumbs
25–40g/1–1½oz/2–3 tbsp butter
30ml/2 tbsp rapeseed (canola) oil
100ml/3½fl oz/scant ½ cup smetana or
   crème fraîche and 4–8 small
   gherkins, to serve

For the buckwheat

350g/12oz/1¾ cups whole
   buckwheat grains
1 litre/1¾ pints/4 cups boiling water
5ml/1 tsp salt
2 large onions
45–60ml/3–4 tbsp sunflower oil

VARIATION The grated potato in the burgers can be replaced with two slices of stale white bread. Remove the crusts and soak in 100ml/3½fl oz/scant ½ cup milk for 5 minutes, until soft.

1 To make the burgers, grate the potato and onion and put in a large bowl. Add the beef, pork, salt and pepper and mix well together until the mixture is smooth.

2 Form the meat mixture into 10–12 equal-sized 2cm/¾in thick burgers and place them on a damp chopping board. (Using a wet surface stops them sticking.)

3 Spread the breadcrumbs on to a plate. Turn the burgers in the breadcrumbs until coated and then place them on a plate or dry chopping board. Set aside.

4 To cook the buckwheat, heat a small frying pan until hot, add the buckwheat and dry-fry for 1–2 minutes. Transfer to a medium pan and add the boiling water and salt. Stir, cover, and cook over a medium heat for 20–30 minutes, until the grains have absorbed all the water.

5 Meanwhile, prepare the onions for the buckwheat. Slice the onions into rings.

6 Heat the oil in a medium frying pan, add the onions and fry, stirring frequently, over a low heat for 5 minutes, or until softened and golden brown.

7 When the buckwheat is cooked, drain and return to the pan. Add the fried onions and stir together.

8 Meanwhile, cook the burgers. Heat the butter and oil in a medium frying pan until hot and the butter has melted. Add three or four burgers at a time and fry, over a medium heat, for 2–3 minutes on each side.

9 Remove from the pan and continue to cook the remaining burgers in the same way. When all the burgers are cooked, return them to the pan, cover with a lid and cook, over a low heat, for 10 minutes.

10 Arrange the burgers in a row on a serving dish and put the buckwheat along each side. Serve hot, with smetana or crème fraîche and gherkins.

Energy 839kcal/3515kJ; Protein 38.9g; Carbohydrate 85.9g, of which sugars 9g; Fat 40.2g, of which saturates 12.9g; Cholesterol 108mg; Calcium 88mg; Fibre 2.9g; Sodium 1284mg.

Beef Stroganoff

This famous dish was created at the time of Catherine the Great by Count Alexander Sergeyevich Stroganov. The Count would invite poor students into his house, and serve them this beef casserole, accompanied by fried potatoes and Salted Cucumbers.

Serves 4

90–105ml/6–7 tbsp rapeseed (canola) oil
6–8 potatoes, peeled and thinly sliced
40–50g/1½–2oz/3–4 tbsp butter
500g/1¼lb beef fillet, very thinly sliced
salt and ground black pepper
Salted Cucumbers (page 79), diced, to serve

For the sauce

30–45ml/2–3 tbsp rapeseed (canola) oil
2–3 onions, thinly sliced
1 chicken stock (bouillon) cube
45ml/3 tbsp tomato purée (paste)
15ml/1 tbsp plain white (all-purpose) flour
2–3 bay leaves
4–5 black peppercorns
300ml/½ pint/1¼ cups water
200ml/7fl oz/scant 1 cup double (heavy) cream
100ml/3½fl oz/scant ½ cup smetana or crème fraîche

1 First make the sauce. Heat the oil in a medium pan. Add the sliced onions and fry over a medium heat for 3–5 minutes. Crumble the stock cube into the onions and fry for a further 1–2 minutes.

2 Add the tomato purée to the pan, then the flour and stir well together. Add the bay leaves and peppercorns and then gradually stir in the water and cream.

3 Slowly bring to the boil, stirring, until the sauce thickens. Simmer for a further 10 minutes. Stir in the smetana or crème fraîche.

4 Meanwhile, fry the potatoes. Heat the oil in a large frying pan. Add the sliced potatoes and fry for 10–15 minutes, turning occasionally.

5 Cover the pan and cook for a further 10–15 minutes, until tender. Season the potatoes with salt to taste.

6 To cook the beef, heat the butter in a frying pan. Add the slices of beef, in batches, and cook quickly, over a high heat, for about 1 minute until browned. Transfer to a plate, season, and keep warm. Repeat until all the meat is cooked.

7 When you are ready to serve, reheat the sauce, add the beef and heat through gently for 2–3 minutes. Serve immediately with the fried potatoes, accompanied by diced Salted Cucumbers.

Energy 919kcal/3810kJ; Protein 32.5g; Carbohydrate 36g, of which sugars 11.7g; Fat 72.6g, of which saturates 34.6g; Cholesterol 194mg; Calcium 94mg; Fibre 3.4g; Sodium 177mg.

Beef Goulash

In Poland, beef is relatively expensive and not always easy to obtain, so the Poles make the most of cheaper cuts with recipes such as this rich goulash, in which the meat is cooked slowly, mushrooms are added to bulk the dish out, and it is enriched with cream.

Serves 4–6

45ml/3 tbsp oil
1.3kg/3lb braising steak
2 large onions, chopped
4 garlic cloves, chopped
2.5ml/¹/₂ tsp salt
2.5ml/¹/₂ tsp ground black pepper
3 allspice berries
2.5ml/¹/₂ tsp paprika
4 fresh bay leaves
1 beef stock (bouillon) cube
5 dried wild mushrooms, rinsed
  and soaked in warm water for
  30 minutes
175ml/6fl oz/³/₄ cup dry red wine
60ml/4 tbsp plain (all-purpose) flour
250ml/8fl oz/1 cup sour cream

1 Preheat the oven to 160°C/325°F/Gas 3. Rinse the meat, then pat dry on kitchen paper and cut into 2.5cm/1in cubes.

2 Heat the oil in a flameproof casserole, add the meat and brown on all sides over a high heat. Remove to a plate using a slotted spoon.

3 Add the onions and garlic to the hot oil in the casserole and fry gently for 5 minutes, or until golden brown. Return the meat to the pan and add the salt, pepper, spices, bay leaves and stock cube. Pour in enough water to just cover.

4 Put the casserole in the preheated oven and cook for about 1¹/₂–2 hours, until the meat is tender.

5 Drain and slice the mushrooms and add to the casserole with the wine. Cook for a further 30 minutes.

6 Mix the flour with the sour cream and stir through the goulash. Cook for a further 10 minutes. Serve.

Energy 508kcal/2119kJ; Protein 50g; Carbohydrate 13.4g, of which sugars 4.6g; Fat 26.4g, of which saturates 11.2g; Cholesterol 162mg; Calcium 78mg; Fibre 1g; Sodium 161mg

Little Beef Pies

These golden little pastries are called pirojki in Russian, and they are an important part of the zakuski table. Pirojki are also served as an accompaniment to soups. In this recipe they are filled with beef, but other fillings such as salmon, potato or cabbage can be used.

Makes 24 little pies

Serves 6–8
1 large onion
30–45ml/2–3 tbsp rapeseed
  (canola) oil
400g/14oz minced (ground) beef
100ml/3½fl oz/scant ½ cup beef stock
30ml/2 tbsp smetana or crème fraîche
1 egg
salt and ground black pepper

For the dough
50g/2oz/¼ cup butter
200ml/7fl oz/scant 1 cup milk
45ml/3 tbsp water
1 small (US medium) egg plus
  1 egg yolk
2.5ml/½ tsp salt
7.5ml/1½ tsp caster (superfine) sugar
5g/⅛ oz easy-blend (rapid-rise)
  dried yeast
400g/14oz/3½ cups plain (all-purpose)
  flour

1 To make the filling, finely chop the onion. Heat the oil in a medium frying pan, add the onion and fry for 5 minutes until softened and golden brown.

2 Add the beef and fry, stirring frequently, for about 10 minutes, until browned.

3 Add the stock to the pan, stir through and then add the smetana or crème fraîche. Stir together, then cover and simmer gently, stirring occasionally, for 10–15 minutes. Leave to cool.

4 Meanwhile, put the egg in a pan, cover with cold water and bring to the boil. Reduce the heat to low and simmer for 10 minutes. When the egg is cooked, immediately drain and put under cold running water. Remove the shell from the egg, then finely chop.

5 When the beef has cooled, stir in the chopped egg. Season with salt and pepper to taste. Set aside, while you make the dough.

6 To make the dough, melt the butter in a pan. Add the milk and water to the pan and heat it to 45°C/110°F. Remove from the heat.

7 Whisk the whole egg in a bowl with the salt and sugar. Add the milk mixture to the egg. Mix the yeast with the flour and stir, a little at a time, into the egg mixture.

8 Knead the dough in the bowl for 5 minutes. Cover with a dish towel and leave to rise in a warm place for 30 minutes, until doubled in size.

9 Grease a large baking sheet. Turn the dough on to a lightly floured surface and knead for 2–3 minutes. Cut the dough into 24 equal-sized pieces and form each piece into a ball. Leave to rest for 5–10 minutes.

10 Flatten each ball to a round measuring 10cm/4in in diameter. Spread 25ml/1½ tbsp of the beef filling in the centre of each round of dough. Fold together and seal the edges at the top. Put them, upside-down with the join facing down, on the baking sheet.

11 Preheat the oven to 230°C/450°F/ Gas 8. Whisk the egg yolk with 15ml/1 tbsp water and brush on top of the pies. Leave to rest for 20 minutes.

12 Bake the pies in the oven for 12–13 minutes, until golden. Transfer to a wire rack and leave to cool.

13 Serve the pirojki warm or at room temperature, on their own or with a bowl of hearty Russian soup.

Energy 411kcal/1719kJ; Protein 17.4g; Carbohydrate 41.7g, of which sugars 3.4g; Fat 20.5g, of which saturates 9g; Cholesterol 117mg; Calcium 120mg; Fibre 1.7g; Sodium 108mg.

Russian Beef-stuffed Cabbage Rolls

Cabbage, whether green or red or white, is a staple food in Russian cuisine, especially in the winter time. These stuffed cabbage rolls, called golubtsy, are made in large quantities and will be happily eaten by the family for two to three days in a row.

Serves 4

1 spring or winter cabbage head
100g/3 ³/₄oz/¹/₂ cup long grain rice
1 onion
30ml/2 tbsp rapeseed (canola) oil
300g/11oz minced (ground) beef
150ml/¹/₄ pint/²/₃ cup water
40–50g/1¹/₂–2oz/3–4 tbsp butter
200ml/7fl oz/scant 1 cup beef stock
200ml/7fl oz/scant 1 cup smetana or
   crème fraîche, plus extra to serve
45–60ml/3–4 tbsp finely chopped
   fresh dill
salt and ground black pepper

1 Cut out the woody stem from the centre of the cabbage head, about 5cm/2in deep. (This will make it easier to break off the cabbage leaves during cooking, see step 3.)

2 Put the cabbage head upside-down in the pan and pour over enough boiling water to completely cover the cabbage. Season with salt.

3 Bring the water back to the boil, then reduce the heat and simmer, breaking off the cabbage leaves one by one as they gradually turn soft.

4 Using a slotted spoon, remove the last cooked leaves from the water, then drain on kitchen paper.

5 Place one leaf at a time on a chopping board and, using a sharp knife, remove the thick stem of the leaf to allow it to flatten but remain in one piece. (This will make it easier to roll the leaves.) You need 12–14 prepared leaves in total.

6 Bring a separate large pan of boiling salted water to the boil, add the rice and stir to loosen the grains at the bottom of the pan. Simmer for about 12 minutes, until tender. Drain into a sieve (strainer) and rinse under cold running water.

7 Meanwhile, finely chop the onion. Heat the oil in a small frying pan, add the onion and fry for 5–10 minutes, until softened and golden brown. Turn into a large bowl and leave to cool.

VARIATION Making cabbage rolls is time consuming so Russians often make Lazy Golubsy. Instead of making rolls, finely shred the cabbage and fry it together with the minced (ground) beef and cooked rice. Add salt and pepper and serve with smetana or crème fraîche.

8 When the onion is cool, add the cooked rice, minced beef and water to the onion. Season well with salt and pepper and mix well together.

9 Place 1–1¹/₂ tablespoons of the mixture in the centre of each cabbage leaf. Fold in the sides and roll lengthways, forming a tight roll.

10 Heat the butter in a frying pan until melted. Add the cabbage rolls and fry for 5–10 minutes, until golden brown. Transfer the rolls to a flameproof casserole, arranging them side-by-side. Add the beef stock, cover, and cook over a low heat for 20 minutes, if using a spring cabbage, and 30–40 minutes if using a winter cabbage.

11 Using a slotted spoon, arrange the cabbage rolls on a serving dish. Stir the smetana or crème fraîche into the stock, bring to the boil and boil for 3–4 minutes. Spoon the sauce over the rolls and garnish with finely chopped dill. Serve with smetana or crème fraîche.

Energy 558kcal/2313kJ; Protein 19.2g; Carbohydrate 28.3g, of which sugars 7.7g; Fat 40.9g, of which saturates 24.1g; Cholesterol 129mg; Calcium 130mg; Fibre 3.2g; Sodium 163mg

Veal Stroganoff

'Stroganoff' dishes are thought to have originated in the 19th century in St Petersburg, where the beef dish was created and named after Count Alexander Sergeyevich Stroganov. The recipe was rapidly assimilated into Polish cuisine, and this version has become a much-loved classic.

4 Add the mushrooms and fry for a further 5 minutes. Transfer the vegetables to a plate and keep warm.

5 Pour the remaining oil into the frying pan and heat. When the oil is hot, add the floured meat strips and stir-fry over a high heat for about 2 minutes, until the meat is brown.

6 Return the vegetables to the pan and add the brandy, mustard, veal or beef stock and seasoning.

7 Simmer for 1 minute, then add the sour cream. Simmer for 1 minute more, until thick and glossy. Serve immediately, garnished with parsley, accompanied by buttered egg noodles or rice.

Serves 4–6

900g/2lb veal fillet
15g/¹/₂oz/2 tbsp plain (all-purpose) flour
2.5ml/¹/₂ tsp cayenne pepper
2.5ml/¹/₂ tsp hot paprika
60ml/4 tbsp vegetable oil
2 small onions, finely chopped
4 garlic cloves, finely chopped
8–10 fresh wild mushrooms, wiped clean and halved
150ml/¹/₄ pint/³/₄ cup brandy
5ml/1 tsp Polish or Dijon mustard
400ml/14fl oz/1²/₃ cups veal or beef stock
400ml/14fl oz/1²/₃ cups sour cream
salt and ground black pepper, to taste
30ml/2 tbsp chopped fresh flat leaf parsley, to garnish
cooked egg noodles or rice, to serve

1 Slice the veal into thin strips – this is easier if you freeze it for 30 minutes first.

2 Mix together the flour, cayenne pepper and paprika in a bowl, and toss the strips of meat in it. Set aside.

3 Heat half the oil in a heavy pan, then add the onions and garlic. Fry gently for 5 minutes, or until soft and brown.

Energy 511kcal/2124kJ; Protein 33.7g; Carbohydrate 9.9g, of which sugars 6.3g; Fat 31.6g, of which saturates 13.6g; Cholesterol 133mg; Calcium 97mg; Fibre 1g; Sodium 434mg.

Veal Kidney Gratin

This spicy gratin with Salted Cucumbers is a real winter warmer, best served steaming hot, straight from the oven. It is served with rice or a piece of good bread. Accompany the dish with a full-bodied red wine for a perfect combination of flavours.

Serves 4

600g/1 lb 6oz veal kidneys
1 onion
150g/5oz button mushrooms
25g/1oz/2 tbsp butter
45ml/3 tbsp rapeseed or
  sunflower oil
4 Salted Cucumbers (page79), peeled
  and diced
45ml/3 tbsp tomato purée
7.5mll/1½ tsp plain white
  (all-purpose) flour
100ml/3½fl oz/scant ½ cup white wine
300ml/½ pint/1¼ cups double
  (heavy) cream
125g/4¼ oz Cheddar cheese
pinch of cayenne pepper
salt
45ml/3 tbsp chopped fresh parsley,
  to garnish

1 Preheat the oven to 240°C/475°F/Gas 9. Dice the kidneys. chop the onion and slice the mushrooms.

2 Heat the butter in a large pan until melted, add the kidneys and fry over a high heat, stirring frequently, until browned on all sides. Remove the kidneys from the pan and keep warm.

3 Return the frying pan to the heat, add the oil and the onion and stir-fry for 2–3 minutes, then add the mushrooms and fry for 10 minutes, stirring occasionally.

4 Stir the Salted Cucumbers and the tomato purée into the mushrooms.

5 Sprinkle the flour into the mushroom mixture and stir until mixed, then stir in the wine. Gradually add in the cream, a little at a time, until smooth.

6 Bring the sauce to the boil, stirring. Reduce the heat and simmer for 2–3 minutes. Add cayenne pepper and salt.

7 Divide the fried kidneys between four ovenproof ramekins and pour the sauce over each. Grate the cheese and sprinkle it over the tops.

8 Bake in the oven for 5 minutes, or until the cheese is golden brown. Serve hot, garnished with parsley.

Energy 735kcal/3094kJ; Protein 40g; Carbohydrate 84g, of which sugars 2.5g; Fat 28.9g, of which saturates 15.4g; Cholesterol 184mg; Calcium 42mg; Fibre 1.5g; Sodium 369mg

Veal Stew with Pearl Barley

This rustic dish from Russia, made with a good piece of meat, is easily prepared for Sunday dinner. Serve it with Salted Cucumbers and a sauerkraut salad.

Serves 4

75g/3oz/6 tbsp butter
600g/1lb 6oz lean, tender, boneless
   stewing veal, diced
2 onions, chopped
10 medium potatoes, peeled and cut
   in half lengthways
200–300ml/7–10fl oz/1–1 ¼ cups
   beef stock
3 sprigs flat leaf parsley
2 bay leaves
4–5 black peppercorns
salt and ground black pepper
Salted Cucumbers (page 79) and a
   sauerkraut salad, to serve

For the pearl barley

15ml/1 tbsp rapeseed (canola) oil
300g/11oz/heaped 1½ cups pearl
   barley
1 litre/1¾ pints/4 cups water
25g/1oz/2 tbsp butter

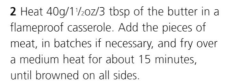

1 To prepare the pearl barley, heat the oil in a pan. Add the barley and stir-fry for 30 seconds. Add the water, bring to the boil then reduce the heat, cover and simmer for 50 minutes, until tender.

2 Heat 40g/1½oz/3 tbsp of the butter in a flameproof casserole. Add the pieces of meat, in batches if necessary, and fry over a medium heat for about 15 minutes, until browned on all sides.

3 Add the remaining butter, onions and potatoes to the pan and cook over low heat for 10 minutes, occasionally stirring. Add the stock, parsley, bay leaves, salt and peppercorns to the pan. Cover and simmer for 30 minutes.

4 Drain the pearl barley and transfer to a serving dish. Stir in the butter until melted and add salt to taste. Serve with the stew, Salted Cucumbers and a sauerkraut salad.

Energy 735kcal/3094kJ; Protein 40g; Carbohydrate 84g, of which sugars 2.5g; Fat 28.9g, of which saturates 15.4g; Cholesterol 184mg; Calcium 42mg; Fibre 1.5g; Sodium 369mg

Fried Calf's Brains

Rich, creamy, and nutritious calf's brains are a real treat. In this classic Polish recipe they are fried with onions, eggs and breadcrumbs, and served on toast.

Serves 4

675g/1½ lb calf's brains
40g/1½ oz/3 tbsp butter
1 large onion, finely chopped
2 eggs, beaten
60ml/4 tbsp fresh breadcrumbs
8 slices hot buttered toast
salt and ground black pepper, to taste
chopped fresh parsley, to garnish

1 Thoroughly rinse the brains under cold running water. Remove the membrane and finely chop.

2 Heat the butter in a large frying pan, add the onion and cook for about 5 minutes, or until golden brown.

3 Add the brains and fry for 5 minutes, stirring, until golden brown.

4 Add the eggs and breadcrumbs and cook for a further 2 minutes, stirring, until the eggs are cooked. Season to taste with salt and pepper.

5 Place the pieces of toast on four serving plates, then top with the hot brain mixture and garnish with chopped parsley.

Energy 521kcal/2172kJ; Protein 27.1g; Carbohydrate 26.5g, of which sugars 2.1g; Fat 34.9g, of which saturates 14.6g; Cholesterol 3850mg; Calcium 90mg; Fibre 1g; Sodium 768mg.

Krakow-style Calf's Liver

Flavoursome and very nutritious, liver is popular all over Poland, especially calf's liver. In this recipe it is served with a white mushroom sauce, giving a lovely contrast of colours and textures. You will need to get your butcher to remove the membrane, or do this yourself, before cooking.

Serves 4–6

900g/2lb calf's liver, rinsed, membrane removed, and sliced into thin pieces
60ml/4 tbsp vegetable oil
chopped fresh parsley, to garnish
black pepper

For the sauce
45ml/3 tbsp butter
1 large onion, sliced
175g/6oz/2½ cups button (white) mushrooms, wiped clean and chopped
15g/½oz/2 tbsp plain (all-purpose) flour
175ml/6fl oz/¾ cup dry white wine
250ml/8fl oz/1 cup sour cream
salt and ground black pepper

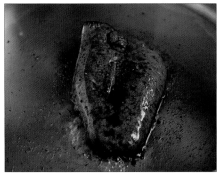

1 To make the sauce, heat the butter in a pan, then add the onion and mushrooms. Cook for 5–8 minutes, or until the onion has softened.

2 Stir in the flour and cook for 1 minute. Add the wine and cook for a further 3 minutes. Add the sour cream and season to taste. Keep the sauce warm.

3 Sprinkle the liver with plenty of black pepper. Heat the oil in a frying pan, add the liver and cook for 1–2 minutes on each side, until brown on the outside but still a little pink in the middle.

4 Transfer to serving plates, pour over the sauce and garnish with fresh parsley. Serve immediately.

Energy 410kcal/1705kJ; Protein 29.5g; Carbohydrate 6g, of which sugars 3g; Fat 27.9g, of which saturates 11.7g; Cholesterol 596mg; Calcium 67mg; Fibre 0.3g; Sodium 288mg.

Baked Lamb

In Russian restaurants, this delicious all-in-one dish of lamb with potatoes, aubergines and tomatoes is cooked in individual dishes, which are brought straight from the oven to the table. Here it is cooked in a single ovenproof dish for convenience.

Serves 4

1 mild chilli
600g/1lb 6oz potatoes, peeled and diced
1 large onion, chopped
1 aubergine (eggplant), sliced
800g/1¾lb boneless lamb
45ml/3 tbsp chopped fresh parsley
4 bay leaves
6–8 black peppercorns
45ml/3 tbsp chopped fresh coriander (cilantro)
3 garlic cloves, chopped
50g/2oz/¼ cup butter
75ml/5 tbsp tomato purée (paste)
1 litre/1¾ pints/4 cups beef stock
3 tomatoes, sliced
salt and ground black pepper

VARIATION The aubergines can be replaced with 2 additional large onions.

1 Preheat the oven to 180°C/350°F/Gas 4. Chop the chilli, discarding the core and seeds. Put the potatoes and onions in a greased roasting pan.

2 Cut the lamb into bitesize chunks. Sprinkle the lamb, aubergine, chilli, parsley, bay leaves, peppercorns, coriander and garlic evenly over the potatoes.

3 Melt the butter in a small pan. Add the tomato purée and fry for 1 minute. Stir in the stock, a little at a time, and bring to the boil. Season to taste.

4 Pour the tomato sauce over the meat and the vegetables. Bake in the oven for about 1 hour. Top the bake with the sliced tomatoes, return to the oven and bake for a further 10 minutes. Serve hot.

Energy 631kcal/2640kJ; Protein 45.3g; Carbohydrate 38.6g, of which sugars 13.9g; Fat 34g, of which saturates 17.2g; Cholesterol 179mg; Calcium 94mg; Fibre 5.8g; Sodium 324mg.

Uzbekistani Pilaff

The cities of Uzbekistan were once important points on the Silk Road from China to Europe, and rice is still a staple part of the diet. Pilaffs, both savoury – consisting of rice, vegetables, meat and spices – and sweet – containing apricots and raisins – are very popular.

Serves 4

60–75ml/4–5 tbsp rapeseed
  (canola) oil
600g/1lb 6oz lean boneless lamb
  steak, cut into bitesize pieces
700ml/1 pint 3½fl oz/scant 3 cups
  water
5ml/1 tsp salt
2 carrots
2 onions
350–400g/12–14oz/1¾–2 cups long
  grain rice
1 whole garlic, with the dry outer skin
  removed, but left intact
5 sprigs fresh parsley, to garnish

1 Heat 15ml/1 tbsp of the oil in a flameproof casserole. Add the lamb and fry, stirring frequently, for about 10 minutes, until brown on all sides.

2 Add the water and salt to the pan, bring to the boil, then reduce the heat and simmer for about 40 minutes, until the meat is just tender.

3 Meanwhile, finely dice the carrots and finely chop the onion. Heat the remaining oil in a separate pan. Add the carrots and onions and stir-fry for about 5 minutes, until softened. Add the rice and stir-fry for about 1 minute, until translucent.

4 Transfer the rice mixture to the lamb and add the whole garlic. Bring to the boil, then reduce the heat, cover and simmer for about 20 minutes, until the rice is tender and has absorbed almost all of the liquid.

5 Serve the pilaff immediately, heaped on to a warmed dish, garnished with parsley.

COOK'S TIP The Uzbekistanis rinse their rice several times in water before cooking it. This reduces the amount of starch and prevents the rice from becoming sticky.

Energy 735kcal/3065kJ; Protein 37.2g; Carbohydrate 81.7g, of which sugars 9.8g; Fat 28.6g, of which saturates 9.2g; Cholesterol 114mg; Calcium 66mg; Fibre 2.9g; Sodium 150mg.

Roast Lamb with Garlic, Rosemary and Thyme

Simply roasting lamb with a selection of aromatic ingredients brings out the best in the meat. In this delicious recipe the lamb is rubbed with a mixture of butter, pepper, cloves and allspice, which lend a distinctive spicy Polish note to the meat.

Serves 6

2kg/4½lb leg of lamb
fresh rosemary
fresh thyme
10 garlic cloves, cut into slivers
5ml/1 tsp black peppercorns
6 whole cloves
6 allspice berries
20g/¾oz butter, softened
redcurrant jelly, to serve

1 Preheat the oven to 200°C/400°F/Gas 6. Place the leg of lamb in a roasting pan. Separate the rosemary into sprigs, and cut the thyme stalks into sections.

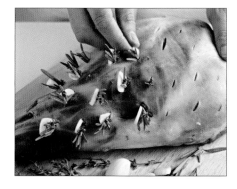

2 Make about 20–30 small, deep slits all over the meat, then push a small sprig of rosemary and thyme and a sliver of garlic into each.

3 Using a pestle and mortar, grind the peppercorns, cloves and allspice to a coarse powder. Combine the powder with the softened butter and smear all over the lamb.

4 Place the roasting pan in the hot oven and cook for 15 minutes. Reduce the heat to 180°C/350°F/Gas 4 and roast the lamb for a further 1½ hours, or until cooked but still slightly pink.

5 Remove the joint from the oven, cover with foil and allow it to rest for at least 15 minutes.

6 Cut the meat into generous slices and serve immediately with redcurrant jelly.

Energy 562kcal/2340kJ; Protein 50.4g; Carbohydrate 0.4g, of which sugars 0.3g; Fat 39.9g, of which saturates 14.1g; Cholesterol 200mg; Calcium 36mg; Fibre 0.6g; Sodium 171mg.

Roast Fillet of Pork with Prunes

Pork is the national meat of Poland, and this recipe of roasted marinated pork fillet stuffed with prunes is a wonderful example of how its delectable flavour can be fully appreciated. Serve with salads for a light lunch, or with Buckwheat Kasha for a more sustaining meal.

2 Preheat the oven to 180°C/350°F/Gas 4. Pour the oil into a roasting pan and put in the oven to heat.

3 Take the pork fillet out of the marinade and lay the chopped prunes along half of the opened-out fillet. Fold the top half over and tie together using string.

4 Place in the hot oil and put into the oven. Roast for about 1½ hours, or until the meat is cooked, basting occasionally with the meat juices.

5 Remove the meat from the oven and allow to rest, covered in foil, for 15 minutes. Remove the string and cut into slices. Spoon over the cooking juices and serve immediately with lettuce and Beetroot Salad.

Serves 4–6

1.8kg/4lb pork fillet (tenderloin)
2.5ml/½ tsp dried marjoram
15ml/1 tbsp caraway seeds
4–5 bay leaves
90ml/6 tbsp white wine
30ml/2 tbsp vegetable oil
225g/8oz ready-to-eat prunes,
  chopped
salt and ground black pepper, to taste
lettuce and Beetroot Salad
  (page 195), to serve

VARIATION This delicious stuffed pork joint also makes an impressive Sunday lunch: serve it with roast potatoes and some greens or spiced red cabbage.

1 Partially cut the pork lengthways leaving one long side attached. Rub with salt, pepper and marjoram, then sprinkle with caraway seeds. Put into a dish and add the bay leaves, then pour over the wine. Leave to marinate for about 2 hours.

Energy 537kcal/2247kJ; Protein 63.1g; Carbohydrate 12.8g, of which sugars 12.8g; Fat 15.8g, of which saturates 7.9g; Cholesterol 207mg; Calcium 38mg; Fibre 2.1g; Sodium 233mg.

Breaded Pork Cutlets

Easy to make and quick to cook, this recipe for pork cutlets dipped in breadcrumbs and simply fried is particularly popular in Poland. Coating the cutlets means that the pork stays moist and tender, without drying out. Serve with mashed potato and red cabbage for a real Polish meal.

Serves 4

4 boneless pork cutlets, fat on, each
   weighing about 225g/8oz
2.5ml/½ tsp salt
2.5ml/½ tsp ground black pepper
115g/4oz/1 cup plain (all-purpose)
   flour
2 eggs, beaten
65g/2½oz/1 cup fine fresh
   breadcrumbs
1 tbsp each of chopped fresh
   rosemary, dill and sage
75ml/5 tbsp vegetable oil
fresh parsley sprigs, to garnish
lemon wedges, mashed potato and
   sauerkraut or red cabbage, to serve

1 Cut slits in the rind of the pork cutlets to prevent them from curling during cooking. Using a meat mallet, rolling pin or the base of a frying pan, pound each cutlet lightly on each side to flatten, then sprinkle each side with salt and pepper.

2 Put the flour and beaten eggs in separate bowls. In another bowl, mix the breadcrumbs with the chopped herbs.

3 Dip the pork cutlets first in the flour, then the egg and then into the breadcrumb mixture.

4 Heat the oil in a frying pan until it is smoking hot, then add the breaded pork and fry on a high heat for 4–5 minutes.

5 Turn the cutlets and cook the other side for another 4–5 minutes until golden brown and crispy all over. Reduce the heat and cook for a further 2 minutes to ensure the pork is cooked right the way through.

6 Garnish with parsley and serve immediately with mashed potato and sauerkraut or red cabbage, and with lemon wedges for squeezing over.

COOK'S TIP It is important that you serve the cutlets immediately, as they will become tough if they are left to stand.

Energy 591kcal/2475kJ; Protein 55.9g; Carbohydrate 34.9g, of which sugars 0.9g; Fat 26.2g, of which saturates 5.6g; Cholesterol 237mg; Calcium 92mg; Fibre 1.3g; Sodium 317mg.

Roast Loin of Pork with Apple Stuffing

A spit-roasted sucking pig, basted with butter or cream, roasted in the oven or outside on a spit, and served with an apple in its mouth, was a classic dish for the Russian festive table. This roasted loin with crisp crackling makes a smaller-scale alternative.

Serves 6–8

1.75kg/4lb boned loin of pork
300ml/½ pint/1½ cups dry cider
150ml/¼ pint/⅔ cup sour cream
7.5ml/1½ tsp sea salt

For the stuffing

25g/1oz/2 tbsp butter
1 small onion, chopped
50g/2oz/1 cup fresh white
    breadcrumbs
2 apples, cored, peeled and chopped
50g/2oz/scant ½ cup raisins
finely grated rind of 1 orange
pinch of ground cloves
salt and ground black pepper

1 Preheat the oven to 220°C/425°F/Gas 7. To make the stuffing, melt the butter in a pan and gently fry the onion for 10 minutes, or until soft. Stir into the remaining stuffing ingredients.

2 Put the pork, rind side down, on a board. Make a horizontal cut between the meat and outer layer of fat, cutting to within 2.5cm/1in of the edges to make a pocket.

3 Push the stuffing into the pocket. Roll it up lengthways and tie with string. Use a sharp knife to score the rind.

4 Pour the cider and sour cream into a casserole, in which the joint just fits. Stir to combine, then add the pork, rind side down. Cook, uncovered, in the oven for 30 minutes.

5 Turn the joint over, so that the rind is on top. Baste with the juices, then sprinkle the rind with sea salt. Cook for 1 hour, basting after 30 minutes, but don't baste after this time, to give the skin a chance to crisp.

6 Reduce the oven temperature to 180°C/350°F/Gas 4. Cook for a further 1½ hours. Leave the joint to stand for 20 minutes before carving.

Energy 504kcal/2114kJ; Protein 67.3g; Carbohydrate 12.3g, of which sugars 7.6g; Fat 19.8g, of which saturates 8.3g; Cholesterol 185mg; Calcium 59mg; Fibre 0.5g; Sodium 205mg

Ukrainian Sausages

These sausages from the Ukraine are called kovbasa – they can be grilled, fried or baked and are wonderful as an appetizer or a main course for lunch or dinner. This pork and beef version can be made several days in advance and kept refrigerated; they can also be cooked from frozen.

Serves 4

450g/1lb pork, such as shoulder
225g/8oz chuck steak
115g/4oz pork back fat
2 eggs, beaten
30ml/2 tbsp peperivka (see Cook's Tip) or pepper vodka
2.5ml/½ tsp ground allspice
5ml/1 tsp salt
about 1.75 litres/3 pints/7½ cups chicken stock
fresh parsley, to garnish
mashed potato, to serve

COOK'S TIP Spicing whisky with peppers to make peperivka is an old tradition in the Ukraine. Add 3 whole cayenne peppers, pricked all over with a fine skewer, to 150ml/¼ pint/⅔ cup whisky or bourbon and leave for at least 48 hours.

1 Mince (grind) the meats and pork back fat together, using the coarse blade of a mincer (grinder), then mince half the mixture again using a fine blade. You can also use a food processor for this.

2 Combine both the meat mixtures with the eggs, peperivka or pepper vodka, allspice and salt. Check the seasoning by frying a small piece of the mixture, then tasting it. Adjust if necessary.

3 Form the meat mixture into four sausages, about 20cm/8in long. Wrap in a double layer of butter muslin and tie securely with string.

4 Bring the stock to a gentle simmer in a large pan. Add the sausages and simmer gently, turning frequently, for 35–40 minutes, or until the juices run clear when the sausages are pierced with a skewer.

5 Leave the sausages in the stock for 20 minutes, then remove and leave to cool. Remove the muslin and sauté the sausages in oil to brown them. Garnish with parsley and serve with mashed potato, topped with butter.

COOK'S TIP Butter muslin is an unbleached linen cloth, which can be bought from most kitchen shops. It is fine enough for the cooking process but robust enough to hold the sausage together.
Peperivka is vodka infused with whole cayenne peppers. To make your own, place 3 washed, dried and pricked peppers in a jar and fill with vodka. Leave for 48 hours before using.

Energy 436kcal/1816kJ; Protein 44.1g; Carbohydrate 0g, of which sugars 0g; Fat 26.5g, of which saturates 9.6g; Cholesterol 227mg; Calcium 28mg; Fibre 0g; Sodium 170mg

Pork Rib Stew with Cabbage

This delicious stew makes the most of an economical cut of pork and the ubiquitous white cabbage, combining flavoursome ribs with a simple broth. It makes the most of typical Polish flavourings – caraway, paprika and garlic – to enhance a warming all-in-one supper dish.

Serves 4–6

40g/1½ oz/¼ cup bacon dripping or
   40ml/2½ tbsp vegetable oil
1.8kg/4lb pork spare ribs
900ml/1½ pints/3¾ cups beef stock
6 black peppercorns
4 bay leaves
5ml/1 tsp caraway seeds
5ml/1 tsp paprika
2 large onions, roughly chopped
2–3 carrots, roughly chopped
3–4 garlic cloves, roughly chopped
175ml/6fl oz/¾ cup dry white wine
1 white cabbage, quartered and
   core removed
chopped fresh parsley or dill,
   to garnish
boiled new potatoes, to serve

1 Heat the bacon dripping or oil in a heavy pan, add the spare ribs and cook over a high heat for 5 minutes, or until brown all over.

2 Add the stock, peppercorns, bay leaves, caraway seeds, paprika, onions, carrots, garlic and white wine.

3 Cover the pan and simmer over a low heat for about 1½ hours. Add the cabbage and cook for a further 30 minutes, until tender.

4 Ladle on to plates, garnish with parsley or dill and serve immediately with boiled new potatoes.

Energy 539kcal/2241kJ; Protein 45g; Carbohydrate 6.1g, of which sugars 5.9g; Fat 35.1g, of which saturates 11.2g; Cholesterol 159mg; Calcium 62mg; Fibre 2.2g; Sodium 161mg.

Honey-roast Ham

This stunning baked ham is often prepared for a Polish Easter Sunday, when the strict Lenten fast is broken with a lavish feast. It can be served hot or cold with a selection of pickles, such as gherkins or beetroot, and horseradish sauce.

Serves 4–6

2.75–3.6kg/6–8lb ham
20 whole cloves
225g/8oz/1 cup clear honey
sweet gherkins, pickled beetroot (beets) and horseradish sauce, to serve

For the marinade
1 litre/1¾ pints/4 cups water
250ml/8fl oz/1 cup cider vinegar
1 onion, sliced
4–5 bay leaves
8 whole cloves
2 cinnamon sticks
8 allspice berries
4–5 dried chillies
5ml/1 tsp yellow mustard seeds
15ml/1 tbsp sugar

1 To make the marinade, put all the ingredients in a large pan with a lid. Weigh the ham and calculate the cooking time, allowing 20 minutes per 450g/1lb of meat.

2 Put the ham in the pan, cover with a lid and simmer for 2–2¾ hours, or until the rind on the ham has lifted away from the meat slightly. Remove the meat from the pan.

3 Preheat the oven to 220°C/425°F/Gas 7. Carefully remove the skin from the ham and discard. Score the fat on the ham with a diamond pattern using a large, sharp knife.

4 Warm the honey gently in a small pan to make a glaze. Do not boil.

5 Place the ham in a roasting pan and press a clove into the centre of each diamond. Brush the ham with honey, then place in the oven and roast for 20–25 minutes until the fat is brown and crispy.

6 Serve hot or cold, with sweet gherkins, pickled beetroot and horseradish sauce.

Energy 595kcal/2482kJ; Protein 68g; Carbohydrate 0g, of which sugars 0g; Fat 35.9g, of which saturates 12g; Cholesterol 242mg; Calcium 26mg; Fibre 0g; Sodium 3442mg

Hunter's Stew

Considered by some to be the national dish, Hunter's Stew, or 'bigos', is one of the most treasured of the Polish recipes. Hearty and sustaining, this stew can be found in many different forms throughout the country, and was originally a game recipe, hence its name. Bigos is cooked in large quantities so it can be reheated – the flavours intensify each time – and is a very good dish to cook in advance.

Serves 6–8

1kg/2¼ lb fresh cabbage, finely shredded
10 dried mushrooms (boletus)
2 onions, chopped
500g/1¼ lb smoked sausage, sliced
1kg/2¼ lb sauerkraut, drained
2 cooking apples, peeled, cored and diced
10 prunes
10 juniper berries, crushed
3–4 bay leaves
10 peppercorns
2.5ml/½ tsp salt
750ml/1¼ pints/3 cups boiling water
500g/1¼ lb roast pork, diced
500g/1¼ lb roast beef, diced
500g/1¼ lb boiled ham, diced
150ml/¼ pint/⅔ cup dry red wine
5ml/1 tsp honey
wholemeal (whole-wheat) or rye bread and chilled vodka, to serve

1 Place the cabbage in a heatproof colander and wilt the leaves by carefully pouring boiling water over it.

2 Rinse the mushrooms, then place them in a bowl with enough warm water to cover. Leave to soak for 15 minutes, then transfer to a pan and cook in the soaking liquid for 30 minutes. Strain, reserving the cooking liquid, then cut the mushrooms into strips.

3 Put the onions and smoked sausage in a small frying pan and fry gently, until the onions have softened. Remove the sausage from the pan and set aside.

4 Put the wilted cabbage and drained sauerkraut in a large pan, then add the cooked onions, along with the mushrooms, mushroom cooking liquid, apples, prunes, juniper berries, bay leaves, peppercorns and salt. Pour in the boiling water, then cover and simmer for 1 hour.

5 Add the cooked sausage to the pan with the other cooked, diced meats. Pour in the wine and add the honey.

6 Cook, uncovered, for a further 40 minutes, stirring frequently. Taste and adjust the seasoning as required. Remove from the heat.

7 Allow the stew to cool, then cover it and transfer to the refrigerator. Leave it overnight. Return to the boil and simmer for 10 minutes to heat through. Serve with wholemeal or rye bread and a glass of chilled vodka.

VARIATION Any meat, such as duck, lamb or venison, works well in this recipe.

COOK'S TIP When reheating, make sure the stew is brought to the boil and thoroughly simmered before serving.

Energy 546kcal/2279kJ; Protein 50.4g; Carbohydrate 24.6g, of which sugars 19.8g; Fat 26.4g, of which saturates 9.7g; Cholesterol 149mg; Calcium 213mg; Fibre 7.7g; Sodium 2122mg.

Polish Stuffed Cabbage Rolls

Golabki, meaning 'little pigeons', are one of the most popular dishes in Poland. Simple to prepare, cheap and very tasty, they can be made ahead in large quantities and reheated.

Serves 4

1 small cabbage
1 small (US medium) egg, beaten
2.5ml/½ tsp freshly grated nutmeg
10ml/2 tsp chopped fresh parsley
10ml/2 tsp vegetable oil
400g/14oz can chopped tomatoes
60ml/4 tbsp boiling water
salt and ground black pepper, to taste

For the stuffing
100g/3¾oz/½ cup long grain rice
15g/½oz/¼ cup dried wild
   mushrooms, rinsed and soaked in
   warm water for 30 minutes
15ml/1 tbsp butter
½ large onion, finely chopped
225g/8oz/1 cup minced (ground) pork
225g/8oz/1 cup minced (ground) beef
1 garlic clove, finely chopped

1 To make the stuffing, bring a large pan of lightly salted water to the boil and cook the rice, according to instructions on the packet. Once the grains are tender, drain and rinse under cold water to prevent them from cooking further.

2 Drain the mushrooms and chop them finely. Heat half the butter in a large pan, then add the onion and fry gently until golden brown.

3 Add the pork, beef, garlic, mushrooms and seasoning. Cook, stirring, until the meat is browned all over, then remove from the heat and leave to cool slightly.

4 Bring a large pan of lightly salted water to the boil and cook the whole cabbage for 10–15 minutes, or until you can insert a knife into the centre easily, but the leaves are not too soft. Lift the cabbage out of the water and leave to cool slightly.

5 Preheat the oven to 190°C/375°F/Gas 5. Add the egg, nutmeg and parsley to the meat mixture and stir to combine well. When it is cool enough to handle, separate the cabbage into individual leaves. Use the tough outside leaves to line an ovenproof dish. Drizzle with oil.

7 Place a spoonful of the filling in each of the remaining cabbage leaves, fold over the edges and roll to form a tight package. Arrange the rolls in a single layer on the oiled cabbage leaves in the dish.

8 Pour over the tomatoes and boiling water, and dot the remaining butter over the top. Cover the dish with a lid or foil. Cook in the oven for about 1 hour. Serve with spoonfuls of the tomato sauce.

Energy 414kcal/1725kJ; Protein 27.6g; Carbohydrate 28.7g, of which sugars 8.2g; Fat 21g, of which saturates 8.5g; Cholesterol 126mg; Calcium 99mg; Fibre 3.4g; Sodium 133mg.

VEGETABLE AND SIDE DISHES

Despite their hearty appetite for meat, Russians in particular have been very inventive when it comes to vegetable dishes. Many of these recipes work well either as an accompaniment to a meat course, or as a meal in their own right. Often the recipes are based on very simple ingredients, but when the vegetables are fresh, well seasoned, and cooked in delicious puff pastry, or in tiny dumplings, they are completely irresistible.

Both Poland and Russia share a love of cabbage, and for the Russians there is no better way to serve it than as sauerkraut. This sharp mixture of fermented cabbage with vinegar makes a satisfying stew for a cold day or a light salad for warmer weather. Sauerkraut is also very popular in Poland. After sauerkraut, perhaps the next best-loved vegetable is the mushroom, which Russians and Poles enjoy picking wild. Then, of course, there is the potato, cooked in many equally enjoyable ways from dumplings to fried potato cakes and beyond!

Cheese Dumplings

Vareniki (meaning 'boiled things') are dumplings, thought to have been inspired by Chinese influences in the Ukraine, which come in all kinds of varieties. These cottage cheese versions can also be made with Italian ricotta, or another fresh cheese, and are similar to gnocchi.

Serves 4

500g/1¼lb/2½ cups ricotta cheese or cottage cheese
2 eggs
200g/7oz/1¾ cups plain white (all-purpose) flour
2 litres/3½ pints/8 cups water
25g/1oz/2 tbsp butter
salt
smetana or crème fraîche, to serve

COOK'S TIP When the dumplings have been boiled, it is important to rinse them under cold running water immediately for a couple of seconds. This is partly to stop them cooking, and also to rinse off some of the starch and stop them from sticking together.

VARIATION Serve these dumplings with fried bacon for non-vegetarians, or as a dessert with smetana and sugar.

1 Put the cheese, eggs and a pinch of salt in a bowl and mix well together. Add the flour and fold in until it is thoroughly combined. The dough should be soft and form into a ball. Remove the ball from the bowl and put on a floured surface.

2 Cut the dough into eight equal pieces and roll each into a sausage shape. Cut each sausage into 2cm/¾in sections.

3 Bring a large pan of water to the boil and add 5ml/1 tsp salt. Put half of the dumplings in the pan and simmer for 2 minutes, until they float to the surface.

4 Using a slotted spoon, remove the dumplings from the pan, transfer to a colander and put under cold running water for a few seconds. Cook the second batch in the same way.

5 Heat the butter in a large pan. Add the drained dumplings and sauté them until thoroughly warmed through and slightly golden. Serve immediately with a bowl of smetana or crème fraîche.

Energy 803kcal/3328kJ; Protein 11.8g; Carbohydrate 38.9g, of which sugars 0.8g; Fat 68g, of which saturates 41.3g; Cholesterol 227mg; Calcium 208mg; Fibre 1.6g; Sodium 450mg.

Grated Potato Dumplings

These Polish dumplings contain a mixture of mashed and grated potato, which gives them an interesting texture. They make an ideal accompaniment to many casseroled or braised meat dishes and are served with delicious little fried cubes of cured pork fat.

Serves 4

1kg/2¼ lb potatoes, peeled
2 eggs, beaten
pinch of salt
115g/4oz plain (all-purpose) flour, plus extra for dusting
15ml/1 tbsp potato flour
150g/5oz pork fat (boczek), cut into 1cm/½ in cubes

1 Chop half the potatoes into chunks, then add to a pan of lightly salted boiling water. Cook for 10 minutes, or until soft. Drain the potatoes, then mash in a bowl.

2 Grate the remaining raw potatoes and squeeze in a sieve (strainer) or in a dish towel to remove the excess liquid. Add to the mashed potato in the bowl.

3 Add the eggs, a pinch of salt and the flours to the bowl, and knead thoroughly to form a dough.

4 Using floured hands, roll spoonfuls of the dough into balls.

5 Bring a large pan of lightly salted water to the boil, then add the dumplings. Cook for 4–5 minutes, or until the dumplings float to the surface of the water.

6 Meanwhile, fry the cubes of pork fat in a hot pan for about 4 minutes, or until golden brown all over. Transfer the cooked dumplings to a serving plate and spoon over the fried pork fat cubes.

COOK'S TIP If you can't find Polish boczek, use a thick slice of pancetta or cured pork belly instead.

Energy 658kcal/2746kJ; Protein 10.3g; Carbohydrate 65.6g, of which sugars 3.7g; Fat 41.1g, of which saturates 16.2g; Cholesterol 130mg; Calcium 71mg; Fibre 3.5g; Sodium 64mg.

Little Deep-fried Potato Pies

Pirojki are an indispensable part of the Russian zakuski table, but can also be served as accompaniments to soup, when a little hole is made in the top and a spoonful of soup is poured in. Pirojki can be baked, but here they are fried so the pastry is deliciously crisp.

Makes 24
Serves 6–8

For the dough
  50g/2oz/¼ cup butter
  200ml/7fl oz/scant 1 cup milk
  45ml/3 tbsp water
  1 small (US medium) egg plus
    1 egg yolk
  2.5ml/½ tsp salt
  7.5ml/1½ tsp caster (superfine) sugar
  5g/⅛oz easy-blend (rapid-rise) dried
    yeast
  400g/14oz/3½ cups plain white
    (all-purpose) flour
  rapeseed (canola) oil for frying

For the filling
  500g/1¼lb floury potatoes
  45–60ml/3–4 tbsp rapeseed
    (canola) oil
  2 onions, finely chopped
  salt and ground black pepper

1 To make the dough, melt the butter in a pan. Add the milk and water and heat it to 45°C/110°F. Remove from the heat. Whisk the whole egg in a large bowl with the salt and sugar.

2 Add the warm milk mixture to the egg. Mix the yeast with the flour and stir it, a little at a time, into the egg and milk mixture to form a soft dough.

3 Knead the dough in the bowl for 5 minutes. Cover with a dish towel and leave to rise in a warm place for 30 minutes, until it has doubled in size.

4 Meanwhile, prepare the filling: peel and cut the potatoes, put in a pan of salted cold water, bring to the boil, then reduce the heat and simmer for 15–20 minutes, until the potatoes are soft.

5 Drain, return to the pan, then leave for 2–3 minutes to allow the steam to evaporate. Mash the potatoes until smooth then transfer to a bowl.

6 Heat the oil in a small frying pan, add the onions and fry, stirring frequently, for about 5 minutes until softened and golden brown.

7 Add the onions to the mashed potatoes and mix. Season with plenty of salt and pepper. Set aside.

8 Grease a large baking sheet. Turn the dough on to a lightly floured surface and knead for 2–3 minutes. Cut the dough in 24 equal-sized pieces and form each piece into a ball. Leave to rest for 5–10 minutes. Flatten each ball to a round measuring 10cm/4in in diameter.

9 Spread 25ml/1½ tbsp of the potato filling in the centre of each round of dough. Fold together and seal the edges at the top. Put them, upside-down with the join facing down, on a floured wooden chopping board.

10 Half fill a deep pan with oil, and heat to 180°C/350°F, or until a small piece of dough when dropped in, rises to the surface immediately. In batches of around four or five, fry the pies in the oil for 2–3 minutes, turn them over gently, and then cook for a further 2–3 minutes, until golden brown.

11 Remove the pies from the pan with a slotted spoon, and place on kitchen paper to drain. Cook all the pies in this way, and serve immediately.

COOK'S TIP The pirojki dough can be made in an electric mixer, fitted with a dough hook, if wished.

Energy 349kcal/1467kJ; Protein 8.5g; Carbohydrate 55.1g, of which sugars 6.3g; Fat 12g, of which saturates 4.6g; Cholesterol 64mg; Calcium 127mg; Fibre 3.1g; Sodium 69mg.

Potato Cakes with Mushroom Sauce

Potatoes are the perfect accompaniment to many Russian dishes and are served fried, boiled, mashed and in gratins, with fish, meat or vegetables. Russians believe potatoes and mushrooms make the perfect combination, and those who do not pick their own mushrooms dry bought ones at home and thread them on a string.

Serves 4

1kg/2¼lb floury potatoes
50g/2oz/¼ cup butter
100ml/3½fl oz/scant ½ cup warm milk
1 egg, beaten
75g/3oz/1½ cups fresh white
  breadcrumbs
15ml/1 tbsp rapeseed (canola) oil
salt

For the mushroom sauce
1 onion, peeled and finely chopped
15ml/1 tbsp rapeseed (canola) oil
25g/1oz/2 tbsp butter
250g/9oz fresh porcini
15ml/1 tbsp plain white (all purpose)
  flour
300ml/½ pint/1¼ cups smetana or
  crème fraîche
salt and ground black pepper

1 For the mushroom sauce, put the soaked mushrooms and the water in a pan and simmer for 40 minutes. Using a slotted spoon, remove the mushrooms from the pan, reserving the water.

2 Heat the oil in a large frying pan, add the onion and fry, stirring frequently, for 3 minutes, or until golden brown.

3 Add the butter and mushrooms and fry, stirring all the time, for a further 5 minutes. Sprinkle the flour over the mushrooms and stir until mixed.

4 Gradually stir all the reserved water into the mushroom and flour mixture, a little at a time, until smooth. Slowly bring to the boil, stirring all the time, until the sauce boils and thickens. Reduce the heat and simmer for 10 minutes.

5 Add the smetana or crème fraîche and simmer for a further 5 minutes. Season with salt and pepper to taste.

6 Peel and cut the potatoes into even pieces. Put in a pan of salted water, bring to the boil, then reduce the heat and simmer for 20 minutes, until soft. Drain, return to the pan and mash until smooth.

7 Add 15g/½oz/1 tbsp of the butter and the milk to the potatoes and mix together until smooth. Leave to cool.

8 Once the potatoes are cool, add the beaten egg and mix thoroughly. Season the potatoes with salt to taste.

9 Wet your hands under cold water, take a handful of the mashed potato and form into a cake. Repeat with the remaining mashed potato to make eight cakes.

10 Spread the breadcrumbs on a plate and turn the cakes in the breadcrumbs to coat on both sides. Set aside.

11 To cook the potato cakes, heat the remaining 40g/1½oz/3 tbsp butter and the oil in a large frying pan, add the cakes and fry over a medium heat, for about 3–5 minutes on each side, turning once, until they are golden brown.

12 Gently reheat the mushroom sauce, and serve the potato cakes hot, accompanied by the sauce.

Energy 389kcal/1637kJ; Protein 8.9g; Carbohydrate 56g, of which sugars 5g; Fat 16g, of which saturates 7.7g; Cholesterol 76mg; Calcium 79mg; Fibre 2.9g; Sodium 274mg.

Potato and Cheese Dumplings

The Polish version of Russian pirojki are pierogi, and they are just as popular. Made from simple, cheap ingredients, they can be served immediately after they are cooked, or allowed to cool and then fried in a little butter. They can be filled with a number of different ingredients.

Serves 4–6

500g/1¼lb plain (all-purpose) flour, plus extra for dusting
2.5ml/½ tsp salt
2 eggs, beaten
45ml/3 tbsp vegetable oil
250ml/8fl oz/1 cup warm water
chopped fresh parsley, to garnish
thick sour cream, to serve

For the filling
15g/½oz/1 tbsp butter
½ large onion, finely chopped
250g/9oz peeled, cooked potatoes
250g/9oz/1¼ cups curd or cream cheese
1 egg, beaten
salt and ground black pepper, to taste

1 To make the filling, heat the butter in a small pan, add the onion and cook for about 5 minutes, or until softened.

2 Push the cooked potatoes through a ricer, or mash in a large bowl. Add the curd cheese and stir to combine. Add the egg, onion and seasoning to taste to the potato mixture and mix well.

3 To make the dough, sift the flour into a large bowl, then add the salt and the two eggs. Pour in the oil and water, and mix to form a loose dough.

4 Turn on to a floured surface and knead for about 10 minutes, until the dough is soft and doesn't stick to your hands.

5 Divide the dough into four equal pieces, then roll each one out thinly with a floured rolling pin. (Cover the portions you are not working on with a dish towel to prevent them from drying out.) Cut the dough into 5–6cm/2–2½in circles using a pastry (cookie) cutter.

6 Place a heaped teaspoonful of the cheese filling mixture in the centre of each of the circles of dough, then fold over the dough and press firmly to seal the edges. The dumplings should be neat and well filled, but not bursting.

7 Bring a large pan of lightly salted water to the boil, add the dumplings and cook for about 4–5 minutes, or until they rise to the surface.

8 Cook for a further 2 minutes, once they have risen, then remove with a slotted spoon and place in a warmed serving dish. Garnish with chopped parsley and serve with thick sour cream.

Energy 419kcal/1768kJ; Protein 11.7g; Carbohydrate 71.6g, of which sugars 2.3g; Fat 11.5g, of which saturates 2.9g; Cholesterol 100mg; Calcium 136mg; Fibre 3.1g; Sodium 57mg.

Mashed Potato Dumplings

These soft little dumplings from Poland are similar to Italian gnocchi and can be served with different toppings. Here they are served with a crisp breadcrumb topping, adding texture and colour to the dumplings. They make an excellent accompaniment to braised meats.

3 Transfer the potato dough to a lightly floured surface and, with damp hands, shape into walnut-sized balls. Flatten the balls slightly and make a small indentation in the centre.

4 Bring a large pan of lightly salted water to the boil, then drop in the dumplings and cook for 5 minutes, or until they are firm to the touch.

Serves 4–6

5 potatoes, scrubbed
225g/8oz/2 cups plain (all-purpose) flour
1 egg, beaten
2.5ml/½ tsp salt
45ml/3 tbsp butter
45ml/3 tbsp fresh white breadcrumbs

1 Cut the scrubbed potatoes into quarters, leaving the skin on for an authentic texture. Place in a pan of boiling water and cook for 10–15 minutes, or until tender. Remove from the heat, drain and leave to cool.

2 Push the potatoes through a ricer, or mash to a paste with a potato masher. Add the flour, egg and salt, and knead to combine.

5 Meanwhile, melt the butter in a frying pan, add the breadcrumbs and fry for about 3 minutes, stirring constantly, or until the breadcrumbs are brown.

6 Drain the dumplings and arrange on a serving dish. Sprinkle the browned breadcrumbs over the top, and serve immediately.

VARIATION Try topping the dumplings with crispy fried onions instead of the toasted breadcrumbs. Slice an onion into thin rounds and fry in olive oil in a large frying pan until crispy. Add a crushed clove of garlic, if you wish.

Energy 313kcal/1321kJ; Protein 7.5g; Carbohydrate 56g, of which sugars 2.8g; Fat 8.1g, of which saturates 4.4g; Cholesterol 48mg; Calcium 69mg; Fibre 2.8g; Sodium 240mg.

Spiced Red Cabbage

Red cabbage is one of the staples of Polish cooking, and this spiced dish has its equivalent in most of the countries of eastern and northern Europe and Scandinavia. The cabbage is braised with apples and spices and makes the perfect accompaniment to goose or duck.

Serves 4–6

1 tbsp butter
1 large onion, sliced
1 red cabbage
2 cooking apples, peeled, cored and
    cut into cubes
7.5ml/1½ tsp caraway seeds
4–5 bay leaves
5–6 allspice berries
30ml/2 tbsp clear honey
juice of 1 lemon
1 glass dry red wine
6 whole cloves
salt and ground black pepper, to taste
chopped chives or parsley, to garnish

1 Melt the butter in a frying pan over a medium heat.

2 Add the sliced onion to the frying pan and fry gently for 5 minutes, or until the onion has softened and is golden brown.

3 Finely shred the cabbage and place in a large, heavy pan, together with 1 litre/1¾ pints/4 cups boiling water.

4 Add the fried onion to the cabbage with the remaining ingredients. Stir well and cover. Cook over a medium heat for 15–20 minutes.

5 Check the mixture towards the end of the cooking time. The cabbage should be tender, the apples should have broken down and the liquid should have reduced by about half.

6 If there is too much liquid, cook uncovered for a further 5 minutes.

7 Add salt and ground black pepper to taste, if you wish.

8 Serve garnished with chopped chives or parsley, or keep in the refrigerator until needed. This dish is even better served the next day, and can also be frozen.

Energy 112kcal/469kJ; Protein 2g; Carbohydrate 17.1g, of which sugars 15.5g; Fat 2.4g, of which saturates 1.3g; Cholesterol 5mg; Calcium 55mg; Fibre 3.1g; Sodium 25mg.

Fried Mushrooms with Root Vegetables

Russians check their hand-picked mushrooms carefully and reserve the most beautiful specimens
for drying or marinating. The rest are often cut into pieces and fried in butter or used in soup.
This is a traditional side dish, which makes a good accompaniment to most meat dishes

Serves 4

350g/12oz fresh mushrooms, such as
  porcini, cut into small pieces
65g/2½oz/5 tbsp butter
2 onions, peeled and chopped
1 turnip, finely diced
3 carrots, finely diced
3–4 potatoes, finely diced
60–75ml/4–5 tbsp finely chopped
  fresh parsley
100ml/3½fl oz/scant ½ cup smetana or
  crème fraîche
salt and ground black pepper

1 Heat a large frying pan, add the
mushrooms and cook over a medium
heat, stirring frequently, until all the liquid
has evaporated. Add half of the butter
and the onions and stir-fry for 10 minutes.

2 In a separate frying pan, heat the
remaining butter until melted. Add
the diced turnip, carrots and potatoes,
and fry for 10–15 minutes, until soft and
golden brown. Do this in two or three
batches if you don't have a big enough
frying pan, as the vegetables need to stay
in a single layer.

3 Mix the mushrooms and the fried root
vegetables together, cover the pan and
cook for about 10 minutes, until the
vegetables are tender. Season to taste.

4 Sprinkle the chopped parsley into the
pan. Stir in the smetana or crème fraîche
and reheat gently. Serve hot.

Energy 361kcal/1503kJ; Protein 5.8g; Carbohydrate 31g, of which sugars 11.1g; Fat 24.7g, of which saturates 15.5g; Cholesterol 63mg; Calcium 94mg; Fibre 5.7g; Sodium 150mg.

Sautéed Wild Mushrooms

Poland is the largest producer of wild mushrooms in Europe, and as in Russia, collecting them is a national pastime. This recipe of fried onions and mushrooms in a sour cream sauce allows the earthy flavours to shine through. It can be served with fried or roasted meat.

Serves 4

60ml/4 tbsp butter
2 large onions, halved and sliced
15ml/1 tbsp plain (all-purpose) flour
250ml/8fl oz/1 cup sour cream
450g/1lb/6½ cups fresh wild
   mushrooms
salt and ground black pepper, to taste
15ml/1 tbsp chopped fresh parsley,
   to garnish

1 Melt the butter in a large frying pan, then add the onions. Cook gently for 5 minutes, or until they begin to brown slightly. Stir in the flour and sour cream.

2 Meanwhile, brush the wild mushrooms to remove any grit, and wash the caps only briefly if necessary. Dry the mushrooms with kitchen paper and slice them thinly.

3 Add the sliced mushrooms to the onion sauce and season to taste. Simmer gently over a low heat for 15 minutes. Garnish with chopped parsley and serve immediately.

Energy 303kcal/1253kJ; Protein 5.5g; Carbohydrate 13.7g, of which sugars 8.4g; Fat 25.6g, of which saturates 15.8g; Cholesterol 69mg; Calcium 98mg; Fibre 2.8g; Sodium 125mg.

Dumplings Stuffed with Mushrooms

These tiny stuffed dumplings are traditionally served in Poland as an accompaniment to borscht or clear soup, or as a light snack with a shot of 95 per cent proof Polish spirit or vodka. Uszka means little ears in Polish, and it is generally thought that the smaller the dumplings the greater the skill of the cook who made them.

Serves 4–6

225g/8oz/2 cups plain (all-purpose) flour, plus extra for dusting
2.5ml/½ tsp salt
1 egg, beaten
30–45ml/2–3 tbsp lukewarm water
chopped fresh parsley, to garnish (optional)

For the filling
115g/4oz/2 cups dried mushrooms, rinsed and soaked in warm water for 30 minutes
25g/1oz/2 tbsp butter
1 onion, very finely chopped
15ml/1 tbsp fresh white breadcrumbs
30ml/2 tbsp finely chopped fresh parsley
1 egg, beaten
salt and ground black pepper, to taste

1 Soak the dried mushrooms in warm water for 30 minutes.

2 To make the filling, drain the soaked mushrooms and chop very finely.

3 Gently heat the butter in a large frying pan, add the onion and sauté for 5 minutes, or until softened.

4 Add the chopped mushrooms to the pan and cook for about 10 minutes, or until the liquid has evaporated and the mixture begins to sizzle.

5 Turn the mushroom mixture into a large bowl, then add the fresh white breadcrumbs, chopped parsley and beaten egg.

6 Season to taste and mix together to form a firm paste, then set aside and leave to cool slightly. (This mixture can be kept in the refrigerator at this stage for up to 24 hours.)

7 Sift the flour into a large bowl, mix in the salt, then make a dip in the middle with the back of a wooden spoon. Pour the beaten egg into the dip and mix into the flour adding enough lukewarm water to form a stiff dough.

COOK'S TIP As with Russian pelmeni, these tiny dumplings can be frozen and then cooked as needed. To do this, at the end of step 6 simply place each dumpling on to a greased baking tray, then freeze. When frozen, transfer to freezer bags. To serve, drop into boiling water and cook for 5–8 minutes.

8 Turn the dough out on to a lightly floured surface and knead until it is pliant but fairly stiff. Leave to rest for 30 minutes. Roll out the dough thinly, to a thickness of about 3mm/⅛in, then cut into 5cm/2in squares.

9 Place a small amount of the mushroom filling in the centre of each square of dough. Fold one corner over the filling diagonally and press the edges together. Fold the two bottom corners of the triangle to the middle and press together to form a 'pig's ear' shape.

10 Bring a large pan of lightly salted water to the boil. Drop in the dumplings and cook for about 3–5 minutes, or until they float to the surface.

11 Lift out the dumplings with a slotted spoon and place on a warmed serving dish. Garnish with chopped parsley, if you like, and serve immediately.

Energy 198kcal/835kJ; Protein 6.4g; Carbohydrate 32g, of which sugars 1.3g; Fat 5.9g, of which saturates 2.8g; Cholesterol 72mg; Calcium 70mg; Fibre 1.5g; Sodium 70mg.

Puff Pastry Cabbage Pie

Crisp puff pastry with a very soft cabbage filling is a favourite dish for Russians to eat on a Saturday night when the whole family is gathered around the table. Russian hostesses pride themselves on their pastry-making, but buying a sheet of ready-made puff pastry is acceptable!

Serves 4–6

300–400g/11–14oz cabbage
40–50g/1½–2oz/3–4 tbsp butter
3 eggs
1 sheet ready-made chilled puff
    pastry, measuring about
    40x20cm/16x8in
salt

For the glaze
1 egg yolk
5ml/1 tsp water
15ml/1 tbsp fresh white breadcrumbs

COOK'S TIP This pie is made with one large sheet of ready-made puff pastry, which can be bought chilled in one roll. The size should be about 40x20cm/16x8in. However, if your pastry sheets are smaller, it is possible to put three smaller sheets together and seal them into one large one.

1 Discard the outer leaves and hard stalk of the cabbage, cut in half and chop finely. Heat the butter in a medium frying pan over a low heat, add the cabbage and stir-fry for 25 minutes until soft, but don't allow it to brown. Set aside to cool.

2 Put the eggs in a pan, cover with cold water and bring to the boil. Reduce the heat and simmer for 10 minutes, then drain and put under cold running water. Remove the shells from the eggs, then chop and put in a large bowl. Add the cabbage, season to taste, and mix.

3 Preheat the oven to 220°C/425°F/Gas 7. Put the sheet of pastry on a dampened baking tray. Spread the cabbage and egg mixture lengthways on one half of the pastry sheet. Brush the edges with water and fold the other side over to enclose. Seal together by pressing with a fork along the join. It should look like a tightly packed loaf.

4 To make the glaze, whisk together the egg yolk and water. Brush the pastry with the mixture and make some small holes in the top with a fork. Sprinkle the top of the pastry with the breadcrumbs.

5 Bake the pie in the oven for 12–15 minutes, until the pastry is crisp and golden brown. Leave the baked pie to rest for 5–10 minutes, then cut into portions and serve.

COOK'S TIP Make sure that the brand of puff pastry you buy is a high quality, all-butter one, or at least containing a high proportion Pf butter.

Energy 333kcal/1388kJ; Protein 7.9g; Carbohydrate 25.3g, of which sugars 3.3g; Fat 23.6g, of which saturates 4.5g; Cholesterol 143mg; Calcium 80mg; Fibre 1.2g; Sodium 276mg.

Sauerkraut Stew with Prunes

Dried fruits are often used in Russian cuisine, not only for desserts but also in main courses. In this dish they add a delicious sweetness to the contrasting sour taste of the sauerkraut. Serve the dish as a main course with potatoes or to accompany baked ham.

3 Add the sauerkraut to the pan and fork it through to mix with the fried onions and melted butter.

4 Add the peppercorns and bay leaf to the sauerkraut and onion mixture. Add the garlic bulb, without peeling or separating into cloves.

5 Transfer the sauerkraut mixture into an ovenproof dish. Add the water and sugar, and season with salt.

6 Bake the sauerkraut in the oven, stirring occasionally. After 30 minutes, stir in the prunes. Return to the oven and bake for a further 20 minutes, stirring two or three times during cooking.

COOK'S TIP Keeping the garlic whole and unpeeled gives a very sweet, gentle garlic tone to the sauerkraut. If you prefer a stronger taste, stir in an additional crushed clove of garlic at the same stage as you add the prunes.

Serves 4

700g/1lb 10oz sauerkraut
2 large onions, sliced
75–100g/3–3³⁄₄oz/6–7¹⁄₂ tbsp butter
5 black peppercorns
1 bay leaf
1 whole garlic bulb, about 10 cloves
200ml/7fl oz/scant 1 cup water
15ml/1 tbsp sugar
8 dried prunes
salt

1 Preheat the oven to 200°C/400°F/ Gas 6. Rinse the sauerkraut under running water if you find it too sour.

2 Heat the butter in a medium pan until melted. Add the sliced onions and fry for 5–8 minutes, stirring occasionally, until soft and golden brown.

COOK'S TIP Sauerkraut is available bottled or canned from large supermarkets.

Energy 239kcal/986kJ; Protein 4.2g; Carbohydrate 21.2g, of which sugars 18.3g; Fat 15.7g, of which saturates 9.8g; Cholesterol 40mg; Calcium 142mg; Fibre 7g; Sodium 1298mg.

Fried Potatoes with Eggs and Onions

A large pan with fried potatoes and onions can make a whole meal for a Russian family, often served with smetana, bread, Salted Cucumbers and maybe a couple of fried eggs. Fried potatoes are also the most common accompaniment to Russian fish and meat dishes.

Serves 4

6–8 potatoes, total weight 1kg/2¼lb, peeled and cut into slices or wedges
60–75ml/4–5 tbsp sunflower oil
50g/2oz/¼ cup butter
1–2 onions, sliced into rings
4 eggs
salt
4 Salted Cucumbers (page 79), sliced, and smetana or crème fraîche, to serve

4 Add the fried onions to the cooked potatoes and season well with salt. Wipe out the small frying pan and return to the heat.

5 Melt the remaining butter in the frying pan and fry the eggs. Place on top of the potatoes and serve with Salted Cucumbers and smetana or crème fraîche.

1 Pat the sliced potatoes dry with kitchen paper. Heat the oil in a very large frying pan, add the potatoes and fry for 3 minutes. Shake the pan or turn the potatoes and fry for a further 5–10 minutes, until golden.

2 Cover the pan with a lid, or with a double thickness of foil, and cook over a low heat for 5–10 minutes, until the potatoes are tender.

3 Meanwhile, heat half of the butter in a small frying pan, add the onions and fry, stirring, for 5–10 minutes until golden.

Energy 477kcal/1990kJ; Protein 11.8g; Carbohydrate 48.2g, of which sugars 8.9g; Fat 27.8g, of which saturates 9.6g; Cholesterol 217mg; Calcium 71mg; Fibre 3.9g; Sodium 176mg.

Courgettes with Smetana

Russians who have their own dacha (country house) grow their own vegetables. Courgette plants usually produce a glut, so during the season they are preserved, salted or marinated, fried and mixed with caviar and also sautéed and served in a creamy, mild smetana sauce.

Serves 4

4 small courgettes (zucchini)
45–75ml/3–5 tbsp plain white
  (all-purpose) flour
30ml/2 tbsp rapeseed (canola) oil
45ml/3 tbsp chopped fresh parsley
200ml/7fl oz/scant 1 cup smetana or
  crème fraîche
salt and ground black pepper
rye bread to serve

VARIATION Try using dill instead of parsley if serving this with fish.

1 Cut the courgettes into 1cm/½in thick slices. Coat the slices in the flour.

2 Heat the oil in a large frying pan, then add the courgettes, working in batches if necessary to keep to a single layer, and fry for about 1 minute on each side or until golden brown. Remove from the pan and keep warm until all the courgettes are fried.

3 Return all the courgettes to the pan. Season the courgettes with plenty of salt and pepper and sprinkle with the chopped parsley.

4 Add the smetana or crème fraîche to the pan, cover and simmer over a low heat for about 5 minutes until the courgettes are soft.

5 Serve the courgettes warm, straight from the pan with rye bread.

COOK'S TIP Courgettes can be frozen. Slice them, blanch in boiling water, dry on kitchen paper, then freeze in a single layer on baking trays. When frozen transfer to freezer bags.

Energy 312kcal/1290kJ; Protein 5.7g; Carbohydrate 13.4g, of which sugars 4.5g; Fat 26.5g, of which saturates 14.4g; Cholesterol 56mg; Calcium 111mg; Fibre 2.5g; Sodium 17mg.

Vegetable Ragoût

Russians prefer to eat their vegetables very soft and very hot. Both are illustrated in this recipe, which may seem simple but, with the addition of vegetable stock and butter, is a very tasty and economical way to serve vegetables. Serve the ragoût with dark rye bread and butter.

Serves 4

3–4 carrots
1 swede (rutabaga)
1 turnip
1 parsnip
10ml/2 tsp sunflower oil
1 large onion, finely chopped
100–200ml/3½–7fl oz/scant ½–1 cup
  vegetable stock or lightly salted
  water
105ml/7 tbsp finely chopped fresh
  parsley
15g/½oz/1 tbsp butter
dark rye bread and butter, to serve

1 Cut the carrots, swede, turnip and parsnip into small chunks. Heat the oil in a flameproof casserole, add the chopped onion and fry over a medium heat, for 3–5 minutes until softened.

2 Add the carrots, swede, turnip and parsnip to the pan and fry, stirring frequently, for a further 10 minutes. Add the stock and bring to the boil. Cover with a lid and simmer for 20 minutes.

3 Add the chopped parsley and the butter to the pan and stir until the butter has melted. Season with salt to taste and serve hot.

VARIATION Add 100g/3¾oz/scant 1 cup fresh or frozen peas to the ragoût 3 minutes before adding the chopped fresh parsley and butter.

Energy 122kcal/506kJ; Protein 2.6g; Carbohydrate 15.9g, of which sugars 13.3g; Fat 5.7g, of which saturates 2.3g; Cholesterol 8mg; Calcium 137mg; Fibre 6.3g; Sodium 68mg.

Buckwheat Kasha

Kasha has been eaten in Poland and other Eastern European countries for centuries as a staple accompaniment to all kinds of roasts and stews. It is often simply served with standard or soured milk, which may be an acquired taste but is thought to be delicious all over the country.

Serves 4–6

300g/11oz/1½ cups buckwheat
500ml/17fl oz/2¼ cups water
pinch of salt
60ml/4 tbsp vegetable oil or
   45g/1½ oz lard

1 Put the buckwheat in a large, heavy pan and add the water, salt and oil or lard.

2 Bring to the boil and cook over a low heat for about 20 minutes, or until the buckwheat has absorbed all the water and the grains are soft.

3 Serve the kasha immediately.

COOK'S TIP Kasha can be made with other grains, but the buckwheat version has a stronger flavour than most. It forms part of the traditional Christmas Eve supper.

Energy 180kcal/746kJ; Protein 2.9g; Carbohydrate 25.7g, of which sugars 0g; Fat 7.8g, of which saturates 0.9g; Cholesterol 0mg; Calcium 10mg; Fibre 1.35g; Sodium 0mg.

Polish-style Cucumber Salad

According to legend, this simple salad, 'miseria', was a favourite dish of Queen Bona Sforza, an Italian princess who married the Polish king Sigismund I in the 16th century. Homesick for her native Italy, the dish made her cry, hence its Polish name, derived from the Latin for 'misery'.

Serves 4–6

2 medium cucumbers
2.5ml/½ tsp salt
120ml/4fl oz/½ cup sour cream
juice from ½ lemon
2.5ml/½ tsp sugar (optional)
1.5ml/¼ tsp ground black pepper
15ml/1 tbsp chives, to garnish

1 Peel the cucumbers, slice them thinly and place in a sieve (strainer).

2 Sprinkle over the salt, leave for a few minutes, then rinse to remove the salt and pat dry with kitchen paper.

3 To make the dressing, mix together the sour cream, lemon juice, sugar, if using, and black pepper.

4 Fold in the cucumber, then place in the refrigerator and leave for 1 hour. Serve as an accompaniment, garnished with chopped dill or chives.

Energy 53kcal/216kJ; Protein 1.3g; Carbohydrate 2.6g, of which sugars 2.6g; Fat 4.1g, of which saturates 2.5g; Cholesterol 12mg; Calcium 44mg; Fibre 0.7g; Sodium 13mg.

Apple and Leek Salad

Fresh and tangy, this simple Polish salad of sliced leeks and apples with a lemon and honey dressing can be served with a range of cold meats or smoked fish as part of a summer meal. For the best result, make sure you use slim young leeks and tart, crisp apples.

Serves 4

2 slim leeks, white part only, washed
  thoroughly
2 large apples
15ml/1 tbsp chopped fresh parsley
juice of 1 lemon
15ml/1 tbsp clear honey
salt and ground black pepper, to taste

COOK'S TIP When buying leeks, look for slim ones with firm white stems and bright green leaves. Avoid those that are discoloured in any way. If you can't find young leeks use older ones but blanch them in boiling water, then rinse in cold running water. This gives a milder flavour.

1 Thinly slice the leeks. Peel and core the apples, then slice thinly.

2 Put in a large serving bowl and add the parsley, lemon juice, honey and seasoning to taste.

3 Toss well, then leave to stand in a cool place for about an hour, to allow the flavours to blend together.

Energy 59kcal/252kJ; Protein 1.9g; Carbohydrate 12.5g, of which sugars 11.8g; Fat 0.6g, of which saturates 0.1g; Cholesterol 0mg; Calcium 27mg; Fibre 3.4g; Sodium 4mg.

Beetroot Salad

The fresh, sweet and nutty flavour of beetroot makes the ideal partner for horseradish, and this salad is often served as a side dish with cold meats, such as ham and Polish sausage. Beetroot is believed to have beauty-enhancing and aphrodisiac properties.

Serves 4–6

4–5 medium beetroot (beets), washed but not peeled
15ml/1 tbsp sugar
60–75ml/4–5 tbsp freshly grated horseradish
juice of 1 lemon
1 glass dry red wine
2.5ml/½ tsp salt
cold meats, to serve

1 Put the beetroot, in their skins, in a large pan, and cover with water. Bring to the boil and cook the beetroots for about 1 hour, or until tender. Remove from the heat and leave to cool.

2 When the beetroot are cool, peel off the skin with your fingers or a sharp knife. Grate the flesh into a large bowl.

3 Add the sugar, horseradish, lemon juice, red wine and salt to the shredded beetroot. Mix together, then transfer to a jar. Store in a cool place for up to 4 months. Serve with cold meats.

Energy 60kcal/253kJ; Protein 1.5g; Carbohydrate 9g, of which sugars 8.5g; Fat 0.1g, of which saturates 0g; Cholesterol 0mg; Calcium 20mg; Fibre 1.6g; Sodium 221mg.

Polish-style Lettuce Salad

This light salad makes an excellent accompaniment to pork or poultry dishes. The egg yolks make a lovely rich dressing – choose free-range eggs with a good golden yolk, if you can. You should serve the salad as soon as it is dressed, as if left for too long it will wilt.

Serves 4-6

2 medium lettuces
200ml/7fl oz/scant 1 cup sour cream
juice of 1 lemon, or 2 tbsp vinegar
1 tbsp sugar
5ml/1 tsp salt
2 hard-boiled eggs
chopped chives and dill, to garnish

1 Divide the lettuces into separate leaves. Wash carefully under running water, then pat completely dry with kitchen paper or a clean dish towel.

2 To make the dressing, in a large bowl, mix together the sour cream, lemon juice or vinegar, sugar and salt.

3 Peel the eggs and carefully separate the yolks from the whites. Crumble the yolks and fold them into the dressing.

4 Just before serving, place the lettuce leaves in a large bowl. Pour the dressing over the leaves, and mix gently with two forks. Transfer to a serving dish.

5 Thinly slice the egg whites and arrange over the top, with the chopped chives and dill. Serve immediately.

Energy 112kcal/465kJ; Protein 3.6g; Carbohydrate 5g, of which sugars 5g; Fat 8.8g, of which saturates 4.8g; Cholesterol 83mg; Calcium 61mg; Fibre 0.6g; Sodium 39mg

Celeriac Salad

This salad combines raw celeriac with onion, apples and carrots in a simple dressing. It goes especially well with cold chicken and turkey. Because the vegetables are raw, it is also bursting with goodness, and adds a fresh crunch to accompany winter dishes.

Serves 4

1 medium celeriac
1 small onion
2 large apples, peeled and cored
2 carrots
juice from 1 lemon
15ml/1 tbsp clear honey
15ml/1 tbsp olive oil
30ml/2 tbsp mayonnaise
15ml/1 tbsp chopped fresh parsley
salt and ground black pepper

1 Finely shred the celeriac, onion, apples and carrots. Transfer to a large bowl and toss to combine.

2 In a separate bowl, combine the lemon juice, honey, olive oil, mayonnaise, and salt and pepper to taste. Pour over the vegetables, add the parsley and toss to combine. Taste and adjust the seasoning as necessary.

Energy 149kcal/623kJ; Protein 1.4g; Carbohydrate 17.1g, of which sugars 16.6g; Fat 8.9g, of which saturates 1.2g; Cholesterol 6mg; Calcium 74mg; Fibre 3.8g; Sodium 55mg.

Sauerkraut Salad with Cranberries

Cabbage is a staple ingredient in Russia and the best soured cabbage can be bought in the market halls, where you are invited to taste both the cabbage and the brine. It is not unusual for a customer to taste up to ten different kinds before making a decision.

Serves 4–6

500g/1¼lb sauerkraut
2 red apples, cut into wedges
100–200g/3¾–7oz/scant 1–1¾ cups
  fresh cranberries or lingonberries
30ml/2 tbsp sugar
60–75ml/4–5 tbsp sunflower oil
2–3 sprigs fresh parsley, to garnish

1 Put the sauerkraut in a colander and drain thoroughly. Taste it, and if you find it is too sour, rinse it under cold running water, then drain well. Transfer to a large bowl and add the apple slices.

2 Add the apples and the cranberries or lingonberries to the sauerkraut. Add the sugar and oil and mix well. Transfer to a serving bowl and garnish with parsley.

Energy 105kcal/437kJ; Protein 1.3g; Carbohydrate 8.8g, of which sugars 8.8g; Fat 7.4g, of which saturates 0.9g; Cholesterol 0mg; Calcium 49mg; Fibre 3.1g; Sodium 493mg.

Fresh Spring Salad

This pretty salad can be served as an accompaniment to most meat and fish dishes. It is a typical home-made Russian dish and is hardly ever served in restaurants. Prepare this salad no more than an hour in advance and only add the dressing just before it is served.

Serves 4

2 eggs
1 large cos or romaine lettuce
1 cucumber, peeled and finely sliced
10 radishes, finely sliced
1 bunch spring onions (scallions), finely sliced
45ml/3 tbsp chopped fresh dill, to garnish

For the dressing
200ml/7fl oz/scant 1 cup smetana or crème fraîche
juice of 1 lemon
15ml/1 tbsp sugar
pinch of salt

1 First make the dressing. Put the smetana or crème fraîche and lemon juice in a small bowl and whisk together.

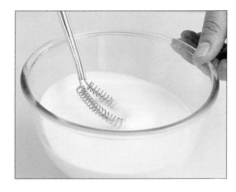

2 Add the sugar and salt to the bowl and whisk again until the sugar is completely dissolved. Set aside.

3 Put the eggs in a pan, cover with cold water and bring to the boil. Reduce the heat to low and simmer for 10 minutes. Drain and put under cold running water. Remove the shells and slice the eggs.

4 Cut the lettuce into pieces and put in a serving dish. Layer the salad by placing the cucumber on top of the shredded lettuce, then the radishes, then the sliced egg and finally the spring onions.

5 Just before serving, spoon the dressing over the salad and garnish with chopped fresh dill.

Energy 268kcal/1107kJ; Protein 6g; Carbohydrate 8.7g, of which sugars 8.5g; Fat 23.5g, of which saturates 14.5g; Cholesterol 152mg; Calcium 96mg; Fibre 1.8g; Sodium 55mg.

DESSERTS AND DRINKS

Despite the hearty nature of many Polish main courses, a dessert is often also served, generally based on fruit and so not too filling but sweet enough to round off the meal. Russians, too, enjoy something sweet to finish dinner, but their desserts more often consist of little cakes or pies. More substantial Polish desserts are based on curd cheese and eggs. Polish Cheesecake is a light baked mixture made with whisked eggs, while Pancakes with Vanilla Cheese are folded round a similar mixture of curd cheese with raisins and vanilla. Russian desserts also often include fruit, either the widely available ones such as cherries, blueberries and apples, or more exotic fruits from one of the warmer former Soviet republics – grenadines, grapes or watermelon. These are combined in delicious concoctions such as cherry compote, or vanilla ice cream with frozen berries and warm fudge sauce.

Bread and Apple Bake

Bread has always been the basic, staple food of Russian cuisine. It is treated with great respect, bought fresh each day and used to the last crumb. This recipe makes a new dish out of old bread – frugal, simple but very good. Sweet, dessert apples are best for this recipe.

Serves 6–8

a loaf of 2–3 days old white bread
60g/2¼oz/4½ tbsp cold butter
1 egg
150ml/¼ pint/⅔ cup milk
6–8 apples
130g/4½oz/⅔ cup caster (superfine)
    sugar

1 Preheat the oven to 200°C/400°F/ Gas 6. Use 10g/¼oz/1½ tsp of the butter to grease a 20cm/8in flan tin (pan).

2 Slice the loaf fairly thickly; you will need around 10 slices. Cut off the crusts.

3 Break the egg into a bowl and beat lightly. Add the milk to the bowl and whisk together. Cut five of the bread slices in half.

4 Dip the halved slices of bread, one at a time, into the milk mixture and place in the flan tin so that they cover the edges. Dip the remaining uncut bread slices in the milk mixture and place tightly in the bottom of the tin.

5 Cut the remaining 50g/2oz/4 tbsp butter into small cubes. Peel and core the apples and cut the flesh into small pieces.

6 Put half of the apples on top of the bread, sprinkle with half of the sugar and half of the butter cubes. Top with the remaining apples, sugar and butter.

7 Bake in the oven for 15 minutes. Lower the temperature to 180°C/ 350°F/Gas 4 and bake for a further 35 minutes, until golden brown. Serve warm, straight from the tin.

Energy 245kcal/1038kJ; Protein 4.6g; Carbohydrate 41.8g, of which sugars 26.1g; Fat 7.9g, of which saturates 4.3g; Cholesterol 41mg; Calcium 77mg; Fibre 1.6g; Sodium 240mg.

Apple Pie

Russians like to finish the day with vechernij chaj – evening tea. Chocolate confectionery, cookies, berries and spoonfuls of jam may be served. If something more substantial is required, a large home-baked pie is served with the steaming hot tea.

Serves 4–6

40–50g/1½–2oz/3–4 tbsp butter
5–6 cooking apples, peeled and sliced
45ml/3 tbsp raisins
1 sheet ready-made chilled puff
  pastry, measuring about
  40x20cm/16x8in
1 egg yolk
5ml/1 tsp water

1 Melt the butter in a medium frying pan. Add the apples and stir-fry, over a low heat, for 5 minutes, until soft. Remove the pan from the heat, add the raisins and mix together. Set aside and leave to cool.

2 Preheat the oven to 220°C/425°F/Gas 7. Put the sheet of pastry on a greased baking tray. Carefully place the apple filling on just half of the pastry, leaving one side free of filling, and a 5cm/2in border around the other three edges.

3 Brush the edges of the pastry with water or milk and fold over the other half to enclose the filling.

4 Whisk the egg yolk and water together to make a glaze. Brush the pastry with the mixture and make some small holes in the top with a fork.

5 Bake the pie in the oven for 12–15 minutes, until golden brown. Allow the pie to rest for 5–10 minutes then cut into slices and serve with a spoonful of smetana or crème fraîche.

Energy 393kcal/1650kJ; Protein 4.1g; Carbohydrate 56.3g, of which sugars 27.7g; Fat 18.4g, of which saturates 11.4g; Cholesterol 46mg; Calcium 68mg; Fibre 2.5g; Sodium 136mg.

Small Blueberry Pies

Delicious little blueberry pies are perfect as a dessert after a Sunday lunch. Alternatively, serve them in the afternoon; seat your guests in the garden and bring out the samovar. Serve these home-made temptations on a Russian tray decorated with fresh flowers, with lots of hot tea.

Makes 10

For the dough
50g/2oz/¼ cup butter
200ml/7fl oz/scant 1 cup milk
45ml/3 tbsp water
2.5ml/½ tsp salt
7.5ml/1½ tsp caster (superfine) sugar
1 small (US medium) egg
400g/14oz/3½ cups plain white
  (all-purpose) flour
large pinch of easy-blend (rapid-rise)
  dried yeast

For the filling
300–350g/11–12oz/2¾–3 cups
  blueberries, fresh or frozen
25g/1oz/2 tbsp caster (superfine) sugar
15ml/1 tbsp potato flour

For the glaze
150ml/¼ pint/⅔ cup smetana or
  crème fraîche
45ml/3 tbsp caster (superfine) sugar
icing (confectioners') sugar, for
  dusting

1 To make the dough, melt the butter in a small pan. Add the milk, water, salt and sugar and heat until warm to the finger. Pour the mixture into a large bowl. Add the egg and mix together.

2 Put the flour and yeast in a large bowl and mix together. Stir in the butter mixture, a little at a time, until combined.

3 Knead the dough in the bowl for at least 5 minutes. Cover the bowl with a dish towel and leave the dough to rise in a warm place for 30 minutes, until it has doubled in size.

4 Turn the dough on to a lightly floured surface. Cut the dough into 24 equal-size pieces and form each piece into a ball. Leave to rest for 5–10 minutes.

5 Meanwhile, prepare the filling. Put the blueberries in a bowl, add the sugar and potato flour and mix together.

6 Preheat the oven to 200°C/400°F/Gas 6. Grease a large baking tray. Flatten each ball to a round measuring about 15cm/6in in diameter.

VARIATION You can vary the fillings for these little pies depending on what fruit is in season: blackberries would work well, as would raspberries or apricots, or try finely chopped apples and a sprinkle of cinnamon. Adjust the amount of sugar to suit the fruit you use.

7 Place the rounds on the baking tray. Place 45ml/3 tbsp of the blueberry mixture in the centre of each round, then fold a small edge up around the mixture.

8 Bake the pies in the oven for 10–15 minutes, until golden brown.

9 Meanwhile, make the glaze. Put the smetana or crème fraîche and the sugar in a bowl and mix together.

10 When the pies are baked, gently spoon a little of the glaze over each pie. Dust the tops with sifted icing sugar. Serve hot or cold.

Energy 371kcal/1559kJ; Protein 4.4g; Carbohydrate 55.8g, of which sugars 25.7g; Fat 16g, of which saturates 4.9g; Cholesterol 8mg; Calcium 93mg; Fibre 3.2g; Sodium 228mg.

Crêpes with a Cheese Filling

Russians love pancakes of all kinds, and these crêpes are deliciously light and crisp. If you omit the sugar and add salt and pepper, this can be adapted to a savoury dish for a main course.

Serves 4

50g/2oz/¼ cup butter
3 eggs
2.5ml/½ tsp salt
2ml/⅓ tsp caster (superfine) sugar
200ml/7fl oz/scant 1 cup warm water
185g/6½oz/1⅔ cups plain white
  (all-purpose) flour
350ml/12fl oz/1½ cups milk
rapeseed (canola) oil, for brushing,
  and frying
smetana or crème fraîche, and caster
  (superfine) sugar, to serve

For the filling

500g/1¼lb/2½ cups fresh cheese, such
  as ricotta or cottage cheese
2 egg yolks
30–45ml/2–3 tbsp caster (superfine)
  sugar

1 Melt the butter. Whisk the eggs, salt and sugar together in a bowl. Add the water, then gradually whisk in the flour.

2 Stir the milk into the egg and flour mixture, a little at a time, and then add the melted butter.

3 Heat a non-stick frying pan over a medium heat. Brush it with a little oil and pour in a thin layer of batter. As soon as the surface has set, turn the crêpe over and cook the other side.

4 Fry the remaining crêpes in the same way, brushing the pan with oil each time and stacking when cooked.

5 To make the filling, put the cottage cheese or ricotta cheese and egg yolks in a bowl and mix together. Add sugar to taste. Place 45ml/3 tbsp of the filling in the centre of each crêpe and fold over to create an envelope.

6 Heat the oil in a frying pan. Add the envelopes, joint-side down, and fry, over a medium heat, for 1–2 minutes. Turn and fry the other sides for 1–2 minutes, until golden brown. Serve the pancakes with smetana or crème fraîche and sugar.

Energy 1054kcal/4371kJ; Protein 17.5g; Carbohydrate 48g, of which sugars 12.7g; Fat 89.6g, of which saturates 47.9g; Cholesterol 394mg; Calcium 332mg; Fibre 1.4g; Sodium 547mg.

Pancakes with Vanilla Cheese

Pancakes are always popular, and these delicious Polish ones are no exception. Filled with a rich rum and raisin cheese mixture, the pancakes are dusted with icing sugar.

Serves 4–6

115g/4oz/1 cup plain (all-purpose)
  flour
45ml/3 tbsp sugar
pinch of salt
3 eggs, plus 2 yolks
350ml/12fl oz/1½ cups milk
225g/8oz/1 cup curd (farmer's) cheese
40g/1½oz/¼ cup raisins
45ml/3 tbsp rum
10ml/2 tsp vanilla sugar or 5ml/1 tsp
  vanilla extract
45ml/3 tbsp vegetable oil
45ml/3 tbsp icing (confectioners')
  sugar, for dusting

1 Sift the flour into a large bowl. Stir in the sugar and salt, and make a well in the centre. In a jug (pitcher) whisk together the 3 eggs and the milk.

2 Gradually add the milk mixture to the flour, beating constantly, until smooth.

3 Put the egg yolks, curd cheese, raisins, rum and vanilla sugar or extract in a bowl and beat well.

4 Heat enough oil to just coat the base of a small frying pan over a high heat and add a ladleful of the pancake batter.

5 Cook for about 1 minute, until golden underneath, then flip over and cook on the other side. Slide on to a plate and keep warm. Continue until you have used all the batter.

6 Place a spoonful of the curd cheese mixture in the centre of each pancake and fold the edges over. Dust the pancakes with icing sugar and serve immediately.

Energy 330kcal/1383kJ; Protein 11.5g; Carbohydrate 31.3g, of which sugars 16.7g; Fat 16.8g, of which saturates 6g; Cholesterol 182mg; Calcium 126mg; Fibre 0.7g; Sodium 68mg.

Baked Cheesecake

Russians love their tea and tea drinking is an ancient Russian tradition. It is popular to have parties where nothing but tea and sweet accompaniments are served. These include cherry jam, gooseberry jam and whole strawberry jam (put in the tea or eaten from special plates), chocolates, fudge and soft spicy ginger cookies. The highlight of the tea is a cheesecake, flavoured with raisins, preserved peel and lemon.

Serves 6–8

15g/½oz/1 tbsp butter
45ml/3 tbsp fresh white breadcrumbs
4 eggs
100g/3¾oz mixed (candied) peel
500g/1¼lb/2 cups cottage or ricotta cheese
90g/3½oz/½ cup caster (superfine) sugar
50g/2oz/scant ½ cup raisins
grated rind of 1 lemon
45ml/3 tbsp semolina
icing (confectioners') sugar, for dusting
smetana, crème fraîche or whipped cream, and fresh berries, such as strawberries, raspberries, blueberries or redcurrants, to serve

3 Add the cottage or ricotta cheese, sugar, raisins, lemon rind and semolina and mix well together.

4 Whisk the egg whites until they are stiff and hold their shape, then carefully fold into the cheese mixture. Spoon the mixture into the prepared tin.

1 Preheat the oven to 180°C/350°F/Gas 4. Use the butter to grease the bottom and sides of a 20cm/8in loose-bottomed cake tin (pan), then pour in the breadcrumbs and tip and shake until the insides of the tin are well coated with the breadcrumbs.

2 Separate the egg yolks from the egg whites into two separate large bowls. Finely chop the candied peel and add to the egg yolks.

5 Bake the cake in the oven for 30–40 minutes, until a skewer, inserted in the centre, comes out dry. Leave the cake to cool in the tin.

6 Slide a knife around the edge of the cake and carefully remove it from the tin. Place on a serving plate and dust with sifted icing sugar.

7 Serve the cheesecake with smetana, or crème fraîche or whipped cream, and fresh berries.

Energy 297kcal/1239kJ; Protein 7.6g; Carbohydrate 27.2g, of which sugars 19g; Fat 18g, of which saturates 9g; Cholesterol 83mg; Calcium 56mg; Fibre 1.1g; Sodium 139mg.

Polish Cheesecake

There are many versions of cheesecake in Poland, including this light, baked version. The raisins and semolina sink to the bottom of the cheesecake and form a kind of base during cooking.

Serves 6–8

500g/1¼ lb/2¼ cups curd (farmer's)
   cheese
100g/3¾oz/scant ½ cup butter,
   softened
2.5ml/½ tsp vanilla extract
6 eggs, separated
150g/5oz/¾ cup caster (superfine)
   sugar
10ml/2 tsp grated lemon rind
15ml/1 tbsp cornflour (cornstarch)
15ml/1 tbsp semolina
50g/5oz/⅓ cup raisins or sultanas
   (golden raisins) (optional)
icing (confectioners') sugar, to dust

1 Preheat the oven to 200°C/400°F/Gas 6. Grease and line a 20cm/8in round cake tin (pan).

2 Cream together the curd cheese, butter and vanilla in a large bowl until combined.

3 In a separate large bowl, whisk the egg whites with 15ml/1 tbsp sugar, until stiff peaks form.

4 In a third bowl, whisk the egg yolks with the remaining sugar until the mixture is thick and creamy.

5 Add the egg yolk and sugar mixture to the curd cheese and butter mixture with the lemon rind and stir to combine.

6 Gently fold in the egg whites, then the cornflour, semolina and raisins or sultanas, if using, taking care not to knock the air out of the mixture.

7 Transfer the mixture to the prepared tin and bake for 1 hour, or until set and golden brown.

8 Leave to cool in the tin, then dust with icing sugar and serve in slices.

COOK'S TIP It is important to use good quality curd cheese in this recipe; it should not taste sour at all.

Energy 347kcal/1448kJ; Protein 10.8g; Carbohydrate 24.8g, of which sugars 21.6g; Fat 23.6g, of which saturates 13.4g; Cholesterol 196mg; Calcium 34mg; Fibre 0g; Sodium 131mg.

Baked Coffee Custards

Unlike their eastern European neighbours, the Polish have a passion for both drinking and cooking with coffee. Here, it is used to lift a simple baked custard to new heights.

Serves 4

300ml/¹/₂ pint/1¹/₄ cups full-fat
   (whole) milk
25g/1oz ground coffee (not instant)
150ml/¹/₄ pint/²/₃ cup single
   (light) cream
3 eggs
30ml/2 tbsp caster (superfine) sugar
whipped cream and unsweetened
   cocoa powder, to decorate

1 Preheat the oven to 190°C/375°F/ Gas 5. Put the milk in a heavy pan and bring to the boil. Add the coffee, remove from the heat and leave to infuse for 10 minutes.

2 Strain the flavoured milk into a clean pan, add the cream and gently heat until just simmering.

3 Beat the eggs and sugar in a bowl until pale and fluffy. Pour over the hot milk mixture, whisking constantly.

4 Pour the custard mixture into individual heatproof bowls or coffee cups and cover tightly with foil. Place them in a roasting pan and pour in enough boiling water to come halfway up the bowls or cups.

5 Carefully place the roasting pan in the oven and cook for about 30 minutes, or until the custards are set. Remove from the roasting pan and leave to cool completely. Transfer to the refrigerator and chill for at least 2 hours.

6 Just before serving, decorate with whipped cream and cocoa powder.

Energy 207kcal/860kJ; Protein 8.5g; Carbohydrate 12g, of which sugars 12g; Fat 14.3g, of which saturates 7.6g; Cholesterol 174mg; Calcium 147mg; Fibre 0g; Sodium 96mg.

Chocolate and Coffee Mousse

A light but intensely chocolatey mousse is always a popular way to end a meal. This Polish version is made with a good strong chocolate and flavoured with coffee and rum, Polish spirit or vodka. You can omit these, depending on your preference.

Serves 4–6

250g/9oz dark (bittersweet) chocolate (minimum 70 per cent cocoa solids)
60ml/4 tbsp cooled strong black coffee
8 eggs, separated
200g/7oz/1 cup caster (superfine) sugar
60ml/4 tbsp rum, or 95 per cent proof Polish spirit or vodka

VARIATION For a slightly less intense mousse, whip 300ml/½ pint/1¼ cups double (heavy) cream until soft peaks form, then fold into the mixture at the end of step 3.

1 Break the chocolate into small pieces and melt in a heatproof bowl over a pan of gently simmering water. Ensure the water does not touch the base of the bowl, or the chocolate may seize.

2 Once the chocolate has melted, stir in the cold coffee. Leave to cool slightly.

3 Beat the egg yolks with half the sugar until it is pale, thick and creamy. Add the rum, spirit or vodka and the chocolate.

4 Whisk the egg whites in a separate bowl until stiff peaks form. Stir in the remaining sugar, then fold into the chocolate mixture. Spoon into glasses. Chill for at least an hour before serving.

Energy 464kcal/1951kJ; Protein 10.6g; Carbohydrate 61.3g, of which sugars 60.9g; Fat 19.1g, of which saturates 9.1g; Cholesterol 256mg; Calcium 70mg; Fibre 1.1g; Sodium 98mg.

Baked Apples with Cinnamon and Nuts

Cream cake may be one of the most popular desserts in Russia, but health conscious young Russians of today appreciate lighter desserts and are as happy to serve baked apples – another old traditional Russian classic dessert.

2 Preheat the oven to 220°C/425°F/ Gas 7. Using a vegetable peeler, peel the apples. Remove the cores, leaving the base of the apple intact. Put the apples in an ovenproof dish.

3 Divide the filling into four, and stuff the apples. Melt the butter in a small pan and pour over the apples to coat.

4 Bake the apples in the oven for about 20 minutes, until soft, but before they collapse. Serve hot, with vanilla ice cream.

Serves 4

4 large, firm apples
15g/½oz/1 tbsp butter
vanilla ice cream, to serve

For the filling
25g/1oz/2 tbsp butter
90ml/6 tbsp blanched almonds
  or hazelnuts
30ml/2 tbsp sugar
5ml/1 tsp ground cinnamon

VARIATION Instead of flavouring with cinnamon, use the same quantity of ground cardamom or vanilla extract.

1 To make the filling, melt the butter. Grind or finely chop the almonds or hazelnuts and put in a bowl. Add the sugar, cinnamon and melted butter and mix together.

Energy 294kcal/1229kJ; Protein 5.3g; Carbohydrate 22.8g, of which sugars 22.2g; Fat 20.9g, of which saturates 6.2g; Cholesterol 21mg; Calcium 66mg; Fibre 4.1g; Sodium 67mg.

Poached Pears with Chocolate

Many types of pear are grown in Poland, and they are either simply eaten raw or gently poached and served with a rich chocolate sauce, as in this recipe. Once cooked, these pears can be frozen in their syrup. To use from frozen simply defrost and then make the chocolate sauce.

Serves 4

4 firm pears, peeled
250g/9oz/1¼ cups caster (superfine) sugar
600ml/1 pint/2½ cups water
500ml/17fl oz/2¼ cups vanilla ice cream

For the chocolate sauce
250g/9oz good-quality dark (bittersweet) chocolate (minimum 70 per cent cocoa solids)
40g/1½ oz unsalted butter
5ml/1 tsp vanilla extract
75ml/5 tbsp double (heavy) cream

1 Cut the pears in half lengthways and remove the core. Place the sugar and water in a large pan and gently heat until the sugar has dissolved completely.

2 Add the pear halves to the pan, then simmer for about 20 minutes, or until the pears are tender but not falling apart.

3 Lift out of the sugar syrup with a slotted spoon and leave to cool.

4 To make the chocolate sauce, break the chocolate into small pieces and put into a pan.

5 Add the butter and 30ml/2 tbsp water. Heat gently over a low heat, without stirring, until the chocolate has melted.

6 Add the vanilla extract and cream, and mix gently to combine.

7 Place a scoop of ice cream into each of four glasses.

8 Add two cooled pear halves to each and pour over the hot chocolate sauce. Serve immediately.

COOK'S TIP Like apples, there are two types of pear: softer dessert varieties and those that can be cooked. Use firm ones, as they will hold their shape when poached, rather than disintegrating.

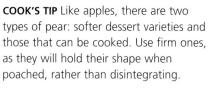

Energy 1014kcal/4255kJ; Protein 8.8g; Carbohydrate 145.1g, of which sugars 143.2g; Fat 46.7g, of which saturates 29.6g; Cholesterol 81mg; Calcium 206mg; Fibre 4.9g; Sodium 152mg.

Plum Dumplings

These traditional sweet dumplings are served everywhere in Poland during the autumn, when plums are at their best. They are sometimes eaten as a meal on their own!

Serves 4

675g/1½lb potatoes, peeled
250ml/8fl oz/1 cup sour cream
75g/3oz/6 tbsp butter
2 eggs, beaten
250g/9oz/2¼ cups plain (all-purpose) flour, plus extra for dusting
8 plums
90g/3½oz/¾ cup icing (confectioners') sugar, mixed with 30ml/2 tbsp ground cinnamon
45ml/3 tbsp breadcrumbs
icing (confectioners') sugar and cinnamon, for dusting

1 Cut the potatoes into even pieces and cook in a pan of lightly salted boiling water for 10–15 minutes, or until soft. Drain, cool, then mash in a large bowl.

2 Add the sour cream, 25g/1oz/2 tbsp butter, eggs and flour to the mashed potato and stir to combine thoroughly.

3 Turn the dough out on to a lightly floured surface and knead lightly.

4 Cut a slit down one side of each plum and remove the stone (pit), keeping the plum intact. Push a teaspoonful of the sugar and cinnamon mixture inside each.

5 On a well-floured surface, roll out the potato dough until it is about 5mm/¼ in thick. Divide into eight 10cm/4in squares.

6 Place a plum in the centre of each square, then bring up the dough and pinch the edges together to completely seal the plum in the dough.

7 Bring a pan of water to the boil, and add the dumplings in batches. Cook for 8 minutes, until they rise to the surface. Remove with a slotted spoon, transfer to a bowl and keep warm while you cook the remaining dumplings.

8 Heat the remaining butter in a large frying pan, add the breadcrumbs and fry until golden brown. Add the dumplings, turn to coat in the crumbs, then transfer to a serving plate and dust with icing sugar and cinnamon. Serve immediately.

Energy 510kcal/2147kJ; Protein 11.1g; Carbohydrate 72.6g, of which sugars 18.6g; Fat 21.6g, of which saturates 12.4g; Cholesterol 115mg; Calcium 147mg; Fibre 5.3g; Sodium 190mg.

Strawberry Mousse

A popular dessert in homes all over Poland, where strawberries are often grown in the garden,
this light fruit mousse is an excellent way to enjoy the strawberry season when they are at their
least expensive. You can also mix in some raspberries to this recipe for a little added tartness.

Serves 4

250g/9oz strawberries, hulled
90g/3³/₄ oz/¹/₂ cup caster (superfine)
  sugar
75ml/2¹/₂fl oz/¹/₃ cup white wine
75ml/2¹/₂fl oz/¹/₃ cup cold water
15ml/1 tbsp powdered gelatine or
  8 sheets leaf gelatine
60ml/4 tbsp boiling water
300ml/¹/₂ pint/1¹/₄ cups double (heavy)
  cream
fresh mint leaves, to decorate

1 Chop most of the strawberries, reserving
a few whole ones for decoration.

2 Transfer the chopped strawberries to a
food processor or blender, add the sugar
and wine, and blend to a smooth purée.

3 Put the cold water in a large bowl and
sprinkle over the gelatine (or immerse leaf
gelatine). Leave for 5 minutes, then add
the boiling water and leave for 2–3
minutes, or until the gelatine has
completely dissolved.

4 Add the strawberry mixture to the
gelatine and mix to combine. Chill for
about 30 minutes, or until the mixture
has thickened.

5 Lightly whip the cream until soft peaks
form, then gently fold into the thickened
strawberry mixture.

6 Spoon the mousse into serving glasses
and chill overnight in the refrigerator. Just
before serving, decorate with a halved
strawberry and some mint leaves.

Energy 478kcal/1987kJ; Protein 7.2g; Carbohydrate 29.4g, of which sugars 29.4g; Fat 40.4g, of which saturates 22.5g; Cholesterol 98mg; Calcium 62mg; Fibre 0.7g; Sodium 34mg

Wild Strawberries with Whipped Cream

Smaller and with a more intense flavour than their domestic cousins, wild strawberries require
little in the way of preparation. In this delectable dish they are simply served with
a dollop of slightly sweetened cream and garnished with mint.

Serves 4

475ml/16fl oz/2 cups double
    (heavy) cream
50g/2oz/¼ cup vanilla sugar
275g/10oz/2½ cups wild strawberries
fresh mint leaves, to decorate

1 Whip the double cream with the sugar
until soft peaks form.

2 Wash and hull the berries, then divide
among four serving dishes.

3 Spoon over the sweetened whipped
cream and decorate with fresh mint. Serve
immediately.

COOK'S TIP Tiny wild strawberries grow on
grassy banks, heaths and open woodland
and have a beautifully sweet flavour. The
plant, which has hairy stems and runners,
is low-growing and the leaves are
toothed, shiny and grow in groups of
three. Look for the ripe berries in mid- to
late summer.

Energy 657kcal/2712kJ; Protein 2.5g; Carbohydrate 19.2g, of which sugars 19.2g; Fat 63.8g, of which saturates 39.7g; Cholesterol 163mg; Calcium 76mg; Fibre 0.8g; Sodium 31mg.

Pashka

This classic Russian recipe is a special Easter treat. The fresh cheese and dried fruit dessert is made by mixing the ingredients together, putting them in a lined mould and letting all the liquid drain away, creating a firm, dome-shaped pudding. The traditional shape is a pyramid, made in a wooden mould, but a coffee filter-holder or a clean plastic flower pot work equally well. Paskha needs to be made a few days in advance.

Serves 6–8

500g/1¼lb/2½ cups ricotta cheese or cottage cheese
75g/3oz/6 tbsp unsalted butter, softened
275g/10oz/1½ cups caster (superfine) sugar
30ml/2 tbsp vanilla sugar
150ml/¼ pint/⅔ cup whipping cream
30ml/2 tbsp smetana or crème fraîche
2 egg yolks
40g/1½oz/generous ¼ cup raisins
grated rind 1 lemon
glacé (candied) orange or lemon and blanched almonds, to decorate

1 If using cottage cheese, push the cheese through a sieve (strainer). Put the ricotta or cottage cheese in a sieve and stand the sieve over a bowl. Leave to drain overnight in a cold place.

2 Line a clean 750ml/1¼ pints/3 cups coffee filter, or a flower pot with a drainage hole, with damp muslin (cheesecloth) allowing the edges of the muslin to overhang the edges.

3 Transfer the drained cheese into a bowl, add the butter, sugar and vanilla sugar and beat together until smooth.

4 Pour the whipping cream into a separate bowl and whisk until it forms soft peaks.

5 Stir the whipped cream into the cheese mixture, then add the smetana or crème fraîche and egg yolks. Whisk until fluffy and smooth. Add the raisins and grated lemon rind and stir together.

6 Spoon the mixture into the lined holder and fold the edges of the muslin into the centre. Cover with a small saucer that fits inside the holder and put a 500g/1¼lb weight on top. Stand in a bowl or soup plate and leave in a cold place, to drain, for one to three days.

7 Remove the weight and saucer. Unfold the muslin and very carefully turn the paskha out on to a serving plate. Remove the muslin. Serve the Paskha decorated with glacé fruits and nuts.

Energy 369kcal/1544kJ; Protein 9.3g; Carbohydrate 41.9g, of which sugars 41.9g; Fat 19.1g, of which saturates 11.5g; Cholesterol 100mg; Calcium 118mg; Fibre 0.1g; Sodium 256mg.

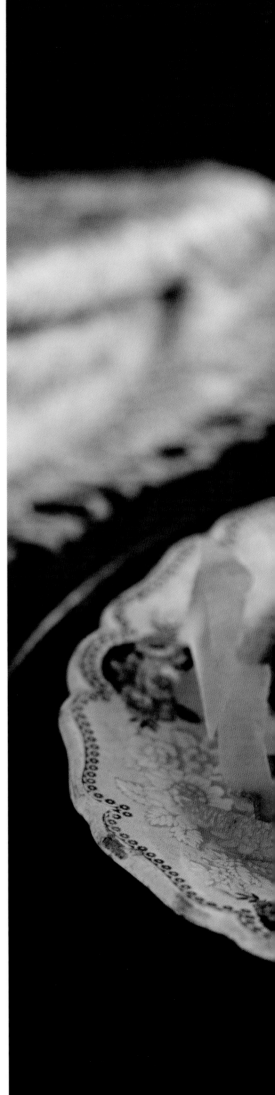

Pear and Raspberry Compote

This simple dessert combines seasonal fruit with typical Polish flavourings, cinnamon and cloves, to make a nutritious dish that can be eaten on its own or served with vanilla ice cream or whipped cream. Omit the raspberry liqueur if you are making this for children.

3 Add the pears to the pan and simmer gently over a low heat for 15–20 minutes, or until the pears are tender.

4 Lift the pears out of the pan with a slotted spoon and arrange on a serving dish. Leave to cool.

5 Meanwhile, remove the cinnamon and cloves from the syrup in the pan.

6 Blend half the raspberries in a food processor, then push through a sieve (strainer) set over a bowl and add the juices to the syrup in the pan.

7 Stir in the remaining raspberries and the raspberry liqueur.

8 Pour the sauce over the pears and leave to cool completely before chilling in the refrigerator. Alternatively, serve the compote warm.

Serves 4–6

900ml/1½ pint/3¾ cups water
350g/12oz/1¾ cups sugar
1 large cinnamon stick
4–5 whole cloves
900g/2lb pears, peeled, cored and
  cut into quarters
275g/10oz/1⅔ cups fresh
  raspberries, rinsed
60ml/4 tbsp raspberry liqueur

1 Place the water and sugar in a heavy pan and heat gently until the sugar has completely dissolved.

2 Add the cinnamon stick and cloves to the mixture, increase the heat and boil for 4 minutes, stirring, until the mixture becomes syrupy.

VARIATION If you don't have any raspberry liqueur use the same amount of brandy.

Energy 331kcal/1408kJ; Protein 1.6g; Carbohydrate 81.9g, of which sugars 81.9g; Fat 0.3g, of which saturates 0.1g; Cholesterol 0mg; Calcium 63mg; Fibre 4.8g; Sodium 11mg.

Dried Fruit Compote

Russian suppers almost always consist of three dishes – a soup, the main dish and a dessert.
To round off an evening meal, a compote is the most popular final course. You can mix the fruit
ingredients to suit your own taste or according to what is available.

Serves 4

250g/9oz/1¼ cups mixed dried fruits
including plums, pears, apples
and apricots
1.5 litres/2½ pints/6¼ cups water
2 cinnamon sticks or bay leaves
60ml/4 tbsp raisins
5ml/1 tsp finely grated lemon or
orange rind
30–45ml/2–3 tbsp sugar

VARIATION To make the Armenian version
of this compote, flavour it with a little
brandy in step 5, and add some roughly
chopped walnuts just before serving.

1 Keeping the fruit types separate, cut
any large pieces of fruit into smaller
chunks. Pour the water into a medium
pan and bring to the boil.

2 When the water is boiling, add the
plums, pears, cinnamon sticks or bay
leaves and return to the boil. Reduce the
heat and simmer for 10 minutes.

3 Add the apples and apricots to the pan
and simmer for a further 10 minutes. Add
the raisins and grated rind and simmer
for 5 minutes more.

4 Remove the fruit from the pan and
transfer to a heatproof serving bowl.

5 Add the sugar to the juices in the pan,
bring to the boil, then boil for 5 minutes,
stirring from time to time until the syrup
thickens slightly.

6 Pour the syrup over the fruit and serve
the compote warm or cold.

Energy 169kcal/721kJ; Protein 2.9g; Carbohydrate 41.1g, of which sugars 41.1g; Fat 0.4g, of which saturates 0g; Cholesterol 0mg; Calcium 57mg; Fibre 4.2g; Sodium 18mg.

Apricot Compote with Almonds

As in Russia, traditional winter desserts in Poland are made with dried fruits, such as plums, apples or apricots, because it was once difficult to buy the fresh variety out of season. This rich apricot compote is warming and nutritious, making it especially popular around Christmas.

Serves 6

350g/12oz/¹/₂ cup dried apricots,
   finely chopped
60ml/4 tbsp water
50g/2oz/¹/₄ cup caster (superfine) sugar
90ml/6 tbsp 95 per cent proof
   Polish spirit
75g/3oz/¹/₂ cup blanched almonds,
   chopped
75g/3oz/¹/₂ cup chopped candied peel
whipped cream and ground
   cinnamon, to serve

1 Place the chopped apricots and the water in a heavy pan, bring to the boil and simmer for 25 minutes.

2 Add the sugar and simmer for a further 10 minutes, or until you have a thick jam-like mixture.

3 Remove from the heat and stir in the Polish spirit, almonds and candied peel.

4 Spoon into serving dishes or glasses and leave to cool, then chill in the refrigerator for at least 2 hours. Just before serving, decorate with whipped cream and dust with cinnamon.

Energy 230kcal/973kJ; Protein 5.1g; Carbohydrate 38.3g, of which sugars 37.9g; Fat 7.4g, of which saturates 0.6g; Cholesterol 0mg; Calcium 93mg; Fibre 5.2g; Sodium 46mg.

Frozen Cranberries with Fudge Sauce

Cranberries are a special treat in Russia and this dessert makes the most of their vibrant, tart flavour by serving them with a deliciously sweet fudge sauce. It is worth making double quantities of the sauce and keeping the rest in a jar for pouring over ice cream.

Serves 4

150ml/¼ pint/⅔ cup whipping cream
100ml/3½fl oz/scant ½ cup milk
30–45ml/2–3 tbsp caster (superfine) sugar
45ml/3 tbsp treacle (molasses)
15g/½ oz/1 tbsp butter
425–500g/15oz–1¼lb/4–5 cups frozen cranberries or lingonberries

VARIATION If frozen cranberries are not available, try serving this fudge sauce with other frozen berries that have a tart rather than sweet flavour, such as a mixture of blackcurrants and raspberries.

1 Pour the cream and milk into a medium pan, add the sugar, treacle and butter, and stir together. Bring to the boil, reduce the heat and simmer for 10-15 minutes, until the mixture is light brown and thick.

2 Put the cranberries or lingonberries in a bowl and leave at room temperature for 10 minutes to thaw slightly. Divide the fruit among four small plates, pour over the fudge sauce and serve.

Energy 264kcal/1100kJ; Protein 2.7g; Carbohydrate 23.2g, of which sugars 23.2g; Fat 18.5g, of which saturates 11.5g; Cholesterol 49mg; Calcium 158mg; Fibre 3.3g; Sodium 70mg

Cranberry Juice

A decanter filled with home-made, sweet and sour cranberry juice is a necessity on the Russian party table, almost as much as the ice-cold vodka and the Russian champagne. These days it can be bought in supermarkets but the home-made variety has a much better taste.

3 Cover the bowl with clear film (plastic wrap) and put in the refrigerator.

4 Put the reserved strained berries in a pan, add the water and bring to the boil. Reduce the heat and simmer for 5 minutes. Strain the berries and discard them, but reserve the juice.

5 Pour the cranberry juices back into the pan. Add the sugar and simmer, stirring all the time, until the sugar has dissolved. Remove the pan from the heat and leave to cool.

6 When cool, mix the juice in the pan with the cold juice from the refrigerator.

7 Return to the refrigerator for 2–3 hours before pouring into a decanter or jug (pitcher) and keep cool until serving time. Serve in tall glasses with ice.

VARIATION Substitute lingonberries for the cranberries, if you wish.

Makes 1.5 litres/2½ pints/6¼ cups to serve 4

500g/1¼lb/5 cups cranberries
1 litre/2½ pints/6¼ cups water
100g/3¾oz/scant½ cup sugar
ice, to serve

1 Put the cranberries in a food processor and blend until smooth.

2 Strain the juice into a bowl, reserving the cranberries.

Energy 143kcal/615kJ; Protein 0.4g; Carbohydrate 37.1g, of which sugars 37.1g; Fat 0.4g, of which saturates 0g; Cholesterol 0mg; Calcium 26mg; Fibre 0g; Sodium 8mg

Honey and Cardamom Drink

It is a well-known fact that Russian gentlemen drink vodka with their food while the women prefer champagne but, for a variation, try this old Russian, alcohol-free honey and cardamom drink as an accompaniment to your Russian meal.

Makes 2 litres/3½ pints/8 cups

150g/5oz/generous ½ cup honey
2 litres/3½ pints/8 cups water
large pinch of dried hops
1 cardamom pod
5ml/1 tsp preserving sugar
10g/¼oz fresh yeast

1 Mix the honey and 350ml/12fl oz/ 1½ cups of the water in a pan. Bring to the boil, then lower the heat and simmer for 2–3 minutes, skimming if necessary.

5 Skim the surface, then pour through a sieve (strainer). Transfer into clean bottles. Store in the refrigerator and drink within a week. Serve chilled.

2 Mix the hops and 150ml/5fl oz/⅔ cup of the water in a separate pan. Bring to the boil, then lower the heat and simmer for 2–3 minutes. Add the honey water.

3 Bring the mixture to the boil and add the remaining water. Remove from the heat and leave the liquid to cool at room temperature until it is about 40°C/104°F.

4 Add the cardamom, sugar and yeast to the pan. Cover and set aside at 8–10°C/ 46–50°F, until the surface is foamy.

Energy 469kcal/1999kJ; Protein 4.2g; Carbohydrate 120.2g, of which sugars 119.8g; Fat 0.1g, of which saturates 0g; Cholesterol 0mg; Calcium 18mg; Fibre 0g; Sodium 22mg.

BAKING

Poles and Russians have a sweet tooth, which is amply satisfied by their many recipes for cakes, cookies and sweet treats. Although people make cakes at home, in Poland especially, bakeries take pride in elaborately decorated confections and pastries to eat as dessert or with coffee as a snack. Afternoon tea is a Russian speciality, with plenty of hot tea – still sometimes served from a samovar – little pots of jam eaten with a spoon, and perhaps a creamy layer cake.

The best cakes and pastries are traditionally made at Christmas and Easter, and both Russia and Poland have special recipes for these festive celebrations, including the traditional Russian Easter cake, kulitj, and Poland's dark, rich Poppy Seed Cake, makowiec. Many of these cakes are made with a yeast dough rather than baking powder, which gives a firm texture and a distinctive flavour that is ideal for combining with dried fruits and spices.

Angels' Wings

This old Polish recipe for deep-fried pastry strips dusted with sugar is traditionally made in large quantities on Fat Thursday, the last Thursday before Lent begins, but also for carnivals, where they are sold in huge quantities.

Serves 4–6

50g/2oz/¼ cup butter, softened
50g/2oz/¼ cup caster (superfine) sugar
3 egg yolks, plus 1 whole egg
250g/9oz/2¼ cups plain (all-purpose)
   flour, plus extra for dusting
2.5ml/½ tsp bicarbonate of soda
   (baking soda)
120ml/4fl oz/½ cup sour cream
pinch of salt
30ml/2 tbsp clear honey
45ml/3 tbsp 95 per cent proof Polish
   spirit or vodka, or rum
15ml/1 tbsp vinegar
vegetable oil, for deep-frying
icing (confectioners') sugar,
   for dusting

1 Beat the butter and sugar in a large bowl. Add the eggs, flour, bicarbonate of soda, sour cream, salt, honey, Polish spirit, vodka or rum, and the vinegar. Beat to combine and form a smooth dough.

COOK'S TIPS
Add a cube of bread to the hot oil to prevent it from spitting while the cookies are cooking.
   These cookies are delicious eaten warm or cold, but for the best result they should be eaten on the same day.

2 Roll out the dough on a floured surface to a rectangle,10cm/4in across, 3mm/⅛in thick. Cut into four 2.5cm/1in strips

3 Cut the dough lengthways, then cut each of these horizontally, on a slight slant, into pieces about 10cm/4in long.

4 Make a 4cm/1½in lengthways slit in the middle of each strip.Lift the lower end of the pastry and pass it through the slit. Gently pull it through the other side and downwards to create a twist.

5 Heat enough oil for deep-frying to 180°C/350°F/Gas 4, then add the pastry strips in batches of two and fry for 5–8 seconds, until they rise to the surface and are golden brown.

6 Remove from the oil immediately, using a slotted spoon, and drain on kitchen paper. Repeat the process with the remaining pastry. Transfer to a serving dish and dust generously with icing sugar.

Energy 364kcal/1527kJ; Protein 7.7g; Carbohydrate 45.7g, of which sugars 14g; Fat 16.2g, of which saturates 8.3g; Cholesterol 203mg; Calcium 104mg; Fibre 1.3g; Sodium 79mg.

Honey and Almond Cookies

These delectable spiced honey cookies are traditionally made at Christmas, although they are also eaten at other times of the year. They keep well if stored in an airtight container.

Makes 20

225g/8oz/1 cup clear honey
4 eggs, plus 2 egg whites
350g/12oz/3 cups plain (all-purpose) flour
5ml/1 tsp bicarbonate of soda (baking soda)
2.5ml/½ tsp freshly grated nutmeg
2.5ml/½ tsp ground ginger
2.5ml/½ tsp ground cinnamon
2.5ml/½ tsp ground cloves
20 blanched almond halves

4 Using a 4cm/½in cookie cutter, stamp out 20 rounds. Transfer the rounds to two lightly greased baking trays.

1 Beat together the honey and whole eggs until light and fluffy. Sift over the flour, bicarbonate of soda and spices, and beat to combine.

2 Gather the cookie dough into a ball, wrap in clear film (plastic wrap) and chill in the refrigerator for 1 hour, or overnight if making in advance.

3 Preheat the oven to 200°C/400°F/ Gas 6. Roll out the dough on a lightly floured surface to a thickness of 5mm/¼in.

COOK'S TIP Ancient Slavic tribes used to make cakes with honey, but it wasn't until the arrival of spices in the 17th century that Polish people starting making these sweet and delicious little morsels.

5 Beat the egg whites until soft peaks form. Brush the tops of the rounds with the egg white, then press an almond half into the centre of each one.

6 Place in the oven and bake for 15–20 minutes, or until they are a pale golden brown. Remove from the oven and allow to cool slightly before transferring to a wire cooling rack.

Energy 112kcal/473kJ; Protein 3.4g; Carbohydrate 22.6g, of which sugars 8.9g; Fat 1.5g, of which saturates 0.4g; Cholesterol 38mg; Calcium 33mg; Fibre 0.5g; Sodium 22mg.

Easter Pastry

Consumed in vast quantities at Easter in Poland, there are many different toppings for these sweet, decorative pastries, including nut paste, almonds, cheese, jams, raisins and coloured icing.

Serves 6

300g/11oz/2²/₃ cups plain (all-purpose) flour
115g/4oz/1 cup icing (confectioners') sugar
250g/9oz/generous 1 cup butter, softened
4 egg yolks

For the filling
500ml/17fl oz/2¹/₄ cups double (heavy) cream
400g/14oz/2 cups caster (superfine) sugar
1 vanilla pod (bean)
400g/14oz/1³/₄ cups unsalted butter, cut into cubes
about 150g/5oz each of almonds and dried fruits, to decorate

1 Sift the flour and icing sugar into a large bowl. Add the softened butter and egg yolks, and mix thoroughly to make a smooth dough.

2 Form the dough into a ball, cover with clear film (plastic wrap) and chill in the refrigerator for 45 minutes.

3 Preheat the oven to 220°C/425°F/Gas 7. Grease a rectangular baking tray. Roll out the pastry and cut a piece that is the same size as the tray. Place on the tray.

4 Cut the remaining pastry into strips and join together. Brush a little water around the edge of the pastry base. Twist the strip of pastry and place around the edge.

5 Bake the pastry base in the oven for about 20 minutes, or until golden brown. Leave to cool slightly, then carefully lift it out on to a large serving dish and cool completely.

6 To make the filling, pour the cream into a heavy pan, then add the sugar and vanilla pod. Gently bring to the boil, then boil for about 5 minutes, stirring constantly, until the mixture is thick.

7 To test whether it is ready, spoon a small amount on to a cold plate. It should set quickly. Remove from the heat and leave to cool slightly.

8 Remove the vanilla pod, then beat in the butter while the cream mixture is still warm. Spread the mixture inside the pastry case, smoothing the top.

9 While the filling is still warm, decorate the top with almonds and dried fruits. You can either simply sprinkle the nuts and fruit over, or you may like to create a pattern.

COOK'S TIP The pastry will keep for up to 3 days in an airtight container in the refrigerator.

VARIATION You can decorate the top with anything you like. Good choices might include crystallized (candied) fruits, drizzles of chocolate, sweets (candies) or coloured icing (frosting). Children, in particular, will enjoy decorating the top.

Energy 1989kcal/8270kJ; Protein 14.9g; Carbohydrate 149.4g, of which sugars 110.6g; Fat 152.2g, of which saturates 86.5g; Cholesterol 480mg; Calcium 270mg; Fibre 4g; Sodium 703mg.

Polish-style Doughnuts

These hot, sweet doughnuts, generously filled with rosehip preserve, are traditionally eaten on Shrove Tuesday, before the restrictions of Lent begin. They are a great favourite throughout Poland. Although they require a little effort to make, the end result is well worth it.

Serves 6

60g/2¼oz fresh yeast
115g/4oz caster (superfine) sugar
500g/1¼lb strong white bread flour,
    plus extra for dusting
250ml/8fl oz/1 cup full-fat (whole)
    milk, slightly warmed
8 eggs, separated
75ml/5 tbsp 95 per cent proof Polish
    spirit or vodka, or rum
15ml/1 tbsp grated lemon rind
pinch of salt
115g/4oz/½ cup butter, melted

For the filling
200g/7oz/⅔ cup rosehip preserve
1kg/2¼lb/6 cups lard or oil
vanilla-flavoured icing (confectioners')
    sugar (see Cook's Tip)

1 Cream the yeast with 15ml/1 tbsp sugar, then add 115g/4oz/1 cup flour and beat well. Gradually add the warmed milk and mix to a smooth batter.

2 Cover with a clean, damp dish towel and leave in a warm place for 30 minutes, or until foamy and risen.

3 Beat the egg yolks with the remaining sugar until thick and creamy.

4 Sift the remaining flour into a separate bowl, then add the egg yolks and sugar, the yeast mixture, the Polish spirit, vodka or rum, lemon rind and salt.

5 Stir to combine, then knead in the bowl until bubbles begin to form. Pour in the melted butter and knead for a few more minutes, or until firm and elastic. Cover with a damp dish towel, then put in a warm place and leave the dough to rise for 30 minutes.

6 On a lightly floured surface, roll out the dough to a thickness of 1cm/½in. Using a 4cm/1½in cutter, cut out rounds. Gather together any pieces of dough that are not used, then reroll and cut out more rounds. Continue in this way until all the dough has been used.

7 To create the filling, place 2.5ml/½ tsp rosehip preserve in the centre of each round, then bring up and seal the edges to make a ball. Cover with a clean dish towel and leave to rise for 1 hour.

8 Melt the lard in a large, heavy, pan and heat until very hot. The temperature is correct when a small amount of the dough rises immediately when dropped into the fat.

9 Carefully lower the balls into the hot fat, two or three at a time. Fry them on one side for about 2 minutes, or until golden brown, then turn over and fry on the other side for about 2 minutes.

10 Test to see if they are done by inserting a skewer a little way in (taking care not to pierce to the centre); if it comes out clean, the dough is cooked.

11 Remove the doughnuts from the fryer with a slotted spoon and drain on kitchen paper. Fry the remaining balls in batches.

12 As they are cooked, allow the balls to cool slightly, then dredge them in icing sugar. Serve immediately.

COOK'S TIP You can flavour icing (confectioners') sugar with vanilla by putting some of the sugar in a sealable jar and adding a vanilla pod (bean). Leave for 2 weeks for the flavour to develop.

Energy 883kcal/3703kJ; Protein 18g; Carbohydrate 109.9g, of which sugars 46.4g; Fat 41.5g, of which saturates 19.4g; Cholesterol 312mg; Calcium 223mg; Fibre 2.6g; Sodium 241mg

Plum Cake

This bread-like plum cake is a traditional harvest treat in Poland, and is still enjoyed today. It freezes well, so if you have a glut of plums make a couple of these cakes for enjoying during the winter months!

Serves 6

225g/8oz/2 cups strong white
  bread flour
7g/¼oz dried yeast
50g/2oz/¼ cup caster (superfine)
  sugar, plus 30ml/2 tbsp
150ml/¼ pint/⅔ cup lukewarm water
50g/2oz/⅓ cup cream cheese
50g/2oz/¼ cup unsalted butter
grated rind of 1 lemon
2 eggs, lightly beaten
450g/1lb plums
cream or ice cream, to serve
  (optional)

For the topping
25g/1oz/2 tbsp butter, melted
15ml/1 tbsp demerara (raw) sugar

VARIATION Any kind of plums can be used for this cake, including the golden yellow type. You can also use fresh apricots or even tinned pineapple when fresh plums are out of season.

1 Put 30ml/2 tbsp flour, the yeast and half the sugar in a bowl. Gradually stir in half the water, then cover with a clean, damp dish towel and put in a warm place and leave for about 30 minutes, or until the mixture starts to rise.

2 Cream together the cream cheese and butter, then stir in the lemon rind and beaten egg. Put the remaining flour and sugar in a second bowl. Add the creamed mixture to the flour and sugar.

3 Add the remaining water to the flour and cream mixture and beat until smooth, for about 15 minutes.

4 Grease a 20cm/8in springform cake tin (pan) and put half the mixture in it.

5 Halve the plums and remove the stones (pits). Dust the plums with a little caster sugar and place half on top of the dough. Add the remaining dough, then place the remaining plums on top, cut sides down.

6 Cover with a damp dish towel and leave to rise in warm place for about 40 minutes, or until doubled in size. Preheat the oven to 200°C/400°F/Gas 6.

7 Bake the cake for 30 minutes. Remove from the oven and brush with melted butter for the topping. Sprinkle with demerara sugar, then return to the oven and bake for a further 15 minutes.

8 Remove from the oven and allow to cool slightly before turning out. Serve warm or cold with cream or ice cream.

Energy 311kcal/1308kJ; Protein 6.4g; Carbohydrate 44.5g, of which sugars 15.9g; Fat 13.2g, of which saturates 7.4g; Cholesterol 89mg; Calcium 86mg; Fibre 2.4g; Sodium 102mg

Cottage Cheese Pancakes

Crispy and delicious, these little pancakes – known as blinis – are very popular in Russia as a dessert. They are traditionally served warm, with fresh berries and smetana. Blinis are used for savoury as well as sweet toppings, and can be eaten with almost anything.

2 Heat the oil in a non-stick frying pan, over a medium heat. Pour a tablespoon of the batter into the pan, adding another one or two spoonfuls, depending on the space in the pan.

3 Fry the pancakes for 1 minute then, using a metal spatula, flip them and cook the other side for a further 1 minute.

4 Transfer the pancakes to a warmed plate and keep warm until you have cooked all the batter.

5 Serve warm with cream, smetana or crème fraîche and fresh berries.

COOK'S TIP You can prepare the pancakes in advance and heat them in the oven at 110°C/ 225°F/Gas ¼ for about 5 minutes, until warm, before serving.

Serves 4

225g/8oz/1 cup cottage cheese or ricotta cheese
45ml/3 tbsp plain white (all-purpose) flour
1 egg, plus 1 egg yolk
30ml/2 tbsp vanilla sugar
15ml/1 tbsp icing (confectioners') sugar
30ml/2 tbsp rapeseed (canola) oil
whipped double (heavy) cream, smetana or crème fraîche and fresh berries, such as raspberries, blueberries or redcurrants, to serve

1 Put the cottage or ricotta cheese in a food processor. Add the flour, egg yolk, vanilla sugar and icing sugar and process until smooth.

Energy 171kcal/716kJ; Protein 4.2g; Carbohydrate 20.7g, of which sugars 12.1g; Fat 8.5g, of which saturates 1.5g; Cholesterol 98mg; Calcium 39mg; Fibre 0.4g; Sodium 45mg.

Polish Honey Cake

Many Eastern European cakes, like this Polish one, which is known as 'Tort Orzechowy', are sweetened with honey and made with ground nuts and breadcrumbs instead of flour. This gives them their characteristic rich, moist texture.

Serves 12

15g/½oz/1 tbsp unsalted butter, melted and cooled

115g/4oz/2 cups slightly dry fine white breadcrumbs

175g/6oz/¾ cup set honey, plus extra to serve

50g/2oz/¼ cup soft light brown sugar

4 eggs, separated

115g/4oz/1 cup hazelnuts, chopped and toasted, plus extra to decorate

COOK'S TIP The cake will rise during cooking but then sink slightly as it cools – this is quite normal.

3 Mix the remaining breadcrumbs with the hazelnuts and fold into the egg yolk and honey mixture. Whisk the egg whites in a separate bowl, until stiff, then fold in to the other ingredients, half at a time.

4 Spoon the mixture into the tin. Bake for 40–45 minutes, until golden brown. Leave to cool in the tin for 5 minutes, then turn out on to a wire rack to cool. Scatter over nuts and drizzle with extra honey to serve.

1 Preheat the oven to 180°C/350°F/Gas 4. Brush a 1.75 litre/3 pint/7½ cup fluted brioche tin (pan), with the melted butter. Top with 15g/½oz/¼ cup breadcrumbs.

2 Put the honey in a large bowl, set over a pan of barely simmering water. When the honey liquifies, add the sugar and egg yolks. Whisk until light and frothy. Remove from the heat.

Energy 188kcal/791kJ; Protein 4.6g; Carbohydrate 23.5g, of which sugars 16.1g; Fat 9.1g, of which saturates 1.6g; Cholesterol 66mg; Calcium 39mg; Fibre 0.8g; Sodium 108mg

Russian Easter Cake

A traditional Russian Easter dinner almost always starts with zakuski and will finish with kulitj, a cake flavoured with cardamom and vanilla, which is often blessed by the priest.

Serves 8–10

200ml/7fl oz/scant 1 cup milk
350–425g/12–15oz/3–3²/₃ cups plain
  white (all-purpose) flour
185g/6¹/₂oz/scant 1 cup caster
  (superfine) sugar
large pinch easy-blend (rapid-rise)
  dried yeast
115g/4oz/¹/₂ cup butter, plus extra
  for greasing
15ml/1 tbsp vanilla sugar
2.5ml/¹/₂ tsp salt
5ml/1 tsp ground cardamom
3 egg yolks
150g/5oz/1 cup raisins

COOK'S TIPS If preferred, the mixture can be made in a large bowl, rather than in a food processor. Cover the cake with baking parchment, halfway through the cooking time, if it shows signs of becoming too brown.

1 Pour the milk into a small pan and heat until warm to the finger. Remove from the heat. Put 325g/11¹/₂oz/scant 3 cups of the flour, half of the sugar and the yeast in a food processor and mix together.

2 Add the warm milk to the processor and mix until combined. Cover and leave to rise in a warm place for about 30 minutes, until doubled in size.

3 Melt the butter, then mix with the remaining sugar, the vanilla sugar, salt and cardamom.

4 Reserve 15ml/1 tbsp butter mixture, then add the rest to the risen dough and mix together until smooth. Add the egg yolks, one at a time, until combined.

5 Generously grease a 17cm/6¹/₂in round, 10cm/4in deep cake tin (pan) or 1.5 litre/2¹/₂ pint/6¹/₄ cup soufflé dish with butter.

6 Transfer the dough to a lightly floured surface and knead in the remaining flour and the raisins. Put the dough into the prepared tin or dish, cover and leave to rise for 30 minutes.

7 Preheat the oven to 180°C/350°F/Gas 4. Brush the dough with half of the reserved melted butter. Bake in the oven for 30 minutes. Brush with the remaining melted butter and bake for a further 20–30 minutes, until risen and golden brown.

8 Remove from the tin or dish and transfer to a wire rack to cool.

Energy 346kcal/1459kJ; Protein 5.3g; Carbohydrate 57.9g, of which sugars 31.3g; Fat 12g, of which saturates 6.7g; Cholesterol 86mg; Calcium 99mg; Fibre 1.4g; Sodium 92mg.

Polish Easter Cake

Served everywhere on Easter Sunday, this bread-like cake is baked in a bundt tin that is said to resemble an old woman's skirts. This gives it the name babka, Polish for grandmother. Finished with a rum or lemon and sugar glaze, it is as pretty as it is delicious.

Serves 4–6

15ml/1 tbsp dried yeast
120ml/4fl oz/½ cup sour cream, slightly warmed
225g/8oz/2 cups strong white bread flour, plus extra for dusting
75g/3oz/⅓ cup sugar
3 eggs, lightly beaten
15ml/1 tbsp vanilla extract
2.5ml/½ tsp almond extract
15ml/1 tbsp grated lemon rind
15ml/1 tbsp grated orange rind
40g/1½oz/¼ cup raisins

For the icing
50g/2oz/½ cup icing (confectioners') sugar
about 15ml/1 tbsp rum or lemon juice

1 In a bowl, combine the yeast with the sour cream. Sift half the flour into a large bowl, then stir in the sugar.

2 Add the yeast mixture, mix, then cover the bowl with a clean, damp dish towel and leave in a warm place for 1 hour, or until doubled in size.

3 Add the remaining flour with the remaining ingredients. Mix to combine, then transfer to a lightly floured surface and knead for 10 minutes, or until smooth and elastic.

4 Grease and flour a 23cm/9in bundt tin (pan). Place the dough in the mould, cover with a damp dish towel and leave in a warm place for 1 hour, or until doubled in size.

5 Meanwhile, heat the oven to 200°C/400°F/Gas 6. Put the cake in the oven and bake for 1 hour, or until the top is golden brown.

6 Leave the cake to cool slightly in the tin, then turn out on to a wire rack until completely cool.

7 Sift the icing sugar into a large bowl and add the rum or lemon juice. Stir to make a smooth icing with a pouring consistency, add a little more liquid if necessary.

8 Place a plate underneath the cake on the wire rack and drizzle the icing over the cake. Leave the icing to set, then slice the cake and serve.

Energy 299kcal/1262kJ; Protein 7.5g; Carbohydrate 54.4g, of which sugars 25.8g; Fat 7.3g, of which saturates 3.4g; Cholesterol 107mg; Calcium 99mg; Fibre 1.3g; Sodium 50mg.

Poppy Seed Cake

This dark, dense cake, made from a sweet dough rolled with an aromatic poppy-seed filling, is made throughout the year in Poland, but especially at Christmas and Easter. Known as makowiec, it has a distinctive taste, as well as appearance, and is absolutely delicious. The cake's filling needs to be soaked for three hours, so give yourself enough time for this.

Serves 6

45ml/3 tbsp sour cream
50g/2oz fresh yeast or 2 packets active
  dried yeast
400g/14oz/3½ cups strong white
  bread flour
115g/4oz/1 cup icing (confectioners')
  sugar, plus extra for dredging
15ml/1 tbsp grated lemon rind
pinch of salt
150g/5oz/10 tbsp butter, melted
  and cooled
3 eggs, beaten

For the filling

500g/1¼lb/5 cups poppy seeds
200g/7oz/scant 1 cup butter
200g/7oz/1 cup sugar
115g/4oz/1 cup chopped almonds
30ml/2 tbsp currants
60ml/4 tbsp honey
45ml/3 tbsp finely chopped
  candied peel
1 vanilla pod (bean)
3 egg whites, lightly beaten
15ml/1 tbsp rum or cognac

1 To make the filling, place the poppy seeds in a fine mesh sieve (strainer) and rinse under cold running water. Boil a kettle and pour boiling water over the seeds. Drain, then transfer to a bowl. Pour over enough boiling water to cover, then leave to soak for at least 3 hours.

2 Drain the poppy seeds, then grind as finely as possible in a blender or with a pestle and mortar.

3 Melt the butter in a pan, then add the sugar, almonds, currants, honey and candied peel. Scrape the seeds from the vanilla pod into the mixture with the poppy seeds, stir to combine, then fry gently for 20 minutes.

4 Remove from the heat, leave to cool, then stir in the beaten egg whites and rum or cognac.

5 To make the dough, mix the sour cream with the yeast in a small bowl. Sift the flour into a large bowl, then stir in the icing sugar, lemon rind and salt.

6 Make a well in the middle of the dry ingredients, then pour in the cooled melted butter, beaten eggs and the yeast mixture.

7 Mix to combine, then turn out on to a lightly floured surface and knead for about 10 minutes, or until smooth and elastic.

8 Roll out the dough to a thickness of about 5mm/¼ in, then spread evenly with the poppy-seed mixture.

9 Roll up the dough to form a loaf shape and place on a greased baking tray. Cover with a clean, damp dish towel and put in a warm place to rise for 45 minutes.

10 About 10 minutes before the end of the rising time, preheat the oven to 190°C/375°F/Gas 5.

11 Pierce the top of the loaf with a large sharp knife, then put in the hot oven and bake for 45–50 minutes, or until golden brown. Transfer to a wire tray and cool.

12 When the cake is completely cool, use a sieve (strainer) to dredge the cake heavily with icing sugar until completely coated. The cake is now ready to be sliced and served.

COOK'S TIP When the cake is dredged very heavily in sifted icing (confectioners') sugar, it has a festive, frosted effect that makes it perfect as an alternative Christmas cake.

Energy 1302kcal/5437kJ; Protein 21.9g; Carbohydrate 124.4g, of which sugars 72.9g; Fat 83.2g, of which saturates 35.9g; Cholesterol 224mg; Calcium 438mg; Fibre 6.6g; Sodium 459mg.

Walnut Gâteau

This fabulously oppulent walnut cake from Poland is deliciously moist, sandwiched together with a delectable cream, which is flavoured with coffee, vanilla and a dash of Polish spirit, vodka or cognac.

Serves 6–8

8 eggs, separated
125g/5oz/²⁄₃ cup caster (superfine) sugar
165g/5¹⁄₂oz/scant 1¹⁄₂ cups walnuts, finely chopped
15g/1 tbsp self-raising (self-rising) flour, sifted

For the filling
75g/3oz/²⁄₃ cup icing (confectioners') sugar, plus extra for dusting (optional)
165g/5¹⁄₂oz/scant 1¹⁄₂ cups walnuts, finely chopped
300ml/¹⁄₂ pint/1¹⁄₄ cups double (heavy) cream
175ml/6fl oz/³⁄₄ cup 95 per cent proof Polish spirit or vodka, or cognac
¹⁄₂ vanilla pod (bean)
30ml/2 tbsp cold strong coffee

1 Preheat the oven to 190°C/375°F/Gas 5. Grease and line a 20cm/8in cake tin (pan). Beat the egg yolks with the sugar until thick and creamy. Stir in the nuts, then fold in the flour.

2 In a separate bowl, beat the egg whites until soft peaks form. Fold a tablespoonful of the egg white into the egg yolk mixture to loosen it, then fold in the remaining egg whites. Pour into the tin and bake for 40–45 minutes, or until risen and brown. Allow to cool, then turn out on to a wire rack.

3 To make the filling, combine the icing sugar and chopped walnuts. Whip the cream until soft peaks form, then fold in the Polish spirit, vodka or cognac with the walnuts and sugar.

4 Split the vanilla pod lengthways, then scrape the seeds into the cream. Add the coffee and stir to combine.

5 Split the cake into two layers. Spread one half with two-thirds of the filling, then position the other layer on top. Spread the remaining cream on top and dust with icing sugar, if using.

Energy 697kcal/2889kJ; Protein 13.2g; Carbohydrate 29.5g, of which sugars 27.9g; Fat 54g, of which saturates 16.4g; Cholesterol 242mg; Calcium 106mg; Fibre 1.5g; Sodium 89mg.

Chocolate and Almond Cake

This rich, dense chocolate cake is filled with a sweet almond paste and coated in glossy dark chocolate icing. It is often served in Poland as a snack with coffee, or as an indulgent dessert for a special occasion. Store in an airtight container in the refrigerator.

Serves 6

6 eggs, separated
115g/4oz/1 cup caster (superfine) sugar
150g/5oz/1¼ cups unsweetened cocoa powder
150g/5oz/1¼ cups ground almonds

For the almond paste
150g/5oz/1¼ cups caster (superfine) sugar
120ml/4fl oz/½ cup water
150g/5oz/1¼ cups ground almonds
15–30ml/1–2 tbsp lemon juice, to taste
½ vanilla pod (bean)

For the icing
115g/4oz good-quality dark (bittersweet) chocolate (minimum 70 per cent cocoa solids), chopped
25g/1oz/2 tbsp unsalted butter, cubed
120ml/4fl oz/½ cup double (heavy) cream
50g/2oz/½ cup icing (confectioners') sugar, sifted

1 Separate each of the 6 eggs, placing the yolks in one large bowl and the whites in another.

2 Add the sugar to the bowl containing the egg yolks. Beat together until the mixture is thick and creamy, then add the cocoa powder and ground almonds, and gently fold together.

3 Grease and line a 20cm/8in springform cake tin (pan). Preheat the oven to 200°C/400°F/Gas 6.

4 Whisk the egg whites until stiff peaks form. Using a metal spoon, gently fold a tablespoonful of the egg white into the egg yolk mixture to loosen it slightly, then fold in the remaining egg whites.

5 Spoon the cake mixture into the tin and smooth the top. Bake for 1 hour, or until a skewer inserted into the centre comes out clean. Leave the cake to cool completely in the tin.

6 To make the almond paste, put the sugar and water in a heavy pan, then heat gently, stirring occasionally, until the sugar has completely dissolved.

7 Bring the sugar and water to the boil and boil for 4–6 minutes, or until a thick syrup forms. Stir in the ground almonds and bring back to the boil.

8 Transfer the paste to a bowl, then add the lemon juice. Split the vanilla pod in half and scrape the seeds into the bowl. Mix well to combine.

9 When the cake has cooled, remove it from the tin and carefully slice into two even layers. Spread the bottom half with the almond paste, then sandwich the second half on top.

10 To make the icing, melt the chocolate and butter in a heatproof bowl over a pan of gently simmering water, ensuring the water does not touch the bowl.

11 Remove the bowl from the heat and gently stir in the cream, then add the sifted icing sugar and stir to combine.

12 Cover the top of the cake with the chocolate icing. Leave to set, then serve cut into slices.

VARIATION If you are making this for a dinner party, you might want to add a splash of rum or brandy to the chocolate icing for an added touch of indulgence.

Energy 892kcal/3726kJ; Protein 23g; Carbohydrate 73.7g, of which sugars 69.3g; Fat 58.4g, of which saturates 19g; Cholesterol 228mg; Calcium 226mg; Fibre 7.2g; Sodium 349mg.

Useful Addresses

AUSTRALIA
Russian Tidbits
113 Koornang Road
Carnegie VIC 3163, Greater Melbourne
Tel: (03) 9572 3911

V & V (Restaurant)
136 Koornang Road, Carnegie VIC 3163
Tel: 613 9568 1621

Polka Deli
22 Post Office Place, Glenroy, Melbourne
Tel: (03) 9304 4700

CANADA
Zia's Deli & Café
2773 Barnet Hwy, Coquitlam
B.C. V3B 1C2, Greater Vancouver
Tel: 604-944-2747
www.coquitlamdeli.com

Wendy's Gourmet Perogies
4532 99th St NW,
Edmonton, AB T66 5H5
Tel: 780-432-3893

NEW ZEALAND
St Petersburg Restaurant
1/333 Parnell Road, Parnell, Auckland
Tel: 09 373 3179
www.russianrestaurant.co.nz

UK
The Apple Tree Polish Deli
18 Lytton Road, New Barnet EN5 5BY
www.theappletreedeli.com

Babushka (Derbyshire)
71 West Bars, Chesterfield S40 1BA
Tel: 01246 555336
www.babushkauk.com

P & K Deli
145 Bond Street, Blackpool
Lancashire FY4 1HG
Tel: 01253 341001
www.pkdeli.co.uk

St Petersburg Restaurant (Manchester)
68 Sackville Street
Central Manchester M1 3NJ
Tel: 01612 366333
www.russiancuisine.co.uk

USA
Ostrowski's Famous Polish Sausage
524 S. Washington St
Fells Point, MD
Tel: 410-327-8935

Polana Inc. (online Polish food)
3512 N. Kostner Ave
Chicago, Illinois 60641
Tel: 773 545 4900
www.polana.com

Green Store Polish Deli
517 McCabe Ave,
Bradley Beach, NJ
Tel: 732-988-4291

Elizabeth's Polish Deli
4108 US Highway 19,
New Port Richey, FL
Tel: 727-842-8535

Pulaski Meat Market
1201 Lenox Ave,
Utica, NY
Tel: 315-732-8007

Moscow on the Hudson
801 West 81st Street,
New York, NY 10033
Tel: 212-740-7397
www.moscowonhudson.com

Babushka
62 Washington Street, Brighton,
MA 02135
Tel: 617-731-9739

Siberia Food Market
259 Main Street, Nashua, NH 03060
Tel: 603-883-4110

Russian Café and Deli
1712 Winchester Blvd,

Campbell, CA 95008
Tel: 408-379-6680

Russianfoods.com
DGV International Inc.
30–60 Review Avenue,
New York, NY 11101
Tel: 917-975-0471
www.russianfoods.com

Markys Gourmet Food Store
687 NE 79th Street, Miami, FL 33138
Tel: 305-758-9288
www.markys.com

Slavic Shop
1080 Saratoga Avenue,
San Jose, CA 95129
Tel: 408-615-8533

Moscow Deli
3015 Harbour Blvd,
Costa Mesa, CA 92626
Tel: 714-546-3354
www.moscowdeli.com

Russian General Store
9629 Hillcroft Street,
Houston, TX 77096
Tel: 713-721-7595

Berezka International Food Store
1215 Commonwealth Avenue
Allston, MA 02134
Tel: 617-787-2837

Bz Bee Market
2322 S El Camino Real
San Mateo, CA 94403
Tel: 650-627-9303

Index

PICTURE ACKNOWLEDGEMENTS
All photography by Jon Whitaker, apart
from the following:
Alamy: 15bl, 17tl, 20t, 21b, 22b, 24t &
bl. Corbis: 14t all, 15t, 15br, 16, 17b, 10
br, 21tr. Istock: pp6, 7tl, 8, 9, 10t, 11, 12,
23t13, 18tr, 19t & b, 20bl, 28t, 30t, 32t,
34t, 38t & bl.
Rex Features: pp18tl & b, 24m, 25b.

TANK

HEAVY METAL AT WAR

PHILIP KAPLAN

Skyhorse Publishing

Skyhorse Publishing books may be purchased in bulk at special discounts for sales promotion, corporate gifts, fund-raising, or educational purposes. Special editions can also be created to specifications. For details, contact the Special Sales Department, Skyhorse Publishing, 307 West 36th Street, 11th Floor, New York, NY 10018 or info@skyhorsepublishing.com.

Skyhorse® and Skyhorse Publishing® are registered trademarks of Skyhorse Publishing, Inc.®, a Delaware corporation.

Visit our website at www.skyhorsepublishing.com.

10 9 8 7 6 5 4 3 2 1

Library of Congress Cataloging-in-Publication Data is available on file.

Cover design by Rain Saukas
Front cover photo: iStock

Back cover photographs courtesy of Philip Kaplan

Previously published as *Chariots of Fire*

Print ISBN: 978-1-5107-0260-8
Ebook ISBN: 978-1-5107-0261-5

Printed in China

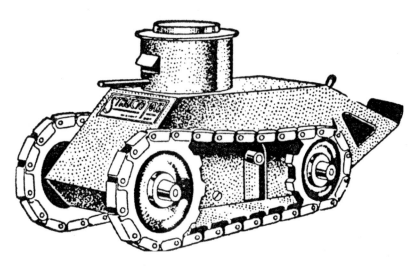

CONTENTS

D-DAY

25P   ADVANCING INLAND FROM OUISTREHAM   6 JUNE 1944

TRAVELLING FORTRESS

She was defined as an enclosed, heavily armored combat vehicle mounted with cannon and guns and movable on caterpillar treads. She was and is the tank.

Mechanized land warfare began with the chariot, the predecessor of the armored car, whose ancestry is much older than that of the tank. Like the tank, the early chariot was operated as a military vehicle by a team or crew consisting of a driver, a bowman who could also hurl a javelin when necessary, and a shield bearer to afford some protection for the others. Archeologists in Russia have established that Bronze Age warriors in Central Asia used chariots as mobile platforms from which they shot arrows and threw javelins at their enemies.

The Hyksos, a little-known warrior race from the region now called Kurdistan, are thought to be the first to have fought using chariots of war. They moved into northern Egypt in 1700 BC to establish a 400-year dynasty with the key to their success being their chariot-based mobile striking force. Eventually, however, they were displaced by a more powerful force, the Egyptian army. The great armies of the Pharoah Thutmose III in 1479 BC, of the Assyrian army in the ninth century BC, and of King Solomon in c. 972-931 were all renowned for their might and the capability of their chariot war units.

It was Cyrus, King of Persia in the sixth century BC, who was credited with the development of the chariot into a first-class fighting vehicle. His long-axled, two-man design was strong and more resistant to overturning than any previous chariot. The axles were mounted with protruding scythes and its horses protected by armor. His chariot was light and extremely fast. And there was also a much larger, wagon-like version which featured a tower-mounted battering ram and had capacity for twenty men. Cyrus believed his forerunner of the tank to have good battlefield potential.

When Alexander the Great invaded India in 327 BC he encountered the forces of the rajah Porus and a battle line of 200 large and powerful elephants. The massive beasts had been made more menacing by the attachment of swords to their trunks and lances to either side of their bodies. These elephants were employed as "infantry tanks" to break the enemy lines and enable supporting cavalry to get through to the opposing forces. A howdah, or fighting cage, was mounted on the back of each animal and carried up to four fighting men. Undoubtedly, the sight of these huge "living tanks" terrified the opposing army and its horses. Alexander was so greatly impressed with the power and presence of the elephants in that military context that he acquired a large number of them for his own force.

The military commander Hannibal is the best-known proponent of elephants in a primary combat role, using them very effectively until his ultimate defeat in battle. At Zama in 202 BC, his Roman opponent Scipio outsmarted him. Hannibal had planned on using his eighty armed elephants in a massive, frightening charge to breach the Roman center, but as the beasts neared the Roman line, the blare of many horns and trumpets rose from the Roman side. Hannibal's elephants were at first bewildered and then terrified. In panic they turned away and retreated through Hannibal's own soldiers. As Alexander had been intrigued by the possibilities the animals seemed

to offer in a combat role, so too were the Romans who soon were to incorporate them into their armies, employing them for the next 200 years.

When the legions of Julius Caesar arrived in what they were referring to as Brittania in 55 BC, they ran into a rude welcome of spear attacks by men in light chariots. According to the Roman leader, the British charioteers drove across the battlefield at great speed, hurling javelins at their enemies from a distance. The attacks caused confusion and disorganization among the Roman ranks. Then the British javelin throwers dismounted to attack their enemies on foot. The chariot drivers meanwhile continued on and then brought their horses to a halt facing away from the action and ready to carry off their comrades in a rapid getaway should it be necessary. These attacks took a high toll of the Romans in both battle casualties and

psychologically. It is thought by some that this demoralizing effect may have led to Caesar's withdrawal from Britain. However, the use of chariots in such roles was, by this time, in decline. Warring societies had concluded that armed soldiers on horseback were of greater value. In all probability, the concept of a man on horseback to gain an intelligence advantage on the battlefield long predates the military use of the chariot. The mounted rider had a height advantage for increased observational capability as well as the speed to approach and escape from enemy forces. As the development of body armor for warriors on the battlefield progressed, their horses were being bred to take a more refined role in combat, and the perceived value of the chariot declined. The horse-mounted cavalry soldier had now become an army's means of breaking the ranks of opposing infantry forces. In the fourteenth century, however, came the

development of firearms, and the function of the cavalry horse in providing mobility for the fighting man was on the way out. Overloaded as both the animal and rider had become with the increasingly heavier armor needed for their protection against the shot from guns, the horse was soon unable to carry his rider efficiently.

So, in the next century, the mounted soldier began discarding his weighty armor as mobility and battlefield agility to evade the missiles of the enemy were coming into favor. The thinking turned to the value of substantial firepower as the way to battlefield success and survival. Though mounted cavalry were an essential part of all armies through the First World War, military planners were, for the most part, looking toward the prospect of a strong, well-made vehicle that would offer ample protection for its crew along with the capability to effectively attack the enemy.

One of the first such vehicles was that of the Italian scientist and physician Guido da Vigevano who, in 1335, designed a windmill-powered cart with an exposed wooden gear train. His device had no real future in development, being wholly dependent on wind for power. But a century and a half later, another Italian, the universal genius Leonardo da Vinci, prepared sketches suggesting development of a dramatic armored fighting vehicle, a bowl-shaped four-wheeled armored car with mounted gun positions and covered with an iron armor plating and a sort of parasol roof. The vehicle was intended to be human-powered by an eight-man crew whose members turned cranks to transfer power to the wheels through a crude form of gearing system. It seems to have lacked an efficient steering capability and had a very low ground clearance which almost certainly would have led to its frequently bogging down. Additionally,

the crew would have soon become exhausted by the effects of the low power-to-weight ratio. Of his design, da Vinci is thought to have remarked: "I am building secure and covered chariots which are invulnerable, and when they advance with their guns in the midst of the enemy, even the largest enemy masses are bound to retreat; and behind them the infantry can follow in safety and without opposition . . . these take the place of elephants and one may hold bellows in them to terrify horses or one may put carabiniers in them. This is good to break up the ranks of the enemy."

For all it left to be desired, the da Vinci design spelled a kind of progress along the way to development of the tank concept, but another four hundred years would pass before a real and viable design would arrive. Meanwhile, in the period between 1419 and 1434, a group of Central European religious dissidents led by Jan

above: "Little Willie" under construction at Foster's Lincoln works in 1915; below: King George V inspecting "Little Willie" in 1918.

Jiska during the Hussite Wars, built and deployed a kind of "war wagon" which was basically a defensive cart offering a level of mobility and armored protection. This "Wagon Laager," as it was called, was constructed with thick, timbered sides and pillbox-like slits through which guns or crossbows could be fired. A tactical defensive circle could be formed by connecting several of the vehicles together, should Jiska's men be threatened with enemy attack while on open ground. In later years, through the nineteenth century, variations on such war carts were notably in use by the Boers in South Africa.

In 1596 the mathematician John Napier designed a "round chariot of metal" which was fully-armored against the musket fire of the time. The power source according to Napier was "those within, the same more easie and more spedie than so many armed men would be otherwise." He called

right: Lt. Col. Ernest Swinton whose 1914 idea led to the creation of the tank; far right: Major J.F.C. Fuller, who foresaw tactics for tanks.

it the "assault car," "the use thereof in moving serveth to break the array of the enemies battle . . . by continual discharge of harquebussiers through small holes, the enemy being abashed and uncertain as to what defence or pursuit to use against a moving mouth of metal."

In 1838 the engineer John George of Saint Blazey, Cornwall, England, petitioned the House of Commons claiming, together with his son, to be the sole inventors of what he referred to as a "modern steam war chariot." He described the vehicle as "coke-burning, with sides armored against muskett and grape shot." It was crewed by three men and was "capable of cutting a twenty-three-foot opening in an enemy rank." It could, he said, "penetrate the densest lines, the firmest cahorts and the most compact squadrons with as much certainty as a cannon ball would pass through a par-

tition of paste board." George and his son proposed bringing a demonstration model of their machine to London for the edification of the Commons which, in the event, expressed no interest in the scheme.

Then, in 1854, the Englishman James Cowan was at work on an armored fighting vehicle when he decided to try enclosing one of James Boydell's traction engines within the iron skin of the machine which was open at the top. The vehicle featured several cannon protruding through gun ports and it moved on short, reinforced board "feet" that were fitted to the circumference of the road wheels, as forerunners of the linked caterpillar tracks on which the tanks and other armored vehicles of the future would roll.

Like the George war chariot, Cowan's steam traction machine failed to impress government authorities in the form of a Select Committee appointed by the British Prime Minister, Lord Palmerston. In the committee's collective view, the Cowan design did not adequately provide internally for the functions of the boiler, the flywheel and the breech-loading guns, other machinery, coal and ammunition storage, or for the driver and gunners. The committee turned down Cowan's design and he immediately referred to them in the press as "washed out Old Women and Senile Old Tabbies."

The most visionary, clever and inventive military-oriented thinkers of the time were essentially agreed that the future of land warfare rested with a type of vehicle that combined great firepower with self-propulsion and greatly improved protection for its crew. Progress was slow, but those minds were definitely on the way to the creation of the tank, a killing machine the world would find irresistible.

The next step along that way was the invention in the 1880s of small internal combustion engines by the Germans Gottlieb Daimler and Karl Benz, leading the world away from steam as the primary power source for the developing armored fighting vehicle. Internal combustion power would prove the only practical choice. The British government, meanwhile, through its War Office, maintained a posture of indifference, ignoring or rejecting various armored fighting vehicle design ideas. In 1895 it gave the ho-hum to a small, open-topped armored car with two mounted machine-guns, the brainchild of American entrepreneur Edward Pennington. The bathtub-shaped contraption featured Pennington's patented pneumatic tires and a quarter-inch-thick armor plate skirt around the hull. The skirt ended eighteen inches above the ground and wore a chain-mail fringe to protect the tires. A driver and two gunners crewed the car, which excited no one in the government and was never produced. The Pennington design was followed by a similar self-propelled fighting vehicle, the Military Scout, a creation of the British inventor Frederick Simms. The Scout was to be powered by a 1.5 hp De Dion engine and was to be armed with an air-cooled Maxim machine-gun. The car was thought promising by many, but not by many in the War Office.

But Simms continued to work on such ideas, developing a small, petrol-powered armored rail-car that was based on Pennington's design. The car actually took part in the Second Boer War and was considered relatively successful in the effort. Simms then went on to design a larger version for the road. It was produced by Vickers and became the first true armored car. Armed with a Vickers-Maxim one-pounder gun at the rear and

"Little Willie" at the Tank Museum, Bovington, Dorset, England.

two Maxim water-cooled machine-guns at the front, the Simms "War Car," as it was known, was capable of a maximum speed of nine mph with its Simms-Daimler sixteen hp engine. The War Car was displayed at the 1902 Crystal Palace exhibition to great acclaim by the press and public. The War Office, though, was once again unimpressed and Simms decided to redirect his interests away from armored fighting vehicle development.

The requirement to be able to move readily across open countryside with ample armor protection drove Richard Hornsby & Sons, developer of a track system for oil-engined tractors, to successfully experiment with a militarized version in 1905. Again, the War Office declined to support the venture beyond that point. Still, with the efforts of Daimler and Benz, and the Hornsby experiment, two key components of the

tank, a reliable power plant and a track system to replace wheels, had been put in place. The years before 1914 saw various limited developments in the field in France, Germany, Italy and Great Britain with the resulting vehicles being used in local conflicts with varying degrees of success. The intransigent, reactionary war ministries and general staffs of the time stolidly maintained their hostile attitudes, delaying and sabotaging such developments wherever possible. Their inability to learn from and properly interpret their own battlefield experience, coupled with their persistent delusions about future tactics and requirements, left them essentially confused and generally ill-prepared for the Great War that was coming.
It should have been abundantly clear to most military commanders at the beginning of the First World War that neither massed ranks of infantry nor charging cavalry could survive in the face of fire from breech-loading, rifled

weapons. Most commanders, though, refused to even consider any alternative to sending their troops "over the top" to cross a pock-marked, denuded wasteland through a withering hail of bullets. "War is good business. Invest your sons," wrote a wag of the day.

The armored car was the first fighting vehicle to enter wartime service. It was built by the Belgians and by the British Royal Navy, and was tested and put into action on the Western Front in 1914. In the thick and sticky mud of the battlefields, however, these new and promising wheeled vehicles were largely unsuitable. In an irony ahead of that conflict, an Australian engineer named Lancelot de Mole had designed a practical armored tank vehicle that was, in fact, superior to that which the British Army would field on the Somme in 1916. But, when de Mole submitted his clever design to the War Office there was virtually no reaction.

So, in 1915, he tried again to interest the decision makers of the War Office and was again rebuffed.

"Caterpillar landships are idiotic and useless. Nobody has asked for them and nobody wants them. Those officers and men are wasting their time and are not pulling their proper weight in the war. If I had my way I would disband the whole lot of them. Anyhow, I am going to do my best to see that it is done and stop all this armored car and caterpillar landship nonsense" declared Royal Navy Commodore Cecil Lambert, Fourth Sea Lord, in 1915. Lambert clearly disapproved of the Royal Navy Armored Car Division, which had been established in October 1914 with the enthusiastic support of the First Lord of the Admiralty, Winston Churchill, to develop a new line of purpose-built armored cars.

From a letter in January 1915 from Winston Churchill to Prime Minister Herbert Asquith: ". . . fit up a small number of steam tractors with small armored shelters, in which men and machine-guns could be placed, which would be bullet-proof . . . The caterpillar system would enable trenches to be crossed quite easily, and the weight of the machine would destroy all wire entanglements . . ."

Urgent diplomatic intercepts: St Petersburg, 29 July 1914, 1 a.m. Czar Nicholas II to Kaiser Wilhelm II: "I FORSEE THAT VERY SOON I SHALL BE OVERWHELMED BY THE PRESSURE FORCED UPON ME AND BE FORCED TO TAKE EXTREME MEASURES WHICH WILL LEAD TO WAR".—Nicky
Berlin, 30 July 1914, 1:20 a.m. Kaiser Wilhelm II to Czar Nicholas II: "THE WHOLE WEIGHT OF THE DECISION LIES SOLELY ON YOUR SHOULDERS NOW. [YOU] HAVE TO BEAR THE RESPONSIBILITY FOR PEACE OR WAR."
—Willy

There's a little wet home in the trench,
That the rain storms continually drench,
A dead cow close by, With her hooves in the sky,
And she gives off a beautiful stench.
Underneath us, in place of a floor,
Is a mess of cold mud and some straw,
And the Jack Johnsons roar as they speed through the air
O'er my little wet home in the trench.
—anon

After the German defeat in the Battle of the Marne, a few Royal Navy units were sent from England to protect the air base at Dunkirk. They were also ordered to assume the rescue of pilots who had been shot down in the area. To that end, the Admiralty Air Department stepped in and provided some armored cars. They bought 100 of the vehicles from Rolls-Royce and shipped some of them directly to France where they were fitted with a box-like arrangement of armor covering the main unit and rear wheels, and other small, raised armored boxes to cover the front wheels and the driver's head. The rest of the Rolls-Royce cars were modified in England where they remained until put into action in the autumn of 1914 where they performed relatively effectively, but also demonstrated that their crews were inadequately protected from overhead sniper fire. That led to development of a new version which incorporated a top-mounted machine-gun turret and overhead armor. The early examples of the new vehicle reached France in December 1914 and were immediately seen to be a great improvement over their predecessors. But, they had come

into service at a point in the war when all significant movement on the battlefields had stopped. The armies of the two enemies were dug in behind wire barriers and fortifications and, while the new armored cars were promising, they were incapable of crossing the trenches or the wire.

Winston Churchill formed the Naval Landships Committee in February 1915 to design and build a new armored tracked vehicle based on a 1914 idea of Lieutenant Colonel Ernest Swinton, Royal Engineers. Swinton believed that a caterpillar-tracked armored vehicle could be created to destroy machine-gun positions and barbed wire barriers and, most importantly, to cross the great trenches and other obstacles on the battlefield with relative ease. The initial trials of the "Machine-Gun Destroyer" as it was referred to, were hugely disappointing, but Churchill and the committee were determined to continue the effort. They purchased two Bullock Creeping Grip tractors and imported them from the United States, and from them developed a new vehicle they called the Lincoln Number One Machine. They then redesigned the track and suspension units and modified the resulting vehicle which was soon delivering the kind of performance sought by the committee. They named the new vehicle Little Willie.

This time, the interest of the British Army was aroused by the possibilities it foresaw for such a machine. What they required, however, was a machine with about twice the capability of Little Willie. It had to be able to cross a trench eight feet wide as well as climb a parapet four and a half feet high. And then, two of the committee members, William Tritton and Lieutenant W.G. Wilson joined forces to come up with a new design, a combination of the best qualities and characteristics of both the Lincoln Machine and

TRAVELLING FORTRESS   11

Little Willie, an entirely new fighting vehicle with tracks that ran around the perimeter of its rhomboid sides. Its overall height was kept to a minimum through the use of sponsons on either side of the vehicle, each mounting a six-pounder naval gun, rather than a a top-mounted turret. It had fixed front and rear turrets, with the front turret accommodating the commander and the driver sitting side by side. The rear turret housed a machine-gun. The vehicle contained four Hotchkiss machine-guns and there were four doors behind the sponsons as well as a man-hole hatch in the top of the hull. To the rear of the hull was attached a two-wheel towed steering tail. This new design was known as Big Willie, but more commonly referred to as Mother. It was eight feet in height and twenty-six feet five inches long, not counting the added steering tail. With a weight of twenty-eight tons, Mother was powered by a 105-hp Daimler sleeve-valve engine.

In February 1916, a trial of Mother was held at the Hatfield Park, Hertfordshire estate of the Marquess of Salisbury. The audience included Minister of Munitions Lloyd George, Field Marshal Lord Kitchener, the Minister of Defence, and some other representatives of the Army and the Admiralty. During the trial, Mother was put through her paces over a specially-prepared obstacle course containing a variety of craters, ditches, streams, wire entanglements and wide trenches, and she acquitted herself well according to the Landship Committee members present. Although Kitchener himself was not especially enthusiastic about what he witnessed that day, the Army representatives were quite impressed and by the end of the event, a production order for twenty-five of the vehicles was awarded to Foster's and one for seventy-five of the machines went to the Metropolitan Carriage, Wagon and Finance Company. Fifty Mothers were to be built with the same armament as the prototype. Strangely, they would thereafter be referred to as "males," with the balance of the vehicles armed with six machine-guns, four of them mounted in smaller side sponsons. These units were called "females." Their role in combat was to protect the males from being swamped by enemy infantry. After the Hatfield Park trial, the King was given a ride in the prototype and emerged saying that a large number of the vehicles would be a considerable asset to the Army.

In the secrecy of the Foster's workshops the workers and executives referred to the unusual new vehicles they were building as "tanks," an odd reference to the new weapons system destined to entirely reform land

A British Mark I with faked Russian lettering at Foster's works, Lincoln, England.

warfare. They were trying to conceal what they were working on. Swinton and Lt. Col. W. Dalby Jones discussed the matter and they considered calling the thing "container" or "cistern" before finally agreeing on "tank," which, they thought, implied some sort of agricultural machine . . . something the company might be expected to produce normally. Foster's personnel even hinted broadly that the new products were to be shipped to Russia. And so the word "tank" entered into common usage and was soon generic for the war machine.

The pressure on the manufacturers to get the Mark I into production inevitably resulted in a vehicle something less than perfect. The makers took this first production tank from drawing board to assembly in just twelve months and, among its many drawbacks was a gravity-fed fuel system which could starve the engine when the vehicle was maneuvering with its front end in a steep, climbing or descending attitude. The fuel tank was positioned inside the vehicle and greatly increased the fire risk. And, in a particularly bizarre design solution, the vehicle required the teamwork of four crew members to steer it, even with the aid of the wheeled steering tail. David Fletcher, Librarian of the Tank Museum, Bovington, England, a leading authority on tanks and author of *The British Tanks 1915-19*: "Four of the crew served the guns; a gunner and loader on each side. The others were all required to operate the controls. The driver, sitting to the right of the commander, was effectively there to make the tank go. Apart from the steering wheel that was almost useless, he had no control whatever over turning, or swinging the tank, to use the contemporary term. He controlled the primary gearbox, clutch and footbrake which acted on the transmission shaft,

along with the ignition and throttle controls. The commander operated the steering brakes and either man could work the differential lock which was above, between and behind them. The two extra men worked the secondary gearboxes at the back, on instruction from the driver, who had to work the clutch at the same time.

"It was, according to the instruction book, possible to steer the tank by selecting a different ratio in each of the secondary gearboxes, although experience soon proved that this would result in twisted gear shafts. Thus, except for slight deviations when the steering brakes were used, the standard procedure for steering was to halt the tank, lock the differential and take one track out of gear. First was then selected in the primary box and the other secondary box, the brake was then applied to the free track and the tank would swing in that direction."

By February 1917, the Marks II and III had gone to war incorporating only minor improvements over the Mk I, but, by April the substantially improved Mark IV had entered service, protected by much better armor. It also featured a vacuum-feed fuel system, a new cooling and ventilation system, an exhaust silencer and a rear-mounted external fuel tank. While the males had the same armament as the prototype, the females were armed with six machine-guns (five Vickers and one Hotchkiss). A total of 420 male and 595 female tanks were produced before the arrival in May 1918 of the Mark V, by far the best and most dramatically advanced version of this pioneering fighting vehicle. The Mk V incorporated an entirely new epicyclic steering system designed by the former Lieutenant, now Major, W.G. Wilson, as well as an extended hull to increase its trench-crossing capability. With enhanced power from

a 150 hp Ricardo engine, the Mk V was capable of 4.6 mph maximum speed, compared to the 3.7 mph top speed of the earlier marks. Mark V production totalled 400 male and 632 female tanks.

The armored strike force of the British Army was forming in 1916 and the Army wisely decided to establish it as a new branch under the overall command of Ernest Swinton. Lt. Col. Hugh Elles, a Royal Engineer officer, was appointed field commander in France. Elles had been GHQ representative for tank development and policy. The new organization was called the Tank Detachment until June 1917 when it was redesignated the Tank Corps and, in 1923, it became the Royal Tank Corps, the award coming from King George V. In 1939, the Royal Tank Corps was renamed the Royal Tank Regiment and became part of the Royal Armored Corps, along with other units, mainly former cavalry regiments.

Elles put together a small staff of officers in 1916 who brought considerable intelligence, enthusiasm and foresight to the war front in France. Realizing the enormous potential of the tank weapon, Elles's key staff, including Captain G. Martel and Major J.F.C. Fuller, predicted the coming battles between opposing tank forces and other advanced tank tactics that were destined to change land warfare forever. It was Fuller who, in 1917, wrote of the tank, "It is in fact an armored mechanical horse."

At dawn the ridge emerges massed and dun, In the wild purple of the glow'ring sun, Smouldering through spouts of drifting smoke that shroud The menacing scarred slope, and, one by one, Tanks creep and topple forward to the wire.
—from *Attack* by Siegfried Sassoon

Well, how are things in heaven? I wish you'd say Because I'd like to know that you're all right. Tell me, have you found everlasting day, Or been sucked in by everlasting night? For when I shut my eyes your face shows plain; I hear you make some cheery old remark—I can rebuild you in my brain, Though you've gone out patrolling in the dark.
—from *To Any Dead Officer* by Siegfried Sassoon

Brought to France under the cover of canvas sheets, the first British tanks entered battle against the Germans in September 1916. In his book, *Tanks In Battle*, Colonel H.C.B. Rogers describes the supplies that were carried into action in the British tanks: "Rations for the first tank battle consisted of sixteen loaves of bread and about thirty tins of foodstuffs. The various types of stores included four spare Vickers machine-gun barrels, one spare Vickers machine-gun, one spare Hotchkiss machine-gun, two boxes of revolver ammuntion, thirty-three thousand rounds of ammunition for the machine-guns, a telephone instrument and a hundred yards of cable on a drum, a signalling lamp, three signalling flags, two wire cutters, one spare drum of engine oil, two small drums of grease and three water cans. Added to this miscellaneous collection was all the equipment which was stripped off the eight inhabitants of the tank, so that there was not very much room to move about."

The training of the crews that went to war in these early tanks had been sub-standard and there had been no instruction in cooperation between the tanks and the infantry. The only point of agreement between the two arms was that the tanks ought to reach their first objective five minutes ahead of the infantry forces and that the primary task of the tanks was to destroy the

"What did you do in the war, Daddy?"

enemy strongpoints which were preventing the advance of the infantry.

In their initial combat action, it was intended to deploy forty-nine British tanks, but only thirty-two were able to take part. Nine of these suffered breakdowns, five experienced "ditching" (becoming stuck in a trench or soft ground) and nine more couldn't keep up the pace, lagging well behind the infantry. But the remaining nine met their objective and inflicted severe losses on the German forces. While accomplishing less than had been hoped for, this first effort of the British tank force produced an important and unanticipated side effect. Those tanks that reached the enemy line made a powerful impression on the German troops facing them, causing many to bolt in fear even before the tanks had come into firing range.

Shrieking its message the flying death
Cursed the resisting air,
Then buried its nose by a tattered church,
A skeleton gaunt and bare.
The brains of science, the money of fools,
Had fashioned an iron slave
Destined to kill, yet the futile end
Was a child's uprooted grave.
—*The Shell* by Private H. Smalley Sarson

When the war is over and the Kaiser's out of print, I'm going to buy some tortoises and watch the beggars sprint; When the war is over and the sword at last we sheathe, I'm going to keep a jelly-fish and listen to it breathe.
—from *A Full Heart* by A.A. Milne

For it's clang, bang, rattle,
W'en the tanks go into battle,
And they plough their way across the tangled wire,
They are sighted to a fraction,

When the guns get into action,
An' the order of the day is rapid fire;
W'en the hour is zero Ev'ry man's a bloomin' 'ero,
W'atsoever 'is religion or 'is nime,
You can bet yer bottom dollar
W'ether death or glory foller,
That the tanks will do their duty ev'ry time.
—from *A Song of the Tanks* by J. Dean Atkinson

The following passage from the book *Iron Fist* by Bryan Perrett describes operational conditions for the crew of the early British tanks in France around the midpoint of the First World War: "Such intense heat was generated by the engine that the men wore as little as possible. The noise level, a compound of roaring engine, unsilenced exhaust on the early Marks, the thunder of tracks crossing the hull, weapons firing and the enemy's return fire striking the armor, made speech impossible and permanently damaged the hearing of some. The hard ride provided by the unsprung suspension faithfully mirrored every pitch and roll of the ground so that the gunners, unaware of what lay ahead, would suddenly find themselves thrown off their feet and, reaching out for support, sustain painful burns as they grabbed at machinery that verged on the red hot. Worst of all was the foul atmosphere, polluted by the fumes of leaking exhausts, hot oil, petrol and expended cordite. Brains starved of oxygen refused to function or produced symptoms of madness. One officer is known to have fired into a malfunctioning engine with his revolver, and some crews were reduced to the level of zombies, repeatedly mumbling the orders they had been given but physically unable to carry them out. Small wonder then, that after even a short spell in action, the men would collapse on the ground beside their

vehicles, gulping in air, incapable of movement for long periods.

"In addition, of course, there were the effects of the enemy's fire. Wherever this struck, small glowing flakes of metal would be flung off the inside of the armor, while bullet splash penetrated visors and joints in the plating; both could blind, although the majority of such wounds were minor though painful. Glass vision blocks became starred and were replaced by open slits, thereby increasing the risk, especially to the commander and the driver. In an attempt to minimise this, leather crash helmets, slotted metal goggles and chain mail visors were issued, but these were quickly discarded in the suffocating heat of the vehicle's interior. The tanks of the day were not proof against field artillery so that any penetration was likely to result in a fierce petrol or ammunition fire followed by an explosion that would tear the vehicle apart. In such a situation the chances of being able to evacuate a casualty through the awkward hatches were horribly remote.

"Despite these sobering facts, the crews willingly accepted both the conditions and the risks in the belief that they had a war-winning weapon."

A British Army corporal said they looked like giant toads. The specter of nearly 400 enemy tanks emerging from the early morning ground fog and mists of Cambrai in north-eastern France on 20 November 1917 must have impressed all who saw it. After years of stalemate and staggering attrition, this first use of massed tanks in warfare was the turning point. British armored commanders had awakened to the possibilities of the tank when imaginatively and skillfully utilized.

For most of 1917 the Allies on the Western Front had been bogged down in their trenches, unable to breach the

The Experimental
Depot for Tanks,
Dollis Hill, London,
a painting by
W.B. Adeney.

German defenses. Now in November, the tank commanders saw an opportunity to break the cycle of despair and hopelessness that hung over the Allied armies. They proposed a massive tank raid to be launched against German positions near the town of Cambrai. They liked the prospects. The terrain of the attack was gently rolling, well-drained land. As their plan called for surprising the Germans with a fast and relatively quiet approach, there was to be no conventional softening-up artillery bombardment in advance of the raid. The commanders had intended that the great tank force would arrive quickly, inflict maximum damage and get out fast, having completed their task in three hours or less. They had presented their plan to Sir Douglas Haig, the British Commander-in-Chief on the Western Front, in August when he was incurring catastrophic losses fifty miles to the north of Cambrai in the swamps of Passchendale. At the time, the optimistic Haig was still looking for a victory and shelved the Cambrai idea. But by the autumn his Passchendale ambitions had sunk in the mud there and he was forced to accept the proposal of his tank men.

The plan called for the great mass of tanks to force a breakthrough between the two canals at Cambrai, capture the town itself as well as the higher ground surrounding the village of Flesquieres and the Bourdon Wood. They were then to roll on towards Valenciennes, twenty-five miles to the northeast. The tanks were carrying great bundles of brushwood which would be used to fill in the trenches that they would encounter when crossing the German defenses of the Siegfried Line. It was intended that the tanks would advance line abreast while the accompanying infantry troops would follow in columns close behind to defend against close-quarters attacks.

Deception and diversion were

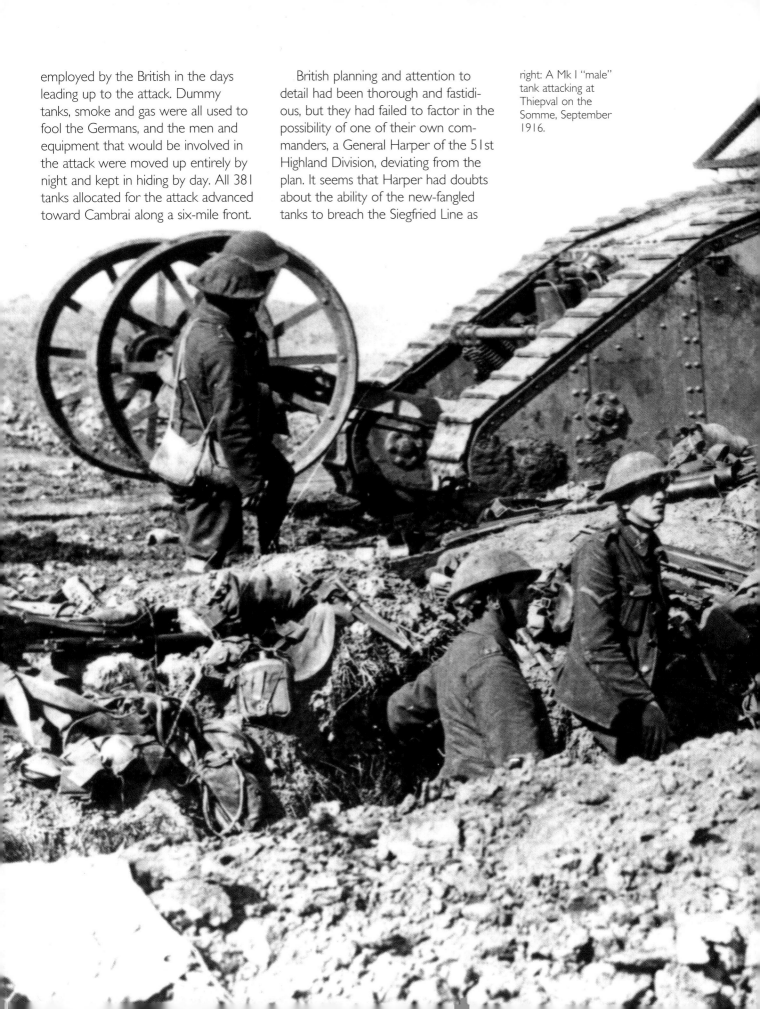

employed by the British in the days leading up to the attack. Dummy tanks, smoke and gas were all used to fool the Germans, and the men and equipment that would be involved in the attack were moved up entirely by night and kept in hiding by day. All 381 tanks allocated for the attack advanced toward Cambrai along a six-mile front.

British planning and attention to detail had been thorough and fastidious, but they had failed to factor in the possibility of one of their own commanders, a General Harper of the 51st Highland Division, deviating from the plan. It seems that Harper had doubts about the ability of the new-fangled tanks to breach the Siegfried Line as

right: A Mk I "male" tank attacking at Thiepval on the Somme, September 1916.

A portrait of Major
General Hugh Elles,
by Sir William Orpen.

quickly as the planners required. On the day of the attack Harper delayed sending his tanks and infantry troops forward until an hour after the rest of the force had left. The delay allowed German field artillery to be positioned with disastrous results for some tank crews. Five burned-out tank hulls were found after the action. Elsewhere along the tank line, however, the armor and infantry had moved swiftly through the German lines, advancing five miles to Bourdon Wood by noon. It had been a brilliant achievement for the British tank crews.

The push continued the next day with the British taking Flesquieres and advancing a further 17 miles. In the next nine days, they won and lost the village of Fontaine-Notre Dame and the surrounding area several times. Then, on 30 November, the Germans counterattacked. Like the British, they struck without the usual initial artillery bombardment, hiding behind heavy gas and smoke screens. The British troops, exhausted by their recent effort, were forced to retreat from the rapidly advancing German forces and in just a few days had to relinquish all of their gains. In the action, the Germans took 6,000 prisoners. Blame for the defeat fell on everyone except those actually responsible—the commanders. There was concern in Whitehall that pointing the finger at their Army commanders would crush the faith of the British people in their military leadership. Still, the British had learned the valuable lesson of how effective tanks and artillery could be when properly employed in concert.

The German offensive of March 1918 began on the 21st and saw the first appearance of their tanks in battle. Designed early in 1917, the A7V was much larger and heavier than the British heavy tank of the day. It weighed thirty-three tons and was operated by a crew of eighteen. The armament consisted of one forward-mounted 57mm gun (roughly equivalent to the British six-pounder) and six machine-guns positioned at the sides and the rear. The maximum armor thickness was 30mm enabling the front of the tank to resist direct hits from field guns at long range, but the overhead armor was too thin to provide much protection. The fitting of the armor plating was such that the hull was very susceptible to bullet splash. The tank's power came from two 150 hp Daimler sleeve-valve engines. Sprung tracks allowed the vehicle to achieve eight mph on smooth and level ground, a high speed for the time. However, the design and the low ground clearance resulted in relatively poor cross-country performance. The Germans built only fifteen A7Vs. In their initial venture into combat, four of the German tanks were used together with five captured British Mk IVs. One month later, thirteen A7Vs participated in the capture of Villers-Brettoneux and in this action the enemy tanks had the same psychological effect on the British infantry as their tanks had had earlier on their German counterparts. Tanks broke the opposing lines.

Shortly after the German success at Villers-Brettoneux, the world's first tank-versus-tank action took place in the same neighborhood. In the early morning light, one male and two female Mk IVs were ordered forward to stem the German penetration. Though some of the British tank crew members had suffered from gas shelling, they all advanced and soon sighted one of the A7Vs. The machine-guns of the two females were useless against the armor of the German tank and both were put out of action. But the male was able to maneuver for

a flank shot and scored a hit causing the German tank to run up a steep embankment and overturn. Two more A7Vs then arrived and engaged the British tank which saw one off. The crew of the second A7V abandoned their tank and fled.

The Cambrai experience undoubtedly saved many lives, influencing the British attack of 8 August 1918, the battle of Amiens, in which 456 tanks finally broke the enemy lines. It was the decisive battle of the war, leading to the German surrender. The battle was launched along a thirteen-mile front. The three objectives were the Green Line, three miles from the start line; the Red Line, six miles from the start and in the center of the front; and the Blue Line, eight miles from the start and in the center. The attack was to begin at 4:20 a.m. with the tanks moving out 1,000 yards to the start line. A thick mist helped the British forces to achieve complete surprise and overrun the German forward defenses.

The main attacks were to be delivered by the Canadian Corps on the right and the Australian Corps on the left, both of them being south of the Somme. The Third Corps was to make a limited advance while covering the left flank. Before the Canadian Fifth Tank Battalion reached and crossed the Green Line objective, it had suffered heavily, losing fifteen tanks. It lost another eleven tanks achieving the Red Line, leaving it only eight machines still operable. The Canadian Fourth Tank Battalion was advancing across firm ground and achieved the Green and Red Lines with ease. Heavy German artillery then took a great toll of the Fourth's tanks, leaving only eleven for the push on toward the Blue Line.

The Australian Corps, attacking with vehicles of the Fifth Tank Brigade, reached the Green Line by 7 a.m., the Red Line by 10 a.m. and they took the

Blue Line an hour later. The tanks had eliminated German opposition up to the Red Line. After that, the Australian infantry poured through the weakened enemy defenses and the tanks were unable to keep pace with them.

After the fighting, most tank crews were suffering the ill effects from having spent upwards of three hours buttoned-up for action. With their guns firing, most of them suffered from headaches, high temperatures and even heart disturbances.

Though it was not immediately apparent, the Allies had won a great victory at Amiens, taking 22,000 German prisoners, and the German High Command realized that it had no more hope of winning the war.

In the Reichstag, the German politicians heard from their military commanders that it was, above all, the tanks that had brought an end to their resistance against the Allies. That evening the downcast Kaiser said to one of his military commanders: "It is very strange that our men cannot get used to tanks." Major (now General) J.F.C. Fuller summed up the result: "The battle of Amiens was the strategic end of the war, a second Waterloo; the rest was minor tactics."

WIPERS

The Ypres Salient at Night, a painting by Paul Nash.

From *The Tank in Action* by Captain D.G. Browne, MC: "From the introduction of tanks in the field, the conditions with which they had to contend had gone from bad to worse. Ypres was the climax. The tanks were sent by scores, and then by hundreds, to drown ineffectually in a morass and the very existence of the corps was imperilled by this misusage. The whole countryside was waterlogged: reclaimed from the sea, for even Ypres once had been a port, its usefulness and habitability depended in normal times upon an intricate system of drainage, for whose upkeep the farmers were responsible, and for the neglect of which they were heavily fined. This drainage had now been destroyed, or had fallen into decay, over the whole area about the front lines. During our reconnaissances in July the deplorable results were not at first apparent. The weather was fine, and the surface soil dry and crumbling: we walked, so far as it was safe, over what seemed to be solid earth covered with the usual coarse grass and weeds; and then, from observation points in well-constructed trenches, peered out through our binoculars upon a barren and dun-coloured landscape, void of any sign of human life, its dreary skyline broken only by a few jagged stumps of trees. From this desolation clouds of dust shot up where our shells were falling. It was much the same as any other battlefield, to all appearances. But even then the duckboards under foot in the trenches were squelching upon water; and a few hours' rain dissolved the fallacious crust into a bottomless and evil-smelling paste of liquid mud. And the rain was the least offender. It was our own bombardment which finished the work of ruin, pulverized the ground beyond repair, destroyed what drainage there was left, and brought the water welling

up within the shell holes as fast as they were formed."

British and Commonwealth soldiers called it "Wipers." Ground gained was measured by the yard; casualties by the thousand.

The following is an account of the third battle of Ypres in World War I. It is rare to come across a memoir of the Great War that is as thoughtful, observant and evocative as this, from The Tank Corps Journal of 1921-22 and attributed only to E. and M.D.:

3:40 a.m. on Y-Z Night. An almost deathly silence spreads over the front, broken only by the occasional bark of an eighteen-pounder or 4.5 howitzer. The crew of Caledonian sit inside their bus awaiting zero hour. Guns have been cleaned, "Spuds" fitted, petrol tank filled, and six brand new plugs are waiting to make 500 sparks a minute each as soon as called upon. A few sections of infantry pass the Tank at intervals, and their voices can be plainly heard from inside. "That's the stuff to gie 'em" and "I wouldn't go over in one of

they things, I'm safer wi' me old tin 'at and 'ipe."

A whistle in the distance, a shower of golden rain from the front line, and with a crash that reverberates throughout the countryside, the barrage, the greatest barrage ever put up, breaks forth.

To those who have never heard a barrage before it comes as a revelation. A thousand grand pianos, ten million drums, and a forest of trees being split by an army of giants, mix these together, and a hurricane at sea for the shriek of the shells as they rush

through the air, and you have a very passable imitation of a barrage.

The first of the Tanks has moved off, but, Caledonian still waits; her job is to take the green line and, if all goes well the red line as well, a total distance of some eleven thousand yards. Her rendezvous is Zonnebeke on the Ypres-Roulers railway where the Boche is reported to be in force, and from where, in all probability, he will launch a desperate counter-attack.

4 a.m. A voice from outside the Tank shouts, "Start up, number four section," and a few sharp barks followed by the running purr of engines shows that all is in readiness for the advance. The first Tank moves slowly forward, followed by Crocodile, Carmanthen, Calcium and Caledonian; it is still almost dark and the drivers, their eyes smarting from the gas which they have passed through only a few hours before, find difficulty in following the track.

A message comes back from the front, "Blue line taken, very few casualties." Caledonian's crew stamp their feet and try to cheer themselves with this news while warming their hands on the exhaust pipes.

Day breaks and the barrage seems almost heavier than before.

Sssssssst—bang. An early balloon has spotted No 4 section coming and has instructed an ever willing 77mm field gun to try its luck. The Tanks at this time, in passing down a partly sunken road in a straight line, are a fair mark and the first shot falls only a few yards ahead of Celtic.

Sssssssssst—bang. Between Celtic and Crocodile this time and near enough to be unpleasant. The crews begin to sit up and take notice, wondering where the next one will fall.

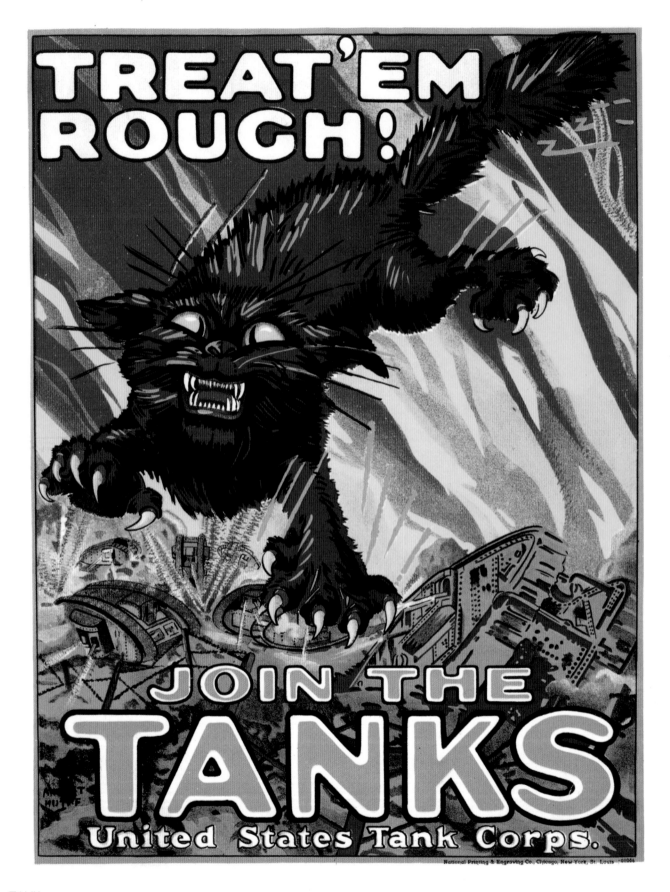

They have not long to wait.

Ssssssssst—bang. A cloud of smoke and dust goes up, hiding for the moment the two first Tanks from the view of the others. Another miss.

Crocodile calmly wags her tail and proceeds—a rather longer pause this time—Fritz must be ashamed of his bad shooting and is going to chuck his hand in. Not a bit of it, a shriek and a bang and the next shell has arrived, bursting under Calcium's sponson. Caledonian's crew hold their breath as they peep from out their reflectors. All to no purpose, however, as soon as the smoke has cleared Calcium is perceived to be holding her course and a surprised gunner looks out of the hatchway to see if Caledonian will be unluckier than the rest.

"All crews took into action two days' ordinary rations in addition to the emergency ration; but this food was supplemented by a few delicasies considered suitable to the festive occasion. Thus most of us carried also oranges, lemons, chocolates, and biscuits, one water-bottle filled with rum, and a bottle of whisky. Personally, I took two bottles of whisky, and was extremely thankful that I did.

"In those days tank equipment was devised and issued on a lavish scale. One took over with the machine a vast assortment of instruments calculated to soften the asperities of a very cramped and uncomfortable mode of warfare, and calling to mind the fittings of HMS Mantelpiece. If we had no zoetropes, excellent carriage clocks, mounted in heavy brass, were the perquisites in more senses than one of every tank commander. The number of these clocks destroyed by shell-fire was so abnormal in the Salient that after that deplorable campaign the issue was stopped, it being felt that the residue of timepieces in stock would serve a more useful purpose and lead a safer life in the numerous offices of Central Stores and Workshops at Erin. A haversack full of spirits, shell-dressings, iodine, and other sinister medical comforts, quite passable binoculars, electric hand-lamps, signalling shutters, six periscopes and an ingenious device like a pair of pantomime braces fitted with batteries, switches and red and green lights, to be used in guiding tanks at night, were also among the treasures thrust upon us in a very open-handed manner. But this halcyon age did not endure for long. Vulgar considerations of waste and expenditure supervened. Before the end of the whereabouts of every spanner and split-pin became a case of acute worry to us all. It should be unnecessary to add that this era of suspicion brought with it a veritable spate of new Army Forms . . . continually superceding each other and never by any chance filled in correctly. We were already in possession of immense logbooks, atrocities known as battle history sheets, and pigeon-message forms. A fully-equipped tank, in short, was a combination of a battleship, an ironmonger's shop, an optician's, a chemist's, a grocer's, and a Government office. We only wanted a typewriter to round off the outfit."
—from The Tank in Action by Captain D.G. Browne

And now I'm drinking wine in France,
The helpless child of circumstance.
Tomorrow will be loud with war,
How will I be accounted for?
—from Soliloquy by Francis Ledwidge, killed in action, 1917

To Caledonian's driver it seemed that she took half an hour to cross the five yards dip where the enemy could spot her. Most of her crew were imitating the action of a University cox, trying to increase her speed from 2 to 20 miles an hour. A muffled report from behind tells them that they are safe. The leading Tanks now begin to branch off across the shell hole desert. Eight are to be in the first wave, followed by five Tanks of No 4 section as "mopper's up." The sun is now well up, but a slight mist hangs over the ground, obscuring the view and blurring the periscopes and reflectors of the Tanks. The planes are flying low, swooping down to within twenty feet of the ground and sounding their "Klaxon" horns. In a few minutes Caledonian is hopelessly lost. The other Tanks of her section are gone right and left, and she has to find the remains of a railway embankment somewhere on her right, and steer a course between "Bill Cottage" and "Douglas Villa."

Both are probably non-existent after this morning's barrage, so it remains to find the embankment, which being about seven miles long and only half a mile away on the right, should not prove very difficult.

The going so far has been good, the best the driver has ever seen so close to the line; it seemed when studying the maps in La Lovie Wood that they would never reach the British front line, so broken did the ground look, but surely they cannot be far from it now, yet there is almost room for a horse and cart to drive between the shell holes.

Wire ahead. Is it British or German? A close inspection reveals the pointed tops to the corkscrews; they are German and the front line has been crossed unknowingly. On the right the railway looms up through the mist, only a hundred yards away, Caledonian is half a mile to the right of her course.

"Neutral left," shouts the driver, "left brake on, sir," and the Tank gradually swings to her new course.

"Neutral right, two up left, two up right; we may as well get a move on while the good ground lasts." And again the Tank moves forward, this time three miles an hour.

Ten minutes of uneventful going brings "Bill Cottage" and "Douglas Villa" into view—two ruins standing about six feet high, their walls spattered with shrapnel and machine-gun fire. The mopping-up parties of the infantry can be plainly seen, dodging shells, dropping bombs into dug-outs lately occupied by the Hun, and gathering prisoners and souvenirs.

A red flare bursts out three hundred yards ahead, quickly followed by another and another, until there is a chain of them miles long.

This is the signal the second wave has been waiting for; the black line has been taken and No 4 section's work has begun. No 1 section should be ahead somewhere, but the only Tanks visible are those of No 9 company returning from the black line. The rest of No 7 company appears to be lost. Two Tanks on the right are badly ditched and Caledonian gives them a wide berth. One of their sergeants comes across to try and borrow Caledonian's unditching boom, but the crew are not to be had, they may

need it themselves later. An officer comes along with the same purpose, but with no better result. "Keep your flaps shut when you get to the top of the hill." He shouts, "they're sniping and machine-gunning pretty badly" and from the blood running down his face it can be well believed. Two hundred yards more and a warning smack on Caledonian's front plate tells the crew to shut all means of entry for bullets.

A tank park in France.

Bang, bang, bang, bang. The sergeant is firing his gun from the right front mounting. *Bang, bang, bang.* Two more join in. The driver, straining his eyes to the right, catches sight of a few grey figures dropping hurriedly into a trench; he must steer for that trench and have them if they haven't beat it down their dug-out. *Tat, tat, tat, tat*—a machine-gun starts pattering on the steel side without much effect; another half minute, however, and someone at the back shouts for the first aid kit. "Who's hit?" "Percy." "Anything serious?" "No, only bullet splashes in the face."

Percy is quickly anointed with picric acid and resumes his seat at the secondary gears. More bursts of fire against the Tank followed by vigorous replies from within. A lonely Boche hiding in a shell hole attacts the driver's attention, the front flap opens a few inches, a revolver barks, and the Boche has paid the penalty of attempting to stop a Tank single handed. *Crrrump*—a five-nine drops ten yards ahead of Caledonian and shakes the ammunition boxes in their racks. An inferno of machine-gun fire breaks out against the front and sides—there must be at least four firing at her. Bullet splinters fly all over the interior and the smell of burning paint mixes with that of hot steel and cordite fumes; the temperature is unbearable and the whole crew are pouring with perspiration.

Hell—! A loud exclamation from the driver calls attention to the fact that he has been hit and requires the first aid bag. It is quickly passed along, but before he has finished swearing about his first "packet" a second bullet enters by way of the observation slit, and striking the driver again, this time in the leg, causing him to break out afresh. By the time he is tied up most of the mirrors in the observation slits

are broken and he and the officer are constrained to keep their direction by means of the periscope, a difficult job, as all who have tried it know. Another loud exclamation, this time from the Tank commander. A bullet has driven a rivet through the front plate and given him a thick lip, this followed almost immediately by another which completely closes one eye. A shell dressing is quickly applied and the advance continues.

The ground is now getting bad and it needs all the skill of the driver to prevent the Tank from becoming ditched.

Another fusillade breaks out against the sides, and the bullet splinters come in in such showers that the gunners have perforce to leave their guns and protect themselves behind the ammunition racks.

The fire redoubles its energy and the second gunner is seen to be bleeding badly from the face. Rivets begin to drop out and the front driving flaps are only hanging by one or two, the bullet-proof glass in the center prism hole is entirely gone and two guns are out of action, ripped to shreds by the storm of bullets.

Two Boches loom up in the direction of Zonnebeke and the front gun is turned on them. A couple of barks and it stops, an armor-piercing bullet from an enemy machine-gun having jammed under the body cover.

"Spare gun up"—the damaged gun is quickly replaced and the firing recommences, this time with better luck. One of the Huns drops his gun and falls headlong and the other dives into a shell hole.

The ground is now very bad indeed and the tracks are continually slipping round without gripping. Altering direction to avoid getting ditched, a round concrete structure appears immediately ahead.

below: A British Mk II moving through Arras
on April 10, 1917; bottom left: A Mk I, derelict
on the Somme battlefield in 1916.

below: A still-operative turret on a damaged Mk I; bottom left: The driver of a Mk I; bottom right: The starboard Hotchkiss gunner of a Mk I.

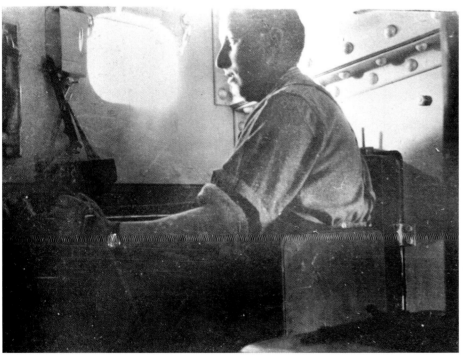

left: A British Mark V Going into Action, a painting by W.B. Adeney.

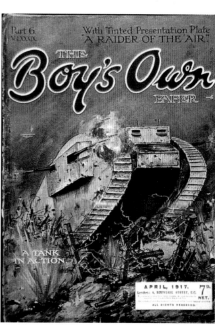

It has a slit about twelve inches deep, four feet from the ground, and through this peeps the nozzle of a machine-gun. The left-hand gunners at once open fire and the offending gun is quickly withdrawn.

To make sure of matters, however, the driver brings Caledonian alongside of the slit, completely preventing any fire from that quarter, and waits for the infantry to arrive and administer the coup de grace with a Mills bomb. This is soon done

and Caledonian continues on her way rejoicing.

The driver, faint from the heat and loss of blood, suddenly perceives a large shell crater immediately ahead. "Neutral right," he shouts to the gearsman, but his wounded leg is unable to work the clutch so that the gears may be withdrawn, and the Tank creeps on towards the hole which is bound to ditch her. Percy struggles vainly at the gear handle, but is unable to make any impression; the driver, wounded

in both hands, endeavors to pull out the primary gear handle, but finding all these efforts useless he shuts the throttle and stops the engine, leaving the Tank on the edge of the crater almost beyond the point of balance.

The enemy, seeing the Tank stop, directs more shell and machine-gun fire onto it, and the interior becomes a perfect inferno.

The driver gives the order to start the engine up again, the engine starts with a roar, but it is useless for the

below: Driver training in a British Mk III in 1917 at Bovington Camp; left: The crew of a French 75 gun in a second-line trench, awaiting their tank target.

driver to continue, with one leg and both arms out of action. The gunners carefully lift him down onto the floor of the Tank, and revive his spirits with rum and sal volatile.

The officer takes the driving seat and endeavors to pull the bus out of the hole, but without success, and he has to give up the job.

All the guns are now out of action and the ammunition boxes riddled with bullet splinters. The enemy fire has slackened somewhat, but it is still far from safe to leave the Tank. The fan having stopped, the heat inside is terrible, and even the unwounded feel it badly. Will the infantry never come up? To make matters worse, an anti-Tank gun opens fire and Caledonian's crew begin to give themselves up for lost.

But hark, another small gun speaks out, this time with a familiar clang about its voice. The driver quickly hoists a periscope and to the joy of all announces that Crocodile is only half a mile away and is firing at the anti-Tank gun. The infantry are now level with the Tank and the enemy fire begins to die down. At last it ceases altogether, and with a sigh of relief the three more seriously wounded members of the crew open the doors and roll out on to the ground. The fresh air is like a tonic and the first driver so far recovers as to make an inspection of the outside.

Not a trace of paint to be seen on the front of the Tank, name all shot away, Lewis guns torn to shreds, peri-

British Mk II tanks at the Battle of Arras, April 1917.

scopes punctured, and the whole of the crew stone deaf and mostly covered with dried blood.

The officer, somewhat dazed from the blow to his head, leads the way for the wounded, leaving the sergeant to take care of the remainder.

On the way they stop and try to hold conversation with Crocodile, but without much effect owing to their deafness. The little party passed down towards the dressing station pursued by machine-gun fire which they fortunately—being deaf—could not hear. On the way they picked up Calcium's driver wounded in the arm and also passed the dead body of poor old "Bunny," the gallant officer of Carmarthen.

Exhausted, they reached a regimental aid post, and after having their wounds dressed were sent rejoicing on their way with a cup of coffee and a packet of "Players." Of the commander of the crew, "Percy" was killed later in the day and Sergeant Richards was wounded, as also were two others, leaving only one of the crew of eight to return to his company to tell the story.

Sergeant Richards was afterwards awarded the Military Medal for his gallantry in remaining with "Percy" after he was wounded, and under heavy fire until the latter died.

"Good-morning, good-morning!" the General said
When we met him last week on our way to the line.
Now the soldiers he smiled at are most of 'em dead.
And we're cursing his staff for incompetent swine.
"He's a cheery old card," grinned Harry to Jack
As they slogged up to Arras with rifle and pack.
But he did for them both by his plan of attack.
—*The General* by Siegfried Sassoon

The skipper and gunner of an American Whippet tank near Verdun, France, in 1918.

PANZER MAN

Before the beginning of the First World War Heinz Guderian, a young German infantry officer elected a technical role for himself with a telegraph battalion in light of his particular interest in the military uses of communications. With the coming of the war, Guderian was given command of a heavy wireless station linked to the cavalry. Improvements to the wireless technology of the day, and the opportunities they afforded, fascinated him and would soon enable commanders to utilize radio communications wherever they happened to be, in a command post, aboard an aircraft, or, once it had been invented, in a tank.

His ability as a commander, came not from recklessness and intuition, as with Erwin Rommel, but from knowledge. He knew exactly how far every tank could go and over which landscape. —George Parada on General Heinz Guderian

Heinz Guderian was born in the Vistula River town of Kulm, south of Gdansk (Danzig, in what is now Poland) on 17 June 1888. His father was a Senior Lieutenant in the Second Pomeranian Jaeger Battalion of the German Army and his assignment took the family to live in Colmar, Alsace, and later to Saint-Avold. Young Heinz was sent to boarding school and then to the Karlsruhe Cadet School in Baden, where his teachers thought him a very serious boy, highly articulate and, at times quite cold. He entered the army with a commission as a Second Lieutenant on 27 January 1908. On 1 October 1913 he married

Margarete Goerne. They had two sons, both of whom fought with the Panzertruppen in the Second World War.

Guderian's obvious promise led to his receiving various divisional and corps staff appointments and, near the end of the First World War, attendance at a General Staff Officer's course where he was the youngest officer. The end of the war left him appalled by the catastrophic loss of life in the trenches. It caused him to focus on developing and refining a theory based on his belief that "only movement brings victory."

He remained on active service after the war and eventually was given a position on the staff of the Transport Troops Inspectorate where he had been chosen specifically to study theoretical uses of motorized infantry in combat, but, as is often the case in military organizations, he was immediately reassigned to another task that was totally unrelated to either his experience or his interests. In his impatience at this surprising and undesired redirection of his career, Guderian decided to spend the bulk of his spare time researching the theory of mechanized warfare and particularly the writings of the tank pioneer, Major General J.F.C. Fuller and military theorist Sir Basil Liddell-Hart. Following his WWI service, Liddell-Hart had developed a concept of mechanized warfare to replace the grinding static warfare he had recently experienced. The ideas of Fuller and Liddell-Hart, combined with Guderian's own theories, to form the basis of what would become his enormous contribution to the development and evolution of armored warfare.

At the end of the First World War, the Versailles peace treaty stipulated that in defeat Germany would not be permitted to develop an effective

A German Panzer Mk III and crew.

army. It forbade Germany the possession or construction of armored vehicles, tanks, or any similar equipment which might be employed in war. Meanwhile, Britain and other nations continued to experiment with tanks and other armored weaponry, though in a somewhat relaxed manner. But the German Army was now subject to the mechanized warfare doctrine of another genius in that field, General Hans von Seekt, who would become another major contributor to the reform and reorganization of the Army.

In the continuing pursuit of their intense interest in tanks and armor, the Germans chose to make secret arrangements with the Soviets in 1928 to share with them a test facility near the Volga River. That sharing also included ideas, technology, and the use of some small tanks acquired by the Russians from the British firm Vickers-Loyds.

Throughout the 1920s and into the 1930s, Germany essentially paid lip service to the various armament restrictions that had been placed on her by the victors at the end of the Great War. In fact, she was maintaining experimental work in the development of a powerful armored warfare capability. Heinz Guderian, in that time, was quite active on the lecture circuit, speaking out on his ideas about the uses and implications of armored warfare, motorized infantry, and aircraft in future conflicts. And in Britain, impressive progress was being made in radio communications for use in tanks and armored vehicles; progress duly observed by Guderian, the man who would one day become known as "the father of the German Panzer force."

Adolf Hitler, who had served for Germany in the Great War, had risen by 1933 to Chancellor of Germany and by 1934, the German firm

Daimler-Benz was well along in the design and construction of a promising new tank prototype, the PzKw Panzerkampfwagen. Early in 1935, Hitler witnessed trials of the new vehicle at the German Army's secret ordnance testing ground at Kummersdorf. He reportedly commented: "That's what I need. That's what I want to have." The PzKw was indeed just what he required, an inexpensive light tank, an impressive new weapon system that he could have in great quantities if production could somehow be achieved in spite of serious rubber, steel and fuel shortages. Still, the optimistic leader of Germany immediately authorized the creation of three panzer divisions.

By that autumn, Heinz Guderian had been made Chief of Staff of the new German armored force. Hitler had been greatly impressed by Guderian's ideas about armored warfare technique, tactics and equipment, and saw to it that Guderian's command received the bulk of the equipment and materials it requested, mainly at the expense of other army organizations that were forced to do without. But even with his favored status and the ear of the German leader, Guderian was unable to obtain many of the tracked armored vehicles essential to his philosophy which required the ability to move motorized infantry overland in concert with his tanks.

The clever, intelligent and determined Guderian sought out and exploited every opportunity, from his early years in the military, through the early years of the Second World War, to expand his knowledge and experience of mechanized warfare. His imaginative, highly advanced concepts kept him at the forefront of the thinking about future tank warfare. More than merely a theorist, he was a hands-on activist, a believer in leading from the

I'LL BE YOUR WALTZING MATILDA IF YOU'LL BE MY VALENTINE?

front. And he contributed heavily to the design, development and manufacture of his tanks, especially to the main design features of the PzKpfw III and PzKpfw IV types (the former intended for attacking soft targets with a short, large-caliber cannon; the latter with a long gun for tank-killing). His was a truly aggressive interest in the tanks his panzers would take into war.

By 1937, Heinz Guderian had been promoted to the rank of General and written and published his book *Achtung—Panzer!* Comment on the book has ranged widely over the years. Of it, Liddell-Hart wrote: ". . . of great interest as a self-exposition of the specialist mind and how it works. He had far more imagination than most specialists, but it was exercised almost entirely within the bounds of his professional subject, and burning enthusiasm increased the intensity of his concentration." Paul Harris wrote: "*Achtung—Panzer!* is one of the most significant military books of the twentieth century. Guderian distilled into it about fifteen years study of the development of mechanized warfare from its origins in the First World War until 1937. He sought to demonstrate that only by the intelligent use of armored formations could Germany achieve swift and decisive victories in future wars, and avoid the ruinous attrition experienced in 1914-18. Although a number of conservative senior officers were skeptical of Guderian's message, by the outbreak of the Second World War it had gained a good deal of acceptance. The panzer (armored) divisions became the cutting edge of the German Army in its spectacular victories of 1939-42."

Achtung—Panzer! certainly impressed Hitler. In February 1938 he promoted Guderian to the rank of Lieutenant-General and put him in command of the world's first armored corps. The new position would provide a showcase for the capabilities of his armored units in 1939, when they were required to perform as the spearhead of the Anschluss, Hitler's annexation of Austria. The impression of ruthless efficiency given to Europe and the world by their role in the bloodless takeover of Austria, however, was a false one. Guderian's armored units suffered from insufficient supplies and an ill-conceived logistics organization. His petrol-engined tanks only managed to keep rolling by taking on fuel from service stations along the invasion route. The tank breakdown rate was reported to be at least 30 percent. Food and ammunition were in critically short supply and the overall experience caused Guderian to rethink and rebuild his entire supply system.

Hitler had planned to send his panzers into Poland early in the morning of 26 August 1939 but cancelled the attack at the last minute on the possibility that something positive might yet

come from his diplomatic maneuvering with Britain, which had guaranteed Poland's integrity. But lacking acceptable progress he rescheduled his Polish adventure. The panzers were alerted on 31 August and the German armored divisions were moved up to forward positions ready for the attack. Guderian: "On the 1st of September at 04:45 hours the whole corps moved simultaneously over the frontier. There was a thick ground mist at first which prevented the air force from giving us any support. I accompanied the Third Panzer Brigade, in the first wave, as far as the area north of Zempelburg where the preliminary fighting took place. Unfortunately, the heavy artillery of the Third Panzer Division felt itself compelled to fire into the mist. The first shell landed fifty yards ahead of my command vehicle, the second fifty yards behind it. I reckoned that the next one was bound to be a direct hit and ordered my driver to turn about and drive off. The unaccustomed noise had made him nervous, however, and he drove straight into a ditch at full speed. The front axle of the half-tracked vehicle was bent so that the steering mechanism was put out of action. This marked the end of my drive. I made my way to my corps command post, procured myself a fresh vehicle and had a word with the over-eager artillerymen. Incidentally, it may be noted that I was the first corps commander ever to use armored command vehicles in order to accompany tanks on to the battlefield. They were equipped with radio, so that I was able to keep in constant touch with my corps headquarters and with the division under my command.

"Messages from the Second (Motorized) Infantry Division stated that their attack on the Polish wire entanglements had bogged down. All three infantry regiments had made a

frontal attack. The division was now without reserves. I ordered that the regiment on the left be withdrawn during the night and moved to the right wing, from where it was to advance next day behind the Third Panzer Division and make an encircling movement in the direction of Tuchel.

"The Twentieth (Motorized) Division had taken Konitz with some difficulty, but had not advanced any appreciable distance beyond that town. It was ordered to continue its attack on the next day.

"During the night the nervousness of the first day made itself felt more than once. Shortly after midnight the Second (Motorized) Division informed me that they were being compelled to withdraw by Polish cavalry. I was speechless for a moment; when I regained the use of my voice I asked the divisional commander if he had ever heard of Pomeranian grenadiers being broken by hostile cavalry. He replied that he had not and now assured me that he could hold his positions. I decided all the same that I must visit this division the next morning. At about five o'clock I found the divisional staff still all at sea. I placed myself at the head of the regiment which had been withdrawn during the night and led it personally as far as the crossing of the Kamionka to the north of Gross-Klonia, where I sent it off in the direction of Tuchel. The Second (Motorized) Division's attack now began to make rapid progress. The panic of the first day's fighting was past."

Guderian was famously the creator of the theory of "blitzkrieg" or lightning war. The main way in which tanks were used in the latter part of World War I—to try and force a hole through the enemy line—had made him realize the validity of his own notion: a powerful, well-supported armored force is best utilized in a high-speed, long-ranging push deep into enemy territory, achieving rapid, sustainable gains while wreaking maximum confusion, chaos, and panic as it travels. He believed in versatility and adaptability in combat, cherishing the radio capability that enabled these qualities. His watchwords were mobility and velocity. In his book, *The Other Side of the Hill*, Basil Liddell-Hart wrote of Guderian: "Sixty per cent of what the German panzer forces became was due to him. Ambitious, brave, a heart for his soldiers who liked and trusted him; rash as a man, quick in decisions, strict with officers, real personality, therefore many enemies. Blunt, even to Hitler. As a trainer—good, thorough, progressive. If you suggest revolutionary ideas, he will say in ninety-five per cent of cases: 'Yes, at once.'"

Guderian: "On the 5th of September our corps had a surprise visit from Adolf Hitler. I met him near Plevno on the Tuchel-Schwetz road, got into his car and drove with him along the line of our previous advance. We passed the destroyed Polish artillery, went through Schwetz, and then, following closely behind our encircling troops, drove to Graudenz where he stopped and gazed for some time at the blown bridges over the Vistula. At the sight of the smashed artillery regiment, Hitler had asked me 'Our dive bombers did that?' When I replied, 'No, our panzers' he was plainly astonished. During the drive we discussed at first the course of events in my corps area. Hitler asked about casualties. I gave him the latest figures that I had received, some 150 dead and 700 wounded for all the four divisions under my command during the battle of the Corridor. He was amazed at the smallness of these figures and contrasted them with the casualties of his

own old regiment, the List Regiment during the First World War: on the first day of battle that one regiment alone had lost more than 2,000 dead and wounded. I was able to show him that the smallness of our casualties in this battle against a tough and courageous enemy was primarily due to the effectiveness of our tanks. Tanks are a life-saving weapon. The men's belief in the superiority of their armored equipment had been greatly strengthened by their successes in the Corridor. The enemy had suffered the total destruction of between two and three infantry divisions and one cavalry brigade. Thousands of prisoners and hundreds of guns had fallen into our hands.

"Our conversation turned on technical matters. Hitler wanted to know what had proved particularly satisfactory about our tanks and what was still in need of improvement. I told him that the most important thing now was to hasten the delivery of Panzers III and IV to the fighting troops and to increase the production of these tanks. For their further development their present speed was sufficient, but they needed to be more heavily armored, particularly in front; the range and power of penetration of their guns also needed to be increased, which would mean longer barrels and a shell with a heavier charge. This applied equally to our anti-tank guns.

"With a word of recognition for the troops' acheivements, Hitler left us as dusk was falling and returned to his headquarters."

I met her paddling down the road, / A vast primeval sort of toad, / And while I planned a swift retreat / She snorted, roared, and stamped her feet, And sprinted up a twelve-foot bank; Whereat a voice cried 'Good old Tank!'
She paused and wagged her armored

tail, / There was a 'Jonah' in the 'Whale,' / Since from her ribs a face looked out; / Her skipper hailed me with a shout, / 'Come on and watch my beauty eat a batch of houses down the street!'
It was pure joy to see her crunch / A sugar factory for lunch; / She was a 'peach' at chewing trees—/ The Germans shuddered at her sneeze—And when she leant against a wall / It shortly wasn't there at all.
I stroked the faithful creature's head; 'What gives her greatest bliss?' I said. Her skipper glibly answered, 'Tanks are crazed about Abdullas . . . Thanks! She waddled off—and on the air Arose Abdulla's fragrance rare!
—*The Ways of Tanks*, from an Abdulla cigarettes ad in the 2 November 1918 issue of *The Sphere*

"On the 6th of September the corps staff and the advance guards of the divisions crossed the Vistula. Corps headquarters was set up in Finckenstein, in the very beautiful castle that belonged to Count Dohna-Finckenstein and which Frederick the Great had given to his minister, Count von Finckenstein. Napoleon had twice used this castle as his headquarters. The emperor first came there in 1807, when he took the war against Prussia and Russia over the Vistula and into East Prussia. After crossing the poor and monotonous Tuchel Heath, Napoleon exclaimed at the sight of the castle, 'Enfin un château!' His feelings are understandable. It was there that he had planned his advance towards Preussisch-Eylau. A mark of his presence was still to be seen in the scratches left by his spurs on the wooden floor. He was there for the second time before the Russian campaign of 1812; he spent a few weeks in the castle in the company

of the beautiful Countess Walewska. 'I slept in the room that had been Napoleon's.'"

With the end of the European war in May 1945, Heinz Guderian surrendered to a U.S. Army unit and became a prisoner of war. While the Russians wanted him to face trial at Nuremburg, the Western Allies did not concur. Guderian spent two years in West German prisons and was finally released in 1948. Thereafter, he wrote his memoirs and other works at his home in Schwangau bei Fussen, where he died on 14 May 1954.

To be prepared for war is one of the most effectual means of preserving peace.
—General George Washington, 1790

The more you sweat in peace, the less you bleed in war.
—Admiral Hyman G. Rickover, U.S. Navy, 1986

Train hard, fight easy . . . and win.
Train easy, fight hard . . . and die.
—unknown

above: General Heinz Guderian, the father of modern tank warfare and Germany's Panzer force.

BLITZKRIEG

The European war will be an industrial war of aircraft, tanks and movement.
—Dwight D. Eisenhower, while an aide to General Douglas MacArthur in the Philippines.

You were given the choice between war and dishonor. You chose dishonor and you will have war.—Winston Churchill, in response to Prime Minister Neville Chamberlain's Munich agreement with Adolf Hitler of 29 September 1938

No one is certain about the exact origin of the word blitzkrieg (lightning war). As defined by the *American Heritage Dictionary of the English Language* it means: A swift, sudden military offensive, usually by combined air and mobile land forces. Credit for coining it has gone variously to *Time* magazine, Adolf Hitler, Sir Basil Liddell-Hart and others. Whatever the origin, historians generally agree that the concept itself is Prussian.

"In the year, 1929, I became convinced that tanks working on their own or in conjunction with infantry could never achieve decisive importance. My historical studies, the exercises carried out in England and our own experiments with mock-ups had persuaded me that tanks would never be able to produce their full effect until the other weapons on whose support they must invariably rely were brought up to their standard of speed and cross-country performance. In such a formation of all arms, the tanks must play the primary role, the other weapons being subordinated to the requirements of the armor. It would be wrong to include tanks in infantry divisions: what was needed were armored divisions which would include all the supporting arms needed to allow the tanks to fight with full effect."
—from *Panzer Leader* by Heinz Guderian

In a few words then, the whole future of warfare appears to me to lie in the employment of mobile armies, relatively small but of high quality and rendered distinctly more effective by the addition of aircraft, and in the simultaneous mobilization of the whole defence force, be it to feed the attack or for home defence.
—General Hans von Seekt, German Army

While it was the vision of von Seekt that led to the birth of the panzer division; it was Heinz Guderian who conceived and fully realized the blitzkrieg tactic. In the 1930s, majority opinion in the German Army held that the tank, while a useful weapon, was not a decisive one. Many senior officers opposed the development of a massive panzer capability which they saw as a threat to their cavalry arm. But Adolf Hitler himself, having experienced and been traumatized by the terrible stalemate warfare of the First World War, conveyed his belief in the blitzkrieg concept when he addressed the audience at the 1935 Nuremberg Party Rally: "I shouldn't negotiate for months beforehand and make lengthy preparations, but—as I have always done throughout my life—I should suddenly, like a flash of lightning in the night, hurl myself upon the enemy." The blitzkrieg approach to warfare brought advantages that the German leader quickly appreciated. He was impressed by the economies afforded through the use of brief and decisive military actions and he needed such speedy, relatively inexpensive victories

to show the German people the effectiveness of his aggressive foreign policy.

Guderian later described his own vision of how a blitzkrieg action might develop: "One night the doors of aeroplane hangars and army garages will be flung back, motors will be tuned up, and squadrons will swing into movement. The first sudden blow may capture important industrial and raw-material districts or destroy them by air attack so they can take no part in war production. Enemy governmental and military centres may be crippled and his transport system disorganized. In any case, the first strategic surprise attack will penetrate more or less deep into enemy territory according to the distances to be covered and the amount of resistance met with.

"The first wave of air and mechanized attack will be followed up by motorized infantry divisions. They will be carried to the verge of the occupied territory and hold it, thereby freeing the mobile units for another blow. In the meantime the attacker will be raising a mass army. He has the choice of territory and time for his next big blow, and he will then bring up the weapons intended for breaking down all resistance and bursting through the enemy lines. He will do his best to launch the great blow suddenly so as

to take the enemy by surprise, rapidly concentrating his mobile troops and hurling his air force at the enemy. The armored divisions will no longer stop when the first objectives have been reached; on the contrary, utilizing their speed and radius of action to the full, they will do their utmost to complete the breakthrough into the enemy lines of communication. Blow after blow will be launched ceaselessly in order to roll up the enemy front and carry the attack as far as possible into enemy territory. The air force will attack the enemy reserves and prevent their intervention."

Two days after German forces rolled into Poland on 1 September 1939 in the beginning of the *Fall Weiss* (Case White) campaign, Britain and France declared war on Germany and by May 1940, Hitler and his war planners had devised and were on the brink of implementing a grand scheme for the conquest of Western Europe. The plan called for a spectacular coordinated strike—an amazing blitzkrieg combining massive armored power, infantry, paratroops, dive-bombers, surprise, speed and deception.

The German Army Group B, made up of thirty Wehrmacht divisions, was positioned along a 200-mile front line

which faced Belgium and Holland and it would be their task to push through the low countries in a four-pronged attack. But it was essentially a diversionary effort. The German planners expected the British and French to immediately move most of their best divisions north and come to the aid of the Dutch and Belgians primarily along the Dyle River in Belgium.

In the south, German Army Group A, the mighty main force of forty-five armor and infantry divisions, were waiting near the Rhine. When the call came it would be their job to break through a gap between the Maginot and Dyle lines, through the forests of the Ardennes and then to race across France to the English Channel where they were to turn northward to support Army Group B, surrounding and entrapping as many as a million Allied soldiers. With that accomplished, the Germans would then concentrate on occupying all of France in a campaign they called *Fall Gelb* (Case Yellow).

The role of German Army Group C, a force of nineteen divisions, was to keep the defenders of the Maginot Line fortifications busy having to respond to a persistent series of attacks and feints.

In 1930, Andre Maginot was the Defence Minister of France as his government was beginning work on an eighty-seven-mile-long system of underground fortifications against any future threat from their German neighbors. Seven years and $200 million later, the massive project was close to completion and was named in Maginot's honor.

Built in defensive layers, the Maginot Line was fronted with tank trap obstacles that lay ahead of a network of pillboxes protected by barbed wire, and behind these were gun emplacements set in ten-foot-thick concrete walls. These were supported by anti-tank guns from 37mm to 135mm and by machine-guns. Huge underground forts were located every three to five miles along the line. These were constructed with several levels with each having elevators, casemates, shell hoists, a command post, sleeping quarters, a guard room, a hospital, munitions magazines, stores, a telephone exchange, a power plant, and a network of connecting tunnels fitted with protective steel doors. The forts were sunk to a depth of 100 feet and each was manned by up to 1,200 personnel.

The French believed that the formidable Maginot Line fortifications of the Franco-German frontier would deter any future German assault or require the Germans to approach France through the Low Countries. Towards the Franco-Belgian border, the Maginot Line dwindled into a smattering of small defensive elements known as the Little Maginot. An important French industrial region lay just behind this relatively weak defense. The Belgian border, however, was strongly defended and the Allies believed (just as Hitler was sure they would) that their best option in the event of German attack would be to move a large force of troops quickly into Belgium when the Germans made their move.

While the German leader was intent on starting his western assault before the worst of the 1939-40 winter began, his meteorologists convinced him to wait until the spring. He ordered preparation of a special panzer corps whose assignment was to launch an assault on the city of Sedan, an important strategic link between the Maginot and Little Maginot lines.

Adolf Hitler, 21 January 1944: To the High Command. "I order as follows: 1. Commanders-in-Chief, Commanding Generals, and Divisional Commanders are personnally responsible to me for reporting in good time: a. Every decision to carry out an operational movement; b. Every attack planned in divisional strength and upwards which does not conform with the general directives laid down by the High Command; c. Every offensive action in quiet sectors of the front, over and above normal shock troop activities, which is calculated to draw the enemy's attention to the sector; d. Every plan for disengaging or withdrawing forces; e. Every plan for surrendering a position, a local strong point, or a fortress. They must ensure that I have time to intervene in this decision if I think fit, and that my counter-orders can reach the front-line troops in time. 2. Commanders-in-Chief, Commanding Generals, and Divisional Commanders, the Chiefs of the General Staffs, and each individual officer of the General Staff, or officers employed on General Staffs, are responsible to me that every report made to me either directly, or through the normal channels, should contain nothing but the unvarnished truth. In future, I shall impose draconian punishment on any attempt at concealment, whether deliberate or arising from carelessness or oversight. 3. I must point out that the maintenance of

signals communications, particularly in heavy fighting and critical situations, is a prerequisite for the conduct of the battle. All officers commanding troops are responsible to me for ensuring that these communications both to higher headquarters and to subordinate commanders, are not broken and for seeing that, by exhausting every means and engaging themselves personally, permanent communications in every case are ensured with the commanders above and below."

General Erich von Manstein, Chief of Staff to German Army Group A, the organization given the task of assaulting Sedan, believed adamantly that those in the German General Staff who thought of the Ardennes as impenetrable and utterly unsuited for tank warfare were wrong. He was certain that the forest offered excellent opportunities for the panzers, with its good roads and many wide fields. He felt that the forest areas themselves provided ideal camouflage cover for the German armored forces against aerial reconnaissance observation. But, with Guderian in total agreement, Manstein also believed that Hitler's idea of committing a single panzer corps to the Ardennes attack was folly and would probably result in a World War I-style stalemate. Manstein and Guderian were convinced that the main emphasis should be on the destruction of the Allied forces in a single swift and decisive panzer strike which could only be achieved through the employment of the bulk of Army Group A.

Guderian: "A conference took place attended by the army and army group commanders of Army Group A, accompanied by General von Kleist and myself in the Reich Chancellery. Hitler was there. Each of us generals outlined what his task was and how he intended to carry it out. I was the last to speak. My task was as follows: on the day ordered I would cross the Luxembourg frontier, drive through southern Belgium towards Sedan, cross the Meuse and establish a bridgehead on the far side so that the infantry corps following behind could get across. I explained briefly that my corps would advance through Luxembourg and southern Belgium in three columns; I reckoned on reaching the Belgian frontier posts on the first day and I hoped to break through them on that same day; on the second day I would advance as far as Neufchateau; on the third day I would reach Bouillon and cross the Semois; on the fourth day I would arrive at the Meuse; on the fifth day I would cross it. By the evening of the fifth day I hoped to have established a bridgehead on the far bank. Hitler asked: 'And then what are you going to do?' He was the first person who had thought to ask me this vital question. I replied: 'Unless I receive orders to the contrary, I intend on the next day to continue my advance westwards. The supreme leadership must decide whether my objective is to be Amiens or Paris. In my opinion the correct course is to drive past Amiens to the English Channel.' Hitler nodded and said nothing more. Only General Busch, who commanded the Sixteenth Army on my left, cried out: 'Well, I don't think you'll cross the river in the first place!' Hitler, the tension visible in his face, looked at me to see what I would reply. I said: 'There's no need for you to do so, in any case.' Hitler made no comment.

"I never received any further orders as to what I was to do once the bridgehead over the Meuse was captured. All my decisions, until I reached

1940, a German Panzer III in France.

Operated by a crew of five, the PzKpfw Panzer III mounted a 50mm gun.

the Atlantic seaboard at Abbeville, were taken by me and me alone. The Supreme Command's influence on my actions was merely restrictive throughout."

Hitler finally agreed to Manstein's approach after the general brilliantly articulated it to him at a High Command dinner. Greatly impressed by the new plan, the German leader immersed himself in a process of refining it with his generals and, on 24 February, declared it ready for implementation in May.

There were ten divisions of the British Expeditionary Force near the Franco-Belgian border in April 1940—about 400,000 men—and just one tank brigade. The Belgians were trying to remain neutral, while the French were boasting confidently that they would beat the Germans when they came, and British Prime Minister Neville Chamberlain was talking about "Herr Hitler" having missed his best chance at a western offensive by not striking right after Poland had fallen.

You'd think, to hear some people talk, That lads go West with sobs and curses, And sullen faces white as chalk, / Hankering for wreaths and tombs and hearses. / But they've been taught the way to do it / Like Christian soldiers; not with haste And shuddering groans; but passing through it / With due regard for decent taste.
—from *How to Die* by Siegfried Sassoon

At dawn on 10 May 1940, the first elements of a German army of more than two million men began to move on Holland, Luxembourg and Belgium. Great masses of tanks and infantry spearheaded the campaign to secure the whole of Western Europe. It was the final day of the so-called Phony War, and the day that Winston Churchill became the new British Prime Minister.

Aircraft of the Royal Air Force and the French Armee de l'Air rose from French airfields to attack the German columns but did little real damage to

the advancing enemy. Everywhere the Germans went, their panzers coursed through the opposition with little apparent effort, except at Rotterdam where determined Dutch resistance held firm. Hitler then ordered a massive air strike on the port city, starting major fires which destroyed nearly 650 acres in the main section. 800 citizens died and more than 75,000 were left homeless. The Dutch forces surrendered after holding out for five days against the enemy assault.

Just north of Liége lay the largest and most heavily fortified example of Belgium's modern defenses, Eben Emael. Positioned near where the Albert Canal merged with the Meuse River, the fort housed a 1,500-man garrison and was defended by two 120mm guns and sixteen 75mm guns capable of covering all approaches to the site—except from above. Before daybreak on the 10th, hundreds of German airborne troops landed near the fort, some of them on the roof of the structure. Their mission included

the placing of explosive charges in ventilators and gun slits, in addition to hollow-charge demolition explosives specially devised to bust the three-foot-thick concrete walls and spread a deadly inferno through the interior and galleries. The fires were supplemented by flame throwers fired into the gun ports. By 7 a.m. the fort had effectively been neutralized and by mid-day on the 11th, the garrison was forced to surrender.

The Allied forces hurried northwards to take up positions on the Dyle and Meuse Rivers, ready to take on the German onslaught. There were thirty-seven British, French and Belgian divisions. The Allies, in particular the French, were aware of the enemy activity in the Ardennes, but were confident that the Germans would require a minimum of ten days to make their way through the heavily wooded region. They also believed that the real defensive test would come at the Meuse, which they were certain they could hold, having

prepared the banks with hundreds of dug-outs with artillery positions behind them. The German armored elements, however, had little trouble with the minefields near the German-Belgian border in the night of 9-10 May, nor with the Allied troops in the zone. German armored divisions reached a point on the Meuse near Sedan in just two days.

13 May, mid-morning. Little remained of the vaunted French defenses on the Meuse. The German armor hadn't needed to fire a shot. Their easy access to the river, which they immediately began crossing on pontoon bridges they had brought with them, had been made possible by the German Air Force whose low-level bombers and Stuka dive-bombers had pounded the French defenders.

General Guderian led the armored units crossing the Meuse: "On the far bank of the river I found the efficient and brave commander of the 1st Rifle Regiment, Lieutenant-Colonel Balck, with his staff. He hailed me with the cheerful cry, 'Pleasure boating on the Meuse is forbidden.' I had in fact coined the phrase myself during the training we had had for this operation, since the attitude of some of the younger officers had struck me as too light-hearted. I now realized that they had judged the situation correctly."

The slower French tanks were no match for the German armor at the Meuse, with the panzers destroying more than fifty in just two hours. German anti-aircraft defenses performed effectively, bringing down 268 of 474 RAF aircraft in France by 14 May.

Guderian: "Once again to the 1st Panzer Division where I found the divisional commander accompanied by his first general staff officer, Major Wenck; I asked him whether his whole division could be turned westwards

or whether a flank guard should be left facing south on the east bank of the Ardennes Canal. Wenck saw fit to interject a somewhat slangy expression of mine 'Klotzen, nicht Kleckern' [a phrase which might be roughly translated as 'Boot 'em, don't spatter 'em'], and that really answered my question. 1st and 2nd Panzer Divisions received orders immediately to change direction with all their forces, to cross the Ardennes Canal, and to head west with the objective of breaking clear through the French defenses. That I might coordinate the movements of the two divisions I next went to the command post of the 2nd Panzer Division, which was in the Chateau Rocan, on the heights above Donchéry. From that vantage point a good view could be obtained over the ground across which 2nd Panzer Division had advanced and attacked on the 13th and 14th of May. I was surprised that the French long-range artillery in the Maginot Line and its westerly extension had not laid down heavier fire and caused us more trouble during our advance. At this moment, as I looked at the ground we had come over, the success of our attack struck me as almost a miracle."

Having crossed the Meuse, the great mass of German armor was able to fan out as it raced west. Many dispirited French troops were cluttering the roads being used by the panzers. Some recalled the derisive shouts from German tankers: "Drop your rifles and get the hell out of here—we don't have time to take you prisoner."

Guderian: "I was pleased to have retained my freedom of movement when, early on the 16th of May, I went to the headquarters of the 1st Panzer Division. I drove through Vendresse to Omont. The situation at the front was not yet clear. All that was known was that there had been

heavy fighting during the night in the neighbourhood of Bouvellemont. So on to Bouvellemont. In the main street of the burning village I found the regimental commander, Lieutenant-Colonel Balck, and let him describe the events of the previous night to me. The troops were over-tired, having had no real rest since the 9th of May. Ammunition was running low. The men in the front line were falling asleep in their slit trenches. Balck himself, in wind jacket and with a knotty stick in his hand, told me that the capture of the village had only succeeded because, when his officers complained against the continuation of the attack, he had replied: 'In that case I'll take the place on my own!' and had moved off. His men had thereupon followed him. His dirty face and his red-rimmed eyes showed that he had spent a hard day and a sleepless night. For his doings on that day he was to receive the Knight's Cross. His opponents—a good Norman infantry division and a brigade of Spahis—had fought bravely. The enemy's machine-guns were still firing into the village street, but for some time now there had been no artillery fire and Balck shared my opinion that resistance was almost over.

"Now, on the previous day we had captured a French order, originating if I am not mistaken from General Gamelin himself, which contained the words: 'The torrent of German tanks must finally be stopped!' This order had strengthened me in my conviction that the attack must be pressed forward with all possible strength, since the defensive capabilities of the French [sic] was obviously causing their high command serious anxiety. This was no time for hesitancy, still less for calling a halt.

"I sent for the troops by companies and read them the captured order, making plain its significance and the

importance of continuing the attack at once. I thanked them for their achievements to date and told them that they must now strike with all their power to complete our victory. I then ordered them to return to their vehicles and to continue the advance."

Being in a point tank in a column is not the healthiest place to be. You never know what to expect . . . what's around the bend, what's just over the rise, what's on your right or your left. You just keep praying. Many a time I would rather have been on foot than in that tank. Those 88s went through the armor like it was paper.
—Charles Shenloogian, World War II U.S. tanker

As Guderian's tank forces advanced rapidly westward, higher-ranking German officers feared that his swift pace was laying his forces open to the possibility of being cut off and trapped by the Allies as he continued to outrun his infantry units. Twice in the first few days after the breakthrough, they ordered his advance halted to allow the infantry time to catch up with the tanks. Guderian clearly disagreed and lobbied heatedly for the freedom to maintain his pace towards the coast. Incredibly, seventy-one German divisions were on the march westward, ten of them armored.

Guderian: "After our splendid success on the 16th of May and the simultaneous victory won by XLI Army Corps, it did not occur to me that my superiors could possibly still hold the same view as before, nor that they would now be satisfied with simply holding the bridgehead we had established across the Meuse while awaiting the arrival of the infantry corps. I was completely filled with the ideas that I had expressed during our conference with Hitler in March, that is to say to

complete our breakthrough and not stop until we had reached the English Channel. It certainly never occurred to me that Hitler himself, who had approved the boldest aspects of the Manstein plan and had not uttered a word against my proposals concerning exploitation of the breakthrough, would now be the one to be frightened by his own temerity and would order our advance to be stopped at once. Here I was making a great mistake, as I was to discover on the following morning.

"Early on the 17th of May I received a message from the Panzer Group: the advance was to be halted at once and I was personally to report to General von Kleist, who would come to see me at my airstrip at 0700 hours. He was there punctually and, without even wishing me a good morning, began in very violent terms to berate me for having disobeyed orders. He did not see fit to waste a word of praise on the performance of the troops. When the first storm was passed, and he had stopped to draw breath, I asked that I might be relieved of my command. General von Kleist was momentarily taken aback, but then he nodded and ordered me to hand over my command to the most senior general of my corps. And that was the end of our conversation. I returned to my corps headquarters and asked General Veiel to come to see me, that I might hand over to him.

"I then sent a message to Army Group von Rundstedt by wireless in which I said that after I had handed over my command at noon I would be flying to Army Group headquarters to make a report on what had happened. I received an answer almost at once. I was to remain at my headquarters and await the arrival of Colonel-General List, who was in command of the Twelfth Army that was following behind us and who had been instructed to clear this matter up. Until the arrival of Colonel-General List all units were to be ordered to remain where they were. Major Wenck, who came to receive these orders, was shot at by a French tank while returning to his division and was wounded in the foot. General Veiel now appeared and I explained the situation to him. Early that afternoon Colonel-General List arrived and asked me at once what on earth was going on here. Acting on instructions from Colonel-General von Rundstedt he informed me that I would not resign my command and explained that the order to halt the advance came from the Army High Command (the OKH) and therefore must be obeyed. He quite understood my reasons, however, for wishing to go on with the advance and therefore, with the Army Group's approval, he ordered: 'Reconnaissance in force to be carried out. Corps headquarters must in all circumstances remain where it is, so that it may easily be reached. ' This was at least something, and I was grateful to Colonel-General List for what he had done. I asked him to clear up the misunderstanding between General von Kleist and myself. Then I set the 'reconnaissance in force' in motion. Corps headquarters remained at its old location in Soize, a wire was laid from there to my advanced headquarters, so that I need not communicate with my staff by wireless and my orders could therefore not be monitored by the wireless intercept units of the OKH and the OKW.

"On the 19th of May we crossed the old Somme battlefield of the First World War. Until now we had been advancing north of the Aisne, the Serre and the Somme, and those rivers had served to guard our open left flank, which was also covered by reconnaissance troops, anti-tank units and combat engineers. The danger from this flank was slight; we knew about the French 4th Armored Division, a new formation under General de Gaulle, which had been reported on the 16th of May and had first appeared, as already stated, at Montcornet. During the next few days de Gaulle stayed with us and on the 19th a few of his tanks succeeded in penetrating to within a mile of my advanced headquarters in Holnon Wood. The headquarters had only some 20mm anti-aircraft guns for protection, and I passed a few uncomfortable hours until at last the threatening visitors moved off in another direction. Also, we were aware of the existence of a French reserve army, some eight divisions strong, which was being set up in the Paris area. We did not imagine that General Frére would advance against us so long as we kept on moving ourselves. According to the basic French formula, he would wait until he had exact information about his enemy's position before doing anything. So we had to keep him guessing; this could best be done by continuing to push on."

The German lightning strike was producing better results than even Hitler had expected. Guderian's panzers had reached Abbeville and Amiens by 20 May and nearly one million Allied troops were isolated in the north by the panzer units racing to the Channel coast. The best elements of the British and French armies, and all of the Belgian army, were cut off and could not be resupplied except through a few of the Channel ports.

In the last days of the blitzkrieg on France, she was also subjected to a short but noteworthy procession of staggeringly inept generals in top command roles. Elderly, exhausted and

essentially devoid of any practical ideas for turning back the invaders, this little parade contributed nothing but more confusion to the sad situation; all soon lost their will, the plot, and finally, the fight.

As the end approached for the Allied forces in France, the BEF's commander, Lord Gort, managed to launch an armored attack aimed at reinforcing the Allied headquarters position at Arras. Gort threw two divisions and seventy-four tanks into the action and had the support of sixty French tanks. The effort caught Rommel's 7th Panzer Division by surprise and gave him a brief fright. But he quickly rallied, and soon had Gort's force reeling from a counterattack with artillery, anti-tank guns and, ulti-

A German PzKw III Panzer tank burns in the North African desert.

mately, his powerful tank force. Forty Allied tanks were destroyed against a German loss of twelve. The advance of the panzers continued unabated to the French coast. With the end of May came the end of the Battle of France and the most powerful and impressive armored sweep the world had ever seen.

Trapped at the French seaside town of Dunkirk, 338,000 troops, mostly from the British Expeditionary Force, along with some French and Belgian units, now faced likely annihilation at the hands of the German invaders. Field Marshal von Rundstedt sat behind the town with his five Army Group A armored divisions, poised to destroy the massive Allied congregation which was gathered

mainly on or near the beaches. He certainly had the firepower and the will to complete the task, but it was not to be. Rundstedt: "If I had had my way, the English would not have got off so lightly at Dunkirk. But my hands were tied by direct orders from Hitler himself. While the English were clambering onto the ships off the beaches, I was kept uselessly off the port unable to move. I recommended to the Supreme Command that my five Panzer divisions be immediately sent into the town and thereby completely destroy the retreating English. But I received definite orders from the Führer that under no circumstances was I to attack . . ."

It seems that Hitler believed that his panzers had been severely strained

in their race across France. He dared not risk them in a direct assault over the difficult terrain around Dunkirk when he needed to deploy them against the remaining French armies to the south. So he gave the job of wiping out the beach-bound BEF to Hermann Goering's Luftwaffe which he felt could easily destroy the enemy forces by bombing them. His misjudgement allowed most of the British troops to be evacuated from the beaches when the Royal Navy, together with an improvised fleet of vessels including coasters, paddle steamers, fishing boats, colliers, yachts and other craft, managed to rescue them. British losses during the evacuation amounted to 68,111 killed, wounded or taken prisoner.

American M3 medium tanks being built in the
Chrysler tank arsenal.

CHARIOTS
OF FIRE

THIS VEHICLE IS FILLED WITH ANTI FREEZE ... MUST NOT BE DRAINED

T252403K

below: A British Churchill Mk 8 95mm Howitzer; top right: A British Matilda tank on display at Bovington Tank Museum; bottom right: A British Crusader in training with a Matilda in the distance.

Great Britain will pursue the WAR AGAINST JAPAN to the very end.

WINSTON CHURCHILL

A Hungarian Turan tank.

A Soviet T-72M tank of the East
German Army.

A row of Western Main Battle tanks; left to right: The British Chieftain and Challenger, the American Abrams, the British Vickers, and the German Leopard II.

right: The French AMX-30 Main Battle tank; far right: The U.S. Army M60-AI Patton Main Battle tank; below: The British Crusader I cruiser tank; bottom right: The British Chieftain Main Battle tank.

The American MIAI Abrams Main Battle
tank at Bovington, England, for trials against
the Challenger, Chieftain, Leopard II and the
Vickers VII main battle tanks.

top left: An M41 Walker Bulldog light tank; left: Sherman tanks in action on the Gustav Line in the Cassino battle of WWII; above right: The Russian T-26 light tank of the inter-war years.

A 1916 drawing by British official war artist Sir Muirhead Bone.

THE RUSSIAN FRONT

What happens to a Russian, or to a Czech, does not interest me in the slightest. What the nations can offer in the way of good blood of our type we will take, if necessary by kidnapping their children and raising them here with us. Whether nations live in prosperity or starve to death interests me only in so far as we need them as slaves for our Kulture: otherwise it is of no interest to me. Whether ten thousand Russian females fall down from exhaustion while digging an anti-tank ditch interests me only in so far as the anti-tank ditch for Germany is finished.
—Heinrich Himmler, October 1943

There were more than 22,000 tanks in the Soviet arsenal by 22 June 1941 when the German invasion of Russia began. At that time the Soviets had more tanks than all the other armies in the world put together—and four times as many as the Germans. But the majority of this armor was obsolete and the Germans knew it. What they didn't know was that their Russian enemy had tested and made operational two new and significantly better tanks in the KV heavy and T-34 medium, and that some of these new tanks were already serving in front-line units. Both were externally well-designed, excellent fighting vehicles that mounted a heavy gun and were protected by thick armor. They did, however, have shortcomings. They were essentially simple, low-technology weapons with little mechanical assistance for the

crews, poor habitability and vision, and a high mechanical breakdown rate. Still, the T-34 cruised through World War II, finishing with very high marks, and is often referred to by experts as the best tank of the war.

Like the Japanese attack on the U.S. battleships moored in Pearl Harbor on 7 December 1941, the German panzer divisions surprised the Russians on a Sunday morning, overrunning the enemy positions and swiftly advancing considerable distances before the Soviets could react. The surprise worked well for the German invaders. Even with the overwhelming number of tanks in the Soviet inventory, only 25 percent were in good working order, and most of their tank officers and men had little experience driving and operating their vehicles. Their units were in the process of being reformed and spare parts and equipment were in short supply.

While the Soviets were unprepared for the fight, the Germans were split over the approach they should take. Heinz Guderian, Erich von Manstein and other German generals strongly favored applying powerful military force to destroy the Red Army, while Hitler and others thought it essential to paralyze Russia's government by seizing political and economic objectives. Hitler finally stipulated "the destruction of the Red Army in western Russia by deep penetrations of armored spearheads."

At the start, the fast-paced panzer attacks seemed to provoke only slow (though courageous) responses by the Soviet armor. The panzer generals knew that it was vital to maintain momentum in their attacks; to keep up pressure on the opposition through quick thrusts followed by bold encirclements of the enemy forces. Manstein: "The farther a single panzer

corps . . . ventured into the depths of the Russian hinterland, the greater the hazards became. Against this it may be said that the safety of a tank formation operating in the enemy's rear largely depends on its ability to keep moving. Once it comes to a halt it will immediately be assailed from all sides by the enemy's reserves.''

When the German attack began, the panzers were able to race through the stunned Soviet tank and artillery units, leaving them crushed in their wake. But the seemingly superior panzer forces were, like any army, heavily dependent

on continuing resupply of fuel, rations and munitions. The progress and security afforded by their momentum could only be assured if the enemy could be kept from interfering with German supply routes. That crucial momentum could also be lost if the rains came and mired the supply trucks in the sticky Russian mud.

The Germans may have had ini-tial advantages in momentum and better organization, but in their early encounters with the KV heavy tank, and later with the T-34, they found to their cost, what a formidable threat the 76mm gun could be. While these Soviet tanks were able to lie back beyond 1,000 yards and penetrate the thickest German armor with the 76mm rounds, German tanks had to fire from within 200 yards to kill a KV or a T-34.

For a while the panzers continued to have their way with the enemy armored units, destroying Soviet tanks with an ease they would never again know in the campaign. For now, they faced only a relative handful of the KVs and T-34s. German forces were benefitting from superior training, leadership, organization, coordination and, not least, highly effective aerial reconnaissance. They invariably knew in advance of any Soviet armored attack, the strength and position of the enemy force.

The Soviets seemed incapable of putting all the necessary elements together to counter the panzers effec-tively, much less grabbing and holding the initiative. They were weakened by inadequate training and incompetent leadership and their tank crews, inept in the handling and operation of their vehicles, had a lot to worry about. They were plagued with frequent mechanical breakdowns due in part to the negligent way they handled the machines. Their tactics were often unsophisticated and at times naïve; their shooting accuracy was uneven at best and there were too few KVs and T-34s available to make an apprecia-ble difference.

In spite of the successes achieved by the panzers to this point, the Germans were awakening to a new reality. As impressive as their gains

Members of a German Panzer platoon on the Russian Front in the Second World War.

had been, with Heinz Guderian's units pushing more than 400 miles in twenty-five days from Brest Litovsk to Smolensk, the Germans were incurring losses 50 percent greater than in their earlier campaigns. Guderian was experiencing tank repair and re-supply problems similar to those of Rommel in the desert war and, after two and a half months of fighting, the spectacularly successful blitzkrieg tactic of the previous two years was coming up short. The advance of the panzers was slowing visibly, and as the horrific winter arrived, the tanks of both sides were less and less effective, imposing ever greater demands on the infantry elements to consolidate the gains made by their tank units and to fend off any enemy tank action.

Moscow remained the prize that Hitler demanded and expected to be his by late October. Now the exhausted German army units were required to behave as though fresh and still vigorous. They were asked to mount a new campaign towards the Russian capital, and to their credit, they did manage a sizeable offensive with Guderian's armies making some gains between Sevsk and Bryansk and at Vyazma, before becoming bogged down on their new front. And then

Panzer IIIs on the Russian Front.

the rains came. The already inadequate road surfaces in the region were turned into quagmires as the rain fell with an intensity normally associated with the tropics. Meanwhile, General Georgi Zhukov, Russia's most successful and powerful military commander of the war, tried in vain to build his armor and crews and develop them into a force capable of performing on a par with the German armor. The incessant rains and ensuing mud kept the Germans from advancing beyond a position 150 miles from Moscow and this delay enabled General Zhukov to reinforce his own armored units and continue to fight a delaying action, adding significantly to the Germans'

problems. While they persisted in their plodding, uneven movement towards the enemy capital, the Germans had clearly lost most of their earlier momentum and, within sight of Moscow they could go no farther. It was then that the weather worsened dramatically and a deep, unyielding freeze set in, paralyzing the now battle-weary tanks of the panzers where they sat. The grease in guns froze as did the oil in the vehicles. The glue-like mud now froze and had to be chipped from the tanks and vehicles with pickaxes.

What Zhukov had going for him at this point was the small but highly effective T-34 and KV tank force which, in fact, had been outperforming the German tanks in the appalling conditions thus far. But he didn't have nearly enough of them to overwhelm the opposition. He also had a large and effective, efficiently placed concentration of anti-tank obstacles giving him a substantial capability for defending Moscow and its environs. As the winter, the worst in 140 years, wore on, the Germans suffered terribly in the numbing cold and the clogging, sucking mud that appeared to reduce all effort and movement, human and mechanical, to slow motion. The Soviets seemed somehow more fit and better able to cope with the brutal conditions. As the snows and bitter cold intensified, the normally impeccable serviceability and performance standards of the German forces and their equipment began to slip. They had come to Russia with the expectation of fighting a relatively brief summer campaign and were ill-prepared for the extremes of winter in the region. They were kitted in summer-weight uniforms and their tanks and other vehicles were not properly winterized. Frozen engine blocks were common; frostbite, trench foot, shock

and exposure brought their men suffering and death on an awesome scale. Their units were achieving less each day, their early success pattern was but a memory and their commanders were rapidly losing faith in and respect for the directions coming to them from Berlin.

Still, the Germans managed a recovery of sorts, though not to the point of really regaining the offensive momentum. By spring they had somehow effected a partial re-supply, repair and reorganization to the extent that they could now readily repel every Soviet penetration and immediately hit back with short, swift tank and infantry assaults which, while not gaining them much, served to hold their positions for the most part. This became German standard operating procedure for most of their remaining operations on the Russian Front. The panzer tankers were forced to run their engines for fifteen minutes every four hours in the horrific Soviet winter, increasing their fuel consump-

tion and putting additional strain on their beleaguered supply system. And running them that way made it impossible to keep their positions secret.

J. Kugies served as a panzer platoon leader and tank commander in the Balkans and on the Russian Front in World War II: "At Tilsit in East Prussia I led a section of five tanks. In the lead tank we were only able to advance at about twelve to fourteen kilometers an hour over the soft marshy roads. Our riflemen marched ahead of us in a wide front to deal with any resistance that I could not break through. Just behind the Russian-Latvian frontier we encountered Soviet soldiers. Our section had been ordered to halt, but due to my defective wireless set, I did not receive the order in our tank and continued to drive on alone. The road soon became blocked by Soviet trucks and my driver had to take us through open terrain. He couldn't stop because of the marshy ground. The Russian truck convoy was escorted by many of their tanks and, before they could turn their turrets toward me I began to fire on them. Their aiming was bad and I managed to shoot nine of them out of action. With their tanks burning, and the crews fleeing, I was then able to destroy an anti-aircraft battery and an artillery position. I crossed a bridge and then closed my hatch cover to prevent any enemy shells from coming in. By this time, my cannon ammunition supply was exhausted and I could only shoot with my machine-gun. We now stayed where we were, alone, for about thirty minutes until our following tanks reached us. After such a dangerous situation, we all had a sip of vodka which, unfortunately, was warm for having been under our gear. Later, we learned that the tanks behind us had stopped often, as ordered, on the marshy ground. They incurred many losses.

"While trying to aid a German infantry reconnaissance patrol which was fighting in a lost cause on 13 August 1941 at the Luga bridgehead, I was wounded. I was nearly out of ammunition and a Russian machine-gun was only five meters ahead of us. I ordered us forward to try and save the reconnaissance patrol. Standing in the hatch, I was pointing in the direction of the Russian machine-gun, which was now firing at us. I was shot three times through my right hand and forefinger and got a graze on the side of my head. My cap was torn to pieces but I was hardly bleeding. As I sank into the tank, I was fired on from a nearby house. I was hit in the right shoulder by splinters and my uniform jacket was torn up. My chief took me immediately to the doctor at a nearby field unit where my wounds were bandaged. I was then flown by JU-52 aircraft to a field hospital

German tank crews in Russia experiencing Molotov Cocktails.

near Dünaburg, followed by a two-day train trip to a military hospital in Germany. I always remember hearing infantry men say to us again and again: 'I wouldn't like to go in your death-boxes,' and we always answered: 'And we don't like to walk.'"

For both sides the effective use of tanks was essential to success in the Russian campaign. Tanks could provide the ability to penetrate the enemy front line, bring vital support to one's over-extended infantry and powerfully defend against penetrations by the enemy forces. The Germans were losing in the contest to field, fight and maintain tanks in this unrelenting, unforgiving situation. By early 1943, the German Panzer force in the Soviet Union was in bad shape. Deteriorating morale and operational inefficiencies, confusion and indecision at the manufacturing, supply and command levels were to blame. In terms

German General Heinz Guderian in his armored vehicle during a battle near Kiev.

of their equipment, the Germans were forced to continue their reliance on the PzKpfw III and IV tanks, of which the III was utterly outclassed by the Soviet T-34, a fact not lost on the T-34 commanders in the field. They strongly urged their superiors to prevail upon the German Ordnance Office to quickly design and build a copy of the T-34 for their use in the East. But Ordnance Office designers scoffed at that approach to a new and capable rival for the Soviet tank and set about planning a new design of their own, the forty-five-ton general purpose Panther.

Hitler's armies had reached the outskirts of Moscow and Leningrad in their most successful push of Operation Barbarossa in 1941. By the summer of 1942, the Führer's primary goal was the Caucasus oilfields which he hoped to capture and thus deprive the Russians of their main fuel supply.

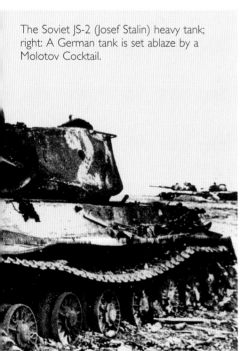

The Soviet JS-2 (Josef Stalin) heavy tank; right: A German tank is set ablaze by a Molotov Cocktail.

To achieve this aim, the German Sixth Army had been directed to capture and occupy Stalingrad and, in so doing, isolate and neutralize this key enemy communications and manufacturing center in southern Russia.

The determination to defend Stalingrad was total and not to be questioned. Every Russian soldier was ordered "Not one step backwards" by Josef Stalin. Waged between August 1942 and February1943, the Battle of Stalingrad was the major Soviet victory of World War II and proved to be the turning point in the war. Hitler himself sealed the fate of his Caucasus campaign in July when he diverted much of the army intended to occupy the oilfields to the already futile struggle at Stalingrad. General Zhukov had amassed a force of nearly a million men which attacked and encircled the German troops in a huge pincer movement on 19 November. The Germans ran out of food and ammunition and were freezing. In the battle 70,000 German soldiers died and 91,000 became prisoners. Near the end of the fight Hitler's commander there, General Friedrich von Paulus, was asked by the Russians to surrender. He had been forbidden by Hitler to attempt to break out of the encirclement and was now urged by the Führer not to be taken alive. On 2 February he gave himself up to the Russians. The German advance in the south was halted and thereafter the Russians were virtually always on the offensive and on the move towards Berlin.

In the belief that the Soviet victory at Stalingrad might have been some kind of aberration, the Germans struggled to recover, regroup and plan a new offensive for May 1943. It was to be called Operation *Zitadelle* (Citadel) and entailed a mighty effort to encircle and destroy the five Soviet armies in the area of the Kursk salient between Orel and Belgorod.

The Battle of Kursk would be the greatest tank battle in history. A win here would buy time for the Germans to gather new strength and perhaps retake the offensive on the Eastern Front, as well as slowing the progress of the Soviets.

But the Russian victory at Stalingrad was no fluke. They would be ready for the enemy at Kursk and would, in fact, receive a gift from Hitler in the form of an extra two months to prepare and set their defenses for the coming attack. The German leader had become so enamoured of what he believed would be his new superweapon, the *PanzerKampfwagen* V—Panther—that, when it was not yet ready for battle by May, he elected to postpone Zitadelle until July.

The Panther was the brainchild of Dr. Ferdinand Porsche, an automotive designer greatly admired by the Führer. It would be, he assured Hitler, superior to the T-34, but in the spring of 1943 it had problems typical of a complex new mechanism, and they had to be worked through. Eventually, it would become one of the great tanks of the war, but not in time for Kursk. And in the interim, Hitler and Porsche strove to advance development of new self-propelled tank destroyers (*Jagdpanzer*); as well as self-propelled infantry support guns (*Stürmgeschütze*). Hitler saw in these new weapons a relatively quick means of expanding his armored capability and possibly re-acquiring the momentum he sought in the East. Dr. Porsche's contribution to this effort was a re-designed version of the Tiger tank, to be known on the-Front as the "Elefant." It was actually called the Ferdinand. This mammoth tank destroyer resembled an oversize Jagdpanzer and was armed with an 88mm PaK gun in a fixed mounting. Like the Jagdpanzer, it came with a whole range of drawbacks including poor crew habitability, a narrow field of fire, no secondary armament, and the complex, costly production

techniques usually associated with a tank. Ninety Ferdinands were built by Krupp and were less than successful in their combat debut. But their cousin, the Tiger, being manufactured by Henschel, showed extremely well in its initial action at Leningrad in late 1942. That performance led to a standardization of both the Krupp and Henschel vehicles in which the 88mm 1.71 gun was fitted.

All of this effort and expense on Jagdpanzers would actually result in less armor (fewer tanks) rather than the expansion that Hitler had wanted, with Germany's motorized infantry and Waffen SS units reaping the benefit of increased armored capability while the key panzer divisions suffered a quantitative reduction in tank strength . . . on the road to Kursk.

At the Kursk salient the Soviets had prepared for their visitors with "Germanic efficiency" and atten-

The burning hull of an M3 Stuart American-built light tank provided to the British and the Russians for use in WWII.

tion to detail. They had established seven defensive lines, laid millions of mines, built an imposing network of anti-tank ditches and dug-in anti-tank strongpoints. At an assembly point nearly 200 miles behind the front line, they had a massive 850-tank force in waiting, the Fifth Guards Tank Army, should it be required. All participating units had been reorganized, manned and re-equipped to full strength or beyond. They were ready for the Germans when the assault began at 7 a.m. on 5 July.

Soviet Intelligence was working well prior to the attack and the German troops found themselves subjected to an intense bombardment

in their assembly areas during the evening of 4/5 July. What followed was a chaotic mixture of tank-versus-tank and hand-to-hand combat lasting for several days. The German Ninth Army on the north flank of the salient went at the Soviets each day with greater intensity, manpower and tank strength until, by 12 July, they had spent their wad and been defeated by the excellent enemy defenses. The Soviet defenders were then able to capitalize on the German failure and move onto the offensive themselves.

The 48th Panzer Korps was operating on the southern end of the salient. They were the first major armored formation to field the PzKpfw V Panther and it was an inauspicious start for the highly touted new tank. Breakdowns were commonplace and crews found their vehicles

A Panzer III rolling on the Russian Front.

regularly becoming stuck in the soft, wet ground, and the Germans were reminded of their famous reference to the Sherman tanks operated in the desert war by the British—"Tommy Cookers"—as the Panthers showed an alarming tendency to catch fire when hit.

Things appeared to improve for the Germans on the southern flank by 11 July when they prepared to engage in the most massive tank battle ever. The "field" was a land-bridge between the rivers Don and Psel at a place called Prochorovka. It was there that the Germans would try to break the Soviet lines and gain access to the open region beyond. It would be the climactic engagement of Zitadelle at what would later be remembered as the "gully of death."

What happened at Prochorovka on 12 July 1943 has been the subject of many books, film and television documentaries. Historians have disagreed about the facts, with wildly varying versions being rendered over the years. The majority, however, generally adhere to the following.

Something between 500 and 700 German tanks, many of them Panzerkampfwagen VI Tigers mounted with 88mm cannon and Panzerkampfwagen V Panthers with their 75mm guns, rumbled out towards the Soviet line at just before noon. They were unaware that the 850 tanks of the Soviet Fifth Guards Tank Army had been moved up during the night of 11/12 July to meet the anticipated assault. When the German tanks encountered the hundreds of more agile T-34 mediums of the Soviets, it resembled a free-for-all in which the T-34s brought chaos and confusion to the German armored units by driving directly into their midst. The close-in tactic effec-

tively neutralized the formidable 88mm guns of the Tigers. The Soviets then went on to outmaneuver the enemy armor, destroying 400 German tanks, including nearly 100 Tigers and many Panthers. It seems probable that Soviet tank losses for the day amounted to many more than the 400 admitted to by Lieutenant-General Pavel Rotmistrov, Commander of the Fifth Guards Tank Army, possibly as many as 650. But at the end of the day, the Soviets prevailed and held the battleground.

The next day Hitler uncharacteristically ordered his principal commanders, Field Marshals Guenther von Kluge and Erich von Manstein, to cancel the operation and begin an immediate withdrawal from the area. Manstein resisted but was overruled. Zitadelle had been an unmitigated defeat and an absolute disaster for the Germans. Their offensive against the Soviets was finished.

Some historians claim that as many as 6,000 tanks, 4,000 aircraft and two million fighting men were involved in the Battle of Kursk. Others state that far fewer tanks actually participated and that only fifteen Tigers and no Panthers were still in action by the 12 July battle at Prochorovka. German and Soviet official reports and press accounts also vary greatly— Soviet Information Bureau: Moscow, Wednesday, 14 July 1943. In the past twelve hours, German assault activity has slackened further with the Red Army increasingly seizing the initiative. Since yesterday evening, German attacks around Belgorod too have decreased in force. General Rokossovsky, on the other hand, has sent new reserves to the front and is attacking in almost all sectors. The panzer spearheads which the Germans drove into the Soviet positions in the first days of the offensive

The German Panzerkampfwagen (armored fighting vehicle) tank was widely used in WWII but was outgunned by the formidable Russian T-34 and was soon supplanted by the better-armed Panzer IV. This example was captured and converted by the Russians.

are shrivelling and the initiative is gradually passing over to the Red Army.

Wehrmacht High Command: Thursday, 15 July 1943. The heavy fighting on the Eastern Front is continuing despite the deteriorating weather. We defeated another enemy force in a concentrated attack near Belgorod, and counterattacks renewed by enemy forces weaker than on previous days have been repulsed with heavy losses to them. East and north of Orel, the enemy continued his attacks Wednesday, with the support of tanks and ground-attack. Attempts by the Soviets to break through German positions have failed under heavy casualties. We immediately mounted counterattacks which are progressing successfully. Along the entire sector of this large-scale battle, we destroyed 336 more Soviet tanks on Wednesday, and our air force shot down 70 enemy planes.

Soviet Information Bureau: Moscow, Thursday, 15 July 1943. The following special communiqué was published this evening: Our troops have now gone on the offensive against the German troops to the north and east of Orel. Our offensive was launched in two directions: southward from the area north of Orel, and westwards from the area east of Orel. North of Orel, our troops have penetrated a 38-kilometer-wide stretch of strongly fortified German defensive positions and have advanced 43 kilometers in a period of three days. Large numbers of enemy fortifications have been destroyed.

A Panzer crewman who was unable to escape his ruined tank near El Alamein.

There are flowers now, they say, at
Alamein;
Yes, flowers in the minefields now.
So those that come to view that
vacant scene
Where death remains and agony has
been
Will find the lilies grow—flowers, and
nothing that we know.
It will become a staid historic name,
That crazy sea of sand! Like Troy or
Agincourt its single fame
Will be the garland for our brow, our
claim,
On us a fleck of glory to the end:
And there our dead will keep their
holy ground.
—from *El Alamein* by John Jarmain,
killed in action 1944

When one thinks of El Alamein, it
is with visions of a mighty clash in
which two vast World War II tank
armies, the British and Commonwealth
forces versus the Deutsches Afrika
Korps and its Italian partners, engage
somewhere in the desert wastes
of Egypt back in 1942. It was Erwin
"Desert Fox" Rommel against Bernard
"Monty" Montgomery. It was M4
Sherman tanks with 75mm guns
and armor-piercing shot, Crusaders,
Stuarts, Grants and Matilda mine-clear-
ing flails against the German Panzer IIIs
and IVs and a lot of obsolete Italian
armor. But equally, it was deprivation,
debilitating heat and crippling, blinding
sandstorms whose grit clogged every
pore and every mechanical seam, frequently rendering men and machines
useless.

The British called the wind *khamsin*,
Arabic for "the hot wind that blows
out of the Sahara." The wind could
raise the temperature by up to 35°
F in just a few hours. It is said that
Bedoin tribal law permitted a husband
to kill his wife after five days of such

conditions. For the soldiers of both
sides, the stinging sand clouds reduced
visibility to zero and made breathing
difficult through their makeshift sand
masks. Odd electrical disturbances
caused compasses to misbehave wildly,
while the hurricane-force gusts often
overturned vehicles and uprooted
telephone poles.

To call conditions for soldiers in the
Western Desert harsh is to understate
them tenfold. When either Allied or
Axis troops reached a place where
they were required to dig in and
establish a position, they frequently
found themselves unable to make an
impression on limestone underlying
the thin sheet of sand. Their only
option was to lie still in their exposed
positions under the sweltering sun,
hoping that they would not be
observed and draw enemy fire. By day
they were prone to attack by swarms
of black flies and at nightfall, when the
temperature plummeted, they suffered
an opposite misery to that of the day.

In the rectangle of desert 500 miles
long and 150 miles wide where most
of the campaign was fought, the coastline was relatively fertile, but inland the
inhospitable wastes supported little
more than prickly camel's thorn, vipers
and scorpions. The only human life
in the area was a handful of nomadic
Bedouin tribesmen. Water, that most
precious resource, was scarce and only
available at widely spaced cisterns or
through the drilling of deep wells. But
the greatest torment of the soldier
was probably the powdery sand that
irritated and inflamed the eyes, ruined
rifle breeches, penetrated tents, covered food and equipment and mini-
mized visibility.

As correspondent in Egypt for
the London *Daily Express*, Australian
writer Alan Moorehead reported the
desert conflict: "Each truck or tank
was as individual as a destroyer, and

each squadron of tanks or guns made
great sweeps across the desert as a
battle-squadron at sea will vanish over
the horizon . . . When you made contact with the enemy you manoeuvred
about him for a place to strike, much
as two fleets will steam into position
for action . . . There was no front line
. . . Always the essential governing
principle was that desert forces must
be mobile . . . We hunted men, not
land, as a warship will hunt another
warship, and care nothing for the sea
on which the action is fought. Always
the desert set the pace, made the
direction and planned the design. The
desert offered colours in browns, yel-
lows and grays. The army accordingly
took these colours for its camouflage.
There were practically no roads.
Nothing except an occasional bird
moved quickly in the desert. The army
for ordinary purposes accepted a pace
of five or six miles an hour. The desert gave water reluctantly, and often
then it was brackish. The army cut its
men—generals and privates—down
to a gallon of water a day when they
were in forward positions. We did not
try to make the desert livable, nor did
we seek to subdue it. We found the
life of the desert primitive and nomadic, and primitively and nomadically the
army lived and went to war."

The American Sherman was the most
successful Allied tank of World War II.
More than 40,000 were built between
1942 and 1946. It first went into
action in the desert war at El Alamein.

In World War II the British 7th
Armored Division called themselves
the "Desert Rats," after the jerboa,
a small desert rodent. They adopted
the animal as their divisional emblem.
Ultimately the name Desert Rats came
to be used to describe the entire
British Eighth Army. In February 1943,

General Bernard Montgomery, the British desert war commander, in a painting by Sir Oswald Birley.

German Lieutenant-General Erwin Rommel, known as the "Desert Fox."

Winston Churchill said of the Eighth Army: "When the war is over it will be enough for man to say, I marched and fought with the Desert Army."

Before Alamein there were almost no victories. After it, there were almost no defeats.
—Winston Churchill

The Suez Canal is a 103-mile channel which crosses the Isthmus of Suez in Egypt and links the Red Sea and the Gulf of Suez with the Mediterranean Sea. The canal was built under the supervision of Ferdinand de Lesseps and opened in November 1869. In 1875 it came under British control and in 1879 the British Prime Minister Benjamin Disraeli purchased the shares in the canal held by the Khedive of Egypt. This assured Britain's ongoing and increasing interest in that country, which she helped to modernize and develop as a protectorate. In 1922 Britain recognized Egypt as an independent ally. The canal was essential to Britain's trade and it was in her vital interest to keep it open and protected. In World War I the Turks tried to attack the canal and were decisively beaten back by British troops. By the 1930s, the presence of an Italian army in neighboring Libya, in support of its Fascist regime's determination to seize the canal, posed an obvious threat in the event of war. In 1936 an Anglo-Egyptian treaty was signed with Britain agreeing to defend the canal until such future time as the Egyptians would be in a position to do so.

After Italy entered the war in spring 1940, the British forces in the Middle East were under the stewardship of General Archibald Wavell. Some historians refer to Wavell as being highly competent but one of the unluckiest British commanders of the war. He always seemed to take command in a theatre just prior to the worst of defeats and then get the bad publicity for it. He was deliberate and determined to plan his operations well and act only when he believed his men and equipment were absolutely sufficient to the task. He considered the comments, criticism and advice coming to him from the British Prime Minister Winston Churchill by the fall of 1940 to be "barracking," a form of heckling, and realized that the PM was losing confidence in him. Still, he was determined not to attack the Italians until he felt that his preparations were complete.

Wavell was planning a five-day raid halting at Buq Buq, twenty-five miles west of Sidi Barrani. He meant to accomplish three things: to test the mettle of the Italians in actual battle rather than in mere skirmishes, to take a few thousand prisoners, and most importantly, to hit the Italians decisively before the Germans could intervene in Libya. The British could field 30,000 men, a mix of Englishmen, Cameron Highlanders, Ulstermen, Sikhs and Hindus, against an Italian force of 80,000.

Just three days after the attack had begun on 9 December, 39,000 Italian soldiers surrendered to or were captured by Wavell's forces. He was amazed and Churchill was tickled pink. Wavell had not intended a major action but now it seemed to have a momentum of its own, and the major port of Tobruk was to be the next British objective. At the same time, the German advance on Greece, to rescue their Italian allies after Mussolini's failed invasion effort, was of great concern to Churchill, and Wavell chose that moment to send a message to the PM questioning British policy towards Greece: ". . . nothing we can do from here is likely to be in time to stop the German advance if really intended. Churchill fired back: "Nothing must hamper capture of Tobruk but thereafter all operations in Libya are subordinated to aiding Greece. We expect and require prompt and active compliance with our decisions."

The Libyan harbor and fortress of Tobruk was captured by the British, along with 25,000 Italian prisoners, on 22 January 1941.

Hitler had become aware of Erwin Rommel in 1937 with the publication of Rommel's book *Infanterie Greift an* (The Infantry Attacks), a widely acclaimed work. In it Rommel explained his aggressive tactical ideas which had evolved from his WWI experiences. The Führer was most impressed and began to follow Rommel's career with great interest. When Germany invaded Poland in the late summer of 1939, he made Rommel commander of the Führer's Headquarters (*Führerhauptquartier*).

Born in Heidenheim in southern Germany on 15 November 1891, Erwin Johannes Eugen Rommel was the son of a mathematics teacher. He entered the German Army in 1910 and made a name for himself in the World War I offensive to the Piave River in 1917, for which he was awarded the *Pour le Merite*.

Rommel was well aware of the conservatism among Hitler's General Staff officers and the gulf it had created between them and their leader. He frequently found himself agreeing with Hitler and opposing the views of the Staff, which continued to enhance Hitler's opinion of him. With the end of the Polish campaign, Rommel asked that he be given command of a Panzer Division and, overruling the objections of his generals, Hitler was pleased to grant the request. In February 1940 Rommel took charge of the 7th Panzer Division, which was then being formed at Bad Godesberg and quickly organized their efficient and demanding training program. His efforts resulted in the best performance by any panzer formation during the invasion of France in May. Hitler showed his pleasure by giving Rommel the first Knights Cross to be awarded to a divisional commander in the campaign. Rommel extended his reputation for bold, aggressive methods when he drove his division to the Channel coast and on to Cherbourg at the amazing pace of forty to fifty miles a day, to take the surrender of the French garrison there. His performance in France, while dramatic, did not impress his detractors in the High Command. They felt that he was inclined to act impulsively rather than with considered judgement, that he failed to cover his flanks or provide proper logistical support for his spearheads, that he was ego-driven and rarely willing to acknowledge the accomplishments of others and, not incidentally, they resented his special relationship with Hitler.

Rommel was propelled by nerve, self-confidence, ego and will. He understood the importance of using his resources to apply and maintain pressure on the enemy, as well as the value of psychological warfare techniques. He was a great improviser and enjoyed involving himself in the minutiae of his planning. He was, for the most part, an inspiring leader who knew how to bluff and deceive his enemy and give the impression of having a more powerful and threatening force than he actually had. He was skillful and quite intuitive, able to get into the mind of an enemy commander and sense the man's interpretation of Rommel's intentions.

In North Africa Rommel's aggressive, audacious exploits earned him the nickname "the Desert Fox" and he soon became a kind of legendary figure credited by many on both sides of the conflict with being superhuman. The British were plainly in awe of his blitzkrieg tactics and, for a time, when a British soldier performed a duty particularly well, his fellow troopers would refer to him as "doing a Rommel."

"We have a very daring and skillful opponent against us, and, may I say across the havoc of war, a great general" said Prime Minister Winston Churchill of Rommel in an address to the House of Commons in 1942.

Late in 1941 Rommel is known to have been sitting in a Libyan farmhouse while an artist was painting his portrait. At one point the area came under attack by British bombers and two bombs fell quite near the farmhouse, making a lot of noise and causing many broken windows and much dust and falling plaster. Undisturbed by the event, Rommel continued to pose, but the fearful artist hesitated in his work as a second wave of bombers approached and the local flak guns roared into action. Rommel, so the story goes, quietly asked the artist if the raid was bothering him. The man replied: "No, Herr General."
"Then carry on, carry on," said Rommel.

In his grand scheme Hitler considered North Africa a low-priority theatre, but he did not want to see his Axis partner Italy pushed out of the region. Field Marshal Heinrich von Brauchitsch, Rommel's immediate superior, informed the general that his new role was to be strictly defensive and that, for the time being, Germany would not be able to provide additional forces to drive the British from their present position in the eastern Libyan province of Cyrenaica. Rommel was, however, promised a fully equipped panzer division by the end of May. But he expected the British to move against his army as early as February and quickly began work on one of his greatest ruses: "It was my belief that if the British could detect no opposition they would probably continue their advance, but that if they saw they were going to have to fight another battle they would first wait to build up supplies. With the time thus gained I

Having planted an explosive charge on this German tank, these British soldiers in Tunisia rush from the imminent detonation.

hoped to build up our own strength until we were eventually strong enough to withstand the enemy attack." To enable his forces to appear as strong as possible and to induce the maximum caution in the British, Rommel ordered a workshop to make dummy tanks of wood and canvas and mount them on Volkswagen chassis. The task was completed by 17 February and Rommel, pleased with the result, awaited the enemy.

The British, however, did not come. Their main focus, and much of Wavell's army, had been shifted to Greece where they began landing on 4 March. That effort reduced British defenses in eastern Libya to a bare minimum. It was not until late March that Wavell refocused on these defenses, "when it was rather too late," and realized with dismay that he had utterly overestimated the protection afforded by the escarpment south of Benghazi: "When I actually went out and saw the escarpment, I realized that it could be ascended almost anywhere and was no protection." He had thought the escarpment would be an effective barrier against tanks. At the end of February Wavell had made a dubious appointment, naming Lieutenant General Philip Neame to

be commander in Cyrenaica. He may have had second thoughts about his choice almost immediately when he learned of Neame's tactical dispositions, declaring them to be "just crazy" and ordering a prompt redeployment.

Rommel, Wavell still believed, would not be able to mount an attack before May. The German had, in fact, been ordered by Brauchitsch in a Berlin meeting on or about 20 March to do nothing before the end of May, but Rommel had other plans. On 24 March he launched a dawn attack of tanks and armored cars on El Agheila, and employing for the first time his "Cardboard Division" of Volkswagen-mounted dummy tanks which, together with his real armor, created huge clouds of dust. The ruse worked like a charm and the British garrison at El Agheila quickly withdrew thirty miles to Mersa Brega in the northeast. On learning of the attack and the lack of a British counterattack, Churchill cabled Wavell on 26 March: "I presume you are only waiting for the tortoise to stick his head out far enough before chopping it off." On 30 March, Wavell told Neame not to be overly concerned about the enemy. "I do not believe he can make any big effort for at least another month." Rommel hit Mersa Brega the next day. His reconnaissance reports showed that the fleeing British force were still on the move northward and not stopping to establish defensive positions. Although under instructions not to open a major offensive before the end of May, Rommel could not resist. Neame's soldiers were in full retreat, 500 miles in a week. The panic and confusion that Rommel had hoped to create in Neame's command had been achieved. Some British troops were referring to their flight as "The Benghazi Handicap" and "The Tobruk Derby."

On 2 April Wavell visited the front to evaluate the situation: "I soon realized that Neame had lost control." Rommel, meanwhile, was busy justifying the contravention of his orders: "It was becoming increasingly clear that the enemy believed us to be far stronger than we actually were, a belief that it was essential to maintain, by keeping up the appearance of a large-scale offensive."

By 7 April Rommel had become obsessed with Tobruk. His men required 1,500 tons of water and food per day, and Tobruk, the only suitable port in Cyrenaica east of Benghazi, was his only practical means of supply. The British were well established there, however, and were busily reinforcing their defenses in anticipation of Rommel's attentions, which he soon offered with reckless abandon. On 14 April his tanks blasted into Tobruk, directly into a trap set for them. He lost seventeen tanks in the action. In the British force at Tobruk, Rommel was up against Major General Leslie Morshead, a fifty-one-year-old Australian known by his troops as "Ming the Merciless" after a character in the Flash Gordon comic strip. On the approach of Rommel's armor, Morshead informed his staff: "If we have to get out we shall fight our way out. There'll be no Dunkirk here. There is to be no surrender and no retreat."

For the 35,000 British, Anzac and Indian defenders of Tobruk, waiting for Rommel meant putting up with endless dysentery, lice, sand fleas, sunburn and boredom. The thrust-and-parry action continued and by late April, Churchill was insisting that Wavell mount a counter-offensive. Wavell's response: "Action before mid-June is out of the question." Churchill was angry and Wavell decided to act with Operation Brevity, a limited effort to establish a launch position for the main

A German panzer crew in North Africa, 1942.

offensive to come. Brevity opened on 15 May. By 27 May the Germans had driven Wavell's forces from Halfaya Pass, an important cut in the escarpment which led onto the Libyan plateau. Brevity had failed.

The British had been thrown out of Greece at the end of April, had taken refuge in Crete to regroup and were now under a considerable German threat there. And Churchill continued to badger Wavell to get on with the major offensive against Rommel, whom the Prime Minister believed was gaining strength by the day. At the same time Wavell was having to fight campaigns in the Axis puppet states of Syria and Iraq. Still, on 15 June he managed to launch Operation

Battleaxe, the long-awaited Cyrenaica main offensive.

For Battleaxe, a reinforced infantry brigade with one and a half squadrons of tanks was to retake Halfaya Pass, while another infantry and armored brigade formation was to move on the German position at Fort Capuzzo. Yet another reinforced armored brigade was to sweep wide to the west towards Sidi Azeiz to protect the British units from Axis forces in the area of Sidi Omar. The Germans, under the command of Hauptmann Wilhelm Bach, had been ordered to let the enemy tanks come into the pass at Halfaya. There they waited, concealed in emplacements all along the cliffside, with 88mm guns that fired twenty-two-

pound shells capable of putting holes twelve inches in diameter in Matilda tanks at a one-mile range. In five failed attempts to punch their way through the pass (which British troops thereafter called Hell Fire Pass), the British force lost eleven of their twelve leading tanks.

Thanks to the initiative of Major General F.W. Messervy, commander of the 4th Indian Division, the rest of the British forces in the pass were withdrawn, saving them from almost certain destruction by Rommel's army. In the disastrous operation, the British had lost ninety tanks, thirty aircraft and 1,000 men. Morale among British troops in the desert war was at an all-time low. To Wavell's admission of defeat, "Am very sorry for failure

of Battleaxe," the reaction of the Permanent Under Secretary to the Foreign Office, Sir Alexander Cadogan was succinct: "The German Army simply has better generals. Wavell and such like are no good against them. It is like putting me up to play Bobby Jones over thirty-six holes." On the morning of 22 June a message arrived for General Wavell from the Prime Minister: "I have come to the conclusion that public interest will best be served by appointment of General Auchinleck to relieve you in command of Armies of Middle East."

The fifty-seven-year-old General Sir Claude Auchinleck was known to his troops in the British Middle Eastern Forces as "The Auk." It was an affectionate and respectful reference to a quick-thinking leader who had a good grasp of both tactical and strategic problems; a man they believed was certainly a match for Rommel. But Auchinleck had one major shortcoming; he was a poor judge of men when selecting his subordinate commanders, a flaw he compounded with misplaced loyalty and a stubborn refusal to deal with his failed choices. In Auchinleck, Churchill had a commander who carried out a war of maneuver against the Axis forces, continually attacking and destroying the Italian units. Rommel was then required to use his German forces to fill in the gaps, further draining his own limited manpower. However, as he was with Wavell, Churchill was impatient with Auchinleck, feeling that the general was not making sufficient progress against the enemy at the necessary pace.

For several months after Operation Battleaxe, relative calm prevailed in the Western Desert. For both sides it was a monotonous period of waiting, watching the enemy across the front and suffering in the intense heat of the high summer and autumn sun. The miserable rations of the German troops, fatty sausage, tinned sardines in oil, and black bread, was surpassed in appeal only slightly by that of the British with their corned beef, hard tack biscuits and ration packs. It was a time of discomfort for all, of resupply and reinforcement for some elements, and of quiet reflection.

On 21 June 1942, after a four-day siege, the Germans recaptured Tobruk and with it 33,000 British troops. By late June Rommel was positioned to drive on to Cairo and Suez. His forces had shoved the British back to the Egyptian border and were threatening Britain's position in the eastern Mediterranean. If Rommel could take Suez he would have a clear path to the oil fields of the Middle East and would then be able to link up with German units in Russia. The British Eighth Army, under Auchinleck, had managed to make a stand at the small coastal town of El Alamein in early July. Alamein was the last defensive position on the western desert front from which the British could hold Alexandria and the Nile Delta. It lay on a forty-mile stretch of sand between the Mediterranean Sea and the salt marshes of the great impassable Qattara Depression. There is a coastal road and a railway line running along the ledges which are bounded on the sea side by salt lagoons. In places the rocky subsoil breaks through the thin sand layer and ends abruptly in a sheer cliff down to the Depression. To the south of the Qattara is the great Sand Sea. The British position then was vulnerable only to frontal attack. There the British and German forces had engaged in a clash now known as the First Alamein, in which the Germans were fought to a standstill.

Now Churchill moved to break Rommel in the desert war. He sacked Auchinleck and said later: "Firing Auchinleck was like killing a magnificent stag." He then appointed General Sir Harold Alexander in overall command and Bernard Montgomery to take charge of the Eighth Army. In Monty he had a man he did not like, but one he believed could get the job done.

General Bernard Law Montgomery was a professional soldier who also had served in World War I. After Alamein, Monty would go on to Italy and later to command land forces in the Normandy invasion of 1944. Born in 1887, the son of a bishop, he was a bible-reading teetotaler. Dogmatic, brusque, overbearing and uncompromising, Montgomery was a natural leader who had excelled at sports in school. In the army his superior officers grudgingly gave him their recommendations for promotion though they found him excessively opinionated and often erratic. By his own admission, he was difficult to get along with: "I am a bit of a cad. One has to be a bit of a cad to succeed in the Army."

Montgomery seems to have cultivated the image of an eccentric, but underneath it all he was undoubtedly a competent military professional who was gifted with the ability to inspire and command the loyalty and obedience of his soldiers. He was small and thin and quite ruthless. He nearly always wore a Royal Tank Regiment beret, a pullover sweater and khaki trousers. He had no experience commanding large formations of armor, but unlike the earlier British commanders in the desert war, he seemed to be constantly visiting his front line units, encouraging them and exuding confidence: "We will finish with Rommel once and for all."

James Mason as Erwin Rommel in a still from *The Desert Fox*, a 1951 film from 20th Century Fox.

The United States and Britain had agreed that the first American troops to go into action should land in the French territories of Northwest Africa in autumn 1942. The idea was to put Rommel in a vice—to squeeze him between the two Allied armies—and the schedule called for an early November starting date. Unlike Wavell and Auchinleck, Montgomery was able to take command at a point when everything he required for victory was coming together . . . air supremacy, strategy and resources. His Eighth Army was quickly becoming a far stronger force than that of his enemy, Monty now had nearly 200,000 men, 2,300 guns, 500 planes and more than 1,000 tanks. Importantly, many of his tanks were new American Shermans which were capable of destroying the German anti-tank guns at a considerable distance. In the Sherman the British had much more of a chance against the German Panzer IV than in their older British Valentines and Matildas.

Battle is the most magnificent competition in which a human being can indulge. It brings out all that is best; it removes all that is base. All men are afraid in battle. The coward is the one who lets his fear overcome his sense of duty. Duty is the essence of manhood.
—General George S. Patton

"I was given a job in the Officers Mess. We were told to get the place tidied up as there were some important people coming to dinner. We found out later that it was to be General Montgomery and some other high-ranking officers. The officer in charge of the Mess had heard from one of the lads that I was the best scrounger in the Company, so he sent for me. He asked me to take the cook with me and go scrounge something special for the dinner. The cook and I borrowed a jeep and travelled about three miles out into the desert where we found a big white house with big letters painted on it that said Out of Bounds to All Allied Forces. Never mind. The cook and I knocked on the door and an old man came to ask what we wanted. We asked him if he had any chickens to sell us and he invited us into the house. He said he would be back shortly. In this big room there was a large and highly polished table about twenty feet long and four feet wide. There were a dozen naked women sitting at the table. The cook and I stood there with our eyes popping out and, after a while, the old man came back carrying a dozen chickens. We showed him a bag of tea that we had brought with us and he agreed to take the tea in exchange for the chickens. He also offered us two of the naked women so they could come with us and work as servants. We told him that we could not accept the women as the Army would not allow that, and we left. When we got back to camp we explained about the chickens and the two women the old man had offered, and the Mess officer laughed and said we should have brought the women with us. At seven that evening General Montgomery and the other officers arrived. After their meal the general and the Mess officer came into the cook house and thanked the cook and everybody for an excellent dinner, shaking hands with us all."
—J. Ellison, Royal Tank Regiment, World War II

Rommel's final attempt to break through the British lines in an effort to reach the Nile Valley was the Battle of Alam Halfa. It was Montgomery's first combat operation in the desert after taking command of the Eighth Army. It would prove a difficult and tense engagement for them both.

On 31 August the German attacked with a powerful tank force along the Qattara Depression. He planned to veer north just behind the Alam Halfa ridge; however, his force was delayed making its way through British minefields, which alerted Montgomery in time to make preparations and take countermeasures. Now Rommel's flanks were threatened by the British 7th and 10th Armored Divisions and he was forced to make his turn earlier than intended, at the ridge itself,

which was lined with heavy British defenses. It was there that the battle was fought. It continued until 2 September when, desperately short of fuel and supplies, Rommel was forced to break off the attack and retreat behind his own lines. The reality of his weakening force (only 203 tanks remaining against 767 British) meant he had to withdraw to regroup. The problem of resupply and re-equipping his armored units was hampering his ability to prepare for the decisive battle that both sides knew was coming. In typical Rommel style, he discarded his offensive mode and went on the defense.

With his remaining 100,000 soldiers he set out to establish a forty-mile defensive front along the Miteirya Ridge to block the space between the coast at El Alamein and the Qattara Depression. He constructed an elaborate five-mile-deep complex of minefields which he called "The Devil's Gardens." The minefields were designed with pathways intended to lure the enemy into the danger areas. They were planted with a half million mines, including Tellers which withstood the weight of a man but exploded under that of a tank or other vehicle, as well as S-mines—deadly anti-personnel devices which,

A PzKpfw III panzer tank of Erwin Rommel's Afrika Korps.

when tripped by a man, would jump into the air and explode at waist height.

To counter the minefield hazard, Montgomery could rely on British ingenuity in the form of the Baron, a tank comprised of an obsolete Matilda hull to which had been fitted a flail which rotated lashing chains well ahead of the tank to detonate mines as the vehicle moved through the field. In addition to his Baron fleet, he had 500 mine detectors. The newly invented device would emit a high-pitched siren-like whine when swept over metal. He also borrowed an idea from his adversary and had an entire fake army base constructed near the southern part of the front. It included cardboard trucks, storage dumps, vehicles and a railway . . . all phony and all in addition to an actual camouflaged base built by his men on the north end of the front.

Then there was luck. Rommel's had been rather bad recently and was getting worse, while Monty's seemed to be improving. The Desert Fox was having trouble with his blood pressure and in September he became ill with jaundice. It required proper treatment and for that he had to return to Vienna. This event was a break for Montgomery and so was the code-breaking activity at Bletchley Park in the English midlands where German Enigma machine messages were being decrypted. The resulting product was called Ultra and one such message indicated that Rommel's immediate replacement was to be Lieutenant General Georg Stumme, a man with command experience on the Russian Front, but none in desert warfare. Nigel Hamilton, in his book *The Full Monty*, on the general's preparation for the decisive clash: "Monty's battle plan for Alamein was scripted five weeks in advance. Major William Mather

remembered the moment. It was September 13, 1942—six days after the end of Alam Halfa. 'It was like a hen giving birth. He walked backwards and forwards on the sands of Burg el-Arab all day, like Napoleon with his head down, his hands behind his back. And he came back into his caravan and in about four hours he wrote the whole operation order for Alamein. That was it.' "

News of Field Marshal Sir Bernard Montgomery having invited his prisoner of war, General Wilhelm von Thoma, Field Commander of the Afrika Korps, to dine with him in his GHQ trailer in North Africa shocked and infuriated many Britons. But Prime Minister Winston Churchill reacted: "I sympathize with General von Thoma. Defeated, humiliated, and . . . dinner with Montgomery."

In defeat, unbeatable; in victory, unbearable.
—Winston Churchill, on Field Marshal Sir Bernard Montgomery

The British code-name for the great Alamein offensive was Operation Lightfoot. The operation began under bright moonlight at 9:40 on the night of 23 October. For five hours the thunder of more than 1,000 British guns reverberated across the wastes. The night sky was lit by the brilliant flashes. The screaming of the shells was a sound that would never be forgotten by the combatants. The next noise the Germans heard was the rumble and squeal of many tanks crawling through the minefields to make routes which were carefully marked by the Allied sappers. They did well, but it was inevitable that most of the large mined area would remain uncleared. The British units were advancing in two widely separated

formations. A main force of tanks and infantry was moving forward on a four-mile front near the coast while a secondary force was creating a diversionary attack well to the south. Again, Nigel Hamilton: "The courage of the infantry at Alamein would go down in history as almost 10,000 assault troops advanced through uncleared minefields and stormed the Axis outposts. The fighting was merciless, no quarter being given, lest taking prisoners slow down the rate of advance. It was brutal, surgical and deadly, the wounded being left where they lay."

British progress through the minefields was slow and arduous. Their vehicles and armor were easy targets for the Germans in the first two days. But by the time Stumme's forces began a counterattack, they were facing a formidable array of British armor. They managed to slow the advance of Montgomery's force, but in the process the 15th Panzer Division lost 75 percent of its tanks by the end of the second day of Lightfoot. During the second day the car carrying Stumme was hit by shell fire and the general was blown from it. Days later he was found there, dead of an apparent heart attack. In the evening of 24 October, Hitler telephoned Rommel to inform him that things were not going well at Alamein and that no one seemed to know what had happened to Stumme. The Führer asked Rommel if he was fit enough to take charge again in North Africa. Rommel headed for Alamein the following day.

Four times over the next two days German and Italian tanks attempted to assault a British position on the small hill called Kidney Ridge. When they tried a fifth time they became the target of British planes which dropped bombs on them for two hours, forcing the Germans to withdraw. Both sides now seemed stalled, unable to advance their position. To break the stalemate, Montgomery quickly devised a new plan which he named Supercharge. He redirected his forces northward and then implemented the plan, a new assault from Kidney Ridge in the evening of 2 November. This time the British armor was truly ensnared in the enemy minefields and suffered mightily under the German guns, losing a further 200 tanks.

Now the stalemate situation was critical for both the British and German forces. Rommel's army was hemmed in along the forty-mile corridor between the Mediterranean and the Qattara Depression. He was again in charge, but saw no other option than immediate retreat. His enemy seemed to have an inexhaustible supply of soldiers, artillery and swift new tanks. He had, perhaps, half as many personnel and only fifty-five tanks remaining. He ordered a retreat but the order was countermanded by Hitler: "Yield not a meter of ground. Your enemy despite his superiority, must also be at the end of his strength." The situation was bad enough for both sides that Montgomery, ordinarily supremely confident, was having second thoughts about his chances of defeating Rommel. Both Monty and Churchill were extremely concerned about the possibility of Rommel's army surviving to resist the Allied invasion scheduled to begin in just four days.

Actually, the British force still had more than 600 tanks, even after incurring losses to the Germans at a rate of four to one. The sheer magnitude of Allied arms was crushing the German effort.

Finally, in the early morning of 4

November, units of the 5th Indian Division and the 51st Highlanders achieved a breakthrough for the British when they forced a gap between Rommel's Afrika Korps and the Italian forces. Rommel's situation now became truly desperate with the probability that the British would be able to cut off the retreat that he knew he must attempt. Hitler finally relented and allowed Rommel to pull out of the battle, but the German's troubles were far from over. He bitterly resented Hitler's earlier "victory or death" order which had compelled him to keep his men fighting twenty-four hours longer than he should have. Now in full retreat, his army had only ten tanks remaining and was forced to fight a series of rear guard actions, gradually giving up Sidi Barrani, Tobruk, and Benghazi—all of the towns they had taken in better times. His soldiers, staff cars, and tanks had clogged the coastal road for two days while Allied planes strafed them and Montgomery's forces pursued them. That pursuit lasted six weeks as Rommel struggled to bring his depleted force all the way back to the German supply base at Tripoli. Montgomery's vehicles were mired in the mud when a sudden, unusually heavy desert rainstorm struck, delaying them. Rommel was trying to bring his remaining forces all the way back to Tunisia and link up there with other German forces in order to re-engage with the British and with the Americans who had by now landed in French North Africa.

When Allied forces reached and entered Tripoli on 23 January, Rommel and what remained of the Afrika Korps had made their getaway by sea, but not before destroying Tripoli's port facilities. In the Battle of El Alamein, Montgomery had lost 13,500 men; Rommel lost 50,000. The British lost

500 tanks but of them only 150 were not repairable. The Germans lost 450 tanks.

Allied invasion troops had successfully made their landings in Algeria and Morocco in November and in April 1943 the two Allied forces linked and prepared to move up into the European continent via the scenic southern route, through Italy. By 13 May the last Axis soldier in Tunisia had surrendered, the Allies had taken 275,000 prisoners. Rommel and 700 other German soldiers had escaped.

The following excerpt is from a letter by Montgomery to Major General A.H. Gatehouse, head of the British Ministry of Supply Mission in Washington, DC on 18 September 1943: "The Eighth Army thanks from the bottom of its heart the Army Ordnance Department and all those factories and the men and women who work in them for what they have done. It wishes them the very best of luck in the future. Wherever we fight in the future our gratitude towards them will ever be fresh in our minds. May it ever remain so both while this war lasts, and afterwards when the United Nations together bring peace and order into being."

Donald Chidson was a member of the British 4th Tank Regiment in North Africa during World War II. Commanding his troop in an attack during the breakout from Tobruk on 22 November 1941, he ordered his tank to move well beyond their objective, to give his accompanying infantry maximum support. His tank came under heavy shell fire and was shortly halted and immobilized. Even so, Lieutenant Chidson and his crew continued to fight, bringing substantial fire on the enemy forces. He radioed his squadron reconnaissance officer, arranging to bring fire onto the enemy positions ahead of his tank. He "ably and cooly directed this fire" read the citation for his MC, "from his tank despite continuous enemy fire directed upon it." Chidson kept on fighting and directing fire on the enemy until help arrived and the tank was towed away for repair. The following day Lt. Chidson's tank again closed on enemy forces and was again heavily shelled and this time attacked with Molotov Cocktails. His driver was seriously burned. With that, Chidson scrambled from the tank in a fury, attacking the nearby enemy troops with his revolver, whereupon several of them surrendered to him. Lt. Chidson was granted the award of an immediate Military Cross.

above right: British Army Lieutenant Donald Chidson; right: The burned-out wreck of a Panzer III which was destroyed by British gunners.

INVASION

Hard pounding this, gentlemen.
—Wellington

"Soldiers, sailors and airmen of the Allied Expeditionary Force! You are about to embark upon the Great Crusade, toward which we have striven these many months. The eyes of the world are upon you. The hopes and prayers of liberty-loving people everywhere march with you. In company with our brave allies and brothers-in-arms on other fronts, you will bring about the destruction of the German war machine, the elimination of Nazi tyranny over the oppressed peoples of Europe, and security for ourselves in a free world. Your task will not be an easy one. Your enemy is well trained, well equipped and battle-hardened. He will fight savagely. But this is the year 1944! Much has happened since the Nazi triumphs of 1940-41. The United Nations have inflicted upon the Germans great defeats, in open battle, man-to-man. Our air offensive has seriously reduced their strength in the air and their ability to wage war on the ground. Our home fronts have given us an overwhelming superiority in weapons and munitions of war, and placed at our disposal great reserves of trained fighting men. The tide has turned! The free men of the world are marching together to victory! I have full confidence in your courage, devotion to duty and skill in battle. We will accept nothing less than full victory! Good luck! And let us all beseech the blessing of Almighty God upon this great and noble undertaking."
—Dwight D. Eisenhower, Supreme Allied Commander, Europe

Two kinds of people are staying on this beach, the dead and those who are going to die—now let's get the hell out of here.
—Colonel George A. Taylor, Commander U.S. 16th Infantry Regiment, 6 June 1944

Since the United States entered the war in December 1941, the Allies had struggled desperately to prepare the way for a long-awaited second front, an invasion of the European continent, to liberate the nations under Nazi occupation. Hitler had been seeing to the fortification of much of Europe, including the massive "Atlantic Wall" stretching from Denmark to the Spanish frontier. But it was still an incomplete barrier, with many gaps, in the summer of 1944 when Allied preparations for the invasion were finally ready. The Germans had other concerns in their efforts to maintain control over Europe in 1944, not least being the ever-increasing activity of resistance organizations, saboteurs and spies in France, Holland, Norway, Poland, Albania, Greece and Yugoslavia. The German satellite states of Hungary and Rumania were restless and engaged in secret contacts with the West. And across the English Channel, in the ports of Falmouth, Dartmouth, Weymouth, Portsmouth and Newhaven, ships, planes, tanks, trucks, ammunition, weapons, food, fuel and all manner of supplies had been assembled in staggering numbers, together with more than 1.5 million Americans, 1.75 million Britons and 150,000 Commonwealth and European troops, most of them fresh and well trained, ready to take part in the greatest invasion of all time. Wags suggested that, with the weight of all that equipment, it was only the porcine barrage balloons

A Sherman tank stands as a memorial in Normandy.

BOLD
AUDACIEUX

that were holding England up and keeping her from sinking.

At a Cairo conference late in 1943, British Prime Minister Churchill and U.S. President Roosevelt had agreed that France would be the venue for the Allied assault on the continent and that the entire operation would be under the command of American General Dwight David Eisenhower who, in January 1944, was named Supreme Commander, Allied Expeditionary Force (SCAEF). Ike, as he was commonly known, had graduated from West Point in 1915 and had made his reputation as a military strategist and coordinator of Allied forces in the North African invasions of 1942. Initially, the land forces would be commanded by British General Bernard Montgomery. The coming operation was to be called Overlord and was scheduled for May, depending upon readiness and the weather. The first day of the operation would forever be known as D-Day.

Eisenhower and his staff were headquartered at Southwick Park near Portsmouth on the south coast of England. There they developed the plan for Overlord, including logistics, determining that a sixty-mile stretch of beaches on the Cotentin Peninsula of Normandy would be the landing area for the assault. While the area lacked sufficient port facilities, was often subject to heavy surf conditions and was much farther from the British embarkation ports than, say, the Pas de Calais coast, it did have certain advantages. It was relatively close to Cherbourg and the Brittany ports. It was less strongly fortified than the Pas de Calais (much the most likely site for a landing) and its beaches had relatively few cliffs, a minimum of clay and depressions, and were fairly well-suited to the landing of troops and equipment and their quick deploy-

ment inland. The solution for the lack of port facilities would come in the form of two immense pre-fabricated concrete harbors called Mulberries, which were towed to the landing area. Other ingenious ideas were devised and perfected to support the landings, including PLUTO (pipeline under the ocean), a flexible pipe system capable of pumping a million tons of fuel a day from England to France, SWISS ROLL and CARPET LAYER, armored vehicles for laying an artificial road surface from the surf across the beach, and flail tanks which used chains on rotating drums to beat the ground and clear paths through minefields. There were the multi-purpose AVREs (Armored Vehicle Royal Engineers) which were converted British Churchill tanks whose tasks included the carriage of sappers to take out pillboxes and other targets at close range, bringing in portable bridges for the use of other tanks, and carrying fascines, as in World War I at Cambrai, to fill in ditches.

The Germans were well aware that the invasion was coming, but could only guess about the date and location of the landings. Allied deception plans included an assault on Norway from Scotland, and landings on the Pas de Calais from ports in the southeast of England.

In addition to the German fortifications, Field Marshal Erwin Rommel had hurriedly prepared a formidable set of obstacles which the Allied troops and landing craft would have to negotiate. They included steel "hedgehogs" to hole the inbound landing craft, iron frames, and wooden stakes set at an angle.

At Omaha, the most difficult, dangerous and heavily defended of the landing beaches, 100-foot cliffs were backed by a pebble bank, dunes and a 200-yard salt marsh that abutted

an escarpment. The salt marsh was heavily mined and criss-crossed with anti-tank ditches. The Atlantic Wall defenses in the area of Omaha included eight large gun emplacements, thirty-five pillboxes, eighteen anti-tank guns and eighty-five machine-guns. 75mm and 88mm guns were posi-

Omaha Beach in stark contrast to its appearance on D-Day, June 6, 1944.

tioned in three-foot-thick concrete emplacements in the cliffs at both ends of the beach. And, unknown to the Allies, the Germans had brought up eight battalions of battle-seasoned troops to defend Omaha. Rommel believed that the first twenty-four hours of the invasion would be deci-sive. But Field Marshal Gerd von Rundstedt, whom Hitler had brought from retirement to run the German forces in the West, had no confidence in the effectiveness of the Atlantic Wall defenses at holding back the Allies, much preferring to maintain substantial reserves inland in order to make a fight at a location favorable to his force. But it was Rommel to whom Hitler had turned to make the extensive shoreline fortifications work. Rommel knew well the ability of Allied air power to interdict German communications. He was certain that, unless the Germans savagely repelled

the Allies at the point of the landings, they were lost.

The one thing that Rommel, Rundstedt and Montgomery all agreed on was that in the end, the great operation in Normandy would be settled by tanks.

The landings were set for 5 June,

but unfavorable weather conditions caused a delay of twenty-four hours. Finally, Eisenhower got what he wanted to hear from his chief meteorologist and, at 4:15 a.m. on 5 June, declared the invasion on for the 6th. He later told his driver, Kay Summersby: "D-Day is on. Nothing can stop us now."

Lord Louis Mountbatten had stated the conditions for success in such an invasion effort: "First, get ashore against no matter what opposition. Second, having got ashore, stay ashore no matter what the weather conditions. Third, stop the enemy from building up his forces against you quicker than you can. Otherwise, he'll throw you back into the sea."

The ships that had brought the Allied troops to Normandy lay as much as twelve miles off the French coast at 3 a.m. on 6 June when the men descended into the landing craft that would bring them in to the beaches. A four-foot swell was being whipped up by an eighteen-knot breeze. Many of the invaders would be miserable with seasickness before they reached the beach. Of twenty-nine amphibious DD (duplex-drive) canvas-sided "swimming tanks" launched from assault ships when still four miles from Omaha beach, twenty-one sank immediately with the loss of nearly all the crews. Three more were lost before reaching the beach, two of them to enemy action. Only two made it to the shore.

Many of the tank crews struggling to make the beaches that day were lost as their tanks were destroyed or crippled by mines, hung up on the myriad German obstacles or bogged down in the sucking sand.

Omaha was carnage. From 6:36 a.m., when the first Americans entered the surf from their landing craft, to 11 a.m., when things finally began to

go their way and U.S. infantry soldiers were climbing the hill, crossing the plateau and swelling the numbers of their companions already engaged in house-to-house fighting in the village of Coleville behind Omaha, the beach had become littered with bodies, parts of bodies, and wounded. Men were struggling to clear the area of tanks, vehicles and equipment, hopelessly backed-up and crowding the limited space to the water's edge.

Those who survived the landings, the subsequent battles inland and the remaining campaign against the Germans would forever remember 6 June as the longest day of their lives. By the end of that day more than 155,000 Allied troops had come ashore across the five invasion beaches, Utah, Omaha, Gold, Juno and Sword, and eighty square miles of France were in Allied hands. All five landing beaches were secured at a cost of 2,500 lives. The British and Canadians at Gold, Juno and Sword, and the Americans at Utah, having had a far easier time on their sands than the men at Omaha, were now advancing inland. Within the first few days after D-Day it was apparent, to some Germans at least, that all hope of driving the Allies back into the sea had gone. "From June 9 on, the initiative lay with the Allies. The first phase of the invasion ended with an obvious military, political and psychological success for the Allies," wrote Lieutenant General Hans Spiedel, Rommel's Chief of Staff. Adolf Hitler's reaction to the predicament of his forces in Normandy was, "Hold at all costs."

With the Normandy beachheads secured, General Eisenhower and his commanders concentrated on the next phase of the operation which included the capture of Cherbourg and the preparations for the Allied advance into France. But first they had to break out of the bocage, a patch-work quilt of tiny fields divided by tall, thick impassable hedgerows that sat on broad-based six-foot-high banks, and were criss-crossed with a tangle of narrow lanes, east and west of the beachheads—not a good place for tanks. Initially, the Americans tried a combination of fighter-bombers, artillery fire and planted explosives to blast gaps through the embanked hedge-rows for their tanks, but they soon developed a better method. Salvaging metal elements from the German beach obstacles, they created a type of plow which they welded to the front of some tanks and were then able to cut through the thick hedge banks.

The Tigers and Panthers of the German armored forces performed optimally when positioned to stand and fight at a range of 1,000 yards or more from their targets. Certainly, the Germans did not want to engage the

Churchills, Cromwells, and Shermans of the Allies in the area of the bocage, where firing ranges would be more like 200 to 400 yards. These Allied tanks were clearly inferior to the Tigers and Panthers in their armor and armament, but the Allies knew that this German advantage would be min-imized if the fighting took place in the bocage. The Germans knew that the best place for the sort of tank battle they wanted was on the large, open plain south of Caen.

In their fine book, *The Battle for Normandy*, Eversleigh Belfield and H. Essame provide the following account

of a British tank crew's experience in the campaign: "To crash straight across country ignoring the easy route, taking in Churchillian [tank] strides small woods, buildings, hills, valleys, sunken roads and, worst of all, those steep high banks which divide up the Norman bocage like the ridges on a monstrous waffle, this was something for which we were not quite prepared by our training in the Dukeries.

"There was no luxury and little comfort about the Churchills, save when driven slowly along a road in the small fields of Normandy among the cider orchards, every move during the hot summer brought showers of small hard sour apples cascading into the turrets through the commanders' open hatches; after a few days there might be enough to jam the turret.

"Five men in close proximity, three in the turret and two below in the driving compartment, all in a

top: Major General Percy Hobart devised various special purpose tanks, the example at left being a "flail" used for clearing paths through minefields; above: A variety of German anti-tank obstacles employed in the Normandy area during the Allied landing operations, 1944.

thick metal oven, soon produced a foul smell: humanity, apples, cordite and heat. Noise: the perpetual 'mush' through the earphones twenty-four hours each day, and through it the machinery noises, the engine as a background, with the whine of the turret trainer and the thud and rattle of the guns an accompaniment. The surge of power as the tank rose up to the crest of a bank; the pause at the top while the driver, covered with sweat and dust and unable to see, tried to balance his forty tons before the bone-jarring crash down into the field beyond, with every loose thing taking life and crashing round inside the turret. Men, boxes of machine-gun ammunition, shell-cases—and always those small hard apples.

"The skill of the driver, and indeed of all those men in the crew, was remarkable: the operator struggling to keep the wireless on net and the guns loaded: the gunner with eyes always at the telescope however much the turret revolved and crashed around him; the hot stoppages in the machine-guns; the commander, with his head only above the hatches, choked with dust, not quite standing, not quite sitting during all those long Normandy days: always the wireless pounding at his eardrums.

"After dark was the time for maintenance, the 3-ton trucks from the echelon came up with petrol, ammunition and food; then the guns had to be cleaned and all repairs finished before first light and stand-to. Thanks to the tanks, repairs were not many, but crews could not go on very long without a rest."

Hitler's armored strength was positioned to take full advantage of the ideal tank terrain near Caen. Montgomery's overview of the situation called for his armored units to engage the panzers near Caen at the

east end of the bridgehead and wear them down prior to hitting them with a surprise attack out of the bocage to the west by American armored units.

Cherbourg was taken on 27 June by the U.S. VII Corps under command of General Joe Collins. With Montgomery's British and Canadian troops holding their position at Caen, Eisenhower ordered the controversial Lieutenant General George S. Patton Jr., who had commanded U.S. troops in North Africa and Sicily and was the highest-ranking armored commander in the invasion force, to take his forces south and east, to surround the bulk of the German army. Patton was the American version of a blitzkrieg commander and quickly completed his assigned run, ready to join with Montgomery in an effort to catch and squeeze the German forces. But the cautious Montgomery moved his forces at a slower pace than that of Patton, which had the effect of allowing a great many enemy armor and infantry units to escape the trap through a corridor at Falaise. While Eisenhower and U.S. General Omar Bradley were dismayed at General Montgomery's apparently leisurely approach, Patton reportedly said to Bradley: "Let me go on to Falaise and we'll drive the British back into the sea for another Dunkirk." Montgomery, however, was probably the shrewdest of all the players, having learned much about his opponent's armored tactics from studying their performances in North Africa and the Russian Front.

Believing that Allied air superiority over the Normandy region denied his tanks the mobility they desperately needed to fight their kind of war there, Rommel was uncharacteristically slow to mount a counter-offensive. When he finally did so, the German armor was overwhelmed by that of the British at Caen, which fell to the

Allies on 9 July. With American forces proceeding effectively from the west near St Lo, and the substantial German losses near Caen, Rommel's armor was now forced to make a fight in the bocage in support of his understrength infantry. Still, in Montgomery's opinion, the Allied effort to crush the enemy in the region was not progressing as it should and he planned a major attack south from Caen, using three armored divisions supported by infantry divisions and preceded by a huge air bombardment. In the assault, Operation Goodwood, his Cromwells, Churchills and Shermans, with their 75mm guns, would have to face the better-armed Tigers and Panthers and the excellent anti-tank guns of the Germans.

Of the nine Panzer divisions in Normandy, seven were gathered to face approximately 1,350 British tanks by 21 July near Caen. On the 19th just 400 German tanks had appeared, but the fighting was disastrous for the Allies who lost 300 tanks in the first three days of the battle. The American M4 Shermans struggled to break out of the thick bocage against the vastly superior German Tigers, but by 25 July momentum had shifted in favor of the Yanks, who were moving south toward Avranches at a steady rate. As Montgomery's Goodwood armored units and infantry were frequently bogged down in traffic delays, Patton's seven fresh armored divisions (100,000 men and 15,000 vehicles) were making enormous gains beyond Avranches by 30 July. By 4 August, Patton's army reached Rennes, the Brittany capital.

On 7 August Lieutenant-General G.G. Simonds launched Totalize, the first key Canadian attack, an effort to drive his tanks from Caen to Falaise through the German lines. Waiting to greet his force en route were many

Tom Hanks as Captain John Miller in a
still from the film *Saving Private Ryan*, a
Dreamworks SKG motion picture.

Tiger tanks and a large number of 88mm guns that could be deadly in the anti-tank role. Simonds intended to attack by night and minimize his tanks' exposure on the broad plain south of Caen. He would run two tank columns, one along each side of the Caen-Falaise road. Many of his lead infantry were to be transported in armored carriers. The Canadians were to move in four parallel columns to the right of the road while the British elements would go as three columns to the left of the road. In the darkness the force would have search-light beams and continous tracers from anti-aircraft guns, as well as their compasses to guide their movement. The way would be paved for them by

Allied heavy bombers hitting German concentrations and by a massive artil-lery barrage. Simonds planned to push about four miles through the German lines before stopping his initial drive.

The Simonds force moved out on the 7th and, as they entered enemy territory, the German troops were thrown into chaos and confusion. Their commander, Major-General Kurt Meyer, rallied them, however, and they began an effective defense. The Allied advance did not resume until the afternoon of 8 August. For the next few days the Canadians were badly beaten up by the Germans who destroyed 150 Allied tanks and halt-ed the Canadian and British armored columns, creating some spectacular

traffic jams as well as filling many of the fields on the plain south of Caen with wrecked, smouldering tanks. The Polish armored division accompanying the Canadians lost twenty-six of its tanks and an entire Canadian armored regiment was wiped out by the Germans. When the faltering Totalize was called off on 10 August, the Allies had gained roughly nine miles of German territory.

Again, from *The Battle of Normandy*: "To those fighting there [on the Caen-Falaise plain] this area seemed to have been dedicated to battle by the Germans, who had evacuated all the inhabitants and most of their livestock. From the end of July until after the middle of August,

Popular songs of the war years.

the sun was so hot here that, by early afternoon, any man touching exposed metal burned his bare skin. Vast numbers of vehicles pounded the dry ground and the dust was so dense that desert veterans recalled their North African days with nostalgia. Driving at anything except a snail's pace raised a huge cloud of this dust and, in the forward areas, shelling and mortaring inevitably resulted. Well-provided with long-range Moaning Minnies, the Germans knew the range to most targets; the huge notices saying DUST CAUSES DEATH emphasized the dangers of speed to all who neared the forward troops. One effect of this chalky dust was to turn everyone's hair grey, youth seemed to

have departed, leaving only an army of prematurely aged and grimy men.

"Dry weather had ripened the tall uncut corn, which could not only hide snipers, but also caught fire easily; many a wounded soldier was literally roasted to death when he lay helplessly on the ground, the corn all around set ablaze by a mortar bomb or a smoke shell. A drought added to the discomfort, little water could be found locally and it had to be brought up in the water trucks, whose arrival came to be the most important event in the day, even more eagerly awaited than the mail from home.

"Finally, the insect life flourished. In the daytime persistent hordes of flies swarmed round the soldiers and

their food; great fat flies bloated from their feasting off tens of thousands of human and animal corpses which lay rotting on the battlefield itself, or its environs; others fed off the large quantities of human excrement which lay on the ground. Stomach upsets became common. By night, the mosquitoes took over to plague the troops. They were larger and more ferocious creatures than any that even the most hardened veterans had encountered elsewhere and seemed to find little inconvenience in making their nightly journey from the Ore or Dives Valleys to the Caen Plain. If a mosquito decided it would dine off your knees, then dine it did, battledress or no battledress; and as it

Britain's Queen Elizabeth with soldiers of an armored division just before the D-Day landings, June 6, 1944.

sucked, its friends would be wriggling happily inside your gaiters to nibble your ankles while others clamped down in hordes upon your wrists and face. They appeared to relish the anti-mosquito paste."

By 7 August Hitler had decided to mount a major panzer counter-offensive to breach the American line at Mortain in order to cross the 25-mile stretch to the coast and re-take Avranches. In so doing, he hoped to cut off Patton's army from its supplies and bring the American general's tank units to a standstill. He expected his panzers to cause such a stir in the rear of the American units as to panic and demoralize them, creating entirely new opportunities for German forces in the Normandy region. The German commander of this operation was Field Marshal Günther Hans von Kluge, who managed to form a panzer group of 185 tanks.

The panzers were now between the proverbial rock and hard place, compelled to take up mobile warfare and in so doing exposed to unrelenting tank-busting attacks from the skies. The effect of these rocket-firing attacks on the Germans was actually more psychological than material. The RAF Typhoons were scoring few hits (and very few actual kills) on the German tanks. The accuracy of the Allied fighter-bomber rocket attacks was minimal against the panzers, though the attacks certainly took a heavy toll of German supply and transport vehicles. Most of the German armor destroyed, disabled or silenced there were victims of ground-based anti-tank fire, mechanical breakdown or had simply run out of fuel.

After these losses, Hitler sacked Kluge. He then appointed Field Marshal Walther Model to command all German forces in Normandy, most

of which had been in some form of retreat for much of the previous week. Most senior German commanders there expected the worst in an Allied trap in what had become known as the Falaise Pocket, where sixteen entire German divisions were, in fact, cut off. The Canadian units had entered Falaise on 16 August and by the 22nd the pocket had been almost completely sealed off by the Allies. In the fighting that followed, an estimated 10,000 Germans died and 50,000 were captured, while 40,000 managed to escape, crossing the Seine near Rouen. The German soldiers thereafter referred to Falaise as "the killing ground." General Eisenhower later said of it: "It was literally possible to walk for hundreds of yards at a time stepping on nothing but dead and decaying flesh."

With the successful Allied breakout from the Normandy bocage, and the progress of the British and Canadians around Caen to the east, Allied armored units would now have to pursue their enemy to Germany on a wide front. Once the pursuit was in full swing, Montgomery's armored forces moved amazingly quickly to seize Antwerp and the vital port facilities there, while his 7th Armored Divison took Ghent. By 5 September the British divisions had accomplished these tasks, having covered 230 miles in just seven days. The U.S. 1st Army had made its way through the Ardennes to the Siegfried Line and the German frontier, while the U.S. 3rd Army, to the right of the 1st, had to overcome fierce resistance by German forces to establish a bridgehead over the Moselle between Metz and Nancy. The Allied armies had now stretched their supply lines to the breaking point. On reaching the Siegfried Line defenses, the Allied pursuit ground to a halt,

as did that of the Russians approaching from the east, giving the Germans a breather in which to regroup and reassemble a substantial armored fighting force.

In the Battle of Normandy, the Germans had suffered more than 300,000 casualties; Allied casualties amounted to nearly 210,000. Ernie Pyle, with the 4th Division in Normandy, August 1944: "I know that all of us correspondents have tried time and again to describe to you what this weird hedgerow fighting in northwestern France has been like. But I'm going to go over it once more, for we've been in it two months and some of us feel that this is the two months that broke the German Army in the west.

"This type of fighting is always in small groups, so let's take as an example one company of men. Let's say they are working forward on both sides of a country lane, and this company is responsible for clearing the two fields on either side of the road as it advances. That means you have only about one platoon to a field. And with the companys' understrength from casualties, you might have no more than twenty-five or thirty men in a field.

"Over here the fields are usually not more than fifty yards across and a couple of hundred yards long. They may have grain in them, or apple trees, but mostly they are just pastures of green grass, full of beautiful cows. The fields are surrounded on all sides by immense hedgerows which consist of an ancient earthen bank, waist-high, all matted with roots, and out of which grow weeds, bushes, and trees up to twenty feet high.

"The Germans have used these barriers well. They put snipers in the trees. They dig deep trenches behind the hedgerows and cover them with

right: The Desert Fox, Field Marshal Erwin Rommel, at left, with Field Marshal Gerd von Rundstedt.

timber, so that it is almost impossible for artillery to get at them. Sometimes they will prop up machine-guns with strings attached, so then can fire over the hedge without getting out of their holes. They even cut a section of the hedgerow and hide a big gun or a tank in it, covering it with brush. Also, they tunnel under the hedgerows from the back and make the opening on the forward side just large enough to stick a machine-gun through. But mostly the hedgerow pattern is this: a heavy machine-gun hidden at each end of the field and infantrymen hidden all along the hedgerow with rifles and machine pistols.

"Now it's up to us to dig them out of there. It's a slow and cautious busi-ness, and there is nothing very dashing about it. Our men don't go across the open fields in dramatic charges such as you see in the movies. They did at first, but they learned better. They go in tiny groups, a squad or less, moving yards apart and sticking close to the hedgerows on either side of the field. They creep a few yards, squat, wait, then creep again.

"If you could be right up there between the Germans and the Americans you wouldn't see very many men at one time—just a few here and there, always trying to keep hidden. But you would hear an awful lot of noise.

"Our men were taught in training not to fire until they saw something to fire at. But that hasn't worked in this country, because you see so little. So the alternative is to keep shooting constantly at the hedgerows. That pins the Germans in their holes while we sneak up on them.

"The attacking squads sneak up the sides of the hedgerows while the rest of the platoon stay back in their own hedgerow and keep the forward hedge saturated with bullets. They shoot rifle grenades too, and a mor-tar squad a little further back keeps lobbing mortar shells over onto the Germans. The little advance groups get up to the far ends of the hedge-rows at the corners of the field. They first try to knock out the machine-guns at each corner. They do this with hand

grenades, rifle grenades and machine-guns.

"Usually, when the pressure gets on, the German defenders of the hedgerow start pulling back. They'll take their heavier guns and most of the men back a couple of fields and start digging in for a new line. They leave about two machine-guns and a few riflemen scattered through the hedge, to do a lot of shooting and hold up the Americans as long as they can.

"Our men now sneak along the front side of the hedgerow, throwing grenades over onto the other side and spraying the hedges with their guns. The fighting is very close—only a few yards apart—but it is seldom actual

hand-to-hand stuff. Sometimes the remaining Germans come out of their holes with their hands up. Sometimes they try to run for it and are mowed down. Sometimes they won't come out at all, and a hand grenade, thrown into their hole, finishes them off.

"And so we've taken another hedgerow and are ready to start on the one beyond. This hedgerow business is a series of little skirmishes like that clear across the front, thousands and thousands of little skirmishes. No single one of them is very big. But add them all up over the days and weeks and you've got a man-sized war, with thousands on both sides being killed."

above: M4 Sherman Allied tanks advancing on Falaise, south of Caen, in the months after the Normandy landings.

TOWARDS THE RHINE

Once in combat, it was virtually impossible to get replacement tank maintenance mechanics, and equally difficult, if not more so, to get trained replacement tank crews. As a result, it was necessary for the ordnance maintenance battalion to develop a two-fold function. We not only did the maintenance, repair, and replacement of the shot-up tanks, but we actually became involved in the training of new tank crews. After severe tank losses and comparable losses in the crews, the armored regiments ran out of good tank crews. It was necessary for the ordnance to take raw infantry recruits who had just come off the boat from the United States and train them to be tank crews. In some cases the training time amounted to only several hours or maybe a day at the most. These inexperienced crews in turn suffered more severe losses due to their lack of training.
—from *Death Traps* by Belton Y. Cooper

It had many defects and teething troubles, and when these became apparent the tank was appropriately rechristened the "Churchill."
—from a speech by British Prime Minister Winston Churchill to the House of Commons in July 1042.

By the end of summer 1944, the Allies had liberated Paris, which was saved from the last-minute devastation ordered by Hitler, when his commander there, General Dietrich von Choltitz, negotiated the surrender of the city, agreeing not to destroy it in exchange for the safe withdrawal of

Personnel of the U.S. Army 60th Infantry Regiment advance with an M4 Sherman tank into Spangle, Belgium, in September 1944.

German tanks on the move in a still from the 20th Century Fox film *Patton*; above right: U.S. tanks advancing to liberate Samree, Belgium, in January 1945.

his occupying garrison. The logistics of liberating the city cost the Allies dearly in personnel commitments, fuel, other resources and, more importantly, time—delaying their advance on the Rhine and Germany.

It was at that point that a major dispute arose between Eisenhower and Field Marshal Sir Bernard Montgomery (later referred to by Ike as "a thorn in my side"). Montgomery strongly favored a direct assault on Germany along a narrow front, followed by a concentrated attack on Berlin, while Eisenhower planned an approach to Germany on an extended front. Ike saw the need to allow his supply system to catch up with his armies which had outrun it, and to consolidate their position along the Rhine, before commencing the final push on Germany, as the highest priority.

In September an extensive Allied airborne operation against the Dutch

towns of Arnhem, Nijmegen and Eindhoven resulted in a shambles and the British First Airborne Division incurred 75 percent casualties in the fighting. This was followed in October by the American capture of the German city, Aachen, which had once been the Frankish capital of Charlemagne's empire. From Aachen, the Yanks entered the Hürtgen Forest where they suffered heavy losses in the snow-covered German minefields.

Despite the many successes of the Allied tank operations in Normandy, it was the inability of the Allies to adequately support their three-pronged attacking forces in the campaign that followed which prevented them from ending the European war in 1944. By September, when the Allies reached the vaunted Siegfried Line, their forces had been considerably weakened by the effort and could no longer be supplied with the fuel, ammunition, food, spares and maintenance essential to continue their advance. The Russians, having similar supply problems in their approach to Germany from the east, were also stalled. This was the break the Germans desperately needed. They took full advantage of it to put together a substantial armored fighting force with which they intended, once again, to shove the Allies into the sea and regain the upper hand. It would be their last real opportunity of the war.

To assemble this impressive armament force, the Germans had to redouble the mobilization of their country, contain the Russian advance in Poland, take thousands of workers from their declining industrial base to replace the heavy manpower losses they were incurring in the fighting, and somehow find the wherewithal to mount, equip, at least partially train, and field nine complete new Panzer divisions and twenty infantry divisions.

While managing the near miraculous resurrection of their armored capability, Hitler's forces could do little to stem the flow of precious oil from their war reserves. Germany's entire infrastructure was in ruins near the end of 1944. Her strategic oil reserves had been reduced to slightly more than 300,000 tons, from more than a million tons in the spring. Allied bombing had crippled her synthetic oil production facilities and, in August, Russian forces approaching the vital Ploesti oilfields of Romania had cut off that source. The shortage compelled the Germans to move their tanks by rail, using the remains of their coal supply, rather than further strain their oil reserves. However, with Allied air superiority growing daily, bombers (and fighters in the ground-attack role) were busy with the destruction of the German railways, making life ever more miserable for those trying to

move panzers to where they would be required. They were forced to confine such rail movements to the night.

Shortly after the D-Day landings, Hitler had sought to recapture the initiative and alter the likely outcome of the war through the introduction of an entirely new terror weapon, the V-1 flying bomb. Referred to by Britons and Americans as "Doodlebugs" or "Buzzbombs," the small, pulse-jet-powered weapons were an early type of cruise missile, but not capable of reaching and striking a specific target with any degree of reliability or accuracy. Still, by the end of the summer of 1944, the V-1s, fired from launch sites on the Channel coast of France, had killed more than 6,000 people in the south of England and destroyed 75,000 buildings. The Nazis followed the V-1 campaign with something much more terrible in September—attacks on Britain by supersonic V-2 rockets which arrived silently and without warning, devastating much greater areas than the V-1s had done. But these terror weapons came too late to change the course of the war for the Germans.

It was probably Hitler's need of V-weapon launch sites in Northern France for further attacks on Britain, together with his desire to recapture the Antwerp port facilities, that most influenced the decision to make his final strike at the Western Allies, rather than the advancing Russians.

He elected to attack through the Ardennes forest of Belgium, owing to the relatively sparse American forces there, and the vagaries of the weather in that region which would virtually guarantee both minimal enemy aerial reconnaissance and opposition. Efficient initial assembly and early mobility for the panzers was practically assured. He hoped to cut the enemy supply lines, split the Allies and crush

their morale sufficiently to redirect the course of the war and force a negotiated peace. He had little respect for the American soldier, believing that this blitzkrieg surprise attack would terrorize and crack the enemy troops. The final planning conference for the operation was held on 11 and 12 December.

" 'Gentlemen, before opening the conference, I must ask you to read this document carefully and then sign it with your full names.' The date was 3 November 1944, and I had assumed that the conference would be merely a routine meeting of the three army commanders who held the northern sector of the Western Front under Field Marshal Model's Army Group B. Each officer present had to pledge himself to preserve complete silence concerning the information which Jodl intended to divulge to us: should any officer break this pledge, he must realize that his offense would be punishable by death. I had frequently attended top secret conferences presided over by Hitler at Berchtesgaden or at the 'Wolf's Lair' both before and after 20 July 1944, but this was the first time I had seen a document such as the one which I now signed. It was clear that something most unusual was afoot.

"The German commanders knew the terrain in the Ardennes well. We had advanced across it in 1940 and retreated through it only a few months before. We knew its narrow, twisting roads and the difficulties, not to say dangers, they could cause an attacking force, particularly in winter and in the bad weather conditions which were an essential prerequisite to the opening of our operation. The main roads contained many hairpin bends, and were frequently built into steep hillsides. To get the guns of the artillery and flak units as well as the pontoons

and beams of the bridging engineers around these sharp corners was a lengthy and difficult business. The guns and trailers had to be disconnected and then dragged around the corner by a capstan mechanism, naturally one at a time. Vehicles could not pass one another on these roads."
—General Hasso von Manteuffel, General Officer Commanding, 5 Panzer Army

"All I had to do was to cross the river, capture Brussels and then go on and take the port of Antwerp. And all this in December, January and February, the worst months of the year; through the Ardennes where snow was waist-deep and there wasn't room to deploy four tanks abreast, let alone six armored divisions; when it didn't get light until eight in the morning and was dark again at four in the afternoon and my tanks can't fight at night; with divisions that had just been reformed and were composed chiefly of raw untrained recruits; and at Christmas time."
—General Sepp Dietrich, General Officer Commanding, 6 Panzer Army

On the morning of 16 December, taking advantage of the cover of heavy fog, eight panzer divisions slashed through the frail Allied defenses along the eighty-five-mile forest front.

At first, the German advance through the Ardennes piled up significant gains against the totally surprised Americans. The campaign became known as the Battle of the Bulge because of the dent the Germans made in the Allied line. But when the panzers approached the American-held town of Bastogne, they encountered a robust defense by members of the 101st Airborne Division under the command of Brigadier General Anthony McAuliffe. Losing his initial

Valentine, self-propelled guns, above: near Nijmegen in February 1945, and below: at the Siegfried Line.

momentum and determined to press the offensive, the area German commander, General von Lüttwitz, issued a surrender ultimatum to McAuliffe on 22 December. It had been typed on a captured American typewriter and read: "To the U.S.A. commander of the encircled town of Bastogne. The fortune of war is changing. This time the U.S.A. forces near Bastogne have been encircled by strong German armored units. More German armored units have crossed the river Roer near Ortheuville, have taken Marche and reached St Hubert by passing through Homores-Sibret-Tillet. Librimont is in German hands.

"There is only one possibility of saving the encircled U.S.A. troops from total annihilation: that is the honorable surrender of the encircled town. In order to think it over, a period of two hours will be granted, beginning with the presentation of this note.

"If this proposal should be rejected; one German artillery corps and six heavy anti-aircraft battalions are ready to annihilate the U.S.A. troops in and near Bastogne. The order for firing will be given immediately after this two-hour period.

"All the serious civilian losses caused by this artillery fire would not correspond with the well-known American humanity."
—General Heinrich von Lüttwitz, General Officer Commanding, XLVII Panzer Corps

General McAuliffe's reply: "Nuts."

Eisenhower ordered General George Patton to come to the aid of the American forces at Bastogne, and his 37th Tank Battalion commander, Creighton Abrams, Jr. spearheaded the armored column that broke the German encirclement of Bastogne. Abrams would go on to become a prominent four-star general, commanding all U.S. forces in the Vietnam War. The current American main battle tank is named in his honor.

In his book, *Soldier*, General Matthew B. Ridgeway stated: "I remember once standing beside a road leading through a pine wood, down a slope to the road junction of Manhay, where a hot fight was going on. That whole Ardennes fight was a battle for road junctions, because in that wooded country, in the deep snows, armies could not move off the roads. This particular crossroads was one of many that the Germans had to take if they were to keep up the momentum of their offensive, and we were fighting desperately to hold it. I had gone up to this point, which lay not far forward of my command post, to be of what help I could in this critical spot. As I was standing there, a lieutenant, with perhaps a dozen men, came out of the woods from the fighting, headed towards the rear. I stopped him and asked him where he was going and what his mission was. He told me that he and his men had been sent out to develop the strength of the German units that had reached Manhay, and that they had run into some machine-gun fire that was too hot for them, so they had to come back.

"I relieved him of his command there on the spot. I told him that he was a disgrace to his country and his uniform and that I was ashamed of him, and I knew the members of his patrol were equally ashamed. Then I asked if any other member of the patrol was willing to lead it back into the fight. A sergeant stepped up and said he would lead it back and see to it that it carried out its mission.

". . . another incident occurred which I remember with regret. In the fierce fighting, the town [Manhay] changed hands several times. The Germans had brought up some flat-trajectory guns, and they started shelling our little group. Fragments whizzed everywhere. One struck an artillery observer who was standing by me, in the leg, and another punctured the fuel tank of his jeep. As this shell exploded an infantry sergeant standing nearby became hysterical. He threw himself into the ditch by the side of the road, crying and raving. I walked over and tried to talk to him, trying to help him get hold of himself. But it had no effect. He was just crouched there in the ditch, cringing in utter terror. So I called my jeep driver, Sergeant Farmer, and told him to take his carbine and march this man back to the nearest M.P., and if he started to escape, to shoot him without hesitation. He was an object of abject cowardice, and the sight of him would have a terrible effect on any American soldier who might see him.

"That's the sort of thing you see sometimes. It is an appalling thing to witness—to see a man break completely like that—in battle. It is worse than watching a death—for you are seeing something more important than the body die. You are witnessing the death of a man's spirit, of his pride, of all that gives meaning and purpose to his life."

The following passage recounts the participation of one American armored unit in the Battle of the Bulge. When Generalfeldmarschall Gerd von Rundstedt launched the German counter-offensive in the Ardennes on 16 December 1944, the principal elements of the U.S. 11th Armored Division were crossing the English Channel to France. The 11th arrived at Cherbourg on the 17th and was ordered south to Lorient and St Nazaire to contain

the enemy forces in those vital sea-
ports.

While en route south, the surprise
German assault through the Ardennes
caused the American command to
redirect the units of the 11th northward on 20 December toward Reims.
Heading to the River Meuse, they
were assigned to defend a thirty-mile
sector between Sedan and Givet and
to hold themselves in readiness as a
mobile reserve force.

Covering more than 500 miles in
just three days, the Division entered
the combat area, was made part of
the VIII Corps of Patton's Third Army
and moved on to Belgium's southern
frontier. They met heavy opposition
on 30 December from the 15th
Panzer Grenadier Division, which had
distinguished itself in the Afrika Korps,
when they attacked the Germans
northeast of Neufchateau. German
forces of the 3rd Panzer Grenadier
Division engaged elements of the
11th in fierce fighting at the towns of
Acul and Chenogne on 31 December,
at Rechrival on 1 January and at
Senonchamps on 2 January 1945.
Through their victories in these intense
engagements, the men of the 11th
succeeded in defending the essential
Neufchateau highway supply link to
Bastogne, keeping the enemy from
cutting off the crucial flow of supplies
to the Americans there.

For the next ten days the men
of the 11th Armored Division had
the jobs of patrolling and protecting
key road junctions and roadblocks,
reconnoitering for tank and infantry
positions in German territory and
lending support to the U.S. 17th, 87th
and 101st Airborne Divisions in the
area. Then on 13th January, the 11th
Armored launched a powerful offensive against the 9th Panzer Division,
the 130th (Lehr) Panzer Division, and
the 26th Volksgrenadier Division at

above: U.S. Army tanker Steve Joseph on his
Sherman.

American Sherman M4A4 tanks moving through the German city of Gelsenkirchen; right: German Lieutnant Ludwig Bauer of 33 Regiment "Prinz Eugen," 9th Panzer Division.

Bertogne. By 16 January, after a fire fight with the 27th Volksgrenadier Division at Velleroux; the 11th occupied the town and linked up with the U.S. First Army at Houffalize, stopping the German advance and containing the famous "bulge" the enemy had made in the Allied line on 16 December at the start of the counter-offensive.

Now the 11th was advancing steadily across Belgium as German forces were withdrawing ahead of it. The Americans reached the border with Luxembourg on 22 January, having liberated two dozen Belgian towns along the way. For their rapid march across France to reach the scene of the fighting in the Ardennes, and their slashing pursuit and engagement of the enemy in the great Battle of the Bulge,

the members of the 11th Armored Division, United States Army, were given the nickname "Patton's Thunderbolts."

"We arrived in Paris on Christmas Day. I was given another tank and we were on our way again, to take the city of Trier. We approached the city in the middle of the night and at dawn we were hit by a barrage. As we started towards the city, the point tank and a half-track were knocked out. Shells were flying all around us. I spotted an 88 and got my gunner on it and knocked it out. Then we were hit with three rounds. One went through the front, killing my driver and starting a fire. He never knew what hit him. Another broke my tracks and the third exploded under the tank near the

escape hatch. I got my badly-wounded assistant driver out and helped him to some medics. I then put out the fire in my tank."
—Charles Shenloogian, World War II U.S. tanker

Although significant combat engagements were still to come, initiative and momentum shifted to the American side on 26 December. By Christmas Eve the prolonged bad weather and thick fog had lifted, permitting Allied fighter-bombers, including the tank-busting Typhoons of the Royal Air Force, to mount a powerful attack on the enemy armor. The Germans had again tried an assault on Bastogne, engaging in a large-scale armored action, but this too was unsuccessful and 5th Panzer Army commander

Hasso von Manteuffel now knew that the German counter-offensive had failed and a retreat was in order. The full-scale pursuit of Hitler's forces toward Germany was under way.

In the Battle of the Bulge, American losses were 10,276 killed, 47,493 wounded and 23,218 missing. The British forces suffered 1,400 casualties with 200 killed. It is believed that German casualties were approximately 100,000 killed, wounded or captured.

The fighting in the Ardennes in late 1944 and early 1945 was among the most savage and intense of the entire war. The aggression of the German forces had been whipped up to a great intensity at the beginning of the campaign by a rumor circulating among them that the American and British armies were about to turn over their German prisoners to the Russians. Therefore, German troops

engaged the Allies in Belgium with unprecedented ferocity and a number of their commanders were subsequently tried for war crimes committed during the campaign. But in the majority of the armored battles, the American forces in their initially defensive role, and later when they were able to take the fight to the enemy, were more prudent than the Germans in the use of their tanks, preserving them and their mobility to a greater extent than did the panzers.

As American armored and infantry forces were advancing on the retreating German units from the south, the British were chasing them from the north. Much of the remaining panzer strength had been rushed to Poland in a vain attempt to hold off advancing Russian armor there. This left only small armored reserves to cope with the on-rushing Allies in the west. By 22 March 1945, there were no more German soldiers fighting west of the Rhine.

The final push is ably described in this account of the U.S. 745th Tank Battalion as it rolled into and across Germany in the last weeks of the war. It is taken from a speech by Captain S. Scott Sullivan to the final reunion of the 745th at Fort Knox, Kentucky, in September 1999. "Mid-February 1945 found the battalion halted, performing much-needed maintenance, and getting ready for a massive attack against the defenses in the Roer River area. The 745th launched the drive to the Rhine River with Able Company being the first to cross the Roer. The battalion moved across the Cologne Plain and encountered stiff resistance. The Germans had laid thousands of mines and hid numerous anti-tank guns to ambush the Americans. As a result, the 745th began to conduct more and more night attacks. The fighting was so severe that, by the end of February,

Able and Dog companies were down to two tanks total—due to the enemy's guns and the deep, muddy sugar beet fields.

"The battalion fought its way from one small village to another—always moving toward their objective, the city of Bonn and its bridge across the Rhine River. In early March, the battalion conducted a night attack to capture this critical bridge. Able company moved in with the elements of the 16th Infantry Regiment and sneaked quietly into the city. They found the bridge and began to secure the area but not before the Germans unfortunately blew it up right in front of them. The battalion continued to clear the city, even destroying a tank and anti-tank gun on the university campus. The ancient city of Bonn was now in the hands of the American Army.

"While the 745th secured the city and conducted resupply and rearming, twenty miles down the river, the 9th Armored Division was luckily able to capture a railroad bridge in the city of Remagen. This allowed the Allies to continue the attack into the very heart of Germany. The 745th moved down to support the expansion of the bridgehead and crossing. They crossed the Rhine and continued the fight. The Germans were putting up a heavy fight, attempting to push us back over the Rhine. Artillery and mortar fire was continuous. As the 745th pushed deeper into Germany, the Wehrmacht threw everything they had at them. The 745th took town after town and repulsed multiple counter-attacks. All of these actions directly contributed to the American Army keeping the bridgehead and building enough combat power to break into the Ruhr Valley and link up with the American 9th Army. As the 745th moved through following the breakout, their job was to eliminate tough pockets

The Red Death, a wartime painting by Adolf
Hoffmeister.

of resistance which were bypassed
earlier.

"The battalion then pushed on
to assist the Big Red One in seizing and clearing the Harz Mountain
area. Here the Germans were well
organized and the mountainous terrain kept tanks mostly on the roads.
The 745th met the challenge, and
from April 12th through 21st fought
bravely and scored record numbers
of kills and prisoners. 1st Platoon,
Able Company's performance on 18
April was an example of how formidable and experienced the 745th had
become. The platoon alone captured
fifty enemy vehicles near Rubeland and
went on to ambush an enemy column

the same day, to destroy thirty more
vehicles and capture a thousand prisoners. The combined effects of actions
like these broke the German will and
mass surrenders began. The German
Army was crumbling and the war in
Europe was nearly over.

"The 745th went on to relieve
elements of the 97th Infantry Division
on the Czech border. It was now the
beginning of May and all indications
were that the Germans were about to
quit. The 745th didn't quit—although
given the mission to defend—they
kept attacking and edging deeper in
Czechoslovakia. They pushed so far
that the division had to give them
orders to stop on May 6th, but not

before Dog Company had made the
historic link-up with Russian forces at
Karlsbad. The German High Command
surrendered two days later—the Allies
had taken Fortress Europe."

Fritz-Rudolph Averdieck was a radio
operator sergeant with Armored
Grenadier Regiment 90 of the
German Army in World War II. He
rode an armored personnel carrier
(*Schützenpanzerwagen* or SPW) which
was used by his commander as a
command center during operations.
The SPW was a light armored vehicle
with half-tracks. It was also used as a
troop carrier, was open at the top and
mounted a machine-gun. The wireless

operator sat beside the driver, with the commander behind him on the carrier: "In early 1945, the last barrier before Berlin was the Seelowe Heights near the Oder River. After incurring heavy casualties in our numerous attacks which failed to throw the Soviet bridgehead back over the Oder, the great Soviet offensive began on 16 April. The superior strength of the enemy overwhelmed our battle-weary troops, and reached the Seelowe Heights. Our weakened regiment counter-attacked, but was unable to regain the old front lines. Nevertheless, we strengthened and held a position on the Heights the night of 19 April. But the continuous Soviet heavy artillery and mortar fire took a heavy toll, tearing large rents in our lines. One thing was clear from the sounds of the ongoing battles. The enemy had already passed us to the north and south on its march to Berlin.

"The remnants of the regiment were retreating in stages toward Berlin. Attempts were being made to delay the advance of the enemy with repeated counter-attacks, but the front had been broken at various points and the Soviets were attacking us with tanks from the rear and on the flanks. A tank attack on our flank the morning of 18 April caused our SPW and remaining vehicles to be sent back a few kilometres to Worin, a small abandoned village. We took up a position behind a house near a crossroads. A rain of mortar shells and artillery salvoes fell on us, wounding some soldiers. The Regimental Commander was seriously wounded and the adjutant took over for him.

"In the late morning, the rest of the regiment came into Worin. Regimental command was now directly at the front. We were at the divisional command post a few hundred metres further into the village and our signal operations were constantly breaking down during this period.

"It was our misfortune to have a mixture of petrol and diesel fuel in the tank and the SPW could only be driven slowly and it had frequent breakdowns. A young lieutenant who had joined us a few days earlier, daringly planned to route the SPW over open ground along a downhill path. We reached the protection of a hollow without incident. We then had to go uphill, however, and the lame carrier came into full view of the enemy, attracting mortar fire and salvoes. The SPW crawled and bucked through it and we were expecting a direct hit in our open turret at any time, which would have been the end of us. After long moments we came to a protected depression and drove behind a barn where a number of other vehicles of various types had gathered.

"As the Russian tanks penetrated into Worin, I decided to leave the village with my lame SPW and, luckily, after crawling up a hill, I reached the edge of a wood. Explosions overhead forced us to move deeper into the forest. We were supposed to be in Müncheberg by that afternoon and columns of vehicles were rolling through the forest toward Jahnsfelde on their way to the main track to Müncheberg. Some of them returned later with the news that we were surrounded and the Russians were only two kilometres to our rear. Jahnsfelde had fallen. We could hear the machine-gun fire of fights on our left and right flanks and there was no way out. The divisional communications unit elected to break out on its own and three of our five men fell into Russian hands. The Russians were now directly behind us and we prepared for the worst, protecting ourselves with our machine-gun. We also got ready to blow up the SPW.

"By the late afternoon, all our infantry, tanks and other vehicles were gathered in the forest. The only hope for us was to take an unknown track to break through to our lines. Our commander, a lieutenant, organized the infantry. The SPW was towed by a Tiger tank. We took up positions at the edge of the wood at dusk and heard the enemy firing behind us. As darkness fell, we moved out of the wood and through the burning ruins of Jahnsfelde. We met no resistance.

"We set up new positions near Müncheberg. Our SPW was brought to a workshop in the rear and repaired during the night. The next day, 19 April, Soviet tanks broke through again and, together with our auxiliaries, we retreated back to Rüdersdorf. Huge columns of wretched, miserable civilian refugees hindered our movement until about 3 a.m. We stayed in Rüdersdorf until noon of the 20th.

"Only ninety soldiers were left of our entire regiment, so a further ninety-man company was assembled from the auxiliary troops, who were normally non-combatants. Men from the Intelligence units were also assimilated into the infantry. This 'support' company moved out and came under continuous Russian air harassment. Shortly afterwards we followed, with two lieutenants, in the SPW. A bomber let loose a hail of bombs on us. We joined the divisional command in the woods near Hennickendorf-Herzfeld as fighters flew low over the trees, but they did not see us.

"In the evening, we were ordered to block the neck of land between two small lakes with our 180-man contingent, but only the ninety-man 'support' company was at hand. At sundown the troops marched out under a hail of explosives and phosphorous bombs. We on the SPW had to use the road frequently, which was lit up by numerous burning flares that we called 'Christmas trees.' We had to wait a long time in the vehicle for the company to catch up with us. It was now just a sixty-man contingent. Thirty soldiers had nipped off and there was no trace of our ninety-man original regiment.

"We took up positions previously held by an SPW company, with two Tiger tanks. Against us were enemy tanks. Earlier, a Stalin tank had broken through the lines after putting a Tiger out of action. It now rattled along the road 100 metres from us and was stopped by anti-tank obstacles. A bazooka shell ricocheted off it with a spray of sparks. The enemy tank tried to retreat but was put out of action by the second Tiger. A nearby petrol and ammunition dump went up in flames and the air crackled with detonations as in a fight. Then the air strikes stopped. We drove the SPW from the road to the edge of a wood and camouflaged it. We were a few kilometres from Rüdersdorf, along a road that passed through fields and pine groves. I tried to sleep with the snapping sounds of the fire from the dump in my ears.

"When I awoke it was dark and I could still hear the rattling sounds, followed shortly by shouts from our left and right along the road. The Russians had broken through again and the 'heroes' of our support company had taken to their heels. The helplessness of our lieutenants had nearly cost us our SPW. Now dawn was breaking.

"Trusting to luck we drove along the edge of the wood. Under machine-gun fire we drove through a ditch. We could hear the enemy tanks as we approached the outskirts of Herzfelde under the protection of a light early morning fog. Some Tigers and 88mm artillery batteries

A still from the United Artists film *The Big Red One*.

from our division had been positioned here and began a duel with some Russian tanks that came out of the woods. We watched as tracer grenades ricocheted off the Russian tanks. A short time later one of our tanks was hit on the side and went up in flames. At least the hazy, rainy weather spared us the fighters. As our regiment no longer existed, the two lieutenants decided to drive to Berlin to search for the Divisional Command or the rest of the support company.

"While underway we observed some peculiarities in the defenses of Berlin. They consisted only of fighting units that had organized themselves independently. Hitler Youth were in position at some places. Strangely, we came under continuous fire along the way over Schönebeck to Schönblick. We now felt that defeat was inevitable. BERLIN REMAINS GERMAN was written on a signboard at the edge of the city. We heard a rumor that the city was preparing for its defense and was full of SS. We found our missing 'support' company in Schönblick in very comfortable quarters, and all of

A painting by C.A.Russell, British Scorpion Mine-Destroying Tanks in France.

us were put off. In the afternoon we were on the road again as part of a long column. With frequent stops, we passed beautiful residences and well-kept gardens with spring flowers, baths and parks. The Russians were already at Köpenick and threatened to cut us off. We met troops moving outwards. Then we passed through Köpenick, over the River Spree and through

Adlershof and Altglienicke into the housing estate of Rudow where we took up quarters. The small fighting units of our division set up their positions at Adlershof. We began our own Battle of Berlin."

Ludwig Bauer was a lieutenant with 33 Regiment, 9th Panzer Division of the German Army. He fought in Russia, on the Western Front in the Ardennes in 1944, and in the Ruhr Basin near the end of the war. His tanks were knocked out nine times and he was wounded seven times. While a commander of the 1st Panzer Regiment, 33, "Prinz Eugen," he was awarded the Knights Cross: "At the beginning of April 1945 I was leading what remained of the Panther Company (5th Tank Regiment, No 33), five Panther tanks. We were in the Seigen area. I was put under the command of a neighboring division and ordered to report to a Captain Adrario in Erndtebrück. After engaging in various operations we took up positions there as it was reported that the Americans were marching towards us with superior strength.

"We had not been out of our tanks for weeks and were dead tired after all of the action. I reported to Captain Adrario and received a special bonus of tobacco for the troops. I intended to take my tanks to a previously reconnoitered position, but the captain was of the opinion that we had had enough for the day. He ordered me to go to a house which was situated diagonally opposite the command post of an infantry unit in the middle of town. There I introduced myself to the company commander. I informed the troop captain of the position of my tank and asked him to wake me and raise the alarm should there be the slightest cause for concern. Then I lay down with my crew in the ground-lev-

el room of a shoemaker. Our tank stood in front of the house. We were only separated from it by the wall of the house.

"I thought I was dreaming. Suddenly, I heard shooting and American voices. It must have been five or six o'clock in the morning. My driver, Gustl Medack, woke me up: 'The Americans have arrived!' At that moment they shot through a window and called out in typically American accents, 'Hello, comrades, come on out. The war is over.'

"As quickly as I could, I snapped on my belt, put on my cap, ran up the narrow staircase. In the tumult that followed, I couldn't tell whether any of my men had followed me. I paused momentarily at the first floor and, with the Americans pursuing me, dashed further up the stairs. Then, standing there, I realized that I hadn't got any shoes on. In my rush to get away I had forgotten them. The Americans then began to search the house. I ended up in the loft. It was a hay store and as they entered it, I crawled into the hay. They shot into the hay a few times and then went downstairs again. Now it was essential that I find out if any of my men had also come upstairs (I later learned that they had all been picked up), so I crawled out of the hay and evaluated the situation. The Americans were talking out on the street. I was able to watch them through a small window in a door which served as a lift for the hay. I could see my tank and what was going on in the street.

"The arrival of the Americans had come as a surprise. As relatively few shots had been fired, either by the German infantry or the tanks which were positioned around Erndtebrück, I suspected that the enemy had been directed in by someone via an unsecured route. In any event, the Americans were there and I estimated their strength to be three companies.

"I stood there, upstairs in the house, without my shoes, my Panther down below. Our infantry had either been picked up or had escaped. What was I to do now? First, I had to find out if any of my crew were still hidden in the house. I crept downstairs and searched through the rooms but found no one. Between two and three hours dragged by. I continued to watch the goings-on through the window. By this time the Americans had completely cleared out the tank. It seemed they only valued things to eat or drink. They emptied a bottle of cognac amidst a lot of noise. They ate the salami sausages that we had received as special rations. They tossed out bags of underwear, papers and photos. Then an officer joined them. I thought that they were going to blow up the tank. Instead, after considerable to-ing and fro-ing, a tank-disabling chemical (an acid) was thrown into the Panther. It caused thick, billowing smoke and, apparently, as far as the Americans were concerned, that was that. My tank was still standing in front of the house, undamaged. I decided to make my getaway with it. I considered the situation and crept down the stairs. I had left our cigarette supply under a bench in the kitchen and, above all, I wanted to have that, come what may.

"In front of the house my tank was surrounded by Americans. Two of their soldiers were observing it from between the hall and the kitchen. After their long march they had made themselves comfortable by removing their shoes. At an opportune moment I grabbed a pair of their shoes, along with my cigarettes, and raced up the stairs. While putting on the shoes and stuffing my pockets with cigarettes, I heard some cursing from downstairs. Obviously, something had been missed.

"In time I could hear the sound of our own artillery shells. I certainly did not want to die there in the loft as a result of this bombardment. The other Panthers of the company had realized what was happening and vacated their positions, some of them firing as they moved off and rolled through the town at about nine o'clock.

"Slowly, peace and quiet returned. It was after twelve o'clock. My heart was pounding as I made my move. I went downstairs and slipped into a neighboring barn, hoping that one of my crew might be hiding there. Unfortunately, I didn't find anyone. I crawled up to my Panther and hauled myself up at the rear. I wriggled my way to the open driver's hatch, diving in head first. Once inside I could barely manage to get into the normal sitting position. I was just about to release the steering mechanism when three American soldiers suddenly arrived and began looking over the tank. Then they climbed up on top and into the turret. Their inspection seemed to take forever, though it was only minutes. One of them actually clambered through the wireless operator's hatch to the inside of the tank where he stayed for a few minutes. He must have been a stickler for detail. He even stuck his head in through the driver's hatch. I had pressed myself as far forward as I possibly could. Still, he could not have been more than 15cm away from me. My heart was hammering so fast I felt sure he must have heard it.

"At last the American jumped down from the tank. It was now or never. I pressed the starter. 550 horsepower roared into action and I ambled off in first gear. The Americans who had been standing in front of the tank, jumped to one side, horrified while I rolled the twenty metres to the main road, turned left and continued away from the locality. I then began having problems with the gears and the clutch, and soon the tank came to a standstill. I finally managed to put it in third gear and roared off. On the way I received three bazooka hits. The suspension of the gun was damaged and it fell down with its muzzle tilting to the front and came to rest on the top of the tank. The camouflage netting which had been resting on the barrel of the gun slipped forward, leaving me with a slit of about 2cm of glass through which I could see.

"I got away from Erndtebrück safely and later stopped on the crossroads to Schameda to get my bearings. I was under way again when, after a bit, I misjudged a bend, turned too sharply to the left and drove down an embankment into a field. I rolled to a stop, intending to remove the camouflage netting which was draped over the driver's hatch and at that moment the tank took a direct hit. It immediately burst into flames and I tried, as quickly as I could, to get out. In doing so, my cap fell off and my hair immediately 'melted.' I felt the air disappear from my lungs. Everything around me was ablaze. After my failed attempts to remove the netting my strength seemed to ebb away and I thought 'Now it's all over.' I fell back onto the seat, exhausted. Then I noticed how the fire engulfing me was beating its way through the mesh netting, and my will to live returned. I tore wildly at the burning netting. At the last possible second I made it out of the tank and landed on the grass. I looked up to see three German soldiers a hundred metres away. Thus I got back to my own company tanks."

Former German Army tank driver Ernst Kröfel: "Suddenly our missing tank, that which my comrade Gustl Medack had driven, came roaring towards us. I was pleased and thought at first that Gustl had somehow got away from the Americans. When the tank was about 1,000 metres from us we could see thick smoke escaping from the engine compartment. The tank had clearly received an American bazooka hit. The tank was moving at high speed. Alongside us on the six-metre-wide road by the forest was a Hetzer [tank destroyer] with its 75mm cannon. We weren't watching it and the commander, a bearded warrant officer, had not spoken to us. Then, as our missing Panther drew closer to us, the Hetzer fired a shot; the Panther received a direct hit and burst into flames. We saw the driver throw himself out of the tank and, because his uniform was on fire, roll himself in the grass. He then came over to us. His face was terribly deformed by the burns and I only recognized him when he was right in front of us. It was Lieutenant Bauer."

Ludwig Bauer: "The Hetzer commander maintained that he had mistaken my tank for one that had been captured by the Americans and that was why he had fired on it. On 10 April 1945 I had survived my ninth hit. After receiving emergency treatment and reporting the incident to the sectional commander in charge, I was admitted to Olpe Hospital. The burnt skin was removed, along with sooty shreds of uniform that were stuck to the skin of my back. I left the hospital a day later so as not to become a prisoner. With my head and hands swathed in bandages, I found my way back to my section where I remained until the fighting ceased."

As they rolled across Germany in late April 1945, elements of the U.S. Army's 12th Armored Division arrived at Landsberg, an area that contained eleven concentration camps. Starting in 1933 with their "model camp" at Dachau, the Nazis systematically constructed such camps throughout Germany and German-occupied Europe, initially to hold political prisoners and, later, Jews, Gypsies and others they considered enemies of or threats to the state. The camps were a source of slave labor for the Nazis and although only a handful of camps in Poland were designed as extermination centers, vast numbers of inmates in the other camps perished from ill-treatment, illness, and malnutrition. Members of the 12th Armored Division recount their experiences on

Shermans advancing on Germany.

arriving at one such Landsberg camp, Kaufering IV, also known as Hurlach.

"The GIs went into Landsberg and collected about 200 citizens and marched them out to the camp. No one there had money unless he was a Nazi. These were fat Nazis, well-dressed. Out at the camp they were divided into two groups. One group dug mass graves. Each grave was thirty feet long and fifteen feet wide, rows of them. The GIs were in charge. Rifle butts and bayonets were used freely. The released Russian had the run of the place. He was one of the busiest people I have ever seen. His working tool was a club similar to a baseball bat. He just wandered back and forth among the civilians, picking out the slackers. He used that working tool. Some time before we got there, the soldiers brought a captured SS man to work. This particular trooper had been a guard at the camp and had beaten the Russian many times. The trooper, it seemed, couldn't stand the pace. His body was added to the ever-growing pile of dead awaiting burial. This big, husky 'superman' was quite noticeable among the emaciated corpses.

"Other civilians were paired off and marched to an area more than a mile away, to bring back the dead. One fellow claimed inability to carry such a heavy load. He was allowed to bring back separate heads, legs and arms found strewn around. We walked the railroad track to find the scene where bodies had been dismembered. Here some sixty inmates had been made to dig their own graves with spoons and dishes. Every one of these prisoners was then violently murdered, chopped to pieces. The axe was still there.

"As we drove away from the camp, we saw some prisoners who had escaped. Either the injections hadn't taken effect or they had been skipped. Some were lying dead, two or three

miles away, and some were walking, the walking dead. They could barely move their legs and were stooped almost double. One fellow I will never forget. He heard our jeep coming before we got to him. With the most painful effort he turned toward us, brought himself to attention and saluted. The amount of effort it cost him to do that was, I'm sure, far more than he could spare."
—Robert T. Hartwig, 12th Armored Division, U.S. Army, World War II

"We gave all the food we had, mostly K-rations, to the survivors, radioed battalion headquarters of what we had witnessed, and moved out."
—A.G. Bramble, 12th Armored Division, U.S. Army, World War II

They carry no shadow in sunlight, the past like a slate
Rubbed out on a future that arrived too late.
Their faces are maps of a landscape, whose ghosts hover
Around them, an arena of ruins that are all like each other.
—from *Stateless Persons* by Alan Ross

A Sherman tank of the U.S. Army in a snow-covered field near Manhay, Belgium, after defeating the partially overturned German Panther ahead of it, during the Battle of the Bulge, December 1944.

GETTING SHARP

When the train arrived at Clarksville, Tennessee, a Second Lieutenant climbed aboard, looked over the recruits and said, "Put your caps on the left side of your heads, one finger above your left eyebrow, one finger above your left ear. Look cocky. You're in the Armored Force now."
—John M. Nugent, tank crewman, World War II

In times of sudden stress, it was any-body's guess
How the wicked always managed to survive
While their more deserving brothers, along with all the others,
Scratched and scrambled just to stay alive.
—from *Trench Fever*, by Robert Swan

We were at Fort Knox, Kentucky, and we had to know our machine-guns. The cadre took us out into the woods to teach us about the .30 calibre machine-gun. We sat around on empty ammunition boxes and went through all the nomenclature of the weapon. Then the sergeant who was teaching us said, 'Everybody, shut up,' and we all shut up. I'm from New York state and I'd never seen a rattlesnake in my life, but the sergeant was from Texas and he took off his jacket, tipped over the ammunition box that I was sitting on and put his jacket over the rattlesnake. Then he cut the rattlers off.
—John R. Schaeffer, U.S. Army tanker, World War II

To the south of Death Valley, in the Mojave desert of California, is the National Training Center of the United

States Army. It is part of the Army's Fort Irwin, an old post where General George S. Patton saw to the training of armored units in the 1940s. Fort Irwin occupies an immense area and, situated as it is in the middle of nowhere, provides a near perfect environment for armored training and battle simulation. It is a giant sandbox, ideal for the war games and maneuvering of the Army's tanks and other armored fighting vehicles.

It was due to the widespread inefficiencies and inadequacies of U.S. Army performance in the Vietnam War that the Army determined to establish a specially tailored training facility that would enable its soldiers to "fight battles" in a monitored, controlled environment. At Irwin they can engage in force-on-force battle training, taking on opposing force (Opfor) units in realistic, highly demanding combat scenarios which are recorded and played back to help the trainees learn from their mistakes and take pride in their achievements.

In the high summer at Irwin the temperature can exceed 110° F, making tank training even more of a challenge than it normally is. The heat, however, is just one aspect of what tankers may endure during their three-to-five-week training stints at the NTC. While there the soldiers' skills are examined in the field, checking proficiency in a whole range of capabilities including maintenance, logistics, weapons operation and vehicle maneuvering. It is a punishing, round-the-clock regime that is grounded in the kind of discipline and standards needed to guarantee that the lessons essential to success and survival in real combat are mastered in these controlled circumstances. At Irwin, the tankers of the U.S. Army hone their skills in the amazing M1 Abrams main battle tank.

The M1 Abrams is operated by a crew of four: a tank commander, a driver, a gunner and a loader. The job of the commander is to be the eyes, ears and mouth of the crew. Of the four, he is the one who communicates with the other tanks, and with his driver and the other crew members, to maintain the tank on course and in its proper position among the other tanks of his platoon. The rest of the crew is dependent on his eyes and his judgement to keep them out of trouble as he constantly scans the area around the tank and directs the driver. He is the only member of the crew whose position offers the sort of visibility required by his broad responsibilities. As tank commander he is also responsible for the daily servicing and maintenance of the vehicle.

Ernest Audino, tanker, U.S. Army: "On my first tank crew qualification, the battalion had a great gunner and a great loader; he was a weight lifter and that guy could really slam rounds in there. We had a fantastic driver too. When we came off the course at about 2:30 in the morning, we came back for our debrief and the tank crew evaluator recounted each engagement for us. As he was giving us the points for each engagement and showing us what we did, I had a little calculator with me and I was adding up the points. As he got to the very last engagement, which happened to be a fifty calibre one, I could see on the video that the last tracer out of my fifty hit that target and gave me points for it, I knew we had qualified and possibly high in the battalion. The crew knew it too. They just erupted. I was very proud of all of them. At this point I had been up for about twenty-four hours. We finished the debrief, pulled off the range and went back to our cots. The next morning at about 06:30 I was in my sleeping bag on my cot and I felt somebody shoving my shoulder: 'Hey,

sir, wake up, wake up.' I could barely see. I was pretty tired. And here were my platoon sergeant and all the tank commanders from my platoon, with a big bucket of ice and water. I still have a picture in my mind of the three tank commanders high-tailing it out of that barracks, and me freezing cold in my underwear chasing 'em out the door.

"Years ago I was in Germany and we were training at night. When it starts snowing, it doesn't really bother us tankers. The snow can get pretty deep when we are rolling cross-country and that really doesn't affect us. But if you happen to cross a road or a trail and you get three or four tanks there, by the time that fourth tank gets through, the snow is usually pretty well packed down. It's ice at that point. So here was this tank company lined up on a tank trail, a dirt road, in the middle of the night and they are getting ready to move. They had been in position for about five minutes, waiting to move. No one is going anywhere at this point. The tanks are stopped, the vehicles are idling, and then the most unlucky tank company commander appeared out of nowhere. Mysteriously, his tank just flipped over. His was one of the tanks in that column and it was as if God said: 'Your tank is flipping over.' He was parked there on that ice and while the vehicle was idling, just imperceptibly, the tank was sliding sideways on the ice towards the shoulder, and then suddenly the shoulder gave way and the tank was upside down. Thank God nobody in that tank was killed, but that tank commander took no end of ribbing for that. The only thing that broke was the barrel of the fifty calibre machine-gun; that got bent in a U.

"When I was notified that I had been selected for this command, I couldn't believe it. I was going to command First Battalion, 33rd Armor. My

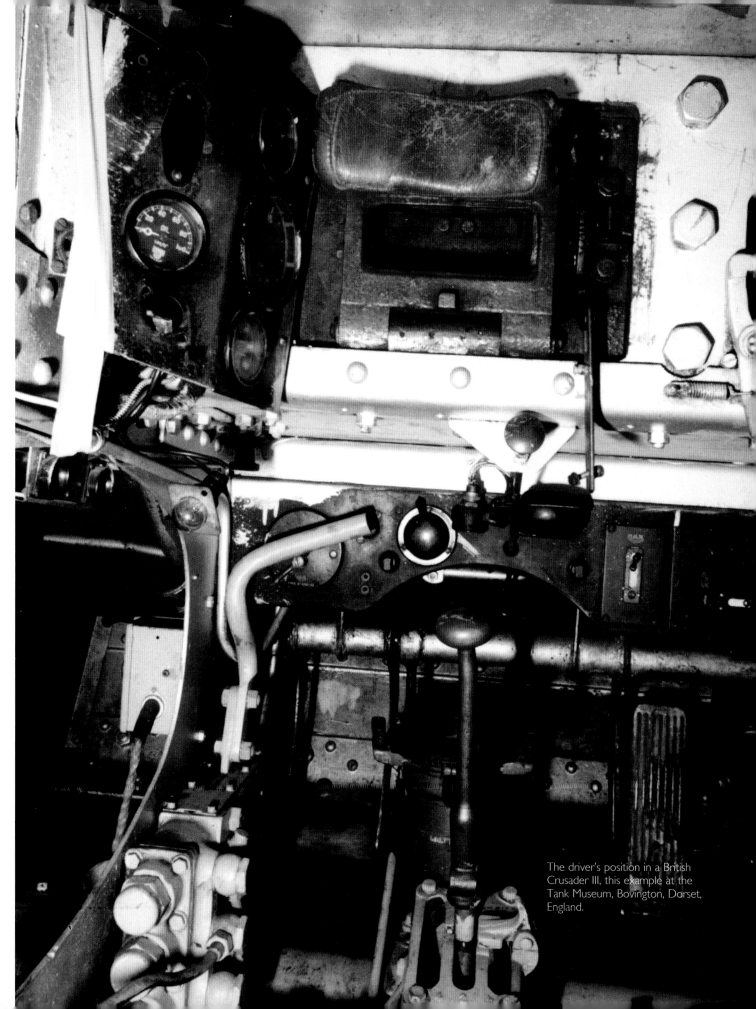

The driver's position in a British Crusader III, this example at the Tank Museum, Bovington, Dorset, England.

The American M3 Lee/Grant medium tank became operational late in 1941. 6,258 of the type were built; bottom right: The wireless operator's position in an M3 Grant tank.

first assignment out of West Point was to this very battalion when it was in Germany. My platoon sergeant was Staff Sergeant Neil Ciotola, who is now our Command Sergeant Major. Even then, we all knew he was the standard. And over the years, whether he knew it or not, he has been the standard by which I have measured NCOs ever since. There are just none better in the army. I've not met one better. He knows tanks, he knows tankers, he cares for them like they are his kids. He's a wonderful man and a great American.

"At the time in Germany, all the tanks were uploaded with all their go-to-war ammunition and tank com-

manders would wear their personal weapons with live ammunition because the terrorist posture was pretty high at the time over there. Wherever we rolled we brought our live ammunition. We were alerted every month, we rolled every month. I remember the phone calls coming in in the middle of the night. With no notice, we rolled. The scouts would leave; they were out the gate in about an hour. The tanks would follow at about two hours. We'd go out to the local dispersal area; we'd move in to the assigned wood line and we'd stay there and wait for orders. That was exciting stuff. We'd spend twenty-four or forty-eight hours there, then we'd go back to bat-

talion. But one time we arrived and the orders came down and I didn't know what to think. I was actually the scout platoon leader at the time. We rolled all the way up to the border, about a sixty-kilometre road march and we spent the next two weeks up there. That was right at Fulda Gap. It was the piece of Germany that was of most interest to us. This was before the wall came down. It was where we expected to fight if we had to fight on a big scale."

"In the Abrams, the driver's seat is in a separate compartment in the forward part of the tank. He is able to steer the vehicle from either of two positions, depending on conditions and the circumstances. With his hatch open and his seat raised to the fully elevated position, his visibility is nearly as good as that of the commander. He is, however, subject to the worst of the sand, dust, and churned-up mud as well as being exposed to enemy lead and steel in the air. When cranked down in the "buttoned up" position, with his seat fully lowered and his hatch closed, he is protected from those hazards, but then becomes dependent on the eyes of his tank commander and the periscopes and night vision device at his position.

"Every time we come out to do an exercise we go through an operation we call Railhead. Companies prepare by tying down the gun tubes so they won't move on a train. We drive them up on the train, which can be particularly hazardous because the tank tracks hang about six inches on either side. We carefully guide them up and then cable them down with shackles and cables, eight in the front, eight in the rear; a really aggravating exercise. Then when we get up to the Yakima area we unbuckle them and carefully drive them off, drive them up here, shoot them and

American-built M3 Lee tanks of a Canadian
Armored unit training in England during WWII.

then repeat the process to go back home again."
—James Jinks, tanker, U.S. Army

"My wife has driven a tank. We used to sponsor spouse driver training classes. It's nice to let the wives see what the husbands do and let the kids see what dad does. And when I arrived in this battalion I was determined to try to do this. We have all these great things and I couldn't live with myself if I let these opportunities to share them with the families go by. So we put together a spouse driver's training program where we would bring spouses with driver's licenses out with us in the field on a specific day. We would give them a one-hour class to orient them to the controls of the vehicle, put them in the driver's hatch, with some tankers, and take them out on the course. We would allow them to do one or two brake tests so they could understand that they had the power to stop that seventy tons. Then we would let them go out on the course for about a kilometre, not really that long, very simple, relatively flat, no challenging terrain. But when the wives came back after driving that 1,500 horsepower, the smiles were from ear to ear. We'd have a photographer right there and the ladies, of course, had their helmets on, beaming. We took pictures of them so that some day, when they are grandmothers, they can point to their picture and say: 'That's when grandma used to drive tanks.' "
—Ernest Audino, tanker, U.S. Army

The Abrams gunner must search for his targets by peering through an optical sight. He is isolated in the tank, with no hatch of his own and sits in front of and slightly lower than the tank commander. He controls the great main gun of the vehicle through control handles that the tankers call "Cadillacs"

because they are manufactured by Cadillac-Gage. Using them, he can adjust the elevation of the gun, traverse the gun through the entire field of fire, control the laser range-finder and fire the weapon. His is a highly skilled role demanding superb coordination.

James Jinks: "Each individual crewman carries a 9mm pistol. We have two M4 carbines. If we go to war we'll have eight fragmentation grenades, eight thermite grenades, twenty-four smoke grenades and a total of forty main gun rounds, and that may not seem like a lot, but is when it's designed to take out enemy vehicles of this calibre of tank. We also have 11,500 rounds of co-ax ammunition as well as a thousand rounds of calibre fifty. In the tank it smells of diesel fuel and cordite, the main gun residue. The system is designed so that the gases from firing don't come back in here, 'cause they are toxic. The cordite has a sulpherous smell; it stinks. There are guys who, when they start smelling it, get excited because they know that it's big-bullet time.

"Hydraulic blast doors . . . if we get hit in the back, all the combustibles, if all that went off at once . . . that protects us. There are big plates on there that blow off, called blow-up panels. When an explosion goes off in there, they'll go about 200 to 300 feet in the air. The crew will be safe inside here. On our Nomex suits . . . the rear end has a couple of sewn-in panels. The Nomex guys you'll see have flaps hanging down on the back of their rear ends. We call those flaps blow-up panels as well."

The job of the loader is to serve the gun, with either the "sabot" or "HEAT" (High Explosive Anti-Tank) rounds, depending on the target. The sabot round is essentially a thin bolt of depleted uranium or tungsten carbide

encapsulated in an aluminum "shoe" or "sabot" that enlarges the bulk of the round to a diameter of the bore of the Abrams main gun. Without its sabot the anti-tank round looks a bit like a big dart. It carries no explosive material. It derives its power from the kinetic energy imparted at the firing and is capable of driving and burning through the armor of another modern tank, causing a deadly shower of "spall" in which fragmentation from the enemy tank's armor is blasted into its interior space, exposing the enemy crew to a terrible flak. This spall phenomenon can result regardless of whether or not the tank's armor has been fully penetrated. In the Persian Gulf War of 1990-91, many hapless Iraqi tank crews fell victim to Abrams-fired bolts as they struggled to put up opposition in their

out-classed Russian T-72s. The HEAT round is basically a cone-shaped liner surrounded by a high-explosive shaped charge, together forming the warhead. When the round strikes a target, the shaped charge drives a jet of molten metal forward at velocities up to Mach 25.

In addition to the loading chore, the loader, when not engaged in his primary role, stands and mans an externally mounted machine-gun near his hatch.

One of the key people in the United States Army, one of those who keeps it ticking over smoothly, is veteran tanker Command Sergeant-Major Neil Ciotola. From a 2002 interview: "When I was growing up I lived in New Jersey. McGuire Air Force Base was right down the highway from us

and there would be 'deuce-and-a-halfs' the old Army trucks, loaded with soldiers in the back and I sat up there in the front seat of the Buick Le Sabre that my dad bought in 1967. I was nine years old and I looked up and waved and a soldier waved back. "What made me join the Army? It was that guy in that deuce-and-a-half who waved back.

"I wanted to be a pilot. My father was in the air force. He used to tell me that I would never amount to anything and that I would have to join the Army. I went ahead and took a flight physical and my eyes weren't good enough. My second choice was armored cavalry. I was eighteen years old and I wanted to be a tanker. It's been twenty-five years now and I've never looked back. If I have any regrets about my job, it's what I've put my

family through doing it. Every time I went to school, I took my wife with me and she studied with me every night. My successes are as much my wife's successes. When I made Staff Sergeant she revelled in it as much as I did. When I made First Sergeant, and it wasn't just the money, it was the prestige, it was the sense of responsibility, it was the people that, not only would I be able to touch but my wife would be able to touch as well. My wife has multiple sclerosis and it has really taken a toll on her in the last five years, but she is still, by any measure, a very vivacious woman. And her goal for me, as well as my goal, has always been to

The tank assembly line at the Chrysler Detroit Tank Arsenal during World War II.

below: Men of the 166th Armored Division, U.S. Army, clean the bore of an M60A3 tank at Fort Knox, Kentucky, 1980; right: An M60 on an a attack exercise in 1977.

become a Command Sergeant-Major in the United States Army. I've been one now for the last five years and she's ready to stop. She's moved with me nine times. That's nine different households she's had to set up. We have a wonderful little boy. He's twelve years old, and my missing his baseball games and stuff like that . . . but he's pretty tolerant. Now my wife wants a home and I owe her that.

"There are a lot of misconceptions about people in the Army . . . that we're a lot of blood-thirsty killers and all that. I've been to combat. I don't want to see it again. I'm tired of getting shot at.

"In my service in the army, I've met some of the most wonderful people in the world, and I just don't ever want to know what it's like to not be a part of that. But I know that I'm coming to the end of my career and that I'll do as I've always done in

the past. I try to give back everything I possibly can. The wonderful thing about the army is, our product is people, and in order for us to be successful, if we want to be here for another 226 years, we have to perpetuate ourselves every day and the only way for us to do that is to give back everything that we know.

"Another wonderful thing about the army is, they forced me to exist with my fellow man, my fellow Americans. Nobody else, other than the armed services, demand that you get to know one another. People tell me the United States Army can't adapt. My men have been out there in minus twelve with the wind-chill factor minus thirty-five. They've been out there changing engines and transmissions, taking their work in ten-minute shifts because their hands start to freeze . . . and people tell me the U.S. Army can't adapt and is soft. They can kiss my ass. They have

no idea what the army is made of. We live in a nation that provides its citizens with many more freedoms and much more latitude than any other nation on this planet.

"People talk about the new army and the old army. I was in the old friggin army. I came in right after Vietnam. My first tank unit was nothing but Vietnam veterans. The problem with the old army was they confused abuse with discipline. But they didn't serve alongside these soldiers, who are every bit as honorable, deserving and capable as those who went before them. Are they selfless? Yes, they are. Are they cut from the same cloth as those who served in World War II? No, they're not. Are we motivated in the same way as this country was motivated then? No, we're not, but we've got to stop living in the past. We need to learn from it, we need to respect it and respect

M60 tanks of the U.S. 63rd Armored Division in Karlshrue, Germany, 1977.

those who did what they did, but, if there's a difference between the soldiers of today and the soldiers of yesterday, sociologically speaking, the kids today want to know why . . . and we'll tell 'em why. When you convince a young man or a young woman that you'll tell them why they have to do something when it's required, when you tell them to execute and execute now, they know because you've treated them that way and they'll execute. There's nothing wrong with the army. Our toys are more expensive, it's harder to keep everybody in all of that nice stuff. It's always gonna be hard to buy that stuff. But fundamentally, philsophically, ethically, morally, there is nothing wrong with the army. I know that the same things went on in the army before, it's just that you can't hide anything anymore. What happens to one person in one unit is everybody's business now.

"When I was a young NCO, I used to think, 'I'm a tanker. I'm the cock of the walk. I'm the King of Battle. I ride in a seventy-ton iron monster. I don't need anybody else.' Well, an M1A1 consumes 500 gallons of diesel or JP-8 in a day, and after that's gone, if you don't have the support facility, you're screwed. You can only eat MREs [Meals Ready to Eat] for so long, you can only exist on one five-gallon water can for so long. If everybody isn't doing their jobs, you're screwed. So, the army isn't about any one particular facet; the army is about people acknowledging that what they do is important, and my job is to make sure that they understand how important each of their jobs are, because if I took out any one facet of my battalion, it would cease to function. Take my medical team away, somebody would die. My job is not only to kick people in the ass, it's also to pat 'em

on the back and give 'em a hug. Just like when the winds are kicking up to fifty and sixty miles an hour, my job is to make sure my First Sergeant gets those tanks around those tents, to keep them from going down, but then after that, it's just to stand there and let my soldiers see me. Wherever my soldiers are, I am.

"When I was a young private in 1977, and my tank had just maneuvered up to an infantry command post and we were talking big shit, this infantry Sergeant First Class who'd had two tours in Vietnam, reached up and literally hauled me out of the turret and dragged me across an open field. He pushed my face into an anti-tank mine and said: 'You see that, you son of a bitch! That's called an M15 anti-tank mine.' He dragged me a littler closer to the tank and said: 'You see that? That's another one.' And he dragged me a littler further and said: 'That's another Goddamned mine. Next time you think you're the King of Battle, you'd better go ahead and pull your head out of your ass and realize that it takes everybody to do this shit.' After I got done wetting myself I got back in my tank and I was a very quiet, submissive, stupid young Private First Class again and I just sat there.

"I am the United States Army. I establish the standards in this unit and the soldiers will abide by those standards. If you cross the line you will answer to the Command Sergeant Major. If you don't accept my perception of what a soldier should be, you will go home. The Marines talk about the few, the proud, and see if you're good enough. You have to be good enough to be a soldier too, whether you're a man or a woman. You have to be deserving to wear the uniform of your nation. We're affable and we're fallible. We make mistakes every day and we do hundreds of things right every day. We're made out to look like the bad guys sometimes. But we're the first one they call when the wife says that her husband is not taking care of her. We take that husband out of there to protect that woman. Somebody said a long time ago that the Army takes care of its own. It takes care of its soldiers, its wives, its children. The system that has been established is a wonderful one that is vested in this sense of integrity that everybody has. My soldiers deserve consistency. That's another thing that I'm supposed to bring. When they wake up, I'm there. Taking PT [physical training], I'm there. It's all about doing the best they can, and the best I can. And they'll get the recognition they deserve. It doesn't necessarily have to be an award or a medal. It just has to be a pat on the back. I hate the fact that the phone rings at least twenty-five times a day

. . . somebody is hurt, somebody got arrested, somebody did this, somebody did that. I hate it. But there's another part of me that . . . I don't know what I would do if I wasn't doing it. They call me because they rely on me. I have to understand the goals and objectives of my battalion commander and I have to help him fulfill the destiny that he has charted for this battalion and I do that by, number one, being his sounding board, number two, being his confidant, number three, being a sanity check, and number four, talking to my non-commissioned officers and articulating the significance of the agenda he has established. Colonel Audino is my fourth Battalion Commander and the only agenda that he has set for himself and this battalion is for them to be a well-trained, combat-ready unit. He loves being around his soldiers and he believes, just like I do, that we have a great privilege and honor, him to be commander of a tank battalion of 557 Americans; me, with the power and authority that I wield and the responsibility that I have as a Command Sergeant-Major.

"I walk out in my uniform in the morning and I have spit-shined jump boots on and starched fatigues and my wife is there and she looks at me and says, 'God, you look good.' I get in front of my battalion and call them to attention and that's how we start off every Monday. I say, 'Listen up, you sons of bitches. This is what we're gonna do. It isn't what you're gonna do; it's what we're gonna do. Get your head out of your ass. Go ahead and shake off the cobwebs. You got any alcohol left in your system, you should have run it off this morning at 6:30. It's time to take a Darvon and drive on. We've got forty-four iron monsters and 150 other vehicles down at the motor pool that need our tender, loving care. We've

A British Valentine tank towing
a Mk IV cruiser tank in mud
recovery trials during WWII.

got people to take care of, we've got equipment to repair and we've got a nation to defend.' "

"I enlisted as a private in 1985 in the California Army National Guard, as a tank crewman. Basic training was fourteen months long for Armor crewmen. I finished second in my class and served as Platoon Leader for my unit. After a 'Team Spirit' deployment to South Korea, I was asked to attend the California Military Academy to become an officer. I finished third in my class and was fortunate to be branched in Armor. I would have gone crazy otherwise. I was trained in M48A5s, M60A3s and M2 Bradleys. I commanded M60A3s. I always wanted a career in heavy metal. Fourteen fifty-two-ton tanks was perfect. I did one National Training Center rotation. The most important lesson of all my training experiences was how important it is to paint a picture of the battlefield so that commanders can act. Planning is essential to prepare for contingencies, but after the shooting starts and the radio goes berserk, it's important that reporting procedures are quick and concise. Of course, the radios hardly ever work like you want them to, so now you know why you spent all night planning for the next day.

"Artillery was available and we trained on the application of artillery all the time. We never spent enough time to get artillery properly implemented at the tank commander level.

The American M48 Patton tank was mounted with a 90mm gun, had a 290-mile range and a top speed of thirty miles per hour.

Having to command a tank or two, read the map, check for artillery, change radio frequencies and make a proper call for fire was very intensive work, especially when guys were supposed to be shooting back, and, oh yes, watch out for that tree. In a battle, everyone is yelling and screaming, especially the gunner and the tank commander. Then you have the loader, who is really stressing because he can't see out of the tank and is getting all his information from the two guys that are screaming stuff like, 'Where is he?', 'He's right there, pointing his gun at us.' 'I don't see him.' 'Fire!' 'I can't. I don't see anything.' 'Just pull the f . . . trigger!'

"I used to laugh at car salesmen who said: 'It's built like a tank.' I would respond: 'So, it requires eight hours of labor for every hour of operation and it breaks down all the time?' There is nothing fun or glorious about breaking down. With proper driving habits, you can avoid a lot of problems. I have never been in a tank that threw a track. Concertina wire wrapped around the idler wheel, yes, but we didn't throw a track. I don't want to count the times I broke track due to maintenance."
—Jeff Babineau, tanker, U.S. Army

To lead uninstructed people to war is to throw them away.
—Confucius, 480 BC

THE NOT SO PACIFIC

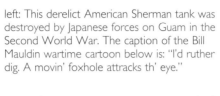

left: This derelict American Sherman tank was destroyed by Japanese forces on Guam in the Second World War. The caption of the Bill Mauldin wartime cartoon below is: "I'd ruther dig. A movin' foxhole attracks th' eye."

Australian Matilda tanks coming ashore on Brunei during the Second World War.

Australian Matildas supporting their infantrymen in clearing the oil refinery at Balikpapan
on July 3, 1945.

Buttoned up and ready for action, an
Australian Matilda rolling through the jungles of
Bougainville in April 1945.

Australian Matilda tanks operating on the island of Wewak, Papua, New Guinea; bottom: American Sherman tanks on a mopping-up patrol near Hollandia, New Guinea.

below: U.S. Army and Marine Corps M4 Sherman tank crews clearing Japanese troops on Peleliu Island; left: An abandoned Japanese tank during the extensive American island-hopping campaign in the western Pacific; pages 168-169: American infantrymen crouching behind a Sherman tank while advancing against Japanese forces on the island of Bougainville in the Solomons in 1944.

U.S. Marines hitching a ride on this American tank in the Korean War.

The Korean War lasted from June 1950 until July 1953 and resulted in a military stalemate; right: U.S. Marine tankers search the Korean highlands for enemy positions; below right: With the aid of these Korean children, this U.S. Army half-track driver manages a quick shave in the field.

Among the most respected armored corps in the world is that of the Israeli Defense Force and Israel is often perceived as one of the leaders in modern tank technology. It was not always so. In its initial combat engagement, on 16 October 1948, the then-battalion-strength Israeli tank organization was ordered into battle against an Egyptian force that had gained control of Lod Airport. In the brief action, Israel's ten French 1930s-era two-man Hitchkiss H39 light tanks all failed embarrassingly, breaking down or ending up in anti-tank ditches, without getting within range of their enemy. These tanks were World War II leftovers, obtained in the Middle East after the conflict. Their two British Cromwell infantry tanks were also quickly out of action.

In those days the Israelis didn't know much about tanks or armored warfare. They did know that they faced a prolonged fight for their very survival against the Arab enemy. They knew that they would have to hold their tiny territory with an unrivalled tenacity and play for time in which to gather strength and improve their fighting capability. They knew, too, that in the coming years they could not possibly prevail in a war of attrition.

GULF AND MIDDLE EAST

The ultra-low design enables the Israeli Merkava main battle tank to hide behind most low obstacles, minimizing its exposure to enemy fire and presenting a very small target.

The slender turret of the Merkava enhances the compact, efficient shape of the special and unconventional tank.

They were the few; the Arabs the many.

The Israelis were extremely limited in equipment, weaponry, ammunition, technology, geography, money and manpower. Their enemy had all the advantages in numbers. Knowing this about their opponents, the Arabs determined to force the Israelis into fighting that defensive war of attrition. The Israelis realized that their only hope was always to control the situation and strike swiftly and powerfully in short campaigns that would be decisive. They had to take and keep the offensive in the struggle to come.

To control the situation, and survive, the Israelis needed to ensure

that their land battles would take place in wasteland regions whenever possible, far from the hard-won cultivated areas where most of their population resided. Somehow, they had to develop a highly effective, technologically sound, well-trained and disciplined armored fighting force, a tall order for a small country with severely limited resources.

Since 1948, the state of Israel has fought six wars with Arab nations of the region. In the course and aftermaths of these conflicts, the Israelis have learned many lessons about tanks and tank warfare. It was in the Sinai Campaign of 1956 that the Israel Armored Corps began to transform

itself from a rather rag-tag outfit to something resembling an efficient and effective war machine.

Late in 1955 the Egyptian government under Gamal Abdel Nasser, the former army officer who had served as prime minister and president of Egypt, and later as president of the United Arab Republic, negotiated a large arms agreement with Czechoslovakia, which led Israel to fear it would have to embark upon a Middle East arms race.

Because the Egyptians were also providing support to the anti-French elements in Algeria, France was disposed to provide armaments to the Israelis in the form of 250 tanks, most of them Shermans. Noting how effective some Shermans had become against German Tigers and Panthers during the 1944 Normandy campaign when the British had retrofitted them with a seventeen-pounder gun, the Israel Armored Corps followed suit and had their Shermans mounted with French CN75-50 guns.

The Israelis attacked the numerically stronger Egyptians in the Sinai desert in late October 1956, following a pattern of horrific attacks and reprisals, and the nationalization of the Suez Canal by Nasser in July—an action which infuriated Britain and France. While there was substantial disagreement among the various Israeli army commanders about how, and even whether, their tanks should be used in the conflict, their 7th Armored Brigade moved out to the southern front of its own volition and quickly spearheaded the initial assault on the Egyptian forces. Impressively, the 7th advanced more than 250 kilometers to the Suez Canal in under 100 hours. On the way, they engaged and destroyed a larger Egyptian armored brigade. The surprising, extraordinarily effective Israeli blitzkrieg contributed mightily to the defeat of the enemy forces by early November, but the victory was also due to the intervention of the French and British whose forces destroyed Egypt's air force on the ground within three days and went on to land at Port Suez in an attempt to seize the canal. The intervention of the United States led to a U.N.-brokered ceasefire on 5 November. But the Sinai Campaign was the turning point for the Israel Armored Corps. The tank had been accepted as a key player in the future defense of the young state.

In the 1967 Six-Day War, the Syrian Army had 70,000 men in six infantry and two armored brigades, as well as one mechanized brigade. They were well deployed along the Golan Heights and were backed up by a sizable mobile reserve. Their armor at the front consisted of forty Russian T-34 and T-54 tanks from a total force of 750 tanks. Most of the early action took place in the Sinai Peninsula while the Syrians confined their activity to shelling Israeli settlements from the Golan positions.

The escarpment of the Golan rises 1,000 meters above the Sea of Galilee and the Jordan Valley. In 1967, three roads climbed the Golan, all of them heavily defended. The slopes had been turned into a virtually impregnable fortress by the Syrians, with defensive positions and fortifications, roadblocks and minefields.

The head of the Israeli Defense Force Northern Command, Major-General David Elazar, had only three brigades available to him when he was called upon to seize the Golan. They were supported by Sherman tanks of the 8th and 37th Armored Brigades on 9 June when General Elazar set out to climb the Golan and clear the Syrian positions.

Syrian resistance was intense as the Israeli infantry and tanks pressed along the mountain track. It was a slow advance with the Israelis suffering many casualties along the way, but the Syrian fortifications were gradually overcome. Several of the Shermans received hits from deadly accurate enemy fire, but they pressed on.

The leading tank battalion was supposed to outflank the heavily defended fortification at Qala, but was hampered by substantial artillery fire as it approached. Instead of being able to outflank the Qala site, the Israelis were held up and engaged with it, and were taking many more casualties.

At this point the second Israeli tank battalion, realizing the predicament of the first, came forward and assaulted the rear echelon stronghold of Zaoura. After securing it, they turned west and attacked the Qala position from the rear. Now the Israeli tanks of the pinned-down battalion were rallied by a young officer and redirected in a renewed attack on Qala. They not only came under intense defensive fire, but encountered a mined anti-tank barrier. The young officer continued the advance, however, and soon three of the Shermans, including his own, were hit. He scrambled down from the tank, ran to another and continued to command from it. The fight went on into the night when, at last, the two tank battalions managed to join up and defeat the Qala fortification, leading to the end of Syrian resistance along the Golan front. The Syrians were in full retreat and the war on the Syrian front was at an end.

The war had begun when, following lengthy skirmishes along the Sinai frontier and the withdrawal of U.N. observers, the Israelis found it necessary to launch a pre-emptive assault on Egyptian positions in the Sinai. The Israelis were taking their own version of blitzkrieg to the Egyptians, who were set in a Soviet-style defense, having been schooled and equipped by the Russians. By 1965 the Israel Armored Corps had accumulated about 1,000 tanks, a combination of American Shermans and Pattons, British Centurions, and French AMX-13s, while the Egyptians had 1,300 tanks, mostly Josef Stalin 3 heavies and T-34s, but their total also included 450 more modern Russian T-54s and T-55s.

Until 1964, the quality of Israeli tank gunnery, and tank maintenance, was at best uneven. With the arrival of the Pattons and Centurions, such a casual approach was no longer tolerable.

These vehicles were far more sophisticated and demanding than the IAC's old Shermans and suddenly a great deal more was required of the crews and personnel. This was the moment when Major-General Israel Tal took command of the IAC and forced through a program of reforms that completely revitalized it. He showed his men how to operate and fight their new tanks with confidence and inspiration. He instilled a high level of discipline, standardized and tightened training procedures and introduced an expertise that had been unknown in the Corps before his arrival. By 1967 the crews of the IAC no longer feared their tanks; they had mastered them and developed a great respect for their capabilities.

In the early action the Israeli Air Force attacked the Egyptian airfields with the aim of eliminating the enemy air arm on the ground, while three IAC tank columns rolled in a surprise attack on Egyptian positions. The Israeli plan called for frightening the Egyptian defenders into retreat. The IAC would then maintain the pressure until the fleeing enemy was exhausted. The Israelis smashed through Egyptian defenses, incurring some losses to enemy tanks, mines and anti-tank guns. But these were essentially token actions on the part of the Egyptians who appeared to lack the will for the fight and tended to crumble after offering only marginal resistance.

The mobility and excellent gunnery of the Israeli tank crews, the surprise factor in their attack, and the immobile defensive stance of the Egyptians in their JS3s and T-34s both contributed to the Israeli triumph in little more than twenty-four hours. By the time Egyptian T-54s and T-55s appeared on the battlefield, it was too late. Although the situation had the makings of a major tank-versus-tank confron-

tation, the Egyptian tank crews were all but hypnotized by Israeli tanks that were outflanking them, rolling through terrain that the Egyptians had thought impassable for tanks. Under massive attack on their exposed flanks, they lost seventy tanks to the Israeli action in less than three hours.

In less than four days of fighting, IAC tanks had defeated and captured 850 Egyptian tanks as well as knocking out thirty-five Jordanian Patton tanks during the invasion of the West Bank and East Jerusalem.

Lieutenant-Colonel David Eshel was a founding member of the Israeli Armored Corps and its Chief of Signals. On retirement, he became proprietor and Editor-in-Chief of the magazine, *Defence Update International.* In his book, *Chariots of the Desert*, he comments on the 1967 conflict: "The Egyptian handling of their armored forces was totally ineffective and unimaginative. With almost three times as many tanks as the Israelis, their armor was kept static, far behind the battle-front. Such armor as was used was engaged piecemeal and reluctantly without precise orders about their objectives. The state of supreme confusion under which the Egyptian Command operated was signified by the handling of their crack 4th Armored Division, a force which, had it been employed decisively, could have caused the Israeli armored commanders considerable headaches. Still, some credit must be handed to the Egyptian formations operating under complete Israeli air supremacy, which deprived them of any operational movements in daylight.

"At the tactical level, the Israeli tank gunners showed that they were more than a match for their Egyptian counterparts, even when heavily outgunned. For example, the 90mm Patton gunners were so effective

Panzer IIIs destroyed by British tanks in the North African desert.

against the monster 122mm JS-3s that they knocked them out without losing a single tank themselves. Similarly, the AMX-13 crews showed that they could out-shoot the 100mm T-55 at night by out-manoeuvring them and penetrating their superior sloped armor from a flank with their 75mm high velocity guns.

"On the other hand, the Israeli armored infantry proved insufficiently trained, as had also been the case in the 1956 war. With the exception of the 9th regular battalion, the rest of the armored infantry performed poorly, a fact which was to have far-reaching consequences in the future shaping of the Israeli armored forces. The Israelis also found out very quickly how badly they suffered from the lack of modern night fighting equipment, in contrast to the well-equipped Egyptian T-55s. Xenon searchlights proved extremely dangerous to the crews.

"There was marked disparity in the standards of tactical leadership between the two sides. Whereas the Israeli commanders led from the front, sometimes even too much so, with brigadiers moving immediately behind their vanguards, ready to intervene at once when necessary, and battalion commanders leading each assault, exercising their battle leadership by personal example, the Egyptian commanders normally remained in their headquarters—confused by conflicting reports from the front and unable to influence the battle by exercising their authority to support actions or to move their reserves to endangered sectors.

"Lack of initiative or motivation caused their armored attacks, those that were executed at all, to peter out at the first enemy response. Egyptian tank crews usually fought buttoned down and so with limited visibility. Hence, at Jebel Libni, a complete bri-

gade of T-55 tanks was outflanked and destroyed. While the Israeli crews sometimes fought for more than sixty hours without rest, the Egyptians were employed on short sorties only. Nevertheless, in spite of their fatigue, the better trained and motivated Israeli crews outfought the relatively fresh Egyptian crews in all battles."

In the years after the Sinai Campaign, the pioneers of the Israeli armor force, and especially Major-General Tal, began the lengthy process of planning and developing a tank weapon of their own, an indigenous vehicle that would be tailored to their particular needs, the Merkava (Hebrew for chariot).

Tal and the Israeli tank planners well understood the predicament that has faced all tank designers since the development of the first British vehicle in World War I; the inevitable compromise between the three great tank requirements: mobility, firepower, and crew protection. It was the substantial losses of tank crews that Israel suffered in their October 1973 War which caused them to give crew protection the highest priority in early planning for the Merkava. Their challenge was to find a way to design in the required degrees of firepower and mobility, but not at the expense of crew survivability. It may have been the only occasion in the history of the tank when a nation has chosen to approach the problem in this way.

Their extensive experience of armored warfare has taught the Israelis much about what happens to tanks and their crews in battle. That experience enabled them to conduct what may be the most thorough and exhaustive studies of ballistics as related to the tank, ever attempted. Their conclusion was that it is just as important for the tank itself to be protected, as its crew—something even more

difficult to achieve. Greater protection, they reasoned, would enable the tank to get in closer to the enemy.

To provide maximum crew protection, the designers of Merkava positioned the entire crew at the center of the tank so that they would be surrounded not just by the armor of the vehicle, but also by all the other elements and materials, for additional layers of shielding from incoming fire. Most modern main battle tanks have the engine located at the rear of the hull. For Merkava it was decided to place the engine and transmission towards the front of the tank, adding another barrier between the crewmen and their enemy. The designers' guiding precept was that every operating part of the vehicle had to function optimally and be positioned in such a way as to add to protection. Even the diesel fuel tanks are designed into the walls of the Merkava hull which consist of an outer layer of cast armor and a welded inside layer, with the fuel contained between the two layers. In a brilliantly innovative concept, the fuel tanks have been developed to generate a hydrostatic pressure on impact from an incoming projectile. This pressure turns the fuel itself into a more resistant medium which actually pushes back at the projectile, turning the projectile's own energy against it.

To further expand the protective characteristics of Merkava, Israeli designers developed a system of panels of high explosive sandwiched between metal plates, which explode outward when hit by an incoming projectile. This Explosive Reactive Armor was in place on the early Merkavas but has been superseded on the most recent generation of the tank by a newer passive system of modular panels that can be quickly and easily replaced.

The Merkava driver is positioned

above: Two wrecked Valentine tanks of 46 Royal Tank Regiment; below: Knocked out and burning, a British Valentine in North Africa.

A still from the 1958 film *Tank Force*, from
Warwick Film Productions.

forward and to the left, with the engine to his right. The engine, a Teledyne Continental AVDS-1790-6A is an uprated version of that used in the American M60 tank, which is also part of the Israeli arsenal. The later generation of Merkava is equipped with an Israeli-designed Ashot transmission system, so efficient that the tank's range has been increased by the changeover from the early mark's Allison to the Ashot. The tops of the tracks are shielded by steel covers which are backed with plates of a "special" armor to protect the tracks and the suspension from damage by HEAT (High Explosive Anti-Tank) weapons.

The turret of the Merkava is well-sloped at the front and has a small cross-section, offering a minimal target to enemy gunners, and it is also protected with a layer of the special armor. Inside the turret, to the right, sit the commander and the gunner, with the loader to the left. While many Merkavas feature an Israeli-produced licensed version of the British 1.7 105mm gun as their principal armament, the current version of the tank has been fitted with a new 120mm high-pressure smoothbore gun that is said to be capable of amazing accuracy. The gun is equipped with a tracking device which can lock it onto a target and keep it aimed accurately even when the tank is moving at speed.

There are other aspects of this impressive vehicle that contribute to it being truly special. It can accommodate additional personnel and has a low-level entrance at the rear, making escape or the ability to evacuate infantrymen under fire easier. It is also one of the most fire-proof tanks. It is believed that few, if any, Merkava crewmen have suffered burns in the tank resulting from combat. This is partly due to the crew being posi-

tioned in a dry, electrically operated fighting compartment, and to the employment of fire-proofed munitions containers. The Merkavas, Marks III and IV, are probably the safest tanks in the world, affording their crews protection and confidence never before known by tankers of any army. The Merkava Mk IV is slightly larger than the Mk III. The IV entered service with the Israel Defense Force in 2004 and the Israel Ministry of Defense is believed to be purchasing up to 400 of the tanks. The IV is capable of carrying eight infantry soldiers or three litter patients, in addition to its four-man crew. It is built with a new all-electric turret and mounts an advanced version of the 120mm gun developed for the Merkava III, which can fire high-penetration projectiles and guided shells and is also able to fire French, U.S. or German 120mm rounds. The commander's station is fitted with a stabilized panoramic day-night sight and an integrated advanced data communications system and battle management system. His station is also equipped with a laser warning system and threat warning display. The Merkava IV is powered by a V-12 diesel engine rated at 1,500 hp, 25 percent more powerful than the engine powering the Mk III. Redesign of the Mk IV hull around the powerpack has resulted in a better field of view for the driver and improved frontal armor protection against air-launched precision-guided missiles, advanced and top-attack anti-tank weapons.

Coming out of a costly eight-year war with Iran, Saddam Hussein presided over a nearly bankrupt Iraq in 1988. He eyed neighboring Kuwait and her $22 billion-a-year oil income with more than casual interest. Kuwait's oil wealth in his pocket would provide just what he needed politically and

The crew of this U.S. Marine Corps M1A1 Abrams main battle tank during the Gulf War Operation Desert Storm.

above: An oilfield fire near the end of the 1990-91 Gulf War.

economically to put Iraq back on her feet and reinforce his power base.

Sensing that the Western nations would raise little more than token complaints, he mustered a force of one million men, 6,000 tanks and 600 aircraft and began massing troops along his border with Kuwait in the summer of 1990. While bridling at his move, Western leaders continued to cling to the hope that Saddam was just blowing smoke, but on 2 August that hope was dashed as Iraqi forces moved into Kuwait and took control of 20 percent of the world's oil resources.

The West was shocked, not only by Saddam's audacious move on his neighbor, but by the chilling implications of the ease with which he had accomplished it. Would he now try to extend his gains by continuing on into Saudi Arabia? Would he be emboldened to attack Israel?

In the evening of 2 August, American senate and congressional leaders, and the U.S. administration, began work on a reaction to the Iraqi move. After much debate they finally agreed on the necessity of developing a "coalition" of allied nations, united in its response to the Iraqi aggression. It would be essential to enlist the participation of Arab countries in this coalition, and, while far from being unanimous in their support, the Arab League did vote to condemn Iraq's actions and her assets in the West were frozen. After some difficult negotiations with the Russians, for whom Iraq had been a good customer over the years, and considerable discussion with Arab states about the matter of deploying American and other Western troops on Muslim territory, the coalition was formed and committed to use all necessary means to force an Iraqi withdrawal from Kuwait by no later than 15 January 1991.

With America taking the lead role in the coalition, U.S. General Norman Schwarzkopf was put in charge of the military operations, Desert Shield and Desert Storm. The chain of command was headed by President George Bush and included Secretary of Defense Dick Cheney and Chairman of the Joint Chiefs of Staff General Colin Powell. The coalition military build-up began immediately. As the planners saw it, it was essential to complete the build-up rapidly, and achieve their goal before March, the beginning of high summer in the Persian Gulf region.

The nightmarish logistics involved in organizing and transporting everything that would be needed to supply and equip the allies proved far more complex and difficult than anyone had imagined. In addition to weaponry, materiel, ammunition, supplies, vehicles and other equipment, there was the matter of coordinating vast numbers of troops and personnel from several coalition nations.

The first phase of the allied effort involved keeping Saddam's forces in a figurative box; denying them any possibility of escalating or widening their adventure, while the allies gathered strength and the wherewithal to begin the second phase. This would involve driving the Iraqis from Kuwait, a job seen by allied planners as potentially very tough. It was believed then that Saddam would welcome the coalition forces with everything he could muster—massed artillery, minefields, flaming oil-filled trenches, and barbed wire, as well as a half million troops and the armored formations of the elite Republican Guard. The use of chemical weapons by the Iraqis was anticipated and extremely high allied casualties were predicted by some.

The coalition "air war" laid the foundation for the ultimate ground war, which Saddam would call "The Mother of All Battles." Using a standard of technology that the Iraqis could only dream of having, the allies

above: Tank Corps, a World War I painting by A.E. Haswell Miller.

began the operation in the evening of 16 January with strikes by cruise missiles and F-117A stealth fighter-bombers, destroying the Iraqi radar installations. The action virtually guaranteed that allied planes and missiles could operate in Iraqi skies with impunity. Within a month most of the objectives of the allied air campaign had been accomplished. The Iraqi supply and transport system, and most of their bridges, were destroyed, as were 1,300 of the 4,000 tanks Saddam then had in Kuwait.

By 22 February the coalition's preparations and build-up for their ground offensive against the Iraqi forces were complete. George Bush gave Saddam one last opportunity to withdraw his troops from Kuwait. The Iraqi leader responded with a boast that "the coalition troops would tumble into the great crater of death." The ground war was on.

On 23 February allied ground troops and armored units rolled

across the Saudi-Kuwaiti frontier. It was immediately apparent that allied estimates of the resistance they would meet were greatly overblown. Allied tank crews rolling to the border came to the dreaded "flaming trenches" and found them to be rather narrower than rumored. American bulldozers quickly filled in crossing points and the tanks rolled on towards Kuwait City, followed by the arrival, some seventy miles inside Iraq, of the U.S. 101st Airborne Division. There they set up a base which was immediately occupied by American infantry and armored cavalry elements

Resistance by Iraqi tank crews proved futile against the vastly superior armor, training, and technique of the allied tankers. The highly capable M1 Abrams American main battle tank was the primary weapon of the coalition armored force. It performed brilliantly against the Soviet-built armor of the other side and easily gave the lie to pre-Gulf War critics who had

claimed that the Abrams was excessively complex, difficult to maintain and out of action for servicing much of the time. In fact, the serviceability rate for the M1 in the Gulf conflict was 90 percent. Only four of the 2,000 M1A1 Abrams tanks in the Gulf War were put out of action in combat. None were destroyed. M1A1s destroyed more enemy tanks than any other weapons system of the war. Every one of the fifty-seven Russian T-72s operated by an Iraqi brigade in their flight from the conflict on 26 February was destroyed by the advancing allied tanks. By that date some 25,000 Iraqi troops had surrendered. Along what came to be known as the "Highway of Hell," hundreds more Iraqi soldiers were killed in their tanks and trucks when coalition aircraft attacked the road, destroying more than 1,000 of the vehicles.

The entire ground action lasted about 100 hours. Iraq lost approximately 25,000 men. Coalition losses amounted to 150 dead. So much for the "Mother of All Battles."

Jeff Dacus, U.S. Marine tanker, Gulf War: "I was a Staff Sergeant at the time. I was Platoon sergeant and a tank commander in 3rd Platoon, Bravo Company, 4th Tank Battalion. My crew was Corporal James Brackett, gunner; Lance Corporal Sean Edler, loader; Lance Corporal Rick Freier, driver. There were four tanks in each of the three platoons and two in the head-quarters section; one for the commanding officer and another for the executive officer. A total of fourteen tanks in the company. My tank was an M1A1 Abrams main battle tank, call sign Titan 4. Our crew nicknamed her Rockin' Reaper after a tattoo on Brackett's arm that showed the Grim Reaper playing a guitar.

"Bravo Company, 4th Tanks, is a reserve unit from Yakima, Washington. They meet once a month for a week-end and two weeks each summer. They were trained on M60A1 tanks when they were called up for Desert Storm. We spent about two weeks, from 26 December 1990 to 15 January 1991, on new equipment training to learn the M1A1. We deployed to Saudi Arabia on 16 January and went into the desert the next day. We

did not come out of the desert until late March.

"The day the war started we had thirteen tanks. One had fuel problems, but we found the parts in the Army's Tiger Brigade and our fourteenth tank joined us as we sat waiting to go across the border. We crossed the border just before five a.m. and led the battalion as we approached the first minefield. The engineers attempt-ed to breach the minefield, but lost three tanks and an amtrak in doing so. Our tanks started through, but the first one hit a mine. The crew was unhurt but the tank was a mobility kill [immo-bilized, but still able to fight]. We went around the vehicle and continued on through the second minefield.

"We engaged in our first combat after reaching an east-west road that was heavily defended by dug-in troops and tanks. Infantry officers request-ed our assistance and my vehicle engaged the Iraqi trenches with coaxial machine-gun fire. Iraqis poured out of their positions after that. Recalcitrant enemy forces were pounded by our tank guns. Dozens of enemy soldiers walked towards and through our company to prisoner of war cages. All the while, our guns engaged the enemy from 2,000 to 3,800 meters. My wingman, Corporal Glen Carter,

right: An abandoned Soviet-built Iraqi T-72 tank south of Kuwait City after Operation Desert Storm; above: Another Soviet-made Iraqi armored fighting vehicle used by Iraq in the Gulf War.

destroyed two enemy tanks at ranges in excess of 3,700 meters. Enemy troops attempting to escape from the Marines to the east of us used small vehicles; Ford Broncos or Toyota Land Cruiser types, to drive past us. Only the first one got by. They were travelling at upwards of sixty miles per hour, but our guns easily destroyed them. We fought until the evening forced us to pull back. Mortar fire and the possibility of artillery had threatened our infantry support and they withdrew, leaving us in the lurch. This was called the Candy Cane engagement because of the red and white striped towers that lined the east-west road.

"We coiled up for the night. Just before six the next morning, Captain Hart recognized the sound of Russian vehicles and two Marines, using thermal sights, spotted a brigade of Iraqi mechanized troops aiming for the logistical trains of our battalion and using a road that served as the boundary between our division, and the First Marine Division to our right. Despite the fact that most of the Marines were asleep, the effect was electric. Our company moved from a coil to a line formation and began firing. Due to morning haze, dust and darkness they never saw us. The guns of their T-72s were slightly elevated, indicating that they were attempting to load. They were obliterated. Our guns hit them from 1,200 to 1,800 meters from the side. The T-72s blew up one after another, their turrets flying into the air. One flew up twenty or thirty feet before crashing back down. Several older tanks were also destroyed. A T-55 took five hits and one round went completely through the turret. We looked at it after the battle and could see sunlight showing through from the other side. It was all over in about ninety seconds. We destroyed thirty-four enemy tanks,

most of them T-72s. We thought they were Republican Guard, but it turned out they were part of the Iraqi 3rd Mechanized Division. Several armored personnel carriers were also flamed. There were few survivors, although Iraqi infantry surrendered when their armor was wiped out. This battle was called the Reveille Engagement because it happened as the Marines were being awakened for a 6:30 jump-off of the day's attack.

"We moved out at about 1300, north towards Kuwait City in poor visibility. We encountered enemy forces retreating and there were many short, sharp engagements. My favorite shot was a 2,000-meter hit on a T-62 while we were moving at thirty kph. My thermal sights went out during the day, which was unfortunate as it was pitch black at 1600 due to oil smoke and dust. We reached our second night's position at an intersection of a fence and the north-south road. We spent the evening destroying enemy vehicles and killing infantry as the Iraqis attempted a counter-attack through their retreating troops. We received only desultory mortar fire in return.

"The next morning we moved on to Kuwait City. There was little opposition. Occasionally, a tank would spot a target and quickly destroy it, but the Iraqis were plainly heading out of town as fast as possible. We reached the edge of the main freeway that afternoon. We would be there for several days, through the ceasefire."

left: Chinese-built tanks of the Iraqi forces in the Gulf War.

IMAGES
OF A WAR:
VIETNAM

Members of the U.S. 11th Armored Cavalry searching the underbrush at Long Binh for hidden Viet Cong combatants in February 1969; above: At Cu Chi, Vietnam, members of the U.S. 4th Cavalry, 25th Infantry Division, test-fire the weapons of the M-551 assault vehicles near their base camp.

above: Bodies of Viet Cong fighters near Long Binh in 1969; right: With a tank of the 11th Armored Cavalry in the lead, members of the U.S. 503rd Airborne Infantry break through the jungle of Thanh Dien Forest in the Iron Triangle, Vietnam.

Combined U.S. tank and infantry forces searching for Viet Cong fighters; right: U.S. Army platoon leaders preparing to advance on Viet Cong sniper positions; below right: 25th Infantry Division troops in a January 1967 search-and-destroy mission.

left: Members of the U.S. 14th Infantry Division searching for Viet Cong near a deserted farmhouse in Phuoc Province, part of a search-and-destroy operation in May 1965; above: Support tanks for the 25th Infantry Division near Saigon in January 1967.

left: A combat tracker team of the 4th Infantry on the trail of fleeing enemy fighters; below: Thanksgiving Dinner in Vietnam, 1968.

below: A member of Company D, 4th
Battalion, 503rd Infantry begins his day with
a wash in a stream north of An Khe; right:
Vietnam Vignette, a 1967 painting by war artist
William L.Prescott.

below: A U.S. Army Pfc. on a quick break during a search-sweep-and destroy operation in 1966; right: Pfc. Ralph Morris, a medic with the 12th Cavalry in Vietnam writing a medical evacuation tag for a battle casualty in May 1966.

TANK STOPPERS

Tanks always create a morale effect on infantry, however often they have seen tanks, or have been told by officers that they will be quite safe if they take cover and let the tanks pass on. It is recognised that infantry can do nothing against tanks. The troops themselves will await a tank attack with calmness. The first essential for the infantry is that they should keep their heads. Anti-tank defence is nowadays more a question of nerves than of material. The German infantry still considers that as soon as the tanks have broken through their line, further resistance is useless. A German Corps order: "Messages concerning tanks have preference over all other telephone calls, including messages regarding aeroplanes."
—from *The Tank in Action* by Captain D.G. Browne, MC

When the tank first entered military service with the British Army in World War I, its primary mission was to break through the enemy defenses and enable British infantry elements to penetrate the German line and engage the opposition in open battle. The early successes caused the Germans to think about ways to defeat the new mechanical threat. Since then the world's armies have concentrated great resources on the design, development, production and utilization of both tank and anti-tank weaponry. Each new, seemingly invincible, tank design has ultimately been countered or seriously threatened, by anti-tank weaponry, whether gun, rocket, grenade, mine or other device.

It was initially thought that a heavily armored tank was more easily put out of action through wounding or killing the crew than through damaging the vehicle itself. The early tank was armored with a form of boiler plate, protecting the crew from rifle and

preceding page: A line of "Dragon's Teeth" anti-tank obstacles at Cripp's Corner, Sussex, England; right: An ex-Finnish Sturmgeschütz III turretless assault vehicle.

machine-gun bullets and small shrapnel fragments. The driver operated the vehicle while peering through a narrow vision slit at the front of the tank, leaving him somewhat vulnerable to fire from German infantry ahead. Even though the likelihood of the enemy actually hitting the driver through that slit was slim, he and the eight other crew members were extremely vulnerable to metal fragment splash from rounds hitting near the slit. They soon adapted chain-mail visors or steel masks to protect against the splash effect.

Next to killing or seriously wounding the crew of a tank, the objective of the opposing force was to stop the vehicle by any means available, making it a stationary target and thus easier to destroy or eliminate as a threat. When a slow-moving tank of 1916 managed to breach the enemy line and advance into the open, it often became relatively easy game for opposing artillery which was likely to stop it.

The First World War brought other anti-tank concepts. Enemy infantry tried lobbing grenades onto the hulls of tanks as they approached, in an effort to injure the crew and cause damage within the vehicle by blowing a hole through its roof. Tank designers were quick to protect against this threat by putting a sloped, triangular "roof" of wood and wire netting over the tank. When a grenade landed on the roof it either exploded away from the hull itself, or fell off and exploded on the ground, doing little or no damage to the tank. Infantry personnel also tried, with varying success, to explode set charges beneath tanks as the vehicles crossed them. Attempts to stop enemy tanks with ditches or trenches often failed as the tanks were designed to cross such gaps.

In its infancy, the tank was probably its own worst enemy, being slow,

underpowered and unreliable. More often than not, it bogged down in mud, succumbed to some insurmountable obstacle or simply broke down mechanically, becoming an easy mark for enemy gunners.

As tanks became faster, more maneuverable, more reliable, better armed and better armored during the 1920s, the efforts to find an effective counter intensified. The designers of anti-tank weaponry now focused on the most vulnerable aspects of their target. Apparent weaknesses in the tank structure such as the tracks, suspension and hatches were quickly exploited. The tank crew was re-targetted with new emphasis put on burning them out of action by attacking the inflammable fuel and ammunition carried in the vehicle. The use of rifle and machine-gun fire to kill the driver either in his open hatch, or through his vision block was also emphasized. Greater attention was paid to finding

weak points in a tank's armor as it became clear that the tank planners of the day were utilizing the heaviest armor on the turret and front of the hull, with thinner plating on the sides, rear and top surfaces.

In 1936 the Spanish Civil War provided a unique opportunity for the testing and evaluation of a wide variety of weaponry, from bomber and attack aircraft through tanks (both light and heavy) and anti-tank systems. Italian and German light tanks were proved highly vulnerable to the relatively small-calibre anti-tank guns of the time, and to an early form of Molotov Cocktail, used by the Soviet-supported Republican forces. The most interesting tank-related lesson of the conflict, in terms of the approaching Second World War, was a German experiment in which their gunners employed a small number of 88mm anti-aircraft guns against a few hapless Soviet BT-4 tanks. So devastating was their effect

left: The interior of a half-track vehicle; below: Matilda Scorpion mine-flail tanks at El Alamein, northwest of Cairo, Egypt.

on the tanks that the future development of German tank armament was dramatically influenced by the experiment.

By the end of the 1930s a new sophistication had invaded the field of tank design. The previous flat-slab look began to give way to a somewhat contoured shape as the advantages of a sloping surface came to light. It was realized that the probability of an enemy round deflecting off such a sloped surface was far greater than was the case with a slab-sided structure. Soon a combination of this "ballistic shaping" and a new welded and cast type of armor was defining the tank weapon for the 1940s. The use of welded seams in place of rivets increased the protection factor for tank crews subtantially by eliminating the possibility of rivets being turned into potentially lethal missiles when the tank hull was struck by incoming rounds.

Tanks were now more powerful and faster, making them more difficult targets for enemy gunners to hit, but new anti-tank guns were able to fire larger, higher-velocity rounds with improved penetration which increased their lethality when a tank was hit. The new rounds soon reached a point of diminishing return, however, when it was discovered that beyond a certain velocity, they actually shattered on impact with the new tank armor, leaving the vehicle relatively undamaged.

As the armor grew in thickness, strength and resistance to penetration, industrialists working on ways to defeat the tank turned their attention to the problems with their ammunition. Part of the trouble with existing anti-tank rounds was the steel of which they were made. The search for a harder, denser, more shatter-resistant material was on in earnest. The solution seemed to be tungsten carbide, but this, although affordable, was considerably heavier than steel and projectiles

made of it therefore achieved much lower velocities than comparable steel rounds. At this point a German idea from the 1920s resurfaced when the Rheinmetall company succeeded in building a light anti-tank gun with a tapered bore. The new gun fired a shell with a tungsten core and a soft steel body mounted with "skirts" which were compressed around the body of the projectile as it travelled through the barrel of the gun. The effect gave both the high velocity and increased penetration power that the makers wanted. The new weapon proved quite effective in the North African desert engagements of 1942.

By 1943 work was under way in Britain on one of the most important anti-tank concepts ever: the Armor-Piercing Discarding Sabot (APDS). A sabot is a lightweight carrier in which a projectile of a smaller calibre is centered so as to permit the projectile to be fired from within a larger calibre weapon. The carrier fills the bore of the weapon from which the projectile is fired and is normally discarded a short distance from the muzzle. The result of this effort, a 3 1/4-pound (at loading) round capable of achieving a muzzle velocity of 1,234 meters per second and penetrating 146mm of armor at a range of 915 meters, made its combat debut in Normandy during June 1944. This was progress and an impressive achievement. But the Germans, whose own supplies of tungsten were so limited that they were unable to allocate any of the precious material for further use in ammunition, had managed to develop and field vehicles in the form of the Tiger II and Jagdtiger (the latter a tank destroyer) with armor capable of standing up to the APDS. Additionally, the 88mm gun of the Tiger II was an overmatch for any tank at a range of 1,500 meters or more, while the 128mm gun of the

Jagdtiger could deliver a round able to smash through armor of 200mm thickness at a 1,000 meter range. Their ammunition was developed without the use of tungsten.

In World War II, several techniques were devised to attack and defeat tanks—methods which often relied on daring, skill, and rather unsophisticated weaponry and which frequently placed the tank-killers at considerable personal risk. A lone soldier might, for example, attempt to sneak up on a tank to toss a grenade at it, or drop one into it through an open turret or hatch.

The turret itself would sometimes be targetted in an effort by an enemy gunner to hit the turret ring, jamming or disabling the turret, and possibly the tank through injury to the crew. With the turret disabled, the tank was often a sitting duck, unable to offer much fight or defend itself. Another choice target was the engine compartment. It was sometimes attacked with explosive charges placed or attached appropriately, but this generally involved an heroic action on the part of the attacker at extremely high risk to himself.

The use of fire as a means of halt-ing a tank by destroying or severely injuring the crew was thoroughly explored in that war. Many approaches to firing tanks were tried, with particular emphasis upon those which would ignite the ammunition and fuel supplies in the vehicle. The fear of being burned to death while trapped inside must have caused many a tank crew to operate their vehicle in a completely buttoned-up condition in combat, to minimize the threat from such attacks. Opposing soldiers facing such closed-down tanks had to lob their Molotov Cocktails above the vehicle's vents in an attempt to fire

below: A Churchill Armored Recovery Vehicle pulling a tracked recovery trailer with a Churchill Mk II tank aboard; right: The ruined remains of a British Mk I tank which was blown apart in the desert near Gaza in 1917.

the interior and either kill the crew or force it to evacuate the tank.

Among the most difficult of targets for the tank attacker were the tracks. These could theoretically be broken or damaged through the use of explosive charges or mines. If the charge failed to immobilize the tank by causing it to throw a track, sufficient damage to the suspension might still halt the vehicle.

It was the Soviets who, in the 1960s, determined to get the very most out of a tank gun by mounting a smooth-bore weapon on it. The idea involved reducing friction and thus gaining greater velocity by eliminating the barrel rifling. Of course, it was the rifling that stabilized the round in flight and added considerably to its accuracy on target. In time the Soviets solved the problem of how to have both velocity and accuracy by what became known as fin-stabilization. It enabled them to use the highly effective Armor-Piercing Discarding Sabot in the form of a long dart with a tungsten core surrounded by a sabot designed for the smooth gun bore. The result was greatly improved penetration and accuracy. In the '60s and '70s, all nations operating tank forces became devotees of the Armor-Piercing Fin-Stabilized Discarding Sabot (APFSDS). The weapon itself was soon enhanced by the replacement of the tungsten core with one of depleted uranium. This nuclear by-product offered significant advances over tungsten, not least being its greater density and punching power.

The next important achievement in the tank v anti-tank competition came with the early '70s British development called "Chobham Armor," a still-secret compound believed to contain steel, plastic and ceramics, with tungsten blocks and rods embedded in it. It is considered most efficient in defeating

A still from the 1967 Universal Pictures film *Tobruk*.

both the APFSDS and the shaped-charge of HEAT (High Explosive Anti-Tank) weapon. A shaped-charge is one in which explosives are "shaped" around the outside of a copper cone. With the explosion of the warhead, the resultant energy is directed inwards and forwards, which creates a stream of gas and molten metal, forcing a metal slug to the front, which then melts through the tank armor. At the same time, Israel was creating Explosive Reactive Armor, a system which has become standard with most major tank users since the 1980s.

There is no more remarkable example of tank versus tank action than that of Hauptsturmführer Michael Wittman against the tanks of the British 7th Armored Division near Villers Bocage, Normandy, on 13 June 1944. Born in Vogelthal, Upper Pfalz on 22 April 1914, Wittman had entered the German Army in 1934 as a regular soldier before transferring to the Waffen SS in 1936. In September 1939 he participated in the Polish campaign as the commander of an armored car and was promoted to Untersturmführer. After his participation in the invasions of France and Yugoslavia, he became a member of an SS Panzer Division and in November 1942 began training on the Tiger E heavy tank. On the Eastern Front he served with 13 Company of SS Panzer Regiment 1 Leibstandarte Adolf Hitler, fighting in the Battle of Kursk, followed by service in Italy and another stint in Russia. Promoted to Obersturmführer in January 1944, he was transferred to Belgium, and then to France in time for the Allied invasion of Normandy.

As commander, 2 Company, SS Heavy Tank Battalion 101, he led a unit credited with destroying 119 Russian tanks and was heavily decorated for his achievements to June 1944.

At dawn on 13 June, only four of the six Tiger tanks led by Michael Wittman were serviceable. They lay in thick cover on a hill above the village of Villers Bocage, perfectly positioned to observe the tanks, personnel carriers and half-tracks of the 7th Armored Division's A Squadron, 4th County of London Yeomanry and A Company, 1st Rifle Brigade as they rolled through the village and halted in a column.

Wittman acted immediately. His lead Tiger emerged from its cover and took up a firing position adjacent to the village main road. His first shot destroyed a British half-track and the wreck lay blocking the road. With his Tiger rolling slowly along a lane parallel to the road, he fired round after round, methodically picking off the enemy tanks and other vehicles. The British tanks returned fire but the majority of their rounds made no impression on the heavily armored Tiger. Now Wittman's tank moved onto the village road itself and travelled into the village where he encountered and destroyed a number of artillery observation Sherman tanks along with a Cromwell attempting to position itself for a shot at the German. Satisfied with the morning's work, Wittman withdrew from Villers Bocage, returning to the cover of the nearby hill.

In renewed tank fighting at the village that afternoon, the panzers faired less well, losing three Tigers and having three immobilized, including Wittman's. But the Germans had clearly won the day, having destroyed twenty-five 7th Armored Division tanks, fourteen personnel carriers, and fourteen half-tracks. The British were forced to withdraw to the west of the village. As a result of this engagement, Michael Wittman was promoted to his ultimate rank of Hauptsturmführer and received the swords to his Knight's Cross. He was also offered an appointment to

a German Officers' Tactical School, which he declined, preferring to remain with his unit. It is generally believed that he was killed on 8 August near Caen while engaged in combat with British Sherman Firefly tanks, but this has been disputed in recent years. It has been claimed that his tank and crew were actually the victims of a rocket attack by an RAF Typhoon fighter-bomber. Other reports indicate that his demise resulted from an attack by heavy artillery.

In the summer of 1983, members of the German War Graves Commission, assisted by French and British volunteers, found the remains of Michael Wittman and his crew. These remains were later buried in a communal grave at the German war cemetery near La Cambe in Normandy.

Stopping tanks isn't always about weaponry. The weapons are the tools required and when one side has superior weaponry, the odds are that it will triumph. But frequently, what tips the odds is human judgement, intelligence, and opportunism. Wittman's Tiger was indeed superior in many ways to the tanks of the 7th Armored Division that June day in 1944, but the factors which led to such a one-sided victory for the Germans were more human than mechanical. The decision on the part of the British armored commander to bring his tank column to a halt at Viller Bocage in a tight nose-to-tail column that morning effectively trapped all of his vehicles where they sat. They were left with no possibility of escape and little ability to defend themselves, much less take up an offensive role against an enemy tank force that was known to be in the area. Wittman, on the other hand, observed, intelligently assessed and seized his opportunity, taking the fullest advantage of its possibilities. It is conceivable that he might have

achieved a similar result had he been in command of a tank less formidable than the Tiger.

The idea for the tank destroyer stemmed from the assault gun, a weapon originally intended by the Germans to accompany advancing infantry and support them by knocking out anything likely to impede their further progress. Conventional wisdom suggested that mounting such a gun on what essentially was a tank chassis provided increased mobility and protection for the crew, as well as a more economical alternative to the tank. This less costly, highly capable vehicle was simple in concept and construction. Lacking a rotating turret, it was easier to build and, with proper armament, proved extremely effective on the offensive as an anti-tank weapon, particularly when employed in an ambush position.

Little good can be said about the results of American and British efforts to build effective self-propelled tank destroyers in the early 1940s. It was not until late 1944 that the U.S. Army became fully operational with its evolved M-36, which mounted a 90mm gun firing a twenty-four-pound armor-piercing shell able to penetrate 122mm of armor at a range of 915 meters. It was also capable of using a tungsten core round which had nearly twice the armor penetration capability of the standard round. The U.S. 2nd Armored Division was quite successful with the M-36 against various panzers in the final assault on Germany in early 1945. U.S. Army enthusiasm for offensive, highly mobile tank destroyer vehicles able to aggressively hunt and kill enemy tanks culminated in the best American example of the war, the M-18. Considerably smaller than the M-36, it weighed far less, had a better gun, and was the fastest tracked vehicle of the war. With relatively light armor protection, M-18 crews counted on their maneuverability, speed and firepower to get the vehicle out of trouble in combat situations. It served with the U.S. and other armies into the 1960s.

Russian efforts to develop an effective counter to the newly introduced German PzKpfw V Panther tank produced an important result in 1943, the SU-85, a clever modification of the very successful T-34 tank. In the SU-85, the T-34 turret was replaced by an armored compartment mounting an 85mm anti-aircraft gun. It was a competent, useful weapon which was eventually redeveloped to accept a Soviet 100mm gun, making it more than a match for any German tank.

The impressive German Panther led directly to development of the Jagdpanther, a tank destroyer of great size (103,000 pounds) and capability. The Jagdpanther, with its 88mm gun, was able to kill any other tank at a safe range of 2,500 meters.

Of the various types of anti-tank

below: A British Mk II "female" tank; left: A ditch-crossing trial in England.

vehicles devised since the 1950s, the best is probably the Austrian SK 105 Jagdpanzer, a light tank design with a 105mm gun. It is equipped with an automatic loader, eliminating one crew member, and fires a shaped-charge round capable of penetrating armor of 360mm thickness at a range of 1,000 meters. Another noble anti-tank vehicle is the Swedish Stridsvagn 103 (S-tank) developed after WWII. An indigenous heavy tank without a turret, its 105mm gun was fixed to the chassis and was aimed by turning the vehicle and adjusting the suspension height.

Following their involvement in the Spanish Civil War, when they provided Polikarpov aircraft to the Republicans and saw the planes used effectively against Italian-supplied tanks, the Soviets directed their Ilyushin design bureau to go to work on a new anti-tank aircraft in 1937. The product of this effort was the Shturmovik ground-attack aircraft.

More than 36,000 Shturmoviks were produced in World War II, and it was perhaps the best anti-tank aircraft of the war. The initial version carried only a pilot, but his vulnerability to attack from the rear led to a two-seat version in 1942 which accommodated a rear gunner for the protection of pilot and plane. Still, the attrition rate of Shturmoviks was terribly high. But their effectiveness against German tanks and other armored vehicles was such that, coupled with Soviet industry's ability to produce the plane in numbers far surpassing the losses incurred, the Shturmoviks ultimately overwhelmed their adversaries. They pioneered successful aerial rocket attacks on German tanks while braving intense anti-aircraft fire.

Certainly, the British Hawker Typhoon ground support fighter-bomber, which suffered a number of early developmental problems, came into its own as a very good and high-achieving machine by the time of

the Normandy landings in mid-1944. Armed with four 20mm Hispano cannon in the wings and eight rocket rails under them, the 400 mph Typhoon became a near-perfect firing platform, excelling in ground attack and pounding German tanks in a performance second to none.

The main American aerial tank-killer in the final year of the Second World War was the Republic P-47 Thunderbolt, a big, heavy, escort fighter that could dive much better than it could climb. The Thunderbolt carried eight .50 calibre machine-guns and two three-tube rocket clusters and was on a par with the Typhoon in its ability to seek out and destroy enemy tanks, trains and other vehicles. But the greatest achievement of the Americans in the field of aerial anti-tank warfare is undoubtedly the Republic Fairchild A-10 Thunderbolt II, also known in the U.S. Air Force as the Warthog. Like its WWII P-47

American Shermans, massed for an assault in Germany, open fire at the beginning of a full-scale offensive against the Reich launched on November 16, 1944.

ancestor, the 1970s A-10 is a rugged aircraft, able to absorb and survive substantial battle damage. It brings a unique, amazingly powerful armament to the combat zone; a 30mm General Electric seven-barrel Gatling-style cannon able to shoot at a rate of up to 4,000 rounds a minute. It carries up to 1,350 rounds of either high explosive, incendiary or armor-piercing shot, the latter having a depleted uranium core with exceptional armor penetration capability. The A-10 delivers sixty-five of these rounds in a two-second burst, a barrage that has devastating effect on most modern tanks. The A-10 is the universally acknowledged king of the aerial tank-killers.

With the coming age of the combat helicopter in the 1960s and 1970s Vietnam War, it became possible to mount a sighting unit on the rotor mast of such an aircraft, together with a small video camera, giving the crew the ability to hide low behind trees or hills while stalking a tank, sight, aim and rise briefly to launch a fire-and-forget missile before departing without ever having been a target themselves. What would become the state-of-the-art attack helicopter of the 21st century, the Boeing McDonnell Douglas AH-64 Apache, an awesome anti-tank weapon, entered development in 1976 armed with the American AGM-114 Hellfire (Helicopter-borne Fire and Forget) missile. With a semi-active laser guidance system, the Hellfire can be launched either directly at its target, or indirectly, when the weapon will seek and find the target. It can follow the Apache laser designator to the target over a range of up to five miles. For the modern tank crew the Hellfire is the most fearsome of threats.

In 1916, German soldiers began using anti-tank rifles and machine-guns, both of which fired armor-piercing (AP) bul-

lets in an effort to cause bullet splash fragments to enter the British tanks and injure their crews. Such weaponry was only marginally successful and, in the early 1930s, a British Royal Artillery Lieutenant-Colonel named Blacker began work on a design for a small, high explosive anti-tank bomb which could be placed over a rod or spigot and launched to a range of about ninety meters. In trials, his "Baby Bombard" failed to impress, but later, in the hands of Major Mills Jefferis, Blacker's notion was revised and reinvented as the Projector Infantry Anti-Tank (PIAT) weapon, an awkward, cranky, extremely demanding device with the reputation of being almost as intimidating to the shooter as it was threatening to the target. Despite its quirks, the PIAT was used effectively by the British Army through much of the Second World War.

Another significant method of attacking tanks in that war was the 60mm anti-tank rocket launcher known as the "Bazooka." The ultimate evolution of work by scientists Robert Goddard and Clarence Hickman, the bazooka was intended to provide the individual American infantryman with an appropriate way of defending against or attacking an enemy tank. It was simply a shoulder-supported steel tube for launching a rocket. It had two grips for aiming and the rear grip housed the trigger. Its rocket was capable of penetrating three inches of steel. It became the Bazooka when U.S. Army Major Zeb Hastings decided to name it after the "musical instrument" used by Bob Burns, the Arkansas Traveller, a radio comedian of the time. The improved M-9 version could be broken down into two sections, making it easier to carry. A larger, 88.9mm version followed which was an excellent anti-tank weapon in the Korean conflict from 1951. It was known as the Super

Bazooka. Nearly half a million bazookas were used by the U.S. Army and Allied armies in World War II.

The Germans also developed a bazooka-type weapon, an 88mm adaptation called Panzerschreck (Panzer Terror) and it was even more effective than the bazooka. But they had an acute shortage of the required nitrocellulose rocket propellant and began development of a shaped-charge alternative. The result was the Panzerfaust (Armored Fist), a disposable anti-tank launcher capable of firing a round that could penetrate 140mm of tank armor and ruined the day of many an Allied tank commander. The Panzerfaust contained a hollow-charge bomb at one end, which was propelled by a small charge of gunpowder and the firing was nearly recoil-less. The early version was difficult to aim and was soon replaced by the Panzerfaust 30, whose warhead had a substantially larger diameter than that of the launch tube. The new bomb had four flexible fins which were wrapped around the boom. The tin section fitted into the tube and the shooter held the launch tube under his arm, aimed and fired. The range of the weapon was about thirty meters. It entered full production in late 1943 and was followed in mid-1944 by two advanced versions offering increased ranges of sixty and 100 meters.

After the war, the Allies learned that the Germans had been making important progress in their development of an anti-tank missile known as the X-7. It was to be the forerunner of all such future weapons. The X-7 could be directed onto its target and deliver a far more destructive payload than that of any anti-tank gun. A French derivative of the X-7 was first used in combat by the Israelis in 1956. They later found themselves on the receiving end of a Soviet version called the Snapper in their 1967 conflict with the Egyptians.

Little was achieved in the area of individual anti-tank weaponry after World War II until the 1960s when the Russians came out with the RPG-2, a weapon similar in style to the Panzerfaust, having a tube which launched an oversized grenade with fins and did so without recoil. While the range of the RPG-2 was just 150 meters, the shot could penetrate up to 180mm of armor. The weapon was later cloned by the Chinese who reworked it to fire a High-Explosive Anti-Tank (HEAT) warhead which could go through 250mm of armor. Then the Russians went one better with the RPG-7, in which the grenade was now powered by a small rocket motor. The warhead was still fired initially by the old recoil-less charge, but once it left the tube its little motor ignited and dramatically accelerated it to the target up to 500 meters away. On arriving it could penetrate 320mm of armor and do appalling damage to the interior of a tank. The secret of its success lay in a new recipe for the explosive and a new way of "packaging" it. The Americans first experienced the effects of the RPG-7 when hit with it by the Viet Cong in 1966. The RPG-7, and an American one-man anti-tank weapon developed at about the same time, the M-72 LAW (Light Anti-Tank Weapon), were also significant in that they caused many nations to re-focus on the need for a really effective advanced one-man anti-tank weapon system. During this period the RPG-7 became the standard type for all Soviet-bloc countries, while the M-72 was adopted by the NATO alliance and some other Western nations. The M-72 was most effective at 300 meters and was able to penetrate 300mm of armor at that range. It was a 66mm rocket launcher made up of two con-

British Matilda tanks of the 1st Armoured Regiment advancing inland on Balikpapan, July 1945.

centric tubes which fired a shaped-charge warhead with a small rocket motor. It was shoulder-fired and was used to great effect in Vietnam and in the 1982 Falklands War.

Among the most interesting weapons of that era is the Swedish Carl Gustav, an 84mm recoil-less anti-tank gun that is fired from the shoulder and can utilize a range of ammunition types to tackle a variety of combat tasks. Another superb weapon is the BILL (Bofors, Infantry, Light and Lethal), which is also a Swedish design. The BILL is a truly revolutionary missile system. It contains a thermal imaging (TI) sight to detect heat from such sources as tank and armored fighting vehicle engines. Wire-guided, the BILL is specifically intended to target the vulnerable upper surfaces of tanks, which

it attacks by overflying the target at low-level. When its guidance computer senses that the missile is in proper position, it detonates a downward-firing shaped-charge which then penetrates the thinner upper surface armor of the tank with deadly effect.

As impressive as the various shoulder-launched shell and rocket projectiles were, they made relatively little difference to the heavy tanks of the day with their massive front armor. Furthermore, in some conditions they could be hazardous to their users. These limitations and drawbacks, together with significant advances in shaped-charge technology, led directly to the development of one of the best weapons yet devised, the British LAW-80 94mm rocket. Incredibly, the LAW-80 warhead can penetrate more than

700mm of armor at an effective range of 500 meters. This amazing weapon is part rocket launcher and part 9mm aiming rifle. The operator simply fires a tracer / explosive bullet from the aiming rifle at the target tank. If his shot is accurate, he selects "rocket" and fires again, this time sending a 3.7-inch missile to the same aiming point hit by his tracer round. If his aiming round missed the target, he fires another tracer, and another, until he hits the tank. He then shoots it with a rocket.

Of the so-called "smart" weapons, two are quite special: the TOW and the MILAN. The TOW (tube-launched, optically tracked and wire guided) is a 1960s product of the American Hughes company and has been steadily upgraded and improved since the initial

A British Crusader tank is knocked out by a German tank and a Crusader crew member bales out; right: A postwar view of a British Churchill 'Toad' flail tank.

model whose range was 2,750 meters. It is the best anti-tank guided missile there is. The current version is able to penetrate armor plate of 800mm or thirty-one inches. The missile, in a sealed tube, is clipped to the back of a launcher tube which is equipped with the sight and guidance system. Refinements have included a shaped-charge warhead version designed to defeat explosive reactive armor, and one which is dedicated to attacking the thinner and more vulnerable upper surfaces of tanks, utilizing special sensors and charges that can fire downward while the warhead overflies the tank. Since establishing itself as the king of sophisticated anti-tank missiles when operated by Israel in the 1973 Arab-Israeli War, it has become the anti-tank weapon of choice in the inventories of

many armies the world over. MILAN (Missile, Infanterie, Légere, Anti-char, or infantry, light, anti-tank missile) is the product of a French / German consortium, Nord Aviation and Bölkow, later joined in the effort by British Aerospace. It is a wire-guided infantry missile fielded by two men. It can be set up and ready to fire in seconds and, once fired, a hit is assured as long as the shooter keeps his sight aligned on the target. The advance MILAN 3 carries a warhead with two shaped-charges. One charge is on an extended probe ahead of the main warhead charge. This "precursor" charge hits and destroys any reactive armor that is protecting the main armor of the target tank. This action is followed instantly by the detonation of the main warhead charge, which can penetrate

more than a meter of armor. MILAN 3 has both day and night thermal imaging capabilities, is efficient at overcoming countermeasures, such as pyrotechnic flares, and is not fooled by distractions such as the heat source of a nearby burning vehicle.

Even though anti-tank weaponry has become more and more sophisticated, there is still a place for the basic tank stoppers: fixed barriers and mines. The tactical minefield became a defense against enemy tanks with the development of contact and pressure mines which were set off by the track pressure over the mine. The most common tank obstacles appeared before World War II at the Maginot Line in France, along the German frontier with Czechoslovakia, in the Low Countries

In England, the original tank "Mother," following her conversion to a petrol-electric drive system, is an abandoned wreck at Bovington; right: The demise of a German tank on the Soviet southwestern front after striking a mine.

and, later, in England. They were called "Dragon's Teeth," made of concrete, often pyramid-shaped (some rectangular) and usually about one meter high. They were laid across probable tank routes, six ranks deep and virtually guaranteed to stop any tank that dared try to cross them. Simple and effective.

In July 2000, it was reported that German landowners along the 650-kilometer Siegfried Line, a system of tank traps, concrete bunkers and gun emplacements from World War II, were furious about government plans to remove the last traces of the Line. The German government had announced that it would be spending millions to erase the fortifications of Nazi Germany's western defense line and that it expected some landowners to pay for the clearance of such facilities from their land, as it would benefit these farmers who would then have more land to farm. Strongly supported by environmentalists who want the Siegfried structures to stay because they are perfect havens for foxes, badgers, and bats, the farmers steadfastly refused to cooperate with the German government in the plan. Enter hundreds of local politicians and war veterans who have joined the argument, taking the view that the Siegfried structures should be preserved as a massive memorial to the thousands of soldiers of both sides who died in the fighting there. They claim that the government is simply out to remove one more reminder of the nation's Nazi past. The enormous stretch of concrete bunkers and anti-tank dragon's teeth became widely known via the wartime song "We're Going to Hang Out the Washing on the Siegfried Line." The German government insists that the remaining structures of the Line must be removed because they are dangerous and the government is liable for any injuries that people suffer there. Farmers who live and work along the Line have been notified by the government that the work of filling in the old bunkers and dragging away the anti-tank defenses was to begin within weeks.

The German WWII military cemetery at La Cambe in Normandy, France, where tank ace Michael Wittman is buried.

The massive Zeppelin Field in the complex of former Nazi rally facilities on the outskirts of Nuremberg. At the end of the war in Europe, the Americans blew up and destroyed the huge wreathed swastika above the columned structure overlooking the enormous stadium. A ruined Sherman tank lies next to the track across from the platform that Hitler had used to address Nazi rallies in the 1930s.

The Royal Tank Regiment memorial statue,
Bovington Tank Museum, Dorset, England.

TANK MAN

Government is not reason, it is not eloquence, it is force; like fire, a troublesome servant and a fearful master.
—George Washington

The tank is more than a killing machine, more than a battlefield menace. In many parts of the world since the Second World War, tanks on the streets have often been the first sign of violent political change, a military coup or the imposition of a repressive regime.

Politicians have long recognized the value of the tank in the intimidation and repression of civilian populations. Its awesome appearance can be traumatizing, especially in an ordinary urban context. Patrick Wright, author of *Tank*, a superb cultural history of the weapon, comments: "People talk about the tank as a rational instrument of warfare—you get lots of them, then you mass them together and you advance—but it's always had a symbolic dimension as well. It is a monstrous object that crawls towards you and you don't know what it can do to you, but it scares you almost to death. It would be quite wrong to ignore this. The symbolic force of this weapon makes it very well attuned to modern peacekeeping-type operations. It may take two months to get it there, but if you put a tank on a bridge things tend to settle down."

In the last half of the twentieth century, ordinary citizens of several nations faced invading tanks and, for a while at least, stood their ground in defiance of clearly overwhelming force and fear.

On 4 November 1956, Hungarian Prime Minister Imre Nagy spoke to his people in a dramatic radio broadcast as Soviet armor assaulted Budapest: "Soviet troops attacked our capital with the obvious purpose to overthrow the legitimate Hungarian government. Our troops are fighting. The government is in its place."

Shortly after the death of Premier Josef Stalin in 1953, the Soviet leadership became aware of a growing disenchantment with the oppressive communist system in the satellite nations, Hungary being a prime example. The Soviets ordered the hardline Hungarian Communist Party boss, Matyás Rakosi, to Moscow for consultation. He was directed to relax the pressures then being applied by his regime on Hungary's industry and collective farms, to soften his "reign of terror" approach, and to work toward a higher living standard for his people. Finally, he was required to ordain fellow communist Imre Nagy as the new Prime Minister. Nagy was a moderate with considerable popular support. He was known for opposing the communist policies of terror and forced industrialization and collectivization. He was a reformer who wanted to liberalize communism in his country, but without any major shift toward capitalism. He began his program in July with what he called "the new stage in building socialism."

In little more than a year after the death of Stalin, the Soviet flirtation with a more relaxed form of communism appeared to be ending as hardline policies came back into vogue. In Hungary, Rakosi saw the opportunity to regain his former stature and embarked on a program to de-stabilize Nagy's government. In March 1955, emboldened by the Russian winds of change, he sacked Nagy and reimposed terror on Hungarians. But with the coming of a new Soviet Communist Party chief, Nikita Krushchev, and his February 1956 denunciation of Stalin, Rakosi's little empire in Hungary began to unravel and by the summer had been dismissed.

Unrest in Hungary, Poland, and elsewhere in the Soviet satellite states was growing rapidly. On 22 October the people of Budapest learned of a change of leaders in the Polish communist party. Wladislaw Gomulka, like Nagy, a relative moderate, was the new party boss, ousting the former Stalinist regime in Warsaw. His rise to power triggered a prompt Soviet reaction. Krushchev flew to the Polish capital as Soviet military forces mobilized to move on the rebellious satellite state. A clash was averted, however, as the clever Gomulka carefully maintained his stance within the federal system of the Warsaw Pact. On hearing of the party changes in Poland, students of the Budapest Technical University were inspired to create a sixteen-point list of demands. They then called for a peaceful gathering on 23 October to demonstrate their solidarity with the people of Poland and declare their demands. Walls all over the city were plastered with posters calling for freedom. The demonstrators were demanding a complete withdrawal of the troops, the abolition of censorship, establishment of a multi-party political system with free elections, economic independence and the re-establishment of traditional national symbols and holidays. They were supported by much of the citizenry. A broad spectrum of politics was represented as leftists, communist reformers, social democrats, religious leaders, conservatives, and even some right-wing elements joined the movement. Ordinary citizens defied the government and got their news by listening to the banned Radio Free Europe. The Hungarian Revolution was under way.

The initial violence occurred when Hungarian secret police opened fire on activists who were attempting to occupy the headquarters of Radio Budapest on the 23rd. Elsewhere in the country revolutionary groups were quickly being formed and a general political strike was organized. Student and general demonstrations erupted in the many town squares where the protestors frequently focused their attentions on dismantling and destroying the hated symbols of repression. Down came Soviet war memorials, red stars, and in perhaps the most defiant of vandalisms, the activists set about the massive statue of Stalin in central Budapest, attacking it with hammers, toppling and decapitating it. In the wake of all this action, Imre Nagy was once again brought in as Prime Minister.

By the 25th the Hungarian situation had worsened significantly. In an ugly scene at the parliament building, unarmed demonstrators were fired on by soldiers in an effort to suppress the uprising. There, and in other parts of the country, hundreds of protestors were killed. Gradually, however, many Hungarian soldiers began changing sides and joining the ranks of the revolutionaries.

Two days after the shootings, Imre Nagy told the nation that he had formed a new government which incorporated non-communists and intended to negotiate the withdrawal of Soviet forces from Hungary. Under new management, Hungarian Radio followed the Nagy announcement with one in which it supported the protestors. But while the Soviet troops had withdrawn from Budapest, they remained poised in the countryside, ready to move forcefully

against the activists. On 1 November, with the troops refusing to withdraw further, Nagy acted by withdrawing Hungary from the Warsaw Pact alliance and declaring his nation's neutrality. By doing so, Nagy renounced the policies of his own party and the international communist movement. The Kremlin reacted immediately.

On 3 November, Soviet Army generals were in discussions with officers of the Hungarian Army about Soviet troop withdrawal. The talks were a sham and the Hungarian delegation was arrested by Soviet security forces. On 4 November, Soviet military forces moved in a savage attack on Hungary and in a few days put an end to the rebellion. Imre Nagy and his top officials, who had sought refuge at the Yugoslav Embassy in Budapest, were given assurances of safe conduct out of the country. When they tried to leave, they were quickly taken into custody by the Soviets who then installed their own puppet government headed by János Kádár, who had won Soviet support by opposing the rebellion.

Now Soviet tanks and armored vehicles clattered down the main streets and boulevards of Budapest, firing indiscriminately as they rolled. Young, armed activists fought back, shooting, shouting and hurling Molotov Cocktails (bottles filled with gasoline) at the tanks. Many homes and buildings were destroyed as the Soviets forceably put down the revolt. Token resistance continued until early in 1957, but the revolution had failed. A new reign of terror had begun. Some 25,000 Hungarians were arrested and incarcerated in the two years following the revolt. Almost 200,000 refugees fled the country to freedom in Britain, the United States and elsewhere.

In 1949, Mao Zedong stood in

Beijing's Tiananmen Square and proclaimed a "People's Republic" on behalf of the people of China. The square, near the Gate of Heavenly Peace leading into the Forbidden City, had been the scene of student demonstrations as early as 1919 and has, since 1949, been the venue where the Chinese leadership reviews the troops of the People's Liberation Army.

Forty years after Mao's proclamation, student and worker members of China's pro-democracy movement gathered to take back Tiananmen Square for a seven-week period in the spring of 1989. They were joined by educators, doctors, soldiers and others and eventually numbered more than one million, many of whom had seen operating democracies while on visits to the United States and Britain.

The demonstration had started on 15 April after the death of Hu Yao Bang, the former Secretary General of the Communist Party of China, who had been demoted and disgraced when he was accused of being in sympathy with student pro-democracy demonstrators in 1987. Thousands of students went to Tiananmen Square to honor Hu Yao Bang and were soon joined by workers and intellectuals. The action of the demonstrators was quickly condemned by the government in a letter to the *People's Daily*, describing the students' behavior as "an act of treason." Police freely used their truncheons to control the demonstrators. This caused many more thousands of students and their supporters to come to the square to denounce the violence and express their anti-government views.

The dissidents produced a daily newspaper which protested against government corruption and demanded political democracy in their country. They broadcast their message, and the speeches of their heroes, from a radio tent in the square and they created a thirty-foot statue which they named the Goddess of Democracy. It was erected to face the massive poster of Mao there. At the southwest corner of the square was a Kentucky Fried Chicken shop which the demonstrators used as their headquarters and meeting place. Their struggle for human rights had been non-violent and a remarkable expression of will and determination.

On 14 May more than 2,000 of the protestors were engaged in a hunger strike as more than 100,000 occupied the square. In the following days their numbers grew rapidly to nearly one million. They began shouting for government reforms and the resignation of the Chinese leader, Deng Xiaoping. Their calls were a supreme embarrassment to the government which, at that moment, was hosting Mikhail Gorbachev, the first Soviet head of state to visit China in thirty years. In a conciliatory gesture, Deng Xiaoping called on the hunger strikers in hospital and then agreed to meet with the student protest leaders. In the meeting Deng did not accede to their demands. He warned the Chinese people of the repercussions that awaited those who became involved in the protest movement. On 20 May the hardline Premier Li Peng branded the protest action "a riot." He declared martial law in Beijing and called in troops from the countryside. By the following day the People's Liberation Army had taken over all newspapers, television and radio stations in Beijing. On the 22nd, the government shut down the satellite feed to North America and Europe.

Key members of the government were divided over what measures they should take to quell the protest. Deng advocated suppression by the use of any force necessary, but others around him wanted no part of that. Unarmed soldiers had no effect on the demonstrators who surrounded their vehicles. By 29 May the government had declared the students and the other demonstrators "hooligans" and "bad elements"; counter-revolutionaries who were liable to be arrested and shot. On 2 June more than 200,000 soldiers had moved into Beijing. Deng's patience was exhausted. He ordered the army to retake Tiananmen Square at all costs. By noon on the 3rd, PLA soldiers had entered the square and were hitting people with truncheons as well as tossing tear gas cannisters to disperse the crowds. In a broadcast the government then warned that it had the right to deal forcefully with the "rioters." The people of Beijing were instructed to stay indoors. At 2 a.m. on 4 June, units of the PLA 27th Field Army surrounded the square and, by 4 a.m. its soldiers had opened fire on the protestors. The army brought in tanks from all directions towards the square and hundreds of the unarmed demonstrators, including many children, were killed. The Chinese Red Cross estimated that up to 2,000 students and civilians died in the tragic action, which quickly attracted worldwide condemnation of the Chinese government.

The next day the shocked and outraged activists steadfastly refused to leave Tiananmen. Elements of the People's Liberation Army occupied the square and were endeavoring to secure their supply lines, as a column of eighteen Norinco Type 69 / 59 main battle tanks advanced down Chang' an Boulevard, the Avenue of Eternal Peace. The BBC's Kate Adie described what happened next: "Just after midday the tanks rolled out of the square. A lone young man stood in front of the first one. The tank faltered; came to a stop . . . it was an extraordinarily purposeful but mundane way of doing things. It seemed impromptu. There he was with his little plastic bag—such a human touch, as if he had been shopping."

Wang Weilin. It may or may not be the real name of the unknown rebel who defied the Chinese Communist regime that day in one of the most courageous acts of all time. He was a slight figure in white shirt and dark slacks. In his left hand he held a shopping bag. He moved towards the approaching tank column and positioned himself directly in front of the lead tank, which stopped and then attempted to swerve to the right around the man, who moved to block it. It then tried to swerve to the left and he moved with it. The man then climbed up onto the front of the tank to speak to the driver. The writer Pico Iyer reported the rebel's words to the driver as: "Why are you here? My city is in chaos because of you."

Little is known about the young man who defied the might and power of his government that day. *Time* magazine cited the unknown protestor as one of the "top twenty leaders and revolutionaries of the 20th century." It is widely believed that he was a nineteen-year-old student. His actual identity is still a mystery, as is his fate. According to the Information Center for the Human Rights and Democracy Movement in China, the Communist Party authorities have never found Wang. They quote Jiang Zemin, the Party General Secretary in 1990, as saying: "We can't find him. We got his name from journalists. We have checked through computers but can't find him among the dead nor among those in prison." When asked about the fate of the young rebel by the American television interviewer

Barbara Walters in a 1992 conversation, Jiang responded: "I think never killed."

The powerful image of The Tank Man, Wang Weilin, or whatever his name may be, posed resolute in front of that Chinese tank, is a familiar one to hundreds of millions of people around the globe. It has become an icon of defiance and one of the most famous and recognized photographs of all time. Of the Tank Man, Patrick Wright has written: "The image has been subject to much interpretation in the West . . . The military historian John Keegan declared it a merely 'poetic image,' a story of 'impersonal armed might of the army lined up against the unvanquished human spirit.' He then breaks to say, drily, "You can write the words yourself." Some newspapers have certainly done that. Tantalized by the image of this man who is universally known and yet almost completely obscure, newspapers have felt obliged to augment the story. One report confirmed Wang's status as a student by putting books in his bag, and there were diverse variations on the words he is said to have shouted at the tanks, from the simple "Go away" of the *Sunday Express* to "Go back, turn around, stop killing my people," elaborated by *Today* a week or so later. In the British Parliament, Neil Kinnock, then leader of the Labour Party said: "The memory of one unarmed young man standing in front of a column of tanks . . . will remain   long after the present leadership in China and what they stand for has been forgotten."

On 4 June 1998, the ninth anniversary of the Tiananmen Square tragedy, United States Senator Paul Wellstone addressed the Senate: "Like everyone who witnessed that brutal massacre, I can not forget the image of that lone courageous figure, Wang Weilin, standing firm and holding his ground against the oncoming PLA tanks. China's leaders have tried to convince the world that freedom and democracy are Western ideals, contrary to Asian values. Their rhetoric would have us believe that maintaining repressive policies is essential to the preservation of their cultural and national identity. The image of Wang Weilin tells a different story; a story of the human spirits' incredible determination and sacrifice for liberty and freedom."

Since the events of June 1989, the Chinese government has sought to mollify the people with the prospect of greater individual material wealth to be achieved through an increase in the pace of economic development, this in lieu of greater political rights. Some personal freedoms have also come to pass, including the right to choose one's job and to relocate. Such gains have functioned as a limited diversion from the political activism of the recent past, but the memory of Tiananmen Square, of the Tank Man and the spirit of the demonstrators there, survives to inspire the peoples of China and the world.

The Tank Man of Tiananmen Square.

PICTURE CREDITS
Photos from the collection of the author are credited AC. Photos from the U.S. National Archives are credited NARA. Photos from the Imperial War Museum are credited IWM. Photos from The Tank Museum, Bovington, are credited BOV. Photos from the Daimler-Chrysler Historical Collection are credited DCHC. P4: IWM/W. B. Adeney; P6: left-AC, right-BOV; P7: AC; P8: top-BOV, bottom-AC; P9:AC; P10: BOV; P12: AC; P13: AC; P16: IWM/W. B. Adeney; P18: AC; P20: IWM/William Orpen; P22: IWM/Paul Nash; PP24-25: all AC; P26: AC; P28: AC; PP30-31: BOV; P32: IWM/W. B. Adeney, right-AC; P34: AC; P35: BOV; PP36-37: BOV; PP38-39: NARA; P40: AC; P41: AC; P42: AC; P45: AC; P46: AC; P49: AC; P50: AC; P52: Punch / Frank Reynolds; P55: BOV; PP56-57: DCHC; P58: BOV; P59: both BOV; P60: AC; P61: BOV; PP62-63: BOV; PP64-65: BOV; PP66-67: all BOV; PP68-69: BOV; PP70-71: all BOV; PP72-73: AC; P75: AC; P76: courtesy J. Kugies; P78: BOV; P79: AC; P80: both BOV; P81: both AC; P83: BOV; P84: BOV; P86: AC; PP88-89: BOV; P91: IWM; P92: AC; P95: IWM; P97: AC; P99: AC; P100: 20th Century Fox; P102: AC; P105: top-courtesy Mrs Donald Chidson, bottom: BOV; P107: AC; P109: AC; P110: both AC; P112: BOV; P113: AC; P115: Dreamworks SKG; PP116-117: all AC; P118: IWM; P120: AC; P121: BOV; p122: NARA; P124: 20th Century Fox; P125: AC; PP127: both BOV; P129: courtesy Steve Joseph; P130: BOV; P131: courtesy Ludwig Bauer; P132: AC/A. Hoffmeister; P134: Lorimar Productions; P136: IWM/C.A. Russell; P139: BOV; P141: BOV; PP142-143: DCHC; P145: BOV; P146: DCHC; P147: BOV; P149: BOV; P150: DCHC; PP152-153: all NARA; P155: BOV; P156: NARA; P158: NARA; P159: AC/Bill Mauldin; P160: BOV; P162: IWM; P163: both AC; P164: BOV; P165: both BOV; P166: AC; P167: BOV; P168: BOV; P170: NARA; P172: NARA; P173: both NARA; P174: BOV; P176: BOV; P179: BOV; P181: BOV; P182: Warwick Film Productions; P184: courtesy Jeff Dacus; P186: USAF Academy Library Special Collections; P187: IWM/A.E. Howell Miller, right: AC; P189: top BOV, bottom: courtesy Jeff Dacus; P190: BOV; P192: NARA; P193: NARA; P194: NARA; P195: NARA; P196: NARA; P197: both NARA; P198: NARA; P199: NARA; P200: NARA; P201: NARA; P202: NARA; P203: NARA; P204: NARA; P205: NARA; P206: AC; P208: BOV; P210: AC; P211: BOV; P212: BOV; P213: BOV; P214: Universal Pictures; P216: BOV; P217: BOV; P218: BOV; P221: BOV; P222: BOV; P223: BOV; P224: BOV; P225: BOV; P226: AC; P228: BOV; P230: AC; P235: Stuart Franklin-Magnum Photos.

ACKNOWLEDGMENTS
The author is particularly grateful to the following for their kind help in the development of this book: Pauline Allwright, Ernest Audino, Fritz-Rudolph Averdieck, Jeff Babineau, Malcolm Bates, A.G. Bramble, Ludwig Bauer, Rex Cadman, Donald Chidson, Valerie Chidson, Neil Ciotola, Jeff Dacus, Daimler-Chrysler Historical Collection, J. Ellison, Chris Everitt, John Ferrell, David Fletcher, Eugene Flowers, George Forty, Will Fowler, Ella Freire, Oz Freire, Flo Garetson, Gaston Gee, Hans Halberstadt, Robert T. Hartwig, Douglas Helmer, Eric Holloway, James Jinks, Steve Joseph, Hargita Kaplan, Margaret Kaplan, Neal Kaplan, Sam Katz, Johannes Kugies, Jacques Littlefield, John Longman, James McMaster, Tilly McMaster, Elise McCutcheon, Judy McCutcheon, Rick McCutcheon, Martin Middlebrook, Steve Nichols, John Nugent, George Parada, Alan Reeves, Heinz Renk, Charles L. Ross, John Schaeffer, Charles Shenloogian, David Shepard, George Hudson Worth, Dennis Wrynn, Grateful acknowledgment is made to the following for the use of their previously published material: Averdieck, Fritz-Rudolph; Bauer, Ludwig; Belfield, Eversleigh and Essame, H., The Battle for Normandy, Pan Books, 1967; Bramble, A.G., Browne, Captain D.G., The Tank in Action, William Blackwood and Sons, 1920; Dacus, Jeff; Eshel, David, Chariots of the Desert, Brassey's, 1989; Guderian, Heinz, Achtung-Panzer!, Arms and Armor, 1992; Guderian, Heinz, Panzer Leader, Penguin Books, 2000;
Hamilton, Nigel, The Full Monty, Montgomery of Alamein 1887-1942, Hartwig; Robert, Liddell-Hart, Basil, The Other Side of the Hill, Papermac, 1993; Mauldin, Bill, Up Front, Henry Holt & Co., 1945; Messenger, Charles, The Art of Blitzkrieg, Ian Allan; Perrett, Bryan, Iron Fist, Arms and Armor, 1995; Ridgeway,

Mathew B. and Martin, Harold, Soldier, 1956; Rogers, Colonel H.C.B., Tanks in Battle, Seeley, 1965; Royal Tank Regiment, The Tank Journal; Sullivan, S. Scott.

BIBLIOGRAPHY
Ambrose, Stephen, Band of Brothers, Simon & Schuster, 1992
Arnold, James R., The Battle of the Bulge, Osprey, 1990.
Barker, Lt Col A. J., Afrika Korps, Bison Books, 1978.
Beevor, Antony, Stalingrad, Viking, 1998.
Belfield, Eversleigh and Essame, H., The Battle for Normandy, Pan Books, 1967.
Blackburn, George, The Guns of Normandy, Constable Publishers, 2000,
Blumenson, Martin, The Patton Papers, 1940-1945, Houghton Mifflin, 1957.
Browne, Captain D.G., The Tank in Action, William Blackwood & Sons, 1920.
Chant, Christopher, Armored Fighting Vehicles of the 20th Century, Tiger Books, 1996.
Campbell, John, The Experience of World War II, Oxford University Press, 1989.
Canby, Courtland, A History of Weaponry, Hawthorn Books, 1963.
Carruthers, Bob, German Tanks at War, Cassell, 2000.
Churchill, Winston, The Second World War: The Grand Alliance, Houghton Mifflin, 1990.
Clancy, Tom, Armored Car, Berkley Books, 1994.
Clancy, Tom, Into the Storm: A Study in Command, G.P. Putnam's Sons, 1997.
Clark, Alan, Barbarossa, Quill, 1965.
Collier, Richard, The War in the Desert, Time-Life Books, 1977.
Cooper, Belton Y., Death Traps, Presidio Press, 2000.
Cooper, Matthew and Lucas, James, Panzer, Purnell Book Services, 1976.
Coppard, George, With a Machine Gun to Cambrai, Cassell, 1999.
Costello, John, Love, Sex & War Changing Values, 1939-45, Collins, 1985.
Crow, Duncan, Modern Battle Tanks, Profile Publications, 1978.
Davies, J.B., Great Campaigns of World War II, Macdonald & Co., 1980.
Delaforce, Patrick, Taming the Panzers, Sutton Publishing, 2000.
Delaney, John, The Blitzkrieg Campaigns, Caxton Editions, 2000.
Deighton, Len, Blitzkrieg, Jonathan Cape, 1979.
Doubler, Michael, Closing With The

Enemy, University Press of Kansas, 1994.
Edwards, Roger, Panzer: A Revolution in Warfare, 1939-1945, Brockhampton Press, 1989.
Eshel, David, Chariots of the Desert, Brassey's, 1989.
Fletcher, David, Tanks and Trenches, Sutton Publishing, 1994.
Fletcher, David, The British Tanks 1915-19, The Crowood Press, 2001.
Flower, Desmond and Reeves, James, The Taste of Courage The War 1939-1945, Cassell, 1960.
Folkstad, William B., The View from the Turret, Burd Street Press, 2000.
Forbes, Colin, Tramp in Armor, Collins, 1969.
Ford, Roger, The World's Great Tanks, Grange Books, 1999.
Forty, George, Afrika Korps At War: The Road to Alexandria, Ian Allan, 1978.
Forty, George, Afrika Korps At War: The Long Road Back, Ian Allan, 1978.
Forty, George, Tank Aces, Sutton Publishing, 1997.
Gardiner, Juliet, D-Day: Those Who Were There, Collins & Brown, 1994.
Gervasi, Tom, Arsenal of Democracy II, Evergreen, 1981.
Green, Michael, M1 Abrams Main Battle Tank, Motorbooks, 1992.
Green, Michael, Patton's Tank Drive D-Day to Victory, MBI Publishing, 1995.
Guderian, Heinz, Achtung—Panzer, Arms & Armor, 1992.
Guderian, Heinz, Panzer Leader, Penguin Books, 2000.
Halberstadt, Hans, Military Vehicles, Metrobooks, 1998.
Hastings, Max, The Korean War, Michael Joseph, 1987.
Haupt, Werner, and Bingham, J.K.W., North African Campaign 1940-1943, Macdonald and Co., 1968.
Hogg, Ian, Tank Killing, Brown Packaging Books, 1996.
Hiolmes, Richard, Battlefields of the Second World War, BBC, 2001.
Hughes, Dr Matthew and Mann, Dr Chris, The T-34 Tank, Brown Packaging Books, 1999.
Jensen, Marvin, Strike Swiftly, Presidio Press, 1997.
Jones, Kevin, The Desert Rats, Caxton Editions, 2001.
Joergensen, Christer, and Mann, Chris, Tank Warfare, Spellmount Limited, 2001.
Lande, D.A., Rommel in North Africa, MBI Publishing, 1999.
Lucas, James, Panzer Army Africa, Purnell Book Services, 1977.
Mauldin, Bill, Up Front, Henry Holt & Co., 1945.
McGuirk, Dal, Rommel's Army in Africa, Motorbooks, 1993.
McKee, Alexander, Caen: Anvil of Victory, Dorset Press, 1964.
Messenger, Charles, The Art of Blitzkrieg, Ian Allan, 1976.
Parker, Danny S., Battle of the Bulge, Greenhill Books, 1991.
Perrett, Bryan, Iron Fist, Arms and Armor Press, 1995.
Rawls, Walton, Wake Up America!, Cross River Press, 1995.
Rogers, Col H.C.B., Tanks in Battle, Smithers, A.J., Excalibur: The Development of the Tank 1909-1939, Leo Cooper, 1986.
Tout, Ken, A Fine Night for Tanks: The Road to Falaise, Sutton Publishing, 1998.
Trewhitt, Philip, Armored Fighting Vehicles, Dempsey Parr, 1999.
Whiting, Charles, Decision at St Vith., Ballantine Books, 1969.
Winchester, Charles, Ostfront: Hitler's War on Russia 1941-45, Osprey Publishing, 2000
Wright, Patrick, Tank, Faber and Faber, 2000.
Zetterling, Niklas and Frankson, Anders, Kursk 1943, Frank Cass, 2000.

Lord William Griffiths, who died 30 May 2015, aged 91, was serving as a Lieutenant in the Second Armored Recce Battalion, British Army, during the run-up to the Battle of the Bulge. In the afternoon of 8 September 1944, at the start of the fight for the Belgian town of Hechtel, his outfit learned that four German Panther tanks were approaching the British tanks' position from the west. Griffiths volunteered to take his tank and crew to investigate, setting off unaccompanied. As he came to a road crossing, one of the enemy tanks opened fire but the shell missed and Griffiths quickly made his way into a nearby wood and waited until the Panther came within range. He then fired three shots, efficiently destroying the German tank. He returned to the road crossing where the other three enemy tanks lay. At that point the three remaining Panthers made off without further engagement. Moving under cover he soon sighted and destroyed two ememy transport vehicles. Griffiths was later awarded an MC (Military Cross) for the action. The accompanying citation noted that "by taking on single-handed the Panther tank there was no doubt that Griffiths had broken up what might have been a serious attack on our left flank, an attack which might have menaced our entire position at Hechtel and altered the decision of the battle."